THE DEVELOPMENT OF TRADITIONAL PSYCHOPATHOLOGY

a sourcebook

MARK D. ALTSCHULE

The Francis A. Countway Library of Medicine
Harvard Medical School

HEMISPHERE
PUBLISHING CORPORATION

Washington   London

A HALSTED PRESS BOOK

JOHN WILEY & SONS

New York   London   Sydney   Toronto

"Freud (1895)," pp. 290–293, is quoted from "On the Grounds for Detaching a Particular Syndrome from Neurasthenia Under the Description 'Anxiety Neurosis,'" *The Standard Edition of the Complete Psychological Works of Sigmund Freud,* Vol. III, revised and edited by James Strachey, by permission of Sigmund Freud Copyrights Ltd., The Institute of Psycho-Analysis, and The Hogarth Press Ltd.; excerpted from Chapter V, "The Justification for Detaching From Neurasthenia A Particular Syndrome: The Anxiety-Neurosis," from *Collected Papers,* Volume I, by Sigmund Freud, Authorized Translation under the supervision of Joan Riviere, Published by Basic Books, Inc., by arrangement with The Hogarth Press Ltd. and The Institute of Psycho-Analysis, London.

Hemisphere Publishing Corporation
1025 Vermont Ave., N.W., Washington, D.C. 20005

Distributed solely by Halsted Press, a Division of John Wiley & Sons, Inc., New York.

Library of Congress Cataloging in Publication Data

Main entry under title:

The Development of traditional psychopathology.

Includes indexes.
1. Psychology, Pathological—Addresses, essays, lectures. I. Altschule, Mark David.
RC458.A44   616.8'9'07   75-15986
ISBN 0-470-02521-2

Printed in the United States of America

Contents _____|

Acknowledgments

My thanks go first to the authors of all the books and articles quoted here. Most physicians, impressed by the wonderfully interesting character of medicine, have a strong urge to tell other physicians about what they have seen, and it is the results of this urge that made this book possible. It is regrettable that only a minority of the more than a thousand works read have been mentioned in the text.

My thanks next go to two men whose generously given help and advice constantly guided me. One was Richard Wolfe, Rare Books Librarian at the Countway Medical Library, who always found more than I asked for but never more than I needed. His instant ability to find the material I was unable to find myself encouraged me to use his services freely, to the obvious benefit of this book. The second, Robert Renehan, Professor of Classics at Boston College, I first called upon for reassurance concerning the available translations of early Greek material I wished to include. I soon found, however, that I was the follower rather than the initiator in this relationship. After his peripheral involvement in the project he regularly called my attention to a great number of items that I had not known about and enriched my overall understanding. Whatever excellence this book may have is in large measure due to these two men.

My secretaries, listed alphabetically, deserve every praise. They were Mrs. Anne Anderson (who also helped with some of the translations from the French), Miss Carol Brandt, Mrs. Mary Byron, and foremost of all Mrs. Irene Horenstein. The last named did almost all the Xerox copying which provided material not only for this book but also for several others.

Introduction

The philosophy underlying all sourcebooks is succinctly expressed by Chesterton's words on history: "Man sees more of the things themselves when he sees more of their origin; for their origin is a part of them and indeed the most important part of them." In tracing our predecessors' path through unfamiliar territory it is often well to avoid obliterating their footsteps because their route may reveal more than does their terminus. The study of such a route indicates not only false directions that must still be avoided but also alternatives that, if followed, might have carried us further forward. This approach creates problems of selection and emphasis in the compilation of any sourcebook, but in the physical sciences the problems are minor for the compiler can start with the science in the twentieth century and work back step by step. This procedure cannot be used in psychiatry, however, because there are great differences of opinion concerning what psychiatry today is—or perhaps should be. A person who by training and allegiance belongs to one of the many schools that contend for leadership in American psychiatry would necessarily have certain attitudes and beliefs that would be reflected in any sourcebook he compiled. Although this bias might enhance the value of the work in some limited respect, it would deprive it of broad usefulness as an historical account of clinical psychiatry up to the beginning of the twentieth century.

Another difficulty is that any writer of a sourcebook is likely to be distracted by the intrinsically interesting qualities of some of the old material. "Fascination," said Cotton Mather, "is a thing whereof mankind has more experience than comprehension." The author of any sourcebook will testify to having to resist the temptation to include all quaint or vivid descriptions of the phenomena under study in addition to those that lead to its comprehension. The choice may rest on whether or not writings of earlier eras are to be interpreted strictly. Was the modern idea of split personality foreshadowed by Alexis of Piemont (1562) when he wrote about children with "The Lunatike disease, which happeneth unto them by reason of a worme with two heads that breedeth in their bodies"? Or is the statue of the two-headed goddess[1] in the National Museum of Anthropology in Mexico City an earlier but more explicit representation of the split personality? Is Alexander of Spain's discussion (in his *De Complexionibus*) of the five ways in which a melancholic person resembled mud essential to our understanding of melancholia? Is it necessary to include the development of modern ideas of the triple mind—superego, ego, and id—from ancient Vedic notions, by way of Plato and his medieval followers, and perhaps from pre-Christian Celtic and Etruscan ideas about the holiness of triads?[2] I think not. A sourcebook must be only what its name indicates, and hence it should include only the material that in the opinion of its compiler contributed to today's comprehension of the problem. Any attempt to do otherwise would only evoke a response similar to Whistler's, when told that "The true critic is enthusiastic for the best in every kind"; he replied, "That's not the critic, that's the auctioneer."

It is sometimes necessary to choose between a first statement that went unnoticed and a somewhat later one, similar in most important respects, that came to be incorporated into the body of systematized medical opinion. In the present work both will be recognized inasmuch as the development of a concept is sometimes better presented in a logical than a chronological order.

Successive editions of a single work also often present problems of selectivity. When a later edition merely adds new cases, inserts responses to critics, or elaborates on the previous edition, reference to the later editions is omitted here. A later edition is cited, however, if it contains revisions so extensive that they constitute in part or in whole a new work, as, for example, in the writings of Haslam and to some extent Kraepelin.

The use by different authors of different words for the same syndrome is too complicated a problem to be disposed of here; it will be discussed where appropriate in the text. Especially noteworthy is the tendency to use ancient Greek words in a new sense despite their established meaning. It perhaps tells more about the users than about the syndrome they are attempting to define. The ancient Greek name, Oedipus, was used in modern Austro-Germanic psychiatry to define a disorder different from that described by Freud when he later used the same word. A related difficulty derives from the different meanings of ordinary language at different times. This problem was minimized here through the use of dictionaries, both English and foreign, of the late eighteenth and early nineteenth centuries.

The present work should not be taken as a kind of sequel to the historical reviews included in many eighteenth- and nineteenth-century clinical works. Among the most remarkable of these is Thomas Arnold's *Observations on the Nature, Kinds, Causes, and Prevention of Insanity, Lunacy, or Madness* (Leicester: G. Ireland for G. Robinson and T. Cadell, 1782 and 1786). Arnold's review is a

[1] This is pictured in I. Bernal, *3000 Years of Art and Life in Mexico* (New York: H. N. Abrams, Inc., 1968), p. 44.

[2] This is discussed in M. D. Altschule, "Only God Can Make a Trio," in *The Roots of Modern Psychiatry* (rev. ed.,) New York: Grune and Stratton, Inc., 1965).

marvelously careful compilation of all the medical authorities up to his time. The historian will find it useful, but it adds little to our understanding of psychopathology today. At best it describes the background of psychiatry as it existed just before the delayed clinical revolution that began in the late eighteenth century and continued for a hundred years. Burton's remarkable *Anatomy of Melancholy,* although it reads like a collection of digressive Augustinian reflections, is the only complete compilation of the writings on that subject up to the seventeenth century and should be studied by those interested in medieval and renaissance psychiatry. The present work gives little space to this period, however, though a few ancient sources are included.

The psychiatric disorders of prominent persons are extensively revealed in history and legend. These illnesses have been discussed in such works as J. R. Whitwell, *Historical Notes on Psychiatry* (London: H. K. Lewis and Co., 1936), R. Burton, *The Anatomy of Melancholy,* and the individual biographies of many notables. Michéa wrote in detail about the hallucinations of many famous persons.[3] One historical figure with psychiatric problems was Queen Elizabeth I, whose terminal illness had severe depressive features, probably secondary to leukemia (the "almonds" of her neck became swollen). The extent to which these illnesses influenced history is interesting but has little importance for the present work.

Fictional descriptions of psychotics are found chiefly in ancient Greek, Elizabethan, and Jacobean dramas.[4] These are significant only in that they portray lay notions of the manifestations of mental disease. Indeed, today's American stage depends so heavily on laymen's interpretations of the Freudian dogma that in the future this dogma may be of interest largely as a literary mode. The literary implications of depression, hypochondriasis, and hysteria in earlier centuries may be surmised from J. F. Sena's *A Bibliography of Melancholy, 1660–1800* (London: The Nether Press, 1970); the number of literary men of that period who experienced these disorders and wrote about them is highly revealing. (Of course those who had more serious illnesses could scarcely have written coherently about them at the time.) In general, however, such literary materials have little relevance for the development of psychopathology and are not included in the present work. It is true that classical Greek dramatists somewhat influenced modern European psychiatry, but though the extent of this influence is difficult to assess, it was probably minor except in the case of the Oedipus legend as misinterpreted by Freud.[5]

There will be only brief discussions of etiologies. For one thing, the etiology of mental disease is unknown although psychogenic hypotheses have been prevalent since antiquity. Caelius Aurelianus in the fifth century A.D. covered much of

[3] See C. F. Michéa, *Du délire des sensations* (Paris: Labé, 1846).
[4] See, e.g., R. R. Reed, Jr., *Bedlam on the Jacobean Stage* (Cambridge, Mass.: Harvard University Press, 1952); also V. Gentili, *Le Figure della Pazzia Nel Teatro Elisabettiano* (Lecce: Edizione Millela, 1969).
[5] See M. D. Altschule, "Greek Revival," in *The Roots of Modern Psychiatry* (rev. ed., New York: Grune and Stratton, Inc., 1965).

modern thinking on this subject when he wrote about mania: "Sometimes it arises from hidden causes, at other times from observable causes." His list of the latter includes "anger, grief, anxiety," as well as "intense straining of the senses and the mind in study, business or other ambitious pursuits." The detailed discussion along these lines in Burton's *Anatomy of Melancholy* provides more extensive coverage.

Purported etiologies have not changed materially in two thousand years, and one important aspect of etiologic concepts still separates them from observational conceptualizations. As Hanson[6] so clearly shows, cause words are always laden with theory and hence speculative to a greater or lesser degree. The present work mentions theoretical considerations only in the broadest, most nonspecific fashion and therefore omits the more specific theorizing of etiologic discussions.

A number of early writers criticized the frequency of careless discussions of etiology. Mandeville, for example, inveighed against theoretical excesses in his book on hypochondriasis and hysteria.

'Tis pride that makes the physician abandon the solid observation of never-erring nature, to take up with the loose conjectures of his own wandering invention, that the world may admire the fertility of his brain; and it is pride in the patient, that makes him in love with the reasoning physician, to have an opportunity of shewing the depth of his own penetration. But if the reasons that are often given by the one, and taken for current by the other, were to be strictly examined into, it would almost induce a man of sense to disown his kind, and make him blush, when he is called a rational creature.

I know that to advance this doctrine is swimming against the stream in our sprightly talkative age, in which the silent experience of pains-taking practitioners is ridiculed, and nothing cry'd up but the witty speculations of hypothetical doctors.[7]

Many physicians today are troubled by the fact that patients with different kinds of mental disorders may have similar psychologic histories. This anomaly is resolved only by those who would interpret everything in psychodynamic terms: The clinical syndrome is then seen as related to the operation of unconscious psychologic factors, while the existence of these factors is surmised on the basis of the syndrome they are supposed to have produced. One eighteenth-century physician, Mead, sought to explain this ancient difficulty by individual differences in the patients' natures, a phenomenon today being studied by geneticists.

There is no disease more to be dreaded than madness. For what greater unhappiness can befal a man, than to be deprived of his reason and understanding; to attack his fellow-creatures with fury like a wild beast; to be tied down, and even beat, to prevent his doing mischief to himself or others: or,

[6] N. R. Hanson, *Perception and Discovery: An Introduction to Scientific Inquiry*, W. C. Humphrey, ed. (San Francisco: Freeman, Cooper, 1969).

[7] R. Mandeville, *A Treatise of the Hypochondriack and Hysteric Diseases: In Three Dialogues* (3rd ed., London: J. Tonson, 1730), pp. iii and iv.

on the contrary, to be sad and dejected, to be daily terrified with vain imaginations; to fancy hobgoblins haunting him; and after a life spent in continual anxiety, to be persuaded that his death will be the commencement of eternal punishment? And to all these may be added this unhappy circumstance, that the disorder is very difficult to be cured. Now, in order to [sic] the clearer comprehension of what I have to say from experience on this disease, I will promise a few hints concerning its nature.

A very frequent cause of this evil is an excessive intention of the mind, and the thoughts long fixed on any one object, even though it be of the pleasing kind. For such intention of mind, such fixed thought, is capable of perverting the rational faculties, as we sometimes observe in studious persons; but when it is blended with some of the passions, as hope, fear, anger, etc. the disorder is heightened; and the madness is accompanied either with melancholy or fury, according to the nature of the cause, and chiefly according to the natural propensity of mind in the patient to this or that passion.[8]

Hill discussed a specific fallacy of etiologic discussions.

Effects are frequently mistaken for causes in the history of diseases, but in none has this error been more common or more fatally injurious than in madness, a certain impatient contempt has pervaded the minds of enquirers on the subject, useful induction has been abandoned for the pride of theory, and pomp of metaphysical reasoning. (In the words of the Editors of the London Medical Review on page iii) "If any one will take the trouble to read the most esteemed works on mental insanity, we have no doubt he will think with us, that the treatises on this subject are more than commonly uninstructive, and that when arrived at the conclusion of his task, he knew little more than when he began it."[9]

Ray's analysis of the sources of error in attempts to establish the etiology of mental disorders was based on the efforts of his predecessors and contemporaries. Today, more than a hundred years later, his criticisms are still valid.

Nothing connected with insanity excites more popular interest than its causes; partly owing, perhaps, to the idea that to learn the cause is the first step towards it cure, but chiefly, no doubt, to an instinctive curiosity to know the why and wherefore of a strange and momentous event. With equal zeal, if not more discretion, the philosopher and the physician have speculated on the subject; and if an imposing array of figures and adverse incidents, embracing almost every human ill, from a blow on the head to a disappointment in love, were always equivalent to true knowledge, we might fancy that we have little to

[8] R. Mead, *Medical Precepts and Cautions,* T. Stack, trans. (London: J. Brindley, 1755), pp. 74-76.

[9] G. N. Hill, *An Essay on the Prevention and Cure of Insanity; with observations on the rules for the detection of pretenders to madness* (London: J. and J. Haddock, 1814), p. 113.

learn respecting the causes of insanity. When we ponder, however, the meaning of certain current words and phrases, and consider the vague and indefinite ideas which they convey, we shall be inclined to suspect, even without any profound acquaintance with the mental movements connected with disease, that we have been mistaking words for ideas,—grasping at a substance and finding only a shadow. The practical importance of the subject requires that it should be rightly understood, and this induces me to enter upon a discussion which might seem, at first sight, more appropriate in a professional treatise.

Our first mistake consists of a vulgar misconception respecting the relations of cause and effect, which is not confined to the ignorant and unthinking. We see it in the common fallacy which supposes that a specific, prominent, well-defined event must necessarily be preceded by some other event equally specific and prominent. This error is the more easily committed, because the imagination is always pleased by discovering an agency whose properties seem to render it abundantly sufficient for the purpose. The mind rests upon it with a certain satisfaction, as if it had arrived at a sure and reliable result. I scarcely need to say how little support is afforded for this notion by the plainest rules of philosophical inquiry. Very often, an event that strongly appeals to the senses, and violently disturbs the present relations of things, may have been prepared by a series of agencies so slight and obscure as to be discovered only by the most keen and penetrating research. They seem to be slight, simply because, with our limited vision, we are unable to discern the whole field of their operations, or measure the results of their mutual dependence. Indeed, there can be no surer way of mistaking the real cause of a signal event than to suppose that it lies upon the surface, ready to be discovered without skilful and laborious research.

We see the same misconception in the common disposition to consider the relation of cause and effect to be determined by proximity or occurrence, or some other casual circumstance, ignoring all distinctions between the necessary and the accidental; and thus we are ever in danger of repeating the process of the untutored mind, by mistaking, in our way, Tenterden steeple for the cause of Goodwin sands. Indeed, it can hardly be denied, that, on this subject, such mistakes have been the rule rather than the exception, both with the wise and the simple. When an attack of insanity takes place, and we look among the occurrences of the past life for the cause of so singular a phenomenon, we seize on the most prominent or peculiar, and easily persuade ourselves that we have found the object of our search. It may be a singular, a remarkable, an extraordinary event, and yet the proof of necessary connection be utterly wanting. That proof seldom can be obtained without an exhaustive investigation of that and many other occurrences in the life of the patient,—the inner as well as the outer life,—and not always, by any means, then. No partial or superficial investigation can lead to a reliable conclusion. So long as a single incident remains untouched, we have no right to pronounce on the sufficiency of any other. But who is willing to take the necessary pains? Who is adequate to such a nice and complicated inquiry? How are its materials to be obtained?

Admitting that the antecedents are thoroughly understood, if that were possible, it would be quite beyond our power to measure the amount of agency exerted by one and another in the production of the disease. The great misfortune, the terrible affliction, the stunning blow, may have had less to do with the final result, than some trouble concealed from the common gaze, deep in the inmost recesses of the inner life. On conversing with those who have recovered from an attack, respecting the incidents which led to it, I have found, oftener than otherwise, that they laid far less stress on the prominent event which had been fixed upon by others as the source of the evil, than on something so slight, apparently, as to have escaped the notice of the most intimate friend. In my observation of insanity, nothing has surprised me more than such revelations of mental experience, completely upsetting, as they did, our own elaborate conclusions respecting the cause of the disease. Not that the revelations of those who have been insane are always reliable, even if they have perfectly recovered, for the very disturbance of mind must necessarily prevent them from reasoning about or even remembering correctly their mental impressions while under the influence of disease; yet, after all due allowance is made, their conclusions may not be more liable to error than those of outside observers. But, well as we may understand these incidents which are obvious to the senses, we can seldom, if ever, be sure that the morbific agency has been exerted by them rather than by those mysterious conditions of the cerebral organism which are indicative of imperfection or tendency to disease, and derived, in the process of generation, from imperfections in the parent or ancestor. . . .

Again occurs a difficulty no less serious than the last. In the series of antecedents which precede an attack of insanity, many of which may seem to be connected by a bond of mutual dependence, by what rule of selection are we led to pronounce this or that the efficient cause,—the *causa causans*? Within what period have we a right to look for the noxious agency? Are we to be confined to the last few weeks? or months? or years? We do not get rid of the difficulty by claiming for our purpose without regard to time or any other circumstance, the incident or event which seems to the mind of a spectator to have had the deepest appreciable effect. We rather substitute for it one still greater. To select any one incident, and leave out of the account entirely the rest, is merely to express an opinion, not to establish a fact. Such a proceeding is worthless, of course, as a matter of science. It can satisfy those only who are dazzled by a show of knowledge.

If driven by force of proof to admit that a multiplicity of incidents are usually concerned, each in its particular way, in producing the ultimate result, we are thus more philosophical in our investigation, more faithful to the truth; but what then becomes of our Tables? Even if, by any device of columns and figures, we could still preserve the tabular form, their statistical character would be utterly gone. To enumerate all the events which precede the attack is to give a history of the case, not to assign its cause.

One source, and perhaps the principal, of the prevalent error, is the habit of regarding insanity as a sharply defined phenomenon, easily separated from all accompanying incidents, like an earthquake or a chemical action, instead of a condition arising from obscure beginnings, culminating more or less rapidly, and declining by imperceptible steps as the darkness of night is succeeded by the light of common day. Any occurrence which can be properly regarded as its cause must necessarily precede the morbid process. But the difficulty is to ascertain that point in the line of sequences which marks the beginning of the diseased action, so that we shall be in no danger of assigning, as a cause, some incident of the morbid process. Of course, the difficulty is all the greater, the longer the duration of the initiatory stage, and the less demonstrative its manifestations. It often happens, in fact, that the first prominent event having, apparently, any connection with the disease, is, clearly, not the cause, but an incident of it; while all before it is too vague, too obscure, too little known, to furnish any light as to the really efficient agency for which we are in search. To avoid mistake on this point requires a knowledge of the patient's history—to mention no other requirement—too minute and thorough to be often obtained. They who have been immediately around him are seldom capable of observing his mental movements correctly, for to do that implies the highest kind of culture, and they may have only the lowest; and yet it is from their reports, chiefly, that the physician is obliged to draw his conclusions respecting the cause. How little reliance can be placed on this source of information daily experience teaches.[10]

Modern etiologic explanations that view psychiatry as a branch of either neurophysiology or sociology are more often polemics than theories at present and hence lie outside the scope of this book.

The present work omits all phrenologic sources, despite the fact that until the late nineteenth century most American and French psychiatrists, and some British, were at least phrenologically oriented. Attempts to relate clinical phenomena to phrenologic dogma produced much feeble writing. Combe, for example, wrote in his famous book on phrenology:

> ___ Monomania or Melancholia is the designation given to a combination of mental symptoms, but which is not indicative of a specific disease. These terms are applied to denote those cases in which only one or a few of the mental powers are deranged, the other remaining entire. But, as already explained, a disease may involve one organ or several without any change of nature; and, therefore, the pathological cause which, affecting one organ, produces monomania, may, by affecting the whole brain, produce general mania, and its nature remain all the time the same. . . .

[10] I. Ray, *Contributions to Mental Pathology* (Boston: Little, Brown and Co., 1873), pp 28-34.

The varieties of monomania known by the names of Religious Melancholy, Hypochondriacal Depression, Nostalgia, Suicidal Mania, etc. have been already accounted for in tracing the relation of the mental symptoms to aberration of function in the primitive powers of the mind, as unfolded by phrenology. Much remains to be done in perfecting this branch of knowledge; but the principle being ascertained, future progress will be more rapid.

After the preceding observations, I need hardly remark, that general MANIA is not a specific disease, but merely an indication that the disease, whatever it may be, implicates the whole brain, and all the faculties of the mind; but it by no means informs us what the kind of morbid action is which is going on in that organ.

When the morbid affection is strictly limited to one or two of the cerebral organs, it often becomes exceedingly difficult to establish its existence in a court of law, as the patient has often a great degree of control over his manifestations, and displays wonderful adroitness in avoiding any exhibition of his infirmity. In regard to the assistance afforded by phrenology in such cases, the same remarks apply as in partial idiocy, and therefore need not be repeated.[11]

When neuroanatomy finally vanquished phrenology it created a vacuum that was filled in the twentieth century by psychodynamic superstitions. Since these superstitions developed after the period covered by this book they are not discussed here. Like phrenology, they deserve to be treated separately in due course.

In spite of this long list of exclusions there remains a huge amount of material produced during the two thousand years prior to 1905 on the nature, development, and course of the different mental disorders whose existence has been recognized— albeit under different names—during that period. Organizing and discussing this material does not commit this editor (or any reader) to the belief that these disorders are diseases, or syndromes, or merely psychologic reaction patterns.

The present work will consist of two parts: general aspects, including theoretical considerations, and clinical observations, including the development of syndromes.

Syndromes were developed mainly between circa 500 B.C. and A.D. 1820; the subsyndromes of melancholy with stupor, paranoia, hebephrenia, catatonia,

---

[11] A. Combe, *Observations on Mental Derangement* (Edinburgh: J. Anderson, 1831), pp. 282-283. This work led the Boston *Medical Magazine* to say: "To throw away figure, and speak in plain language and sincerity, we have read no production on mental derangement which we consider so valuable as the volume before us; none which unfolds, so much to our satisfaction, the philosophy of the disease, or leads to so rational a mode of preventing and removing it."

Andrew quoted with approval (p. 219) from his brother George's *System of Phrenology:* "The discoveries of the revolution of the globe, and the circulation of the blood were splendid displays of genius, interesting and beneficial to mankind; but their results, compared with the consequences which must inevitably follow Dr. Gall's discovery of the functions of the brain (embracing, as it does, the true theory of the animal, moral, and intellectual constitution of man) sink into relative insignificance." The opponents of phrenology were likened to the opponents of Copernicus, Gallileo, Newton, and Harvey. Gall was a Viennese, and the hysterical enthusiasm with which his ideas were received in Boston and some other cities foreshadowed events a hundred years later.

neurasthenia, and anxiety neurosis were isolated during the rest of the nineteenth century. The separation of one syndrome from another implies a classification, but the finicky hairsplitting pursued by some mid-nineteenth-century psychiatrists led to a state of complete anarchy that ended only with Kraepelin's writings. It must be remembered, however, that Kraepelin's authority in this regard stemmed from the widespread recognition of his outstanding qualities as a clinician. His classification, though rigid and unnatural, therefore, submerged those of lesser men. Of the classifications superseded by Kraepelin's some today seem irrational, some are unintelligible, and all are solipsistic except when clearly derivative. Classifications like Cullen's are clearly modeled after Linné's taxonomic schemes. Others represent attempts to organize clinical data so as to accord with ideas of mental processes current in the nineteenth century. Haslam's comments, however, effectively dispose of the latter.

The difficulty of proposing a satisfactory theory of the human mind, must have been felt by every person, who has touched this delicate string since the days of Aristotle, and failure must be expected in him who attempts it: yet the endeavour is laudable, and miscarriage is not linked with disgrace. . . .

Enquiries of this nature have been usually conducted by commenting on the numerous and discordant authorities which have treated on metaphysical subjects; these persons, however they may differ on many points, appear to be pretty generally agreed, that the human mind possesses certain faculties and powers; as imagination, judgment, reason, and memory. They seem to consider these, as so many departments, or offices of the mind, and therefore class men according to the excellence or predominance of these powers. One man, is said to be distinguished by the brilliancy of his imagination; another, by the solidity of his judgment; a third, by the acuteness of his reason; and a fourth, by the promptitude and accuracy of his recollection.

As far as I have observed respecting the human mind, (and I speak with great hesitation and diffidence,) it does not possess, all those powers and faculties with which the pride of man has thought proper to invest it. By our senses, we are enabled to become acquainted with objects, and we are capable of recollecting them in a greater or less degree; the rest, appears to be merely a contrivance of language.

If mind, were actually capable of the operations attributed to it, and possessed of these powers, it would necessarily have been able to create a language expressive of these powers and operations. But the fact is otherwise: The language, which characterizes mind and its operations, has been borrowed from external objects; for mind has no language peculiar to itself.[12]

Symptoms of the Disease. On this part of the subject, authors have commonly descended to minute particularities, and studied discriminations. Distinctions have been created, rather from the peculiar turn of the patient's

[12] J. Haslam, *Observations on Madness and Melancholy* (London: J. Callow, 1809), pp. 7-9.

propensities and discourse, than from any marked difference in the varieties and species of the disorder. Every person of sound mind, possesses something peculiar to himself, which distinguishes him from others, and constitutes his idiosyncrasy of body and individuality of character: in the same manner, every lunatic discovers something singular in his aberrations from sanity of mind; but who are subject to relapses, which would render it improper, and even dangerous, to trust them at large in society: and with those, who are upon the curable establishment, a recurrence of the malady very frequently takes place. Upon these occasions, there is an ample scope for observing the first attack of the disease.[13]

These attempts stand in marked contrast to the classifications of others.[14] That of Areteus, for example, had nothing to do with notions of the nature of mind as expounded by ancient Greek psychologists. His classification is remarkably modern; though never stated in the following form, it was easily derived from his writings by Whitwell:

1. Epilepsy and associated mental conditions
   a) Ordinary
   b) Hysterical[15]
2. Melancholia
3. Mania
   a) Ordinary
   b) Recurrent
   c) Divine
4. Phrenitis
5. Alcoholic or drug delirium
6. Senile dementia
7. Secondary dementia

So long as classifications are based solely on clinical considerations—and no etiologic, anatomic, or biochemical classifications are today acceptable in psychiatry—they will be determined by physicians in active clinical practice.

The works of the nineteenth-century psychiatrists make it clear that perhaps as many as fifty percent of their psychotic patients had cerebral syphilis. Many of the physicians were unaware of this disease but today it is recognized from the post-mortem descriptions. Some patients diagnosed as having syphillis were treated

---

[13] Ibid., pp. 39–41.

[14] Good discussions of these ancient psychologies are to be found in B. Rand, *The Classical Psychologists* (Boston: Houghton Mifflin Co., 1912); R. B. Onian, *The Origins of European Thought about the Body, the Mind, the Soul, the World, Time, Fate* (Cambridge: Cambridge University Press, 1951); B. Snell, *The Discovery of the Mind,* T. G. Rosenmeyer, trans. (Cambridge, Mass.: Harvard University Press, 1955); R. J. Herrnstein, and E. G. Boring, eds., *A Source Book in the History of Psychology* (Cambridge, Mass.: Harvard University Press, 1966).

[15] Hystero-epilepsy was a common diagnosis in the late nineteenth century and the early part of the twentieth. Today the syndrome is called hyperventilation tetany.

with mercury and developed mercury psychoses. Patients with these so-called organic disorders, as well as some with tumors, cysts, cerebral hemorrhages, or epileptogenic lesions, had psychopathological symptoms identical with those which today are considered purely functional. This nonspecificity of syndromes received comment that was often ambiguous or tangential but on occasion more forthright.[16] According to Ball:

Insanity properly speaking is absolutely distinct from the delirium of the acute diseases. There are no anatomic lesions in insanity; those found are the consequences and not the causes of the illness.[17]

Leuret faced the same problem and came to a basically different but operationally similar conclusions, expressed in three striking chapter headings:

I. If it is true that insanity depends on a change in the brain, we ignore completely the nature of this change.

II. Moral treatment, generally used, is not considered anything but an adjunct of physical treatment.

III. Among the insane, intelligence and the feelings cannot be restored to their regular type without the help of moral treatment; and this method of treatment is the only one that has any direct influence on the symptoms of insanity.[18]

As a corollary, Krafft-Ebing's words offer a more modern view.

A diffuse disease of the cerebral cortex must necessarily induce a change of consciousness and the psychic personality. Hence the psychosis appears not simply as a disease of the brain, but also as an abnormal alteration of the personality.[19]

Some of the syndromes under consideration in the present work were poorly defined and elusive. This was inevitable since the definition of disorders was based on one observer's selection and characterization of items from the speech and behavior of patients. Attempts to define diseases in terms of such subjective phenomena alone usually fail. They succeed only if such phenomena are meticulously described and uniformly defined. Such precision is not characteristic of psychiatric writings, as the reader will quickly learn. Nevertheless it has been possible to bring some order out of chaos without resorting to a Procustean bed.

A question naturally arises about why the manic-depressive psychosis was recognized as an entity centuries before the other main psychiatric syndromes. The

[16] For a modern discussion of this matter see H. G. Wolff and D. Curran, "Nature of Delirium and Allied States: The Dysergastic Reaction," *Archives of Neurology and Psychiatry,* 1935, *33*, 1175.

[17] B. Ball *Leçons sur les maladies mentales* (Paris: Asselin et cie., 1880), p. 23.

[18] F. Leuret, *Du traitement moral de la folie* (Paris: J. B. Baillière, 1840).

[19] R. von Krafft-Ebing, *Text-Book of Insanity Based on Clinical Observations for Practitioners and Students of Medicine,* C. G. Chaddock, trans. (Philadelphia: F. A. Davis, 1904), p. 23.

explanation is that, although definitions may differ somewhat with time and place, in the main depression and elation are easily recognized when they exceed the limits of normal day to day variations in mood. In contrast, disordered thinking, manifested by delusions, is much harder to recognize unless it is extreme. In its milder forms this disorder is marked only by deviations from the norm in occupation, ambition, manners, attitude toward education, personal behavior, etc., and as such may be considered merely a personal idiosyncrasy or an antisocial attitude. These diagnostic difficulties are especially likely to arise in a highly complex society where these behavior patterns may simply be manifestations of a considered unwillingness to respond to social stresses in accepted—usually stereo- typed—ways. Hence simple observations of behavior were often not helpful in diagnosing thinking disorders. It was not until the development of associationist psychology in the eighteenth century that the interpretation of thinking disorders was given direction.

Classical Greece gave us the concept of manic-depressive psychosis but failed to identify what is today called schizophrenia. Delusions and hallucinations were recognized but not as symptoms of a specific disorder. In the Middle Ages both soul-psychology and demonology were believed capable of explaining all ills. The dominance of this kind of thought prevented any rational approach to the study of psychiatric phenomena. When the syndromes of today's psychiatry began to crystallize in the writings of nineteenth-century psychiatrists, progress was delayed by strict adherance to formal classifications. Dementia, for example, was considered a sequel rather than a disorder in itself. Thus, although the preceding illnesses may have been manifested by distorted thinking and perception (including hallucina- tions), they were called hysteria, mania, or melancholia in accordance with their other chief manifestations.

Psychiatry, like every other branch of human knowledge, has accommodated itself to developments in human institutions and changes in human ideas. The writings chosen for inclusion in the present work may have only limited interest for historians because they are selected, fragmented, and out of context. To persons working in the field of mental diseases, however, they show how today's concepts grew, not *de novo,* but out of observations made on patients during the last two thousand years. It is worth noting that the clinical phenomena are remarkably uniform despite the massive social and psychologic changes that have occurred. As Petrarch observed, and as Burton commented approvingly, "We change language, habits, laws, customs, manners, but not vices, not diseases, not the symptoms of folly and madness, they are still the same." (We shall leave to others any conclusion that social and psychologic factors do not determine the symptoms.) Some of the earlier writings also show how a useful clinical concept was marred by subsequent solipsistic revisions at the hands of great dogmatists; in such instances a return to some earlier usage might be in order.

This sourcebook is a history of clinical thinking in which the clinicians speak for themselves. Only the order of their presentation is dictated by this editor. In any case credit is given where it is due, and thus is avoided the harsh judgment of

Synesius, who said, "It is a worse crime to steal dead men's works than their clothes." Nevertheless it must be recognized that this book is like a pawnbroker's shop—furnished with other men's goods.[20]

---

[20] I am responsible for the translations unless otherwise noted in the references. For the most part I was aware of no difficulties in making them; on a few occasions, however, I have felt for Sieveking, Romberg's translator, who wrote in a footnote: "We have thought it right to attempt a translation of this passage, as containing a quintessential view of our author concerning hypochondriasis, but we are bound to confess our inability to comprehend his real meaning."

PART I

GENERAL ASPECTS AND THEORETICAL CONSIDERATIONS

APPROACHES TO GENERAL ASPECTS OF MENTAL DISEASE

Post-Hippocratic psychiatric writers on mental disease could readily recognize the clinical patterns that constituted syndromes, but the causes of mental disorders created problems that were (and still are today) largely insoluble. The problem of etiology has been approached in several ways. One was to study the precursors of the mental disorder, some of which were easily recognized, e.g., alcohol excess, drug abuse, and, some centuries later, syphilis and the mercury used to treat it. The eighteenth- and nineteenth-century authors also collected post-mortem material, adding a variety of brain lesions to their list of etiologic factors. Much of this post hoc data is of dubious value. Other observations that also arouse skepticism are lists, often very long, of psychologic or social factors that at least seemed to precede the onset of the illness. Burton's *Anatomy of Melancholy* contains the longest and perhaps most varied early list of this kind. As the amount of this material expanded again in the late eighteenth and early nineteenth century a few authors, notably Haslam (see page 103) began to wonder whether it was possible to distinguish between the early manifestations of mental disorders and psychosocial causes. This problem was not settled then nor is it yet.

Another approach treated the phenomena of mental disturbances as exaggeration, distortion, or suppression of normal mental processes. Since knowledge of normal psychology was almost entirely theoretical, based on fragmentary observation, the clinical use of material derived from the concepts of normal psychology was either vague or fragmentary.

The next pages will show how clinicians, principally of the eighteenth and nineteenth centuries (the post-demoniac era), used psychological concepts then current to interpret mental disorders.

The Unconscious Mind

1

Early in the nineteenth century widespread interest in reflexes, especially spinal, led to much theorizing on the reciprocal relations between brain and viscera, with the reflexes seen as indicating not only the pathway but also the process of this relationship. This material, however important historically for the study of the reflex, is not a source of today's psychiatric thinking and will not be considered here. Griesinger's use of this material came a little closer to psychiatric thinking; he wrote about psychic reflexes that involved the hypothetical "highest" (thinking) centers of the brain and their role in mental disease. Griesinger's treatise (1843) was well received and repeatedly referred to, even as late as the 1890s, but it had no basis in observation and remained mere speculation.[1]

Griesinger (1845)

Griesinger's more solid contribution to the concept of the unconscious mind came from his clinical observations. For example, he emphasized the fact that the patient's illness was the outward culmination of a prolonged, more or less submerged process in which many factors participated.

> ... As regards the mental sphere, we must faithfully and intelligently comprehend the relation of the predispositions and congenital peculiarities of disposition, the degree of education, and the governing inclinations of the individual—his mode of life and views of the world, his outward position and the nature of his thoughts; thus endeavouring to gain a full picture of the history of the individuality. Only in this way is an insight into the true history of these diseases possible; only thus can we succeed in grasping at their beginnings those

[1] W. Griesinger, "Über psychischen Reflexactionen, mit einem Blick auf das Wesen der psychischen Krankheiten," *Archiv für physiologischen Heilkunde,* 1843, 2, 72–108.

fine threads which have ultimately entwined themselves into delirious conceptions; only thus can we, in many cases where insanity appears suddenly and
apparently without motive, recognise the far-back commencement of the
preparation for the disease, and the almost mathematical necessity of its
occurrence.[2]

Maudsley (1867, 1883)

After a British controversy about who had discovered the unconscious mind had
simmered down, Maudsley was able to digest the content of the arguments and
ignore the specific claims to priority. He gave most credit for expounding the idea,
if not for making the discovery, to Beneke, who wrote in Germany a generation
before the British controversy broke out.

Consciousness gives no account of the essential material conditions which
underlie every mental manifestation, and determine the character of it. . . . The
quality of the ideas which arise in the mind under certain circumstances, the
whole character, indeed, of our insight at the time, is notably determined in
great part by the feeling which may then have sway; and that feeling is not
always objectively caused, but may be entirely due to a particular bodily
condition, as the daily experience of every one may convince him, and as the
earlier phenomena of insanity so strikingly illustrate.[3]

There is an appropriation of external impressions by the mind or brain, which
regularly takes place without any, or only with a very obscure, affection of
consciousness. . . . The impressions which it thus receives and retains do not
produce definite ideas and feelings, but they nevertheless permanently affect the
mind's nature; so that as an individual consciously provides his food, and then
leaves the due assimilation of it to the unconscious action of the organism, in
like manner may he consciously arrange the circumstances in which he will live,
but cannot then prevent the unconscious assimilation of their influence, and the
corresponding modification of his character. Not only slight habits of movement
are thus acquired, but habits of thought and feeling are imperceptibly organized;
so that an acquired nature may ultimately govern one who is not at all conscious
that he has changed. Let any one take careful note of his dreams and he will find
that many of the seemingly unfamiliar things with which his mind is then
occupied, and which appear to be new and strange productions, are traceable to
the unconscious appropriations of the day. . . .

It is a truth which cannot be too distinctly borne in mind, that consciousness
is not co-extensive with mind. From the first moment of its independent

[2] W. Griesinger, *Mental Pathology and Therapeutics*, from the 2nd German ed., C. L.
Robertson and J. Rutherford, trans. (London: The New Sydenham Society, 1867), p. 129. This
was little changed from the first edition of 1845.

[3] H. Maudsley, *The Physiology and Pathology of the Mind* (New York: D. Appleton and Co.,
1867), p. 13.

existence the brain begins to assimilate impressions from without, and to re-act thereto in corresponding organic adaptations; this it does at first without consciousness, and this it continues to do unconsciously more or less throughout life. Thus it is that mental power is being organized before the supervention of consciousness, and that the mind is subsequently regularly modified as a natural process without the intervention of consciousness. The preconscious action of the mind, as certain metaphysical psychologists in Germany have called it, and the unconscious action of the mind, which is now established beyond all rational doubt, are assuredly facts of which the most ardent psychologist must admit that self-consciousness can give us no account.

Everything which has existed with any completeness in consciousness is preserved, after its disappearance therefrom, in the mind or brain, and may reappear in consciousness at some future time. That which persists or is retained has been differently described as a residuum, or relic, or trace, or vestige, or again as potential, or latent, or dormant idea; and it is on the existence of such residua that memory depends. Not only definite ideas, however, but all affections of the nervous system, feelings of pleasure and pain, desires, and even its outward reactions, thus leave behind them their residua, and lay the foundations of modes of thought, feeling, and action. Particular talents are sometimes formed quite, or almost quite, involuntarily; and complex actions, which were first consciously performed by dint of great application, become by repetition automatic; ideas, which were at first consciously associated, ultimately call one another up without any consciousness, as we see in the quick perception or intuition of the man of large worldly experience; and feelings, once active, leave behind them their unconscious residua, thus affecting the general tone of the character, so that, apart from the original or inborn nature of the individual, contentment, melancholy, cowardice, bravery, and even moral feeling, are generated as the results of particular life experiences. Consciousness is not able to give any account of the manner in which these various residua are perpetuated, and how they exist latent in the mind; but a fever, a poison in the blood, or a dream, may at any moment recall ideas, feelings, and activities which seemed for ever vanished. The lunatic sometimes reverts, in his ravings, to scenes and events of which, when in his sound senses, he has no memory. . . .

It has been before said that mind and consciousness are not synonymous; it may now be added, that the existence of mind does not necessarily involve the activity of mind. Descartes certainly maintained that the mind always thinks; and others, resting on that assumption, have held that we must always dream in sleep, because the mind, being spiritual, cannot cease to act; for non-activity would be non-existence. Such opinions only illustrate how completely metaphysical conceptions may overrule the best understanding; so far from the mind being always active, it is the fact that at each moment the greater part of the mind is not only unconscious but inactive. Mental power exists in statical equilibrium as well as in manifested energy; and the utmost tension of a particular mental activity may not avail to call forth from their secret repository the dormant energies of latent residua, even when most urgently needed: no man can call to mind at any moment the thousandth part of his knowledge. How utterly helpless is consciousness to give any account of the statical condition of mind! But as statical mind is in reality the statical condition of the organic element which ministers to its manifestations, it is plain that if we ever are to know anything of inactive mind it is to the progress of physiology that we must look for information.

Consciousness reveals nothing of the process by which one idea calls another into activity, and has no control whatever over the manner of the reproduction; it is only when the idea is made active by virtue of some association, when the *effect* solicits or extorts attention, that we are conscious of it; and there is no power in the mind to call up ideas indifferently. If we would recollect something which at the moment escapes us, the best way of succeeding confessedly is to permit the mind to work unconsciously; and while the consciousness is otherwise occupied, the forgotten name or circumstance will oftentimes flash into the memory. . . .

Not only is the actual process of the association of our ideas independent of consciousness, but that assimilation or blending of similar ideas, or of the like in different ideas, by which general ideas are formed, is in no way under the control or cognizance of consciousness. . . .

But the process of unconscious mental elaboration is sufficiently illustrated in daily experience. In dreams some can compose vigorously and fluently, or speak most eloquently, who can do nothing of the sort when awake. . . .

It has been previously said that mental action does not necessarily imply consciousness, and again, that mental existence does not necessarily involve mental activity: it may now be affirmed that the most important part of mental action, the essential process on which thinking depends, is unconscious mental activity. We repeat, then, the question: how can self-consciousness suffice to furnish the facts of a true mental science? Consciousness is not a faculty or substance, but a quality or attribute of the concrete mental act; and it may exist in different degrees of intensity or it may be absent altogether. In so far as there is consciousness, there is certainly mental activity; but it is not true that in so far as there is mental activity there is consciousness; it is only with a certain intensity of representation or conception that consciousness appears. What else, then, is the so-called interrogation of consciousness but a self-revelation of the particular mental act, whose character it must needs share? Consciousness can never be a valid and unprejudiced witness; for although it testifies to the existence of a particular subjective modification, yet when that modification has anything of a morbid character, consciousness is affected by the taint and is morbid also. Accordingly, the lunatic appeals to the evidence of his own consciousness for the truth of his hallucination or delusion, and insists that he has as sure evidence of its reality as he has of the argument of any one who may try to convince him of his error; and he is right: to one who has vertigo the world turns round. A man may easily be conscious of freewill when, isolating the particular mental act, he cuts himself off from the consideration of the causes which have preceded it, and on which it depends.[4]

It is surprising how uncomfortable any one may be made by the obscure notion of something which he ought to have said or done, but did not, and which he cannot for the life of him now remember. There is a dim feeling of some impulse unsatisfied, an effort, as it were, of the lost idea to get into consciousness—a certain activity of it not sufficient to excite consciousness, but sufficient to react upon the unconscious mental life, and to produce a feeling of discomfort or vague unrest, which is relieved directly the idea bursts into consciousness.[5]

It behoves us here to settle clearly in our minds the relation of consciousness to ideational activity, or at any rate to be on our guard against considering consciousness as co-extensive with such activity. When the whole energy of an idea that is excited passes immediately outwards in ideomotor action, then there is scarce any, or there may be no, consciousness of it; in order that there may be consciousness of the idea, it is necessary not only that its excitation reach a certain intensity, but that the whole force of it do not pass immediately outwards in the reaction. . . .

The interference of consciousness is often an actual impediment in the association of ideas, as it notably is to the performance of movements that have attained the complete ease of an automatic execution. It happens that we try hard to remember something, and are unable by the utmost effort of volition, and the strongest direction of consciousness, to do so: we thereupon give up the attempt, and direct our attention to something else; and, after a while, the result for which we strove in vain, flashes into consciousness: the automatic action of the brain has worked it out. . . . An active consciousness is always detrimental to the best and most successful thought: the thinker who is actively attentive to the succession of his ideas is thinking to little purpose; what the genuine thinker observes is that he is conscious of the words which he is uttering or writing, while the thought, unconsciously elaborated by the organic action of the brain, flows from unpenetrated depths into consciousness.[6]

It is obvious then, not only how desires become the motives of action, but how they are gradually evolved into their complete form out of the unconscious organic appetites. In the desire of the adult there is necessarily some sort of *conception* of what is desired, though it is at times a not very definite one; but in the child, as in the idiot, we frequently witness a vague restlessness evincing an undefined want of, or desire for, something of which itself is unconscious, but which, when obtained, presently produces quiet and satisfaction: the organic life speaks out with an as yet inarticulate utterance. Most striking is that example of

[4] Ibid., pp. 14–24.
[5] Ibid., p. 113.
[6] Ibid., pp. 118–120.

the evolution of organic life into consciousness which is observed at the time of puberty, when new organs come into action; when vague and ill-understood desires give rise to obscure impulses that have no defined aim, and produce a restlessness which, when misapplied, is often mischievous: the amorous appetite thus first declares its existence.[7]

Again, the desire naturally attaching to a certain aim is often transferred after a time to the means by which that aim is attained, so that there ensue in this way manifold secondary formations . . .[8]

. . . Consciousness reveals the particular state of mind of the moment, but does not reveal the long series of causes on which it depends. It is a deliberate fooling of one's self to say that actions depend upon the will, and then not to ask upon what the will depends.[9]

Maudsley believed that some appreciation of the unconscious background of morbid conscious states might be surmised from a careful anamnesis. In this he echoed Griesinger.

It is evident, then, that if we had a complete knowledge of the inner nature of an individual, if we could penetrate that most exquisitely organized fabric of thought which by reason of his particular life-experience has been grafted on the original capabilities, it would be possible to foretell with certainty his mode of thought and conduct under any given circumstances—a prediction which, as it is, those who know a man best often fail not to make, with close approximation to truth. But inasmuch as no two minds are originally exactly alike, and as no two persons have precisely similar experiences, the specialty of human conditions being infinite in variety, we cannot obtain the exact and complete elements for a correct and definite judgment of the operation of a given cause upon any individual. None the less true is it that every cause does operate definitely by as stern a necessity as any which exists in physical nature.

Once more, then, is it rendered evident how necessary to a complete psychology of the individual is the consideration of the circumstances in which he has lived, and in relation to which he has developed, as well as the observation of his habits of thought, feeling, and action. From what has been said of ideas and their associations, it is obvious that in the same language, when used by different people, there must often be considerable difference in regard to the fulness and exactness of the ideas conveyed by it.[10]

It is obvious, however, that even in the sound mind the quantity and quality of the volition depend upon the fulness of the reflection, and that any hindrance to the due association of ideas will *pro tanto* affect the will: if the particular

[7] Ibid., p. 132.
[8] Ibid., p. 142.
[9] Ibid., p. 149.
[10] Ibid., pp. 124–125.

volition were to be resolved by a retrograde metamorphosis into its component elements, there would be an explication or unfolding of all the ideas and desires which had gone to form it; and, going still further back in the analysis, there would be a revelation even of those particular relations in life which the individual's definite organization of ideas, the character of his *ego,* implies.[11]

Maudsley denied vigorously that the use of free association was of any value in uncovering unconscious material. However he offered no method of his own.

The method of interrogating self-consciousness may be employed, . . . without carrying it to a metaphysical extreme. Empirical psychology, founded on *direct* consciousness as distinguished from the *transcendental* consciousness on which metaphysics is based, claims to give a faithful record of our different states of mind and their mutual relations, and has been extravagantly lauded, by the Scotch school, as an inductive science. Its value as a science must plainly rest upon the sufficiency and reliability of consciousness as a witness of that which takes place in the mind. Is the foundation then sufficiently secure? It may well be doubted; and for the following reasons:

(*a.*) There are but few individuals who are capable of attending to the succession of phenomena in their own minds; such introspection demanding a particular cultivation, and being practised with success by those only who have learned the terms, and been imbued with the theories, of the system of psychology supposed to be thereby established.

(*b.*) There is no agreement between those who have acquired the power of introspection: and men of apparently equal cultivation and capacity will, with the utmost sincerity and confidence, lay down directly contradictory propositions. It is not possible to convince either opponent of error, as it might be in a matter of objective science, because he appeals to a witness whose evidence can be taken by no one but himself, and whose veracity, therefore, cannot be tested.

(*c.*) To direct consciousness inwardly to the observation of a particular state of mind is to isolate that activity for the time, to cut it off from its relations, and, therefore, to render it unnatural. In order to observe its own action, it is necessary that the mind pause from activity; and yet it is the train of activity that is to be observed. As long as you cannot effect the pause necessary for self-contemplation, there can be no observation of the current of activity: if the pause is effected, then there can be nothing to observe. This cannot be accounted a vain and theoretical objection; for the results of introspection too surely confirm its validity: what was a question once is a question still, and instead of being resolved by introspective analysis is only fixed and fed.

(*d.*) The madman's delusion is of itself sufficient to excite profound distrust, not only in the objective truth, but in the subjective worth, of the testimony of an individual's self-consciousness. Descartes laid it down as the fundamental proposition of philosophy that whatever the mind could clearly and disctinctly

[11] Ibid., p. 161.

conceive, was true: if there is one thing more clearly and distinctly conceived than another, it is commonly the madman's delusion. No marvel, then, that psychologists, since the time of Descartes, have held that the veracity of consciousness is to be relied upon only under certain rules, from the violation of which, Sir W. Hamilton believed, the contradictions of philosophy have arisen. On what evidence then do the rules rest? Either on the evidence of consciousness, whence it happens that each philosopher and each lunatic has his own rules, and no advance is made; or upon the observation and judgment of mankind, to confess which is very much like throwing self-consciousness overboard—not otherwise than as was advantageously done by positive science when the figures on the thermometer, and not the subjective feelings of heat or cold, were recognised to be the true test of the individual's temperature.

It is not merely a charge against self-consciousness that it is not reliable in that of which it does give information; but it is a proveable charge against it that it does not give any account of a large and important part of our mental activity: its light reaches only to states of consciousness, and not to states of mind. Its evidence then is not only untrustworthy save under conditions which it nowise helps us to fix, but it is of little value, because it has reference only to a small part of that for which its testimony is invoked. May we not then justly say that self-consciousness is utterly incompetent to supply the facts for the building up of a truly inductive psychology?[12]

When we experience a state of consciousness that we are not able to refer to an exciting cause, as we refer the sensation of sound to the external body, we invent a faculty as the cause of it.[13]

[12] Ibid., pp. 9–11.
[13] H. Maudsley, *Body and Will* (London: Kegan, Paul, Trench and Co., 1883), p. 73.

Unconscious Psychologic Manifestations of Sexuality

2

The idea that repressed, distorted, or diverted sexual drives are a main cause of mental and emotional disorders is widely regarded as a great twentieth-century discovery. Actually the idea is one of the oldest in the history of medicine.

Burton (1621)

Robert Burton summarized the writings of the two thousand years that antedated his own.

> Because Lodovicus Mercatus, in his second book *de mulier. affect. cap.* 4, and Rodericus à Castro, *de morb. mulier. cap.* 3, *lib.* 2, two famous physicians in Spain, Daniel Sennertus of Wittenberg, *lib.* 1, *part.* 2, *cap.* 13, with others, have vouchsafed in their works, not long since published, to write two just treatises *de Melancholiâ Virginum, Monialium et Viduarum,* as a particular species of melancholy (which I have already specified) distinct from the rest; (for it much differs from that which commonly befalls men and other women, as having one only cause proper to women alone) I may not omit in this general survey of melancholy symptoms, to set down the particular signs of such parties so misaffected.
> ... This melancholy may happen to widows, with much care and sorrow, as frequently it doth, by reason of a sudden alteration of their accustomed course of life, &c. To such as lie in childbed *ob suppressam purgationem;* but to nuns and more ancient maids, and some barren women for the causes aforesaid, 'tis more familiar, *crebriùs his quam reliquis accidit, inquit Rodericus,* the rest are not altogether excluded.
> Out of these causes Rodericus defines it with Areteus, to be *angorem animi,* a vexation of the mind, a sudden sorrow from a small, light, or no occasion, with a kind of still dotage and grief of some part or other, head, heart, breasts, sides,

154987

back, belly, &c., with much solitariness, weeping, distraction, &c., from which they are sometimes suddenly delivered, because it comes and goes by fits, and is not so permanent as other melancholy.

... They complain many times, saith Mercatus, of a great pain in their heads, about their hearts, and hypochondries, and so likewise in their breasts, which are often sore, sometimes ready to swoon, their faces are inflamed, and red, they are dry, thirsty, suddenly hot, much troubled with wind, cannot sleep, &c. And from hence proceed *ferina deliramenta,* a brutish kind of dotage, troublesome sleep, terrible dreams in the night, *subrusticus pudor et verecundia ignava,* a foolish kind of bashfulness to some, perverse conceits and opinions, dejection of mind, much discontent, preposterous judgment. They are apt to loathe, dislike, disdain, to be weary of every object, &c., each thing almost is tedious to them, they pine away, void of counsel, apt to weep, and tremble, timorous, fearful, sad, and out of all hope of better fortunes. They take delight in nothing for the time, but love to be alone and solitary, though that do them more harm; and thus they are affected so long as this vapour lasteth; but by and by as pleasant and merry as ever they were in their lives, they sing, discourse, and laugh in any good company, upon all occasions, as so by fits it takes them now and then, except the malady be inveterate, and then 'tis more frequent, vehement, and continuate. Many of them cannot tell how to express themselves in words, or how it holds them, what ails them, you cannot understand them, or well tell what to make of their sayings; so far gone sometimes, so stupefied and distracted, they think themselves bewitched, they are in despair, *aptæ ad fletum, desperationem, dolores mammis et hypochondriis.* Mercatus therefore adds, now their breasts, now their hypochondries, belly and sides, then their heart and head aches, now heat, then wind, now this, now that offends, they are weary of all; and yet will not, cannot again tell how, where or what offends them, though they be in great pain, agony, and frequently complain, grieving, sighing, weeping, and discontented still, *sine causâ manifestâ,* most part, yet I say they will complain, grudge, lament, and not be persuaded, but that they are troubled with an evil spirit, which is frequent in Germany, saith Rodericus, amongst the common sort; and to such as are most grievously affected (for he makes three degrees of this disease in women), they are in despair, surely forespoken or bewitched, and in extremity of their dotage (weary of their lives), some of them will attempt to make away themselves. Some think they see visions, confer with spirits and devils, they shall surely be damned, are afraid of some treachery, imminent danger, and the like, they will not speak, make answer to any question, but are almost distracted, mad, or stupid for the time, and by fits; and thus it holds them, as they are more or less affected, and as the inner humour is intended or remitted, or by outward objects and perturbations aggravated, solitariness, idleness, &c.

Many other maladies there are incident to young women, out of that one and only cause above specified, many feral diseases. I will not so much as mention their names, melancholy alone is the subject of my present discourse, from which I will not swerve. The several cures of this infirmity, concerning diet, which must be very sparing, phlebotomy, physic, internal, external remedies, are at large in great variety in Rodericus à Castro, Sennertus, and Mercatus, which whoso will, as occasion serves, may make use of. But the best and surest remedy of all, is to see them well placed, and married to good husbands in due time, *hinc illæ lachrymæ*, that is the primary cause, and this the ready cure, to give them content to their desires. I write not this to patronize any wanton, idle flirt, lascivious or light housewives, which are too forward many times, unruly, and apt to cast away themselves on him that comes next, without all care, counsel, circumspection, and judgment. If religion, good discipline, honest education, wholesome exhortation, fair promises, fame and loss of good name, cannot inhibit and deter such (which to chaste and sober minds cannot choose but avail much), labour and exercise, strict diet, rigour and threats, may more opportunely be used, and are able of themselves to qualify and divert an ill-disposed temperament. For seldom should you see an hired servant, a poor handmaid, though ancient, that is kept hard to her work, and bodily labour, a coarse country wench troubled in this kind, but noble virgins, nice gentlewomen, such as are solitary and idle, live at ease, lead a life out of action and employment, that fare well, in great houses and jovial companies, ill disposed peradventure of themselves, and not willing to make any resistance, discontented otherwise, of weak judgment, able bodies, and subject to passions, (*grandiores virgines*, saith Mercatus, *steriles et vidiæ plerumque melancholicæ,*) such for the most part are misaffected, and prone to this disease. I do not so much pity them that may otherwise be eased, but those alone that out of a strong temperament, innate constitution, are violently carried away with this torrent of inward humours, and though very modest of themselves, sober, religious, virtuous, and well give (as many so distressed maids are), yet cannot make resistance, these grievances will appear, this malady will take place, and now manifestly show itself, and may not otherwise be helped. But where am I? Into what subject have I rushed? What have I to do with nuns, maids, virgins, widows? I am a bachelor myself, and lead a monastic life in a college, *næ ego sane ineptus qui hæc dixerim,* I confess, 'tis an *indecorum,* and as Pallas a virgin blushed, when Jupiter by change spake of love matters in her presence, and turned away her face; *me reprimam,* though my subject necessarily require it, I will say no more.

And yet I must and will say something more, add a word or two *in gratiam Virginum et Viduarum,* in favor of all such distressed parties, in commiseration of their present estate. And as I cannot choose but condole their mishap that labour of this infirmity, and are destitute of help in this case, so must I needs inveigh against them that are in fault, more than manifest causes, and as bitterly tax those tyrannizing pseudo-politicians' superstitious orders, rash vows, hard-hearted parents, guardians, unnatural friends, allies (call them how you will), those careless and stupid overseers, that out of worldly respects, covetousness, supine negligence, their own private ends (*cum sibi sit interim benè*) can so severely reject, subbornly neglect, and impiously contemn, without all remorse and pity, the tears, sighs, groans, and grievous miseries of such poor souls committed to their charge. How odious and abominable are those superstitious and rash vows of Popish monasteries! so to bind and enforce men and women to vow virginity, to lead a single life, against the laws of nature, opposite to religion, policy, and humanity, so to starve, to offer violence, to suppress the vigour of youth by rigorous statutes, severe laws, vain persuations, to debar them of that to which by their innate temperature they are so furiously inclined, urgently carried, and sometimes precipitated, even irresistibly led, to the prejudice of their soul's health, and good estate of body and mind; and all for base and private respects, to maintain their gross superstition, to enrich themselves and their territories, as they falsely suppose, by hindering some marriages, that the world be not full of beggars, and their parishes pestered with orphans; stupid politicians, *hæccine fieri flagitia?* ought these things so to be carried? better marry than burn, saith the Apostle, but they are otherwise persuaded. They will by all means quench their neighbour's house if it be on fire, but that fire of lust which breaks out into such lamentable flames, they will not take notice of, their own bowels oftentimes, flesh and blood shall so rage and burn, and they will not see it: *miserum est,* saith Austin, *seipsum non miserescere,* and they are miserable in the mean time that cannot pity themselves, the common good of all, and *per consequens* their own estates. For let them but consider what fearful maladies, feral diseases, gross inconveniences, come to both sexes by this enforced temperance, it troubles me to think of, much more to relate those frequent abortions and murdering of infants in their nunneries (read Kemnitius and others), their notorious fornications, those Spintria, Tribadas, Ambubeias, &c., those rapes, incests, adulteries, mastuprations, sodomies, buggeries of monks and friars. See Bale's visitation of abbeys, Mercurialis, Rodericus à Castro, Perer Forestus, and divers physicians; I know their ordinary apologies and excuses for these things, *sed viderint Politici, Medici, Theologi,* I shall more opportunely meet with them elsewhere.

> "Illius viduæ, aut patronum Virginis hujus,
> Ne me forte putes, verbum non amplius addam."[*][1]

[*]"Lest you imagine that I patronize that widow or this virgin, I shall not add another word."

In addition to these remarks Burton has about 300 pages on "Love Melancholy." The role of sexual factors as causes of mental disorders will not be explored further, however, since etiology is not included in this sourcebook. Moreover, these sexual manifestations, although usually recognized as unconscious, were for the most part explained as the result of the maldistribution or aberrance of humors or,

[1] R. Burton, *The Anatomy of Melancholy . . . A New Edition Corrected and Enriched by Translation of the Numerous Classical Extracts* (Boston: Dana Estes and Co., n.d.), Vol. 2, pp. 45–52.

in the middle of the nineteenth century, irritation of the nerves that connected the uterus with the central nervous system. This vast material is not a source of modern ideas and may thankfully be omitted.

The concept of a symbolic expression of unconscious sexual manifestations is a preoccupation of a large group of psychiatrists, at least in this country. The sources of this notion—regardless of its validity—must therefore be presented here.

Cabanis (1802)

As imagination is his dominant faculty, as it exercises a powerful reaction on the organs that furnish these fantasies, man is the one among all living beings in whom puberty can be most accelerated by vicious stimuli, and whose ordinary course most distorted by all the external circumstances that give false direction to the imagination. Thus, in the bad morals of the cities, one does not give puberty the time to appear; one outruns it, and its effects ordinarily are confused with precocious practices of libertinage. In the midst of strict and pious families, where they direct the children's imagination toward religious ideas, one often sees among them amourous melancholia being confounded with ascetic melancholia and ordinarily also one or the other acquires, in this setting, a considerable degree of strength; sometimes they produce the most disastrous explosions, and leave ineffaceable traces afterwards.[2]

These words appear unchanged in the editions of 1805, 1824, 1828, 1830, and 1843, although other portions of the text underwent extensive revision. The book is quoted in many early and mid-nineteenth-century psychiatric works and hence must have been widely read. Indeed, the above comments are cited in the writings of many later authors.

von Feuchtersleben (1845)

One of the authors who repeated the words of Cabanis was von Feuchtersleben, who was himself widely read.

The erotic delusion, unknown to the patient herself, often assumes the color of the religious; among which may be classed the numerous examples of a mystically exalted love. [3]

Ryan (1831)

Not all authors pursued this line. One whose writings took a different direction was Ryan.

[2] P. J. G. Cabanis, *Rapports du physique et du moral de l'homme* (Paris: Crapelet, 1802), Vol. 1, pp. 108–109.

[3] E. von Feuchtersleben, *The Principles of Medical Psychology* [Vienna, 1845], H. E. Lloyd, trans., and B. G. Babington, ed. (London: The New Sydenham Society, 1847), p. 281.

But there may be ... a total disrelish for the procreative act, even by well-informed, interesting, and lovely women. I have been consulted in four remarkable cases of this description, and in all the subjects were excessively vain of their personal appearance, and fond of admiration, and having the strongest passion for dress and shew, but a complete frigidity to venereal enjoyments. They would talk most ardently of dress during the conjugal act, and suffered it without the smallest enjoyment.[4]

Dickson (1874)

Other authors, notably Dickson, also related sex-deprived emotional difficulties to the role forced upon women by society.

But one of the greatest moral exciting causes is to be found in the artificial life which we lead in the present day. Many of its influences conduce to insanity, and not the least of these is the unnatural condition of continence, which prudential considerations enforce upon a great number, particularly upon women. Apart from the fact that the percentage, in the number of women over men, in this country is nearly three, a large number of men will not marry from prudential reasons, and thus a large percentage of women never have the chance of marrying and fulfilling the reproductive act. The desire for fulfilling the act of reproduction is strongly implanted in women, and the non-satisfaction of it is reflected back upon their nervous systems; and though statistics showing this as a cause of insanity have not, yet, been furnished with regard to the question, nevertheless, the cases which come before the physician strongly tend to prove the truth of his *a priori* conclusion on this point.

The operation of the cause is even more powerful now than it was two or three generations back. In the present age a premature development is cultivated. Girls are forced into positions of womanhood at tender ages, and taught to regard marriage as the one aim of life.

> "Motus doceri gaudet Ionicos
> Matura virgo et fingitur artibus;
> Jam nunc et encestos amores
> De tenero meditatur ungui."[*]
>
> "The ripening virgin joys to learn,
> In Ionic dance to turn,
> And bend with plastic limb;
> Still but a child, with evil gleams
> Incestuous love's unhallowed dream,
> Before her fancy swims."

[*]Horace *Odes,* Book III, Ode vi.

[4] M. Ryan, *Lectures on Population, Marriage, and Divorce as Questions of State Medicine* (London: Renshaw and Rush, 1831), p. 48.

Is it then a wonder if disappointment on this head adds its weight to the deterioration resulting from the unaccomplished design of nature? The necessity for the performance of the sexual act is one of the most constant of natural laws, running throughout animals and plants. Nature will not be deceived. If you rob her in one place you must pay her back in another. And if you deprive an organization of one of its most important functions you must expect to see deterioration as the result of the deprivation.

The girl of the period, cultivated to early sexual maturity, and with an education fitting her only for frivolities, as though dress and enjoyment were the aim and end of existence, and encouraging in her, selfish impulses and sensibilities, is early disappointed if she does not marry; she then feels a craving for something which she, perhaps, cannot explain; as a rule she seeks for satisfaction in anything that is attractive, and too often, contemplation and brooding over her supposed miseries suggest devotion and religious exercise, as the nepenthe to soothe her morbid longing. But ill-timed, and ill-judged religious exercises soon develope excitement; this perhaps soon subsides in the more healthy and vigorous; but if the subjects are predisposed to insanity, the religious excitement soon becomes fanaticism.[5]

Georget (1820)

Other authors, like Georget, made more general comments.

The need for sexual union, so demanding because it is the only one that is strongly curbed . . . if it is not satisfied by a marriage always eagerly desired, can take on an entirely different character than that of their true cause, and in this way can make one ignorant of the source.[6]

Maudsley (1867)

Maudsley examined sexual factors from several angles. He not only discussed socially mediated sexual inhibition in a number of places but also emphasized the occurrence of sexual drives in prepubertal children.

Now, therefore, when the luxuries thought necessary in social life are so many and costly that marriage is much avoided by men, there is a cruel stress laid upon many a gentle nature. In this disappointment of their life-aim, and the long train of consequences, physical and moral, which it unconsciously draws after it, there is, I believe, a fertile source of insanity among women. It is not only that women of the better classes, not married, have no aim in life to work for, no opening for the employment of their energies in outward activities, and are driven to a

---

[5] J. T. Dickson, *The Science and Practice of Medicine in Relation to Mind: The Pathology of Nerve Centers and the Jurisprudence of Insanity* (New York: D. Appleton and Co., 1874), pp. 381–383.

[6] M. Georget, *De la folie: Considerations sur cette maladie* (Paris: Crevot, 1820), p. 162.

morbid self-brooding, or to an excessive religious devotion or a religious enthusiasm which is too often the unwitting cloak of an exaggerated and unhealthy self-feeling; but, through the character produced by the position which they have so long held in the social system, their organic life is little able to withstand the consequences of an unsatisfied sexual instinct. Disturbances of all sorts ensue, and social customs debar them from the means of relief which men have both in active employment and in unmarried sexual indulgence. . . . Let it not be supposed, however, that all these things take place consciously in the woman's thoughts, feelings, and actions: the sexual passion is one of the strongest passions in nature, and as soon as it comes into activity, it declares its influence on every pulse of the organic life, revolutionizing the entire nature, conscious and unconscious; when, therefore, the means of its gratification entirely fail, and when there is no vicarious outlet for its energy, the whole system feels the effects, and exhibits them in restlessness and irritability, in a morbid self-feeling taking a variety of forms, and in an act of self-abuse which on the first occasion may, I believe, be a sort of instinctive frenzy, of the aim of which there is only the vaguest and most dim notion.[7]

Let me now say a few words with regard to the perversion of the instinct of propagation. It is necessary first to guard against a possible objection that this instinct is not manifest till puberty, by the distinct assertion that there are frequent manifestations of its existence throughout early life, both in animals and in children, without there being any consciousness of the aim or design of the blind impulse. Whosoever avers otherwise must have paid very little attention to the gambols of young animals, and must be strangely or hypocritically oblivious of the events of his own early life. It is at puberty that the instinct makes its appearance in the consciousness of man, and thereupon generates knowledge of its aim, and craves for means of gratification; in like manner as, in the course of development through the ages, the blind procreative instinct which is immanent in animal nature finally undergoes a marvellous evolution within human consciousness.

As we have exhibitions of this blind impulse in the healthy child, it is quite natural to look for exaggerated and perverted manifestations of it in the insane child. These we do not fail to meet with: while the enthusiastic idealist is greatly shocked by disgusting exhibitions of unnatural precocity in children of three or four years of age, and exclaims against them as if they were unaccountable and monstrous, they are not without interest to the scientific observer, who sees in them valuable instances on which to base his generalizations concerning man, not as an ideal but as a real being.[8]

In every large asylum are to be met women who believe themselves to be visited every night by their lovers, or violently ravished in their sleep; and in some of

[7] H. Maudsley, *The Physiology and Pathology of the Mind* (New York: D. Appleton and Co., 1867), pp. 203-204.
[8] Ibid., pp. 284-285.

these, as in St. Catherine de Sienne and St. Theresa, a religious ecstasy is united with their salacious delusions. Indeed, a religious fanaticism carried to a morbid degree is not seldom accompanied by a corresponding morbid lewdness; while religious feeling of a less extreme kind in some women, especially certain unmarried and childless women, is very much a uterine affection.[9]

Donkin (1892)

About this time the role of repressed sexual desires, particularly in hysteria, began to figure in psychologic discussions.

On the vulnerable nervous material of the hysterical subject many exciting agents work to produce disorder. Prominent among these are great and sudden emotions, such as fear in all its forms—a notable element in the hysteria of childhood; disappointment; forcibly repressed desires, especially sexual.[10]

[9] Ibid., p. 241.
[10] H. B. Donkin, "Hysteria," in D. H. Tuke, *Dictionary of Psychological Medicine* (Philadelphia: P. Blakiston, Son and Co., 1892), Vol. 1, p. 625.

The Meaning of
Psychotic Thinking

3

Locke (1690)

Speaking with tongues was once (and sometimes is still) regarded as evidence of holiness. Considered quite different from the obscenities spewed out by some psychotic persons, this gibberish was thought to reveal possession by one or more demons. John Locke, in 1690, first called attention to the fact that the verbal productions of the psychotic made sense when examined closely.

How far idiots are concerned in the want or weakness of any, or all of the foregoing faculties, an exact observation of their several ways of faltering would no doubt discover: for those who either perceive but dully, or retain the ideas that come into their minds but ill, who cannot really excite or compound them will have little matter to think on. Those who cannot distinguish, compare, and abstract, would hardly be able to understand and make use of language, or judge or reason to any tolerable degree; but only a little and imperfectly about things present, and very familiar to their senses. And indeed any of the forementioned faculties, if wanting, or out of order, produce suitable effects in men's understandings and knowledge.

In fine, the defect in naturals seems to proceed from want of quickness, activity, and motion in the intellectual faculties, whereby they are deprived of reason; whereas madmen, on the other side, seem to suffer by the other extreme: for they do not appear to me to have lost the faculty of reasoning; but having joined together some ideas very wrongly, they mistake them for truths, and they err as men do that argue right from wrong principles. For by the violence of their imaginations, having taken their fancies for realities, they make right deductions from them. Thus you shall find a distracted man fancying himself a kind, with a right reference require suitable attendance, respect and obedience: others, who have thought themselves made of glass, have used the caution necessary to preserve such brittle bodies. Hence it comes to pass that a man, who is very sober, and of a right understanding in all other things, may in one particular be as frantick as any in Bedlam; if either by any sudden very strong impression, or long fixing his fancy upon one sort of thoughts, incoherent ideas have been cemented together so powerfully, as to remain united. But there are degrees of madness, as of folly; the disorderly jumbling of ideas together, is in some more, some less. In short, herein seems to lie the difference between idiots and madmen, that madmen put wrong ideas together, and so make wrong propositions, but argue and reason right from them; but idiots make very few or no propositions, and reason scarce at all.[1]

Leuret (1834)

The logic of psychotic thinking was mentioned casually by other authors, but it remained for François Leuret to attempt a systematic study of it.

There are people whom we call insane and in whom the disorder consists in that their ideas, deprived of a regular association, join each other at random and give rise to the most unsuitable formations. Sometimes it is a natural bond, which enfeebled or damaged, permits ideas to err by chance; sometimes it is a new bond that forms, and causes ideas of opposite nature to adhere to each other.[2]

The ideas born in the mind of the patients I have called incoherent have strength and correctness; but they last too short a time, they give way to other ideas before their consequences can develop. In the normal world, a slight degree of this disorder, produces what is called a lack of the spirit of order, and, in a more advanced degree, giddiness. Among those considered psychotic, because of this incoherence, the disorder is more pronounced, it can proceed until the words have an arrangement that makes no sense, until the syllables form no word. The myriads of ideas and feelings that succeed each other follow a fixed order in the healthy person, happen almost without order in the mind of the patients, and are rendered, in their incoherence by writings, or spoken words, and by gestures, or sometimes simultaneously by all three forms of expression. This is not all: with happy words can coincide an air of sadness, tears and sobs, and conversely, with an air of good humor, the words express sad ideas; or furthermore with solid ideas, with habits of regular work, and which demand great attention, completely incoherent thoughts; and contrary to all this, actions in complete disorder, exaggerated emotions, bizarre in character or their inappropriate development, the suddenness of their decline, the variation in their duration, with a faculty of understanding that is clear, intact, and well ordered.[3]

---

[1] J. Locke, *An Essay concerning Human Understanding* (19th ed., London: T. Longman and others, 1793), Vol. 1, pp. 140-141.

[2] F. Leuret, *Fragments psychologique sur la folie* (Paris: Crochard, 1834), p. 4.

[3] Ibid., pp. 6-7.

There is still another incoherence that is evident, and of which absent-minded men are frequent examples. Having reached the initial ideas of the subject with which they occupy themselves, these giants of science disdain intermediate points. One might believe that they proceed at random, because one cannot follow their steps: to these who recognize their power and who see their purpose, they go from peak to peak to place on the culminating point they have discovered, a beacon that is a sign of new progress for the human spirit.

The works they create distinguish genius, if ignorance did not mistake it.

Among the insane the incoherence is not often sufficiently great that it is evident at first, and if one gives them the time to explain themselves, if one takes the trouble to examine their writings, one sometimes finds a natural interpretation for some things that at first sight had seemed absurd. By calculated reticenses, or by purposeful elisions, they make unintelligible for others some things that they understand fully.[4]

I will recall in three main rubrics what I have to say on the subject. Abnormal cohesion and the fixity of false ideas divide themselves:

1) as regards psychic matters or objects of thought;
2) as regards external objects or of sensation;
3) as regards organs or the personality of the thinking subject.[5]

There follow many pages of analyses of passages, both written and oral, that are printed verbatim. It goes without saying that these analyses in no way resemble modern interpretations of anal, oral, or genital drives. Hence this material is not a useful source, although it contains principles of psychotic thought which are relevant.[6]

von Feuchtersleben (1845)

The idea that the mind might express itself allegorically was stated specifically by von Feuchtersleben to explain some unconscious effects of mental states on bodily function.

For the body would experience nothing of the heavenly contact of the intellect, if the latter were not enabled to make itself known to it through the medium of figurative language, and, if we are to recognise them as applicable to ourselves, all the reciprocal relations of the body to thought, which will further engage our attention in these lectures, can and must lie only in the first traits hitherto developed, of this figurative language.[7]

[4] Ibid, p. 8.
[5] Ibid., p. 46.
[6] J. Séglas also wrote on the distorted language of psychotic persons in *Les troubles du langage chez les aliénés* (Paris: Alcan, 1892).
[7] E. von Feuchtersleben, *The Principles of Medical Psychology* [Vienna, 1845], H. E. Lloyd, trans., and B. G. Babington, ed. (London: The New Sydenham Society, 1847), p. 127.

The Ego

4

The ego concept has received the close attention of philosophers for centuries.[1] It finally entered clinical psychiatry in the mid-nineteenth century and later became dominant in some schools of twentieth-century psychiatry.[2] The first formal and extensive expression of the concept was made by Griesinger in 1845, but it did not spring full-blown from his mind. It had been foreshadowed in the writings of many people for centuries in the ideas that a foreign self supplanted the normal one in insane persons and that the same might happen normally in dreams.

The first idea is exemplified by Sophocles' statement in his *Life:* "If I am Sophocles, I am not mad; and if I am mad, I am not Sophocles." Many references to the foreign-ego notion are to be found in the New Testament: see Mark 16:9, "Now when Jesus was risen early the first day of the week he appeared first to Mary Magdelene out of whom he had cast seven devils," and Luke 8:2, "Mary, called Magdelene, out of whom went seven devils." Luke 8:29-33 clearly describes the demoniac possession of a psychotic man, called Legion because of the great number of devils in him, who is freed of demons by Jesus. "For he had commanded the unclean spirit to come out of the man . . ."

For hundreds of years both before and after these events demoniacal possession was held responsible for mental disorders ranging from severe psychosis to mere

---

[1] The word *ego* (Ich, le moi) was not universally accepted. G. Moore favored *Ipseity* (*The Use of the Body in Relation to the Mind,* London: Longman, Brown, Green and Longmans, 1846). Ipseity recalls the *thisness* that Duns Scotus had used in the thirteenth century to describe the properties that make for the individuality of objects. Another author, D. Noble, preferred *Me-ity* (*The Human Mind in Its Relations with the Brain and Nervous System,* London: J. Churchill, 1850).

[2] The view of Dreisch, Husserl, and other philosophers of the era regarding the ego concept were discussed, with generally negative conclusions, by C. W. Morris, *Six Theories of Mind* (Chicago: University of Chicago Press, 1932), pp. 175-178, 208-212.

laziness (a specific Noonday Demon was blamed for the latter). Medieval ideas of demoniacal possession could be shown to relate to more recent beliefs that mental disease is caused by the irruption of the demon-like "old Adam" (according to von Feuchtersleben) or to the demoniac id (according to Freud). Such a discussion would be of more interest to medievalists than to modern physicians and psychologists, however, and will be ommitted here.

The peculiar behavior of the ego during sleep is noted by many philosophers. As Immanuel Kant emphasized two centuries ago, their interpretations of the nature of dreams are diverse to the point of absurdity. Since Plato's philosophy came to dominate European thought, however, his views on the subject are widely held. In *The Republic* (Book IX) he describes how the rational part of the soul loses its mastery when a person sleeps, and the "wild animal part, sated with meat or drink, becomes rampant, and pushing sleep away, endeavors to set out after the gratification of its own proper character. You know that in such moments there is nothing that it dares not to do, released and delivered as it is from any sense of shame and reflection." Philosophers from Montaigne ("I believe it to be true that Dreams are the true Interpreters of our inclinations," *Essays*, III, 13) to Maury ("our innate instincts and impulses, when sleep overmasters reflection and considerations of policy, are set free to have all their own way," *La Magie et l'astrologie*, 1877) continued to assert that dreams were the expression of a primitive, infantile, or feral part of the personality which is normally repressed. This highly romantic and titillatingly wicked notion has long been regarded with skepticism by biologists, who have known since Lucretius and Buffon (*Birds*, IX, 151) that horses and dogs dream. In recent years physiologic studies of human dreams have all but demolished the idea that they are mere wish fulfillments. (In this vast literature a dream is now referred to as a REM, a period of rapid eye movement.) Moreover, with the growing permissiveness of American parents and educators and the new morality, behavior that was once considered reprehensible is now acceptable and even fashionable. The id is therefore deprived of many unfulfilled desires, and dreams can no longer be explained according to Plato's notions.

Locke (1690)

Although German philosophers of the eighteenth and nineteenth centuries and their psychiatric followers seemed to regard the ego as a thing, most English writers did not. John Locke, for example, expounded a different view in 1686 that was widely adopted via the writings of Hume during the next 150 years.

> For if we take wholly away all consciousness of our actions and sensations, especially of pleasure and pain, and the concernment that accompanies it, it will be hard to know wherein to place personal identity. .... To ask at what time a man has first any ideas, is to ask when he begins to perceive; having ideas, and

perception, being the same thing . . . If it shall be demanded then, when a man begins to have ideas; I think the true answer is, when he first has any sensation.[3]

Elsewhere in the same work, however, Locke seemed to raise the possibility that the self might in fact be material.

> To find wherein personal identity consists, we must consider what person stands for; which I think, is a thinking intelligent being, that has reason and reflection, and can consider itself as itself, the same thinking thing in different times and places. . . .
> . . . Self is that conscious thinking thing (whatever substance made up of, whether spiritual or material, simple, or compounded, it matters not) which is sensible, or conscious of pleasure and pain, capable of happiness or misery, and so is concerned for itself, as far as that consciousness extends.[4]

Hume (1739)

Hume was much more forthright in his denial of the substantiality of the self. His *Treatise of Human Nature* presented the ego as an abstraction. Hume's definitive pronouncements represented a final version of sensist philosophy and were adopted with little change by many others, both in England and in France.

> For my part, when I enter most initimately into what I call *myself*, I always stumble on some particular perception or other, of heat or cold, light or shade, love or hatred, pain or pleasure. I never can catch *myself* at any time without a perception, and never can observe anything but the perception. When my perceptions are removed for any time, as by sound sleep, so long am I insensible of *myself*, and may truly be said not to exist. And were all my perceptions removed by death, and could I neither think, nor feel, nor see, nor love, nor hate, after the dissolution of my body, I should be entirely annihilated, nor do I conceive what is further requisite to make me a perfect nonentity. If any one, upon serious and unprejudiced reflection, thinks he has a different notion of *himself*, I must confess I can reason no longer with him. All I can allow him is, that he may be in the right as well as I, and that we are essentially different in this particular. He may, perhaps, perceive something simple and continued, which he calls *himself*; though I am certain there is no such principle in me.
> But setting aside some metaphysicians of this kind, I may venture to affirm of the rest of mankind, that they are nothing but a bundle or collection of different perceptions, which succeed each other with an inconceivable rapidity, and are in a perpetual flux and movement.[5]

[3] J. Locke, *An Essay concerning Human Understanding* (19th ed., London: T. Longman and others, 1793), Vol. 1, p. 84.

[4] Ibid., pp. 333, 340.

[5] D. Hume, *A Treatise of Human Nature* (New York: Dutton, Everyman's Library, 1968), Vol. 1, p. 239.

It is evident that the identity which we attribute to the human mind, however perfect we may imagine it to be, is not able to run the several different perceptions into one, and make them lose their character of distinction and difference, which are essential to them. It is still true that every distinct perception which enters into the composition of the mind, is a distinct existence, and is different, and distinguishable, and separable from every other perception, either contemporary or successive. But as, notwithstanding this distinction and separability, we suppose the whole train of perceptions to be united by identity, a question naturally arises concerning this relation of identity, whether it be something that really binds our several perceptions together, or only associates their ideas in the imagination; that is, in other words, whether, in pronouncing concerning the identity of a person, we observe some real bond among his perceptions, or only feel one among the ideas we form of them. This question we might easily decide, if we would recollect what has been already proved at large, that the understanding never observes any real connection among objects, and that even the union of cause and effect, when strictly examined, resolves itself into a customary association of ideas. For from thence it evidently follows, that identity is nothing really belonging to these different perceptions, and uniting them together, but is merely a quality which we attritube to them, because of the union of their ideas in the imagination when we reflect upon them. Now, the only qualities which can give ideas a union in the imagination, are these three relations above mentioned. These are the uniting principles in the ideal world, and without them every distinct object is separable by the mind, and may be separately considered, and appears not to have any more connection with any other object than if disjoined by the greatest difference and remoteness. It is therefore on some of these three relations of resemblance, contiguity, and causation, that identity depends; and as the very essence of these relations consists in their producing an easy transition of ideas, it follows that our notions of personal identity proceed entirely from the smooth and uninterrupted progress of the thought along a train of connected ideas, according to the principles above explained.[6]

The whole of this doctrine leads us to a conclusion, which is of great importance in the present affair, viz. that all the nice and subtile questions concerning personal identity can never possibly be decided, and are to be regarded rather as grammatical than as philosophical difficulties. Identity depends on the relations of ideas; and these relations produce identity, by means of that easy transition they occasion. But as the relations, and the easiness of the transition may diminish by insensible degrees, we have no just standard by which we can decide any dispute concerning the time when they acquire or lose a title to the name of identity. All the disputes concerning the identity of connected objects are merely verbal, except so far as the relation of parts

[6] Ibid., p. 245.

gives rise to some fiction or imaginary principle of union, as we have already observed.[7]

The general development of the controversial ego concept more properly belongs in a work on general psychology, and only the medical application of the concept is appropriately discussed here.

Heinroth (1825)

Perhaps the earliest psychiatric writer to attempt a systematic formulation that would give the ego a role in psychiatry was Heinroth.[8] He proposed a concept of *Person* that seems superficially akin to certain aspects of ego psychology but is actually much different. Heinroth's concept had no discernible effect on today's clinical thinking although it somewhat resembles some of Adolph Meyer's ideas, which may be only coincidental. It will therefore be discussed only briefly here. Heinroth held that mental disorders are diseases of what he called the Person. (He ignored the fact that *person* and *personality* came from the word for mask, as used in the theater of the classical era. The mask told the audience what the actor represented, regardless of what he really looked like or was.) According to Heinroth the Person, an indivisible synthesis of mind and body, willfully enters into mental disorder, which Heinroth considered a state of servitude or at least unfreedom. Heinroth emphasized that the Person has an individual conscience and also a relation—only vaguely stated—with all of life everywhere in the universe. In this he echoed ancient doctrines of a collective mind or Logos that pervades the entire universe. This part of his doctrine was completely unoriginal, and although it was adopted by such disparate thinkers as John Dewey and Jung they probably took it from Plato, not Heinroth.

Mental disorder represented, to Heinroth, a state of moral guilt because the Person had willfully rejected the way of life his (Christian) conscience had outlined for him. It is evident that Heinroth considered the Person as a moral entity more than an ego in today's psychologic sense.

Broussais (1828)

Perhaps the earliest physician to discuss the ego concept in modern terms was Broussais, one of the most original if not one of the soundest medical thinkers of his time. After an early career as a privateersman and a noncommissioned officer in Napoleon's army, he entered medicine and eventually became head of the veterans' hospital and professor of medicine and general pathology in Paris. He was best

[7] Ibid., p. 248.
[8] J. C. A. Heinroth, *System der psychisch gerichtlichen Medizin* (Leipzig: Hartman, 1825). For a scholarly account of Heinroth's concept and its significance see O. M. Marx, "J. C. A. Heinroth (1773-1843) on Psychiatry and Law," *Journal of the History of the Behavioral Sciences*, 1968, pp. 163-179.

known as an ardent convert to phrenology, and his more solid contributions to psychiatry received less notice then and later. (He also became famous for his insistence on repeated massive bleeding for all illnesses, and as a result was held to have caused more deaths than all of his emperor's battles). His book was translated by Thomas Cooper, who had a mind of considerable energy and originality himself. While president of South Carolina College he stated that materialism, along the lines presented by his friend Priestley and others, had actually been the doctrine of Jesus and the Apostles. Two grand juries indignantly brought these writings to the attention of the state legislature, which refused to discuss these views except to say that they had been known when he was given his appointment at the college.

You say to yourselves, "no man observes unless he be furnished with all the means and apparatus of observation: le moi, the myself which is within a man, ought to be presumed in that situation." Stop, gentlemen, take care that your moi (myself) does not come forth suddenly, a Minerva armed cap a pie: remember what has just been proved, that the word moi, myself, cannot designate any thing but a phenomenon which shews itself under certain given conditions, consisting in—1st, The existence of a perfect brain, well grown, and of adult age. 2dly In the fact of certain stimulations, at first internal, subsequently external, transmitted to the brain. It is only under these conditions that le moi, myself, exists at all; nor can any myself be compared but with itself.[9]

The perception of ones self, or the phenomena of *le moi*, is always the same; although this *moi* may perceive itself in joy, or in suffering. It is not the same with that of the object which the external sense makes known: this perception becomes diversified, according as the attention remains longer fixed upon the object itself.[10]

... insanity, having become a powerful habit, *le moi*, personal consciousness, can no longer distinguish it from a normal state while the irritation continues. ... Insanity may be considered as complete when the impressions made on the senses, as the conversations for instance addressed to patients, are unable to bring back *le moi*, their personal consciousness, from its delusion.[11]

When an insane person, recovered, relates what he has done, and declares that he has been deceived by false images of things; when he proves that his conclusions from the facts which seemed real to him, were properly deduced; in a word, while he preserves the remembrance of the fit, we may believe that he preserves his feeling of identity, but that his consciousness has been cheated by false images, the result of cerebral irritation. But when he is alternately reasonable and insane, or reasonable on one point and insane on another,

[9] F. J. V. Broussais, *On Irritation and Insanity* [1828], T. Cooper, trans. (Columbia, S.C.: McMorris, 1821), p. 104.

[10] Ibid., p. 120.

[11] Ibid., pp. 242-243.

without any possibility of disabusing him, what, in this case, are we to think of his identity (moi) and his consciousness? Is it enough to induce us to believe that a monomaniac is reasonable, that he can judge accurately of the temperature or the shape of a body? Can we conclude that he possesses a consciousness of his identity (de son moi) because he gives proper answers in relation to his wants? Suppose we grant thus far, where is his reason, and his self consciousness, when he declares that he is a dog, an owl, a bottle, a leathern jug, a mile stone, a grain of mustard, &c.? Will it be said he has a double moi, a double consciousness, the one for just ideas, the other for false ones? In the case, for instance, of a patient who believes himself to be some animal, we may in strictness allow him the identity of a dog or an owl, but what are we to do with the identity of a mile stone, or a bottle? If we refuse him the double identity, the double consciousness, will it be pretended that he possesses only the consciousness of a normal state obscured by disease? Two replies may be made to this:

1st. We may allow a consciousness oppressed by disease to one who furnishes occasional proofs of reason; but can we make the same allowance to one who for many years has furnished no such proof? Where is the identity, the consciousness of a man in a state of dementia, who, after having long lived in a state completely brutish, dies without having afforded any proof that he has retained his reason? Some there are who have recovered it at the last moment, but whither had it retired during so long an absence? The malady had repressed it, may be the reply: well; I proceed then to the second answer.

2d. In advancing that identity (le moi) and consciousness have been repressed by the malady, let us know distinctly what the malady is. We may conceive of it as of a Being of determined figure, which compresses or oppresses another Being equally marked and determined, called moi, myself, or else another Being of the same nature, called consciousness. How then are we to represent this moi, this consciousness, and this malady, so as to assert anything reasonable concerning them? I shall not push this discussion further, contenting myself with a reference to the first part of this work; but we may conclude from what has been advanced, that if we would avoid ontology, we must not assert generally and absolutely that an insane man preserves or has lost his reason, that he preserves or has lost his consciousness of identity (de son moi,) that the feeling of identity is oppressed under the weight of a malady, and that its tendency is to re-establish itself, as takes place after cure, and sometimes at the last moment of life; that if it does not appear, it exists nevertheless, since it is a simple substance, indestructible, &c. Metaphorical language like this, teaches nothing, and only prolongs the reign of illusion, and adds strength to fanaticism. We must speak simply matter of fact: we may say that a madman sometimes has reason and sometimes not; that he sometimes has, and sometimes has not self consciousness; that when he is cured he recovers his reason, and that he may sometimes possess it a short time before death, but that he often dies without ever recovering it; that the cause of these differences lies in the words *reason, self-consciousness,* which in fact express nothing but the action of the nervous substance of the encephalon, an action liable to change so long as life remains. To this we must add that as the patient neither enjoys the faculty of reason constantly, nor always correctly, he has no regular normal relation to other men.[12]

Griesinger (1845)

Wilhelm Griesinger wrote his remarkable psychiatric text when he was only twenty-seven years old. One of the greatest clinicians of all time, he made a number of brilliant clinical observations in other branches of medicine: the nature of hookworm anemia, the association of pulsus paradoxicus with pericarditis, the occurrence of post-traumatic psychomotor epilepsy, etc. He became professor of medicine at Berlin but unfortunately died soon after. Griesinger viewed the ego as an executive entity, a concept that became, by way of Vienna, a cornerstone of American psychiatry a century after it was first propounded. Early in his career and thereafter he had the dubious pleasure of seeing his works brazenly plagiarized.

> Several of the most recent writers on insanity have been so well pleased with the first edition of my book that they have assumed into their writings not only the ideas and doctrines, the arrangement and examples contained in it, but have even taken, without restraint, as their own, simple excerpts of whole sections.[13]

§ 26. But as the sensations and feelings are the more easily converted into instincts in proportion to their strength, so *Will* is developed out of the single perceptions the more easily according to the strength and persistence with which they enforce themselves. On this account the strongest ideas, at the end of their transition, pass forcibly in actions. It is a fortunate provision, however, in mental life, that every perception does not attain to this degree of strength. Then, according to the laws of the association of ideas, there arise the contrasting perceptions; they draw after them further perceptions related to them, and there arises in consciousness a conflict. The whole mass of ideas which represents the *I* (§ 28) comes into exercise, and gives the final decision according as it impedes or favours that first idea. This opposition in consciousness, which in the end is decided by the *I,* is the fact of the liberty of the individual.

The assumption of absolute liberty, as well as the results that flow from it, is erroneous. The liberty of an individual is always relative, and different men are free in different degrees. Originally the individual is in no respect free; he becomes so, first, by being possessed of a mass of well-ordered and easily-evoked perceptions, out of which there is formed a strong kernel, the *I*. There are two general conditions necessary to the freedom of human action. In the first place, an unobstructed association of ideas whereby, around the ideas presented, which

---

[12] Ibid., pp. 258–259.

[13] W. Griesinger, *Mental Pathology and Therapeutics,* (from the 2nd German ed., C. L. Robertson and J. Rutherford, trans.) (London: The New Sydenham Society, 1867), pp. viii–ix.

are transformed into will, other ideas originating may be gathered, and may be opposed to the former. In the second place, a sufficiently strong I (§ 28), that can give the decision by its mass of ideas, strengthening one set of the opposing perceptions, and thereby relatively weakening the other. With those weak in perception and mentally dull, freedom is to a great extent absorbed in the dreamlike monotony of custom. The man of weak mind is less free, since the living association is absent from his perception, and opposing ideas are not, or only very slowly, awakened. A child is less free as his perception is active, since no strong I has as yet been formed, that could send a powerful, firmly combined mass of perceptions into the conflict.

In a medico-legal aspect, it is very important for the physician to have clear views upon the nature of human liberty, so much obscured by abstract modes of treating the subject. The contents of this paragraph are mainly devoted to this purpose. Liberty, therefore, consists essentially in an influencing and transformation of the (occasional) will; in (occasional) masses of ideas pressing into reflection by the aid of other ideas, and especially by the entire mass of combined ideas belonging to the I; in the control which the I exercises over the tendencies actually existing; therefore, in the possibility of self command. The more compact and united the I is in itself, the more decided is the character; on that account the more decidedly does each one call into exercise, by his affirmation or negation, the ideas which are already floating in the mind. So is the saying to be understood, that "true liberty consists in limitation,"—namely, by means of the I. Where this limitation fails, the ideas that occasionally spring up, often depending only on the sensitive excitations present at the moment, or only passing desultorily (capricious), press unhindered towards the motory side, and enforce their accomplishment. By the most varied bodily influences, however, this limiting power of the I may be restricted, diminished, or quite abolished.

When an individual makes moral motives the rule of conduct in his actions, this can only be done inasmuch as by frequent reproduction and practice he unites the masses of perceptions which are referable to his moral law with all his ideas, so that they, with every strong motion of the thoughts, accompany them into consciousness. They form then an essential constituent element of the measure of perception of his I; and if a conflict arise in the consciousness, they not only immediately step forward, but they also over all the contents of the I, upon the whole, have the advantage. In the immoral man, on the other hand, the egotistical and malignant thoughts have gradually so rooted themselves that they always are ready to step forward, and the I is occupied by that whose chief mass is, upon the whole, to the bad side. Of course it is not supposed that such an individual on this account acts wickedly in every case; in him also the association of ideas is an active principle, and, inasmuch as it suggests to his mind the contrasts of his evil thoughts, half-smothered emotions, half-erased images, and the remembrance of better days, with the good advices received in youth, step into consciousness, and a violent conflict may result. In the end, indeed, the I

favours the wicked side; were it to favour the good, the man would not be immoral; still, he is a man whom certainly it would be unsafe to trust too much, although in this case he may have overcome his evil desires. The strength of the opposing moral motive can, however, never beforehand be estimated. There is no man absolutely bad . . . .

§ 27. The normal reciprocal action of the perception, whereby, through the ideas actually in the mind, other contrasting, or in general limiting, ideas are awakened, whereby all proceeds with moderate strength and rapidity, so that, in general, a conflict can arise in consciousness, so that thought and reflection, and therewith a survey of past and future, are possible, is best designated as the state of *Reflection.* One easily perceives how this is an essential condition of all liberty.

Now there are many states where this reflection is weakened or destroyed. This appears to a greater or less extent, first, in the emotions (§ 30), which are still considered physiological states; then, in almost all pathological states of the brain. Alcoholic intoxication, sympathetic cerebral irritations, most of the deeper organic diseases of the cerebral substance—in short, all the diseases of the brain with which we have here to do as mental diseases—disturb the free exercise of the perception, and thereby limit, or completely destroy, the reflecting power. They effect this in many ways; sometimes certain desires and instincts, through disease of the brain, are directly increased to excessive intensity (sexual instinct destructiveness), and are transformed into will and actions without any other ideas being able to control them; sometimes all perception proceeds with such rapidity, that, in the confusion of ideas, there is no one so powerful or lasting as even to originate an actual conflict in the consciousness. Frequently we see both these conditions in the maniacal states, where, in the latter case indicated, the slightest excitation from without often decides the nature of the actions. Sometimes the perception is so sluggish, and the *I* so weak, that from this source the conditions of an internal conflict are wanting; for example, in dementia. Sometimes, in consequence of cerebral affection, certain false connections of ideas, erroneous conclusions, become so persistent, and so interweave themselves with the whole mass of ideas of the *I*, that their contrasts are competely effaced from the soul, and they therefore press themselves into all conclusions; and the *I*, falsified though these fixed ideas, is now forced always to decide according to their sense: this is the case in monomania, also in many maniacal and melancholic states. The determination and the deed often follow in these cases with great placidity, and with apparently sufficient deliberation and choice of means; notwithstanding the inward reflection is wanting, because the false opinions have acquired the strength of irresistible motives, and the patient cannot rid himself entirely of them.[14]

§ 28. In the course of our lives, in consequence of the progressive combination of the perceptions, there are formed great masses of ideas which

[14] Ibid., pp. 44–46.

constantly become more associated. Their peculiarity in individuals does not depend merely upon the special contents of the single perceptions excited by sensitive impressions and outward events, but also by their habitual relations to the instincts and will, and by the persistent restricting or extending influences which arise out of the whole organism: even the child comes to receive from his, as yet comparatively simple, mass of ideas, a general impression, then, as soon as the material is sufficiently developed and strengthened, he begins to employ an abstract impression, the *I*.

The *I* is an abstraction in which traces of all former separate sensations, thoughts, and desires are contained, as it were, bundled together, and which, in the progress of the mental processes, supplies itself with new material; but this assimilation of the new ideas with the pre-existing *I* does not happen at once—it grows and strengthens very gradually, and that which is not yet assimilated appears as an opposition to the *I* as a *thou*. Gradually it confines itself no longer to a single complexity of ideas and desires which respresents the *I*, but there are formed several such masses of ideas united, organised, and strengthened; two (and not only two) souls then dwell within the man, and this changes or is divided according to the predominance of the one or of the other mass of ideas, both of which may now represent the *I*. Out of this, internal contradiction and strife may result; and such actually occurs within every thinking mind. In happy harmonious natures this conflict is spontaneously and rapidly brought to an end, since in all these various complex perceptions, there is developed, in common, several general, in all recurring, fundamental intuitions, still obscure, and which cannot be easily expressed, whereby there is given to all the spheres of the thought and will a harmonising fundamental direction. Faith on the one hand and empiricism on the other may serve as examples of such various fundamental directions. It is the highest object of self-education not only to acquire such general and solid fundamental directions, but to elevate them gradually as much as possible by thought into consciousness, and so, in the firm possession of such, to attain to the elaborated first propositions of all thought and will adequate to the particular individual nature.

At different times our *I* presents different characters, according to age, various duties of life, occurrences, momentary excitations of this or that mass of ideas, which at the time represents the *I*, being more developed than others and occupying the foreground. "We are another and still the same." My *I* as physician, my *I* as a scholar, my sensuous *I*, my moral *I*, &c.,—that is, the groups of perceptions, instincts, and directions of the will which are expressed by these words—can come into opposition with each other, and repel each other, at different times. Not only must inconsistency and disorder of the understanding and will result, but also—on account of the continued limiting influence of the others—complete want of energy in each of these features of the *I* would ensue, did not some of these more obscure or apparent fundamental directions return to all of these spheres.

One of the most evident, and in relation to mental dieseases most instructive, examples of an entirely physiological renewal and transformation of the *I* is afforded by the mental events which occur during the period of puberty. With the awakening of activity in a hitherto dormant part, and with the complete organic revolution which then takes place in a comparatively short time, great masses of new sensations, instincts, obscure or more definite perceptions and impulses, come into consciousness. These gradually pervade the whole sphere of perception, and become constituent permanent parts of the *I*. Thereby it is thoroughly altered and renewed, and the sentiment of self undergoes a radical change. But, indeed, until this assimilation is completed, this penetration and transition of the old *I* can scarcely take place without much pressure on the consciousness and tumultuous agitation; that is, not without great emotion. This period of life is therefore especially the time for emotions arising from within, without being excited by external influences.

§ 29. It is not without a purpose that we have selected this example which illustrates insanity by many analogies. In it also there is usually developed, with the commencement of the cerebral disease, masses of new sensations, instincts, and perceptions, proceeding from within outwards, which were hitherto, at least in their present form, unknown to the individual; for example, sensations of great anxiety with which there is combined the idea of persecution. At first these stand opposed to the old *I* in the character of a foreign *thou* often exciting amazement and fear. Frequently their forcible entrance into the whole sphere of the perception is felt as if it were the possession of the old *I* by an obscure and irresistible power, and the fact of such forcible possession is expressed by phantastic images. But this duplicity, this conflict of the old *I* against the new inadequate groups of ideas, is always accompanied by painful opposing sensations, by emotional states, and by violent emotions. Herein in great measure, lies the foundation of the fact taught us by experience, that the first stages of the great majority of mental diseases consist in predominating affections of the sentiments, generally of a painful kind.

If the immediate cause of the new and abnormal state of the perception—the cerebral affection—be not removed, it becomes fixed and persistent; and because connections are gradually formed throughout with the groups of perceptions of the old *I,* and since frequently other masses of perceptions more capable of resistance are completely destroyed and effaced through the cerebral disease, the resistance of the old *I,* the struggle in consciousness, ceases by degrees and the emotions are allayed. But now, through these connections, through that introduction of abnormal elements of perception and will, the *I* itself is falsified, and has quite changed its nature. Then the patient can again be calm, and his thoughts sometimes formally correct; but these abnormal erroneous ideas push themselves into every part of it as irresistible premises; because they have over all formed connections, the patient has become in no respect what he formerly was, but quite another man—his *I* has become new and false. At other times it appears that several new groups of ideas, having little coherence amongst themselves, are formed, each of which may represent the *I*, and thus the unity of the individual may be quite lost (many demented monomaniacs). In so far as in these conditions all emotion has ceased, we may rightly designate them simply false thought—diseases of the understanding.

In the preceding remarks we have expressed in few words the ordinary course of events in insanity from its commencement to its termination in incurable dementia. What has been said does not, of course, apply to every case; for example, not to the dementia ensuing immediately after wounds of the head; and also, where the morbid phenomena, on the whole, follow this course, there are presented many intermediate cases and deviations. In particular, through the deeper and further progress of an organic brain disease—for example, that chronic inflammation of the cortical substance which ends in atrophy—the course is so curtailed, that dementia ensues so rapidly as not to admit of the formation of a new *I;* or recovery or death takes place before this can happen. We shall recur to this subject in the third book (on the varieties of insanity).

We may also here call attention to the great influence which the state of the former (old) *I* must have in these conditions. A weak *I* will be sooner subdued by the new abnormal perception than a strong one. A slow imperceptible penetration of the old groups of ideas by the new will certainly cause much less emotion; but, inasmuch as it offers to the *I* less opposition, the latter is the more readily subdued and absorbed. The duration of the disease is of all circumstances the most important. The new groups of perceptions are dangerous to the *I* in proportion as their contents are related to the old; their union will then be easier, but the combination of the two states, contrasted with the earlier, will be proportionately less striking. All these statements are fully confirmed by everyday experience.

In the state of health, the various groups of ideas which can represent the *I* find a fundamental element of unity, above all, in the complexus of ideas of the body proper. And if, in the course of life, this physical sensation of self is in various ways subject to change (disease, age, &c.), so does the joint perception of the same body serve as a point of union for the remaining perceptions, and as a centre from which the motory acts proceed. But there are abnormal conditions, particularly in mental disease, in which the general bodily feeling quickly and sensibly changes, so that hereby this fundamental sensuous element of the old *I* undergoes a total transformation. Then for the first time does the patient lose his former personality; this he no more recognises as his distinguishing feature—then for the first time the patient considers himself a different person than he actually is. It is very essential to distinguish this from those changes which the *I* undergoes through simple occupation by new ideas and aims, produced by the disease of the brain, without essential change in the physical sensation of self.

§ 30. A simple difference in the perception, familiar to all, consists in this—that it sometimes proceeds quietly as calm imagination or thought, while at others it is accompanied by great disturbance, by a general state of mental disquietude. In the first case, the masses of perceptions which represent the *I* act towards the thought which is present in the consciousness as quiet onlookers, as in being perceived they are only feebly and slowly changed by it, and when obscure opinions thereby result relating to the demands or limitation of the *I* (pleasure or displeasure), these also are of but slight intensity. In the second case, any striking occurrence in the consciousness, as a mass of perceptions suddenly presented, or a sudden urgent desire, enters with violence. By these occurrences, separate groups of perceptions are promptly evoked, which bring others along with them; whilst others are rapidly, but not without opposition, repelled, and the *I* must necessarily be affected by them pleasurably or painfully according as they promote or impede it. . . .

Emotion may accompany calm thought: scientific thought can, for example, when the allied ideas meet in a favorable manner, be accompanied by a sense of pleasure, by the feeling of success. But the emotions are much more lively when, through a sudden change occurring within the consciousness, the masses of ideas belonging to the *I* fall into violent oscillation, and the *I* thereby suffers an abrupt or restless change. These affections of the *I* are called the *emotions:* in the first case they are joyful, in the second of a sad nature. In all the sentiments, emotions occur as essential constituents, although every sentiment does not occasion emotion. There are sentiments, more lasting and stable, which have no emotion, as the sentiments of self, country, family. The sentiment of the *I* can proceed even to instantaneous suppression; one becomes "out of himself."

As in the emotions, only the relations of tension and movement in certain masses of perceptions, and the manner in which the *I* is excited by these events, come into consciousness; so they have no definite existence that can be expressed in words, but they call forth desires, and are in turn evoked by them. The sentiments, since they consist of rapid changes in the relations of tension and movement in the perceptions, are naturally always bound to the emotions.

Restrained or expanded effort affects the *I* much more than the same conditions in pure perception, and the most sudden and violent agitations result from the sudden arrest of efforts in progress. When, for example, our calm scientific thought is impeded by an unexpected external hindrance, we may indeed be annoyed; but when our will is opposed, when the execution of plans designed and determined by the *I* is hindered, this excites much more violent emotions—anger, disappointment, &c. We frequently observe that thwarted plans and determinations of the will—for example, an occupation enforced while all the inclinations of the individual are directed towards engagements of quite a different nature—become the causes of lasting emotions, and of insanity thereby developed. We know the case of a man who became insane because he was forced to be a butcher, while he desired to become an ecclesiastic. Examples of this kind are to be found in all asylums.

§ 31. The question, what properly speaking the affections and the sentiments are, and what position they hold in the mental life, is of great importance to the understanding of insanity (which so frequently, and for so long a time, consists principally of a disorder of the affections). Our perception and effort are always subject to progressive change; we only, however, speak of a sentiment, when the mass of perceptions which represents the *I* is subjected to a violent shock and brought into collision, which (§ 30) never can occur without emotion. In this disturbance of the tranquility of the mind, there is no further agitation than that of the wonted calm which our *I* maintains towards the perceptions present, than of the manner in which, above all, the multifarious masses of perceptions and efforts which we feel within us behave towards each other. This usual tranquility is not, however, absolute quiet or inactivity, but is the result of regulated moderate activity, which simultaneously represents the acquired amount of mental power and the ordinary direction of the mental life: it may be called the *mental tone*. . . .

We call the man *impressible*, whose *I* is easily moved, and in whom, accordingly, agreeable or disagreeable feelings—sympathy, compassion, benevolence, aversion, &c.—are readily excited. Agreeable as is this characteristic, yet this danger follows, that the sentiments willingly attach themselves to these obscure excitations, so that they do not succeed each other in a clear train of thought, and that the habit of clear thinking is lost, and the individual governed by mere sentiment, of whose influence he cannot divest himself, but thereby orders his actions and frames his life. This is the impressible character in the bad sense. He is called *unimpressible*, whose *I* is not easily affected by pleasure or pain, either on account of great weakness and dulness of all the mental powers (apathetic, very phlegmatic men), or because, upon contact of the *I* with the perception present, there is simultaneously produced distinct opinions in clear ideas instead of obscure sentiments (intelligent men). The man is *strong-minded*, in whom there is developed a firm tone of mind, who is not immediately moved by every mental excitation, he, indeed, feels events as agreeable or disagreeable, and they are accompanied by obscure opinions relating to the promotion or hindrance of the *I*; but the *I* itself, however, is not so easily shaken; he is not easily subject to general mental disquietude, to anger and ill-humour, and in joy and pain moderation is maintained. There is, on the other hand, *weakness of mind*, where reactions of the *I*, extended, but wanting in energy, are easily evoked; nearly every perception excites a sentiment; joy and sadness succeed each other with the utmost ease, and emotions become necessary to mental life: the diminished sensibility then frequently demands new and strong irritation, as finding pleasure in shocking and fearful events, and the *I* is at rest only in times of exhaustion and sleep.

It is easy to recognise the identity of the last-mentioned case with what, in the sensitive motory sphere, is called irritable weakness, and is considered the most important disposition and fundamental state in many nervous diseases (for example, the spinal neuroses). This state is well called weakness, since with the single and one-sided increase of excitability there is accompanied an absolute diminution of power in the functions. In convulsions, the voluntary muscular movement is weak; in constant emotion, the thought and the will are weak and languid. These states are not only very frequently combined with each other, as in the tendency to emotions and the increased tendency to convulsions in many hysterical persons, but they also very often originate simultaneously in both spheres from the same causes, have in their course the same consequences, and the principles of their treatment are throughout analogous.

§ 32. Upon the nature, method, and facility with which the I is affected in the form of emotions and sentiments, depends certainly a considerable part of the modes of reaction, and therewith the individual peculiarities of men. In so far as the peculiar modes of the individual lie in the inner world of the disposition, and this is not opposed by the versatility of the mental states, the peculiar manner in which this change proceeds is the characteristic; it is this which gives the fundamental complexion and tone to our disposition. The disposition is a certain mode of behaviour of the I, the fixed steadfast kernel of our individuality, with which the results of our whole mental history are associated. This may, indeed, be shaken in the emotions, but not impaired or destroyed; what else can be affected in the emotions than that group of ideas, the I? The I can be detached, and completely destroyed, in serious disorganisations of the brain (in dimentia); it may succumb, and a new one arise in its place (monomania); but even this is only the case (§ 29) when the emotions which necessarily accompany the lesion and destruction of the old I have been completely pacified.

The nature and the manner in which the mass of ideas representing the I is affected by what passes within the consciousness, or presses into it, determines the nature and manner of the self-sensation. Moderate and lasting changes of consciousness are, again, the foundation of the various modifications of the dispositions; when they take place suddenly and energetically, and are accompanied by considerable disturbance of the mental equilibrium, they constitute the foundation of the mental affections. The objects of consciousness can only be of a twofold nature, pleasurable or painful; the one, when the groups of perceptions of the I, the interests of our inner life, are favoured and advanced, through the events in consciousness, in their free course, their adequate relations, and especially in their transition into efforts; the other, when hereby they are repressed, subverted, and limited. From the slightest changes in the disposition up to the most violent emotion, only two kinds are possible: either a state of furtherance and expansion of the I, which affords pleasure, therefore it is in harmony with the new occurrences in consciousness, and seeks to retain them; or a state of limitation and depression, where the group of perceptions of the I, in their flow and transition into effort, are impeded and repressed, sometimes take to flight, sometimes perseveringly strive to enter; here the I is in a negative relation to the new perceptions. Accordingly, all the dispositions and emotions divide themselves into two great classes—the expansive (and at the same time affirmative), and the depressing (and at the same time negative, accompanied by abhorrence). To the one belong joy, gladness, pleasure, frolic, hope, humour, merriment, &c.; to the other, anger, malice, dejection, sadness, sorrow, shame, fear, horror, &c.[15]

In the emotions calm deliberation is impossible. The *I* itself, having fallen into a vacillating and disturbed condition, does not possess the composure necessary to consider the facts present in consciousness with sufficient concentration and attention. That state in which this consideration is possible, and actually takes place, is called *the reason*. In order to this consideration, and therefore also to deliberation, there is requisite a reciprocal definiteness of the perceptions, leisure and delay, composure and reflection. The contrasting perceptions (§ 26) must be capable of becoming effective, and requisite calm must be afforded to the *I*. Neither of these occur in mental disease. Through the cerebral affection, dispositions and instincts are produced which become points of origin of emotions. If out of these, again, false opinions arise, they cannot be rectified, and the patient cannot see his error; at first, because the persistent emotions do not permit the calm necessary to allow the contrasting perceptions sufficiently to develope themselves, and the longer it continues the more do its results, the false judgments, become fortified and consolidated; later, however, because those false judgments have become integral fundamental parts of all the groups of ideas of the *I*.

In every fully developed mental disease it is therefore impossible for the patient to recognise the falseness of the morbid perceptions. This fact is confounded to a very great extent with loss of reflection, spoken of in § 27. But by that even the insane have also lost their reason, and on the ground so well stated by Herbart, that "their thoughts do not admit of being disturbed in their special course by means of external or internal opposition." Also in health, all kinds of caprices, false opinions, foolish thoughts, pass through the brain; but one can, if he be not actually in a state of emotion, calmly accept or reject them.

Recovery from insanity ordinarily takes place only in the primary period, which, however, often continues for a series of years, during which it principally depends on emotional states. Inasmuch as through removal of the disease of the brain, or of its more remote organic causes, the morbid dispositions and emotions disappear, the false judgments which were based upon it must likewise disappear, and the group of perceptions of the, now no longer shaken, *I* enter immediately into their old direction. Should, however, the organic causes of the cerebral disease not have been removed until the false opinions have entered into manifold combinations with the groups of perceptions of the *I*, the patient may certainly recover; but his recovery will be a longer and much more gradual psychological process, until, through strengthening of the former normal direction of the thoughts, the connections which the false opinions had contracted with the *I* gradually loosen, and eventually are entirely dissolved.

[15] Ibid., pp. 48–56.

Many convalescents do not recover completely until they return to their homes and to their former relations of life, employments, &c. When, however, the old *I* is vitiated, corrupted, and falsified on all sides by the morbid false ideas—when, besides, the group of perceptions of the former *I* is so completely repressed (forgotten), that, without any trace of emotion, the patient has exchanged his whole personality, and has scarcely any remembrance of it, then recovery is next to impossible, and only occurs in rare cases through excitation of violent emotions, and thereby through a kind of mechanical training (as attempted, for example, by Leuret), continuously to repel the *appearances* of the insanity. Naturally, this can only be attempted where the brain has not as yet sustained any deep organic lesion: where this is present, as in many of these states, especially in secondary dementia, all hope of recovery is past.[16]

Observation shows that the great majority of mental diseases are first manifested, not by senseless discourse or extreme acts, but by morbid changes of disposition, anomalies of the self-sensation and the sentiments, and consequent emotional states. And, indeed, the earliest stages of insanity generally consist in an aimless feeling of ill-humour, discomfort, oppression, and anxiety, owing to the fact that the new groups of ideas and instincts resulting from the cerebral affection are usually at first exceedingly obscure. On this account, the disturbance of the normal process of thought and will, and the new mental states obtruding on the *I*, are first felt simply as vague modifications of the sentiment and disposition. The diminished power and energy of the *I*, the contraction of its sphere of ideas, produces an indefinite state of mental pain, and, from its vagueness, great irritation of the feelings. The new morbid perceptions and instincts produce divisions of the mind, a feeling of division of the personality, and of imminent annihilation of the *I*. The mental pain discovers itself in some of the familiar forms of agitation, anxiety, sadness, and entails all the forementioned consequences of a radically changed reaction towards the external world, and of a disturbance in the motory function of the mind. Perversions of the natural feelings, aversion and hate towards those formerly loved, outward insensibility, or a morbid fondness clinging to a single object, but without the depth and tenderness of the normal sensation, and subject to rapid and capricious changes, are here ordinary appearances. The increased sensibility involves everything, because, indeed, it is painfully affected by everything, and from the mournful complexion that pervades all his views and opinions, the individual puts an evil interpretation upon everything present, and discovers in the future nothing but evil. Distrust and suspicion are engendered by the feeling of diminished power of resistance, and are constantly excited by bodily feelings of anxiety. Everything appears strange to him, because he acts strangely towards every mental impression, because he himself feels altered, and he feels a strong inclination to ascribe his condition sometimes to the direct influence of the outer world—to believe that he is pursued, influenced, charmed,

[16] Ibid., pp. 58–59.

governed by secret influences—and at others to refer to his former life for the causes, and to accuse himself of a variety of serious crimes, depravities, and misdeeds, of which his present position is the necessary consequence. . . .

The anomalies of emotion which have been hitherto described are to be regarded essentially as appearances of abnormal emotional irritability. There are also, however, abnormal states of dulness, and even of total loss of emotion. Here either the occasional perceptions are no longer connected with the changes in the relation of tension of the quiet masses of perceptions of the *I* which occur in the healthy state—there is little or no disturbance of the emotions generally—or it may be that these events occur indeed, but they are no longer known to the individual, and therefore have no existence to him. To all that formerly interested him he is now equally indifferent, and he is no longer capable of being much affected by any new sentiment; participation and interest, pain and pleasure, love and hate, cease. Apathy and indifference to everything beyond the satisfaction of his sensuous requirements succeed. Intelligence can thereby be tolerably maintained, but generally a greater or less degree of dementia is apparent.[17]

The false ideas and conclusions, which are attempts at explanation and vindications of the actual disposition in its effects, are spontaneously developed in the diseased mind according to the law of causality; on the part of the individual the explanations do not imply reflection, still less are such conclusions formed by the tedious form of syllogism. At first the delirious conceptions are fleeting; the *I* perceives them, it may be terrified by them, acknowledge their absurdity, and yet feel quite unable to rid itself of them, and struggles with them; gradually, by continued repetition, they gain more body and form, repel opposing ideas and form connections with similar masses of perceptions of the *I;* then they become constituent parts of it, and the patient cannot divest himself of them, or only in some degree by exchange with similar false perceptions. The excited, lively, and happy insane ideas are naturally received by the *I* much more easily and completely; it yields to them after a short resistance, and then it occasionally gives itself over to the insane perceptions, half-conscious imagination in a world of happy dreams arises.[18]

As, however, insanity presents a similarity sometimes superficial, sometimes profound, sometimes qualitative to the various states of dreaming; so the psychical process by means of which the individual, when the cerebral disease is removed, returns to healthy life, presents various modifications. Sometimes recovery resembles simple waking; when the individual astonished seeks, as it were, to know himself, the masses of ideas belonging to the disease soon disappear, and the old *I* returns uninjured and unimpaired to its former place. At other times, the already united connections loose themselves with greater

[17] Ibid., pp. 63–66.
[18] Ibid., p. 71.

difficulty, and as the old *I* is but slowly strengthened, recovery consists again of a painful struggle, in which the individual awakened frequently requires the instruction and advice of another will to strengthen his. Not unfrequently, even then all traces of the morbid state do not disappear, and the patient for a long time retains, as vestiges of the past, certain ties, oddities, aberrations, and perversions. From this point it may frequently be observed that the patient undergoes a decided change of character. . . . Those cases are very interesting where, shortly before death, the mental health completely returns or becomes decidedly improved. This occurs most frequently in mania, seldom in melancholia, and almost never in the secondary forms—chronic mania and dementia. In those cases where serious anatomical changes have already taken place in the brain, and the morbid perceptions have completely pervaded and destroyed the *I*, the fundamental requisites of return to normal thought seem to be wanting. The length of time required for this cannot be estimated.[19]

The chief point is invariably this—that, in the great majority of cases, there appears with the mental disease a change in the mental disposition of the patient in his sentiments, desires, habits, conduct, and opinions. He is no more the same; his former *I* becomes changed, he becomes estranged to himself (alienated). In order to prove that this change has taken place in the patient, it is necessary that his former habits and character should be made known to the physician. . . .[20]

von Feuchtersleben (1845)

The very year in which Griesinger was publishing his extensive discussion of the ego von Feuchtersleben was contenting himself with a few sentences of definition, and scarcely any more of fragmentary clinical comment.

> . . . the Ego of the mental physiologist is not the Ego of the metaphysician. The Ego of which we speak consists of body and mind, the other is an abstraction of the most spiritual personality.[21]

Romberg (1851)

In common with other early neuropsychiatrists Romberg mentioned the ego only in passing.

> Diagnostic errors are frequent from psychical hyperaesthesia being confounded with melancholia and hysteria. The characteristic peculiar to the former, as to insanity generally, consists in an alienation of the feeling of

---

[19] Ibid., pp. 111-112.

[20] Ibid., p. 114.

[21] E. von Feuchtersleben, *The Principles of Medical Psychology* [Vienna, 1845], H. E. Lloyd, trans., and B. G. Babington, ed. (London: The New Sydenham Society, 1847), p. 77.

identity and consciousness as regards sensations and impressions, and this in melancholia is combined with a tendency to self-negation (negirendem Affect). In hypochondriasis, on the contrary, the egotistic principle is exalted.[22]

Hysteria is distinguished from insanity by the fact, that in all acts of intellect, subjectivity (the ego) is the ruling genius; self-consciousness is never alienated in the sensations, impressions, and desires.[23]

Carpenter (1874)

Carpenter contributed some interesting observations on the similarity of cannabis intoxication to endogenous psychosis with respect to the involvement of the ego. His *Principles of Mental Physiology* is a separate printing of part of his *Principles of Human Physiology* which had gone through many editions in the previous twenty-five years.

It is singular how closely the ordinary history of the access of *Monomania* corresponds with that of intoxication by Hachisch. A man who has been for some time under the strain of severe mental labour, perhaps with the addition of emotional excitement, breaks down in mental and bodily health; and becomes subject to morbid ideas, of whose abnormal character he is in the first instance quite aware. He may see spectral illusions, but he knows that they are illusive. He may hear imaginary conversations, but is conscious that they are empty words. He feels an extreme depression of spirits, but is willing to attribute this to some physical cause. He exhibits an excessive irritability of temper, but is conscious of his irascibility and endeavours to restrain it. He has strange thoughts respecting those who are most dear to him, suspects his wife of infidelity, his children of wilful disobedience, his most intimate friends of injurious designs; but he has still intelligence enough to question the validity of these suspicions, and shrinks from giving them permanent lodgment in his breast. Dark visions of future ruin and disgrace flit before him; but he may refuse to contemplate them, may be reasoned into the admission of their utter baselessness, and may second the efforts of his friends to direct his thoughts and feelings into a different channel. It is in this stage that change of scene, the withdrawal from painful associations, the invigoration of the bodily health, and the direction of the Mental activity towards any subject that has a healthful attraction for it, exert a most beneficial influence; and there can be no doubt that many a man has been saved from an attack of Insanity, by the resolute determination of his Will *not* to yield to his morbid tendencies.—But if he should give way to these tendencies, and should dwell upon his morbid ideas instead of endeavouring to escape from them, they come at last to acquire a complete

---

[22] M. H. Romberg, *A Manual of the Nervous Diseases of Man,* from the German ed., 1851, E. H. Sieveking, trans. (London: The New Sydenham Society, 1853), Vol. 1, p. 184.

[23] Ibid., Vol. 2, p. 89.

mastery over him; and his Will, his Common sense, and his Moral sense, at last succumb to their domination. The visual appearances which he at first dismissed as unreal, become to his mind objects of actual sight; the airy words are conversations which he distinctly hears, and to which he gives full credence, however repugnant their import may be to his sober sense; his suspicions of wife, children, and friends acquire the force of certainties, although they may not have the slightest basis of reality; the conviction of impending ruin is ever before him, and he makes no effort to escape from it; no reasoning can now dispel his delusions; no proof, however clear to the sane mind, can demonstrate the groundlessness of his notions. His temper, now entirely uncontrolled, becomes more and more irritable; the slightest provocations occasion the most violent outbreaks; and these are excited, not merely by the exaggeration or misinterpretation of actual occurrences, but by the fictions of his own imagination. No conception can be too obviously fallacious or absurd, as judged by the sound intellect, to command his assent and govern his actions; for when the directing power of the Will is altogether lost, he is as incapable as a Biologized or Hypnotized subject, of testing his ideas by their conformity to the general result of his previous experience, or of keeping his emotions under due control.

But, it may be said, if Insanity be the expression of disordered *physical* action of the Cerebrum, it is inconsistent to expect that a man can control this by any effort of his own; or that *moral* treatment can have any efficacy in the restoration of mental health. Those, however, who have followed the course of the argument expounded in this Treatise, will have no difficulty in reconciling the two orders of facts. For whilst the disordered physical action of the Cerebrum, *when once established,* puts the automatic action of his mind altogether beyond the control of the Ego, there is frequently a stage in which he has the power of so directing and controlling that action, as *to prevent the establishment of the disorder;* just as, in the state of perfect health, he has the power of forming habits of Mental action, to which the nutrition of the Brain responds, so as ultimately to render them automatic. And so, the judicious Physician, in the treatment of an insane patient, whilst doing everything he can to invigorate the bodily health, to ward off sources of mental disturbance, and to divert the current of thought and feeling from a morbid into a healthful channel, will sedulously watch for every opportunity of fostering the power of self-control, will seek out the motives most likely to act upon the individual, will bring these into play upon every suitable occasion, will approve and reward its successful exercise, will sympathize with failure even when having recourse to the restraint which it has rendered necessary, will encourage every renewed exertion, and will thus give every aid he can to the re-acquirement of that Volitional direction, which, as the bodily malady abates, is alone needed to prevent the recurrence of the disordered mental action. It is when the patient has so far recovered, as to be capable of being made to feel that he *can* do what he *ought,* if he will only *try,* that moral treatment becomes efficacious. And thus the judicious Physician, when endeavouring either to ward-off or to cure Mental disorder, brings to bear upon his patient exactly the same power as that which is exerted by an Educator of the highest type.[24]

Maudsley (1867, 1883)

Certainly Maudsley's writings comprise the best of the nineteenth-century writings of the critical school.

With regard to the supreme centres of our mental life, from the residua of past thoughts, feelings, and actions, which have been organized as mental faculties, there results a certain physical tone in each individual. This is the basis of the individual's conception of the *ego*—the affections of which, therefore, best reveal his real nature—a conception which, so far from being, as is often said, fixed and unchanging, undergoes gradual change with the change of the individual's relations as life proceeds. Whosoever candidly reflects upon the striking modification, or rather revolution, of the *ego,* which happens at the time of puberty both in men and women, will surely not find it hard to conceive how the self may imperceptibly but surely change through life. The education and experience to which any one is subjected likewise modify, if less suddenly, not less certainly, the tone of his character. By constantly blaming certain actions and praising certain others in their children, parents are able so to form their character that, apart from any reflection, these shall ever in after-life be attended with a certain pleasure; those, on the other hand, with certain pain.[25]

What we call the *ego,* is in reality an abstraction in which are contained the residua of all former feelings, thoughts, volitions,—a combination which is continually becoming more and more complex. That it differs at different times of life, and in consequence in different external relations, those who would most zealously uphold its so-called identity do unconsciously admit when they acknowledge that, through religious influence or otherwise, any one may be made "quite another man," may be "converted," or be "regenerate." When the *ego* is transformed in correspondence with changed external circumstances, the changes are so gradual as to be imperceptible at the time; but a rapid transformation of the *ego* may sometimes be effected by a great event, internal or external, as, for example, when, with the development of puberty, new ideas and impulses penetrate the old circle and become constituent parts of it, producing no little subjective disturbance until the assimilation is completed and an equilibrium established. When a great and sudden revolution in the *ego* is produced by an external cause, it is most dangerous to the mental stability of the individual and very apt to become pathological: nothing is more dangerous to the equilibrium of a character than for any one to be placed in entirely

---

[24] W. B. Carpenter, *Principles of Mental Physiology* (New York: D. Appleton and Co., 1874), pp. 672-675.

[25] H. Maudsley *The Physiology and Pathology of the Mind* (New York: D. Appleton and Co., 1867), pp. 113-114.

changed external circumstances without his inner life having been gradually adapted thereto; and madness, when its origin is fairly examined, always means discord between the individual and his circumstances. He who, having unexpectedly received a sudden great exaltation in life, is not made mad by his good fortune, cannot realize his new position for some time, but gradually grows to it; he who from some subjective cause believes that he has received a great exaltation in life while external circumstances are not correspondent, is mad—the transformation of his *ego* being pathological.[26]

Furthermore, it is plain that the degree of development which the mind has reached must determine in no slight measure the features of its disorder; the more cultivated the mind the more various and complex must be the symptoms of its derangement; while it is not possible that the undeveloped mind of the child immediately after birth should exhibit ideational disorder of any kind. Consider what an infinitely complex development the cultivated mind has been shown to be, and what a long series of processes and what a variety of interworkings of so-called faculties even its simpler conceptions imply; it will then be easily understood how great and varied may be the confusion and and disorder of its morbid action.[27]

The *ego* is not a constant but a variable. It represents the aggregate of sensations clearly or obscurely felt at any given moment, whether springing from the original constitution or from the acquired nature and habits of the organism; these sensations themselves representing the sum of silent multitudes of activities that are going on below the threshold of consciousness, and which, albeit unperceived and unfelt immediately, vibrate subtilely in the most intimate and intricate interactions of organic depths, and in the result affect deeply the *tone* of consciousness.[28]

... it is made evident that disorganisation of the union of the supreme cerebral centres must be a more or less dissolution of the conscious self, the *ego,* according to the depth of the damage to the physiological unity. Even if any one organ of the body be defective, it is a breach in the supreme unity of consciousness, for it is a deprivation to the extent of its deficient energy, and a disturbance to the degree that its work is thrown upon other organs: it is like a horse in a team that does not do its exact share of the work uniformly. The constant feeling of personal identity on which metaphysicians lay so much stress as a fundamental intuition of consciousness, discerning in it the incontestable touch and proof of a spiritual *ego* which they cannot get into actual contact with in any other way, may be expected to be sometimes wavering and uncertain, in other cases divided and discordant, and in extreme cases extinguished. But that is a dismayful expectation to entertain concerning the 'I,'

[26] Ibid., p. 159.
[27] Ibid., p. 290.
[28] H. Maudsley, *Body and Will* (London: Kegan, Paul, Trench and Co., 1883), p. 80.

the 'ego'—the *ens unum et semper cognitum in omnibus notitiis*—of which they thus protest we have more or less clear consciousness in every exercise of intelligence. Look frankly then at the facts and see what conclusion they warrant. Is there the least sign of a consciousness of his *ego* in the senseless, speechless, howling, slavering, dirty, defenceless, and utterly helpless idot, whose defective cerebral centres are incapable of responding to such weak and imperfect impressions as his dull senses are able to convey, and incapable of any association of the few, dim and vague impressions that he does receive? No doubt his body, so long as it holds together by the ministering care of others, may be said to be an *ego* or self; but from the human standpoint what a self! It is not a mental *ego*, since the central organic mechanism in which the lower bodily energies should obtain higher representation, and mental organisation take place—the before-mentioned synthesis, sympathy, and synergy be effected— is either altogether wanting or hopelessly ill constructed. The miserable specimen of degeneracy does not and cannot therefore in the least know that he is a self, or feel that a human self is degraded on him.[29]

It is a common event in one sort of mental disorder, especially at the beginning of it, for the person to complain that he is completely and painfully changed; that he is no longer himself, but feels himself unutterably strange; and that things around him, though wearing their usual aspect, yet somehow seem quite different. I am so changed that I feel as if I were not myself but another person; although I know it is an illusion, it is an illusion which I cannot shake off; all things appear strange to me and I cannot properly apprehend them even though they are really familiar; they look a long way off and more like the figures of a dream than realities, and indeed it is just as if I were in a dream and my will paralysed. It is impossible to describe the feeling of unreality that I have about everything; I assure myself over and over again that I am myself, but still I cannot make impressions take their proper hold of me, and come into fit relations of familiarity with my true self; between my present self and my past self it seems as if an eternity of time and an infinity of space were interposed; the suffering that I endure is indescribable:—such is the kind of language by which these persons endeavour to express the profound change in themselves which they feel only too painfully but cannot describe adequately. An observer of little experience, or one who has made little good use of his experience, judging these complaints by a self-inspective standard, is sure to think that the distress and impotence are largely fanciful or at any rate much overstated, and that they might be got rid of if the will could be stirred to proper efforts; not able to realise in his own experience such an extraordinary mental state, he cannot enter into real sympathy with it or believe thoroughly in it. But if he has never had the delirium of a fever go give him practical experience of strange conscious states and to confound and alarm him with the most singular distractions of self, let him call to mind what has doubtless happened to himself more than once when

[29] Ibid., pp. 302–303.

he has been awakened suddenly out of sleep and been helplessly unable for a few moments to realise who he was or where he was or whether he was at all, although seeing around him the usual objects, cognising but not recognising them, hearing words distinctly but apprehending them not; let him then imagine this brief and passing phase of consciousness to persist, and to be his ordinary mental state; and he will in that way obtain far juster notions of the extraordinary states of abnormal consciousness than he will ever get by the sharpest and most skilful inspection of its ordinary states.[30]

An interesting and very striking example of changed personal identity is furnished by a form of mental derangement which, as it revolves regularly through two alternating and opposite phases, was called by French writers circular insanity, but is better called alternating insanity. An attack of much mental excitement with great elation of thought, feeling, and conduct is followed by an opposite dark phase of depression, gloom, and apathy, each state lasting for weeks or months, and the usual succession of them recurring from time to time after longer or shorter intervals of sanity. Between the two states the contrast is as striking as could well be imagined: in the one the person is elated, exultant, self-confident, boastful and overflowing with energy; talks freely of private matters which he would never have mentioned in his sound state, and familiarly with those above and below him in station whom, when himself, he would not have thought of addressing; in like manner writes many and long letters full of details of opinions, affairs, and plans, to persons with whom he has a slight acquaintance only; spends money recklessly, though not reckless in that way by natural disposition; projects bold and sometimes wild schemes of adventure; is ready and pleased to harangue in public who never made a public speech before; is careless of social proprieties and even disregards moral reticences and restraints; listens to prudential advice but heeds it not, being inspired with an extraordinary feeling of well-being, of intellectual power, of unfettered thought and will. An actual disruption of the *ego* there is not, but there is an extraordinary exaltation of it, in fact an extreme moral rather than an intellectual alienation. The condition of things is much like that which goes before an ordinary outbreak of acute mania, when there is great mental exaltation without actual incoherence, alienation of character without alienation of intelligence, but it is not, like it, followed by turbulent degeneracy; for when the excitement passes off there supervenes the second phase, that of extreme mental despondency and moral prostration.

How changed the person now from what he was! As self-distrustful as before he was self-sufficient; as retiring as before he was obtrusive; as shy and silent as before he was loud and talkative; as diffident as before he was boastful; as impotent to think and act as before he was eager and energetic to plan and to do; as entirely oppressed with a dominating sense of mental and bodily incapacity as before he was possessed with an exultant feeling of exalted powers.

[30] Ibid., pp. 307–308.

To all intents and purposes he is a different person, another *ego*, at any rate so far as consciousness is concerned—subjectively though not objectively—since in all relations he feels, thinks, and acts quite differently.[31]

An interesting fact which cannot fail to attract attention is that during the exalted state of this alternating derangement the person does with almost exact automatic repetition the things that he did, and has the thoughts and feelings that he had, in former exalted states, and during the prostrate state that he thinks, feels and does exactly as he did in former prostrate states. In the one state, however, he has not a clear and exact remembrance of the events of the other; not probably that he forgets them entirely, but that he has only that sort of vague, hazy and incomplete remembrance which one has oftentimes of the events of a dream, or that a drunken man has, when sober, of his drunken feelings and doings. How indeed could he remember them clearly, since it is plain he would be compelled, in order to do so, to reproduce exactly in himself the one state when he was actually in the other? It is impossible therefore he should realise sincerely the experiences of the one during the other, though he may know as a matter of fact that they occurred to him, and, feeling some shame for what he remembers, and misgivings concerning what he does not remember, be unwilling to recall them and speak of them.

Nearly related to these cases, and probably belonging to the same category, are the examples of so-called double consciousness that have lately attracted psychological attention.[32]

These are the usual features of the recurrent mental exaltations and torpid depressions that characterise alternating insanity; and it is the common order of events in such cases for the lucid intervals to become shorter, rarer and less complete, until the disease takes a continuous course with periodically changing phases. One may doubt perhpas whether all the events of her abnormal states were as clean swept from the memory as the reporter of the case assumes, since those who suffer as she did, having a dull, painful, and at the same time confused consciousness of having done and said foolish things during their states of excited alienation, will say they forget them rather than attempt to bring back to their minds what they would gladly forget and willingly be thought to have forgotten. The natural self, ashamed of the abnormal self, is unwilling as it is certainly in great measure unable to identify itself with it, confessing however by this very sense of shame a vague consciousness of identity.[33]

In spite, then, of aught which psychological theory appealing to its own internal oracle may urge to the contrary, it is incontestably proved by observation of instances that there are states of disordered consciousness which, being quite unlike states of normal consciousness, are not to be measured by

---

[31] Ibid., pp. 310–311.
[32] Ibid., p. 312.
[33] Ibid., p. 313.

them, and the events of which may be remembered only dimly, hazily felt rather than remembered, or completely forgotten. The lesson of them is the lesson which has been enforced over and over again on physiological grounds—namely, that the consciousness of self, the unity of the *ego,* is a consequence, not a cause; the expression of a full and harmonious function of the aggregate of differentiated mind-centres, not a mysterious metaphysical entity lying behind function and inspiring and guiding it; a subjective synthesis or unity based upon the objective synthesis or unity of the organism. As such, it may be obscured, deranged, divided, apparently transformed. For every breach of the unity of the united centres is a breach of it: subtract any one centre from the intimate physiological co-operation, the self is *pro tanto* weakened or mutilated; obstruct or derange the conducting function of the associating bonds between the various centres, so that they are dissociated or disunited, the self loses in corresponding degree its sense of continuity and unity; stimulate one or two centres or groups of centres to a morbid hypertrophy so that they absorb to them most of the mental nourishment and keep up a predominant and almost exclusive function, the personality appears to be transformed; strip off a whole layer of the highest centres—that highest superordinate organisation of them that ministers to abstract reasoning and moral feeling—you reduce man to the condition of one of the higher animals; take away all the supreme centres, you bring him to the state of a simply sentient creature; remove the centres of sense, you reduce him to a bare vegetative existence when, like a cabbage, he has an objective but no subjective *ego.* These are the conclusions which we are compelled to form when, not blinking facts, we observe nature sincerely and interpret it faithfully, going to plain experience for facts to inform our understandings, instead of invoking our own imaginations to utter oracles to us.[34]

Meynert (1884)

Meynert occupies a special place in the history of the ego concept because he was the only physician ever to give the development of the ego a rational explanation. Although discussions of the ego (das Ich, le moi) filled many pages of the psychologic literature in the last years of the eighteenth and the first of the nineteenth centuries, very little was said about its development. Many psychiatrists simply said that in the newborn infant instinct reigns alone but is very limited, and experience modifies and adds to it. The role of sensory impressions in the formation of the ego was emphasized by most late eighteenth- and early nineteenth-century philosophers who belonged to the sensist school, but it remained for Theodor Meynert, a neuropsychiatrist, to suggest a reasonable—or at least testable—mechansim. His ideas in this regard have been almost totally ignored.

Starting with the ideas of the eighteenth-century English and French scientists, who held that the development of the ego depended on receiving sensory

[34] Ibid., pp. 314–315.

impressions, Meynert suggested the special role of touch sensation in early infancy. He pointed out that the infant who touched himself received *two* touch sensations, whereas the infant who touched another, or was touched by another, received only *one* touch sensation. This quickly established a difference between self and nonself. The same might be said about the sense of hearing, i.e., the perception of sounds produced by self phonation and those created by others. Sensory phenomena that distinguish self and nonself would rapidly become integrated with other sensory impressions that do not directly make this distinction but would thereby come to do so. Hence the sense of self would commence to develop long before introspective thought processes and would in fact direct these introspections.

Meynert also objected to the metaphysicians' notion of the ego and advanced a neurophysiologic formulation in his book.

> ... [The cortical] centres, connected with one another by every variety and length of association-bundles, are nothing special, their "memories" are defined by the peculiarities of localization referred to above. The sum of these "centres" constitutes the "individuality," the "ego" of abstract-psychologists. I attach some importance to the word "individuality," because it is founded upon the anatomical structure of the cortex, and the simple physiological process which enters into our present discussion. Individuality implies the sum of firmest associations, which under ordinary circumstances are wellnigh inseparable; the aggregate of "memories" forming a solid phalanx, the relation of which to conscious movements can be defined apparently with mathematical precision. This unequal activity of the fore-brain, constituting individuality, varies as regards contents and degree with each person; it is designated also as the *character* of the individual. It has been justly observed, if the character (individuality) of a person were entirely known we would be able to predict the thoughts and deeds of such an individual, however complicated they might be.[35]
>
> The nature of the *ego* does not depend upon any definite order of memories; it is determined simply by the most firmly fixed memories. As soon as we apply the test of more complicated relations to the formation of the *ego*, we must bear in mind that the *ego* can be influenced only by images of permanent intensity, which are associated at the same time with other and as firmly fixed images. The idea of *individuality* is an artificial one, though valuable from a practical point of view, for the degree of intensity by which these images and their connections adhere to this conception will not admit of accurate measurement; and it is plainly impossible to say that at a certain intensity a presentation becomes a factor of the *ego*, and not yet at another. There is but one safe stand to take on this question, and that is to attribute to the ill-defined conception of individuality only those presentations which, as soon as the "character" of an individual is known, will enable us to predict his deeds; whence it follows that

[35] T. Meynert, *Psychiatry: A Clinical Treatise on Diseases of the Fore-Brain* [1884], B. Sachs, trans. (New York: G. P. Putnam's Sons, 1885), pp. 167–168.

the deeds of the individual obey certain laws. On the other hand, these same conscious deeds, as they are not mere copies of acts suggested by reflex movements, remain incomprehensible as long as the character of the individual is known. This very mystery attending the deeds of others is another and highest expression for the freedom of the will.[36]

Spitzka (1883)

Spitzka was able to digest vague and abstruse material and thereby make it useful to clinical medicine. He used the ego concept to describe clinical phenomena but never specifically accepted the ego as a substantial entity.

It is the multitude of impressions and experiences registered in the organ of the memory that constitute the conscious *ego*. *Healthy consciousness is that condition in which the individual, while registering the impressions of the outer world to which his attention is directed at the time, correlates these with the summarized observations of the past.* The sum of the observations constituting the *ego* is continually increasing; the scope of the *ego* becomes wider with every added impression, every correction of a perceptional or conceptional error, and with every new experience. The *ego* of the child is a different one from that of the adult; but it is the nucleus around which the *ego* of the adult is to gather. In other words, the *ego* of an individual is throughout the same complex unit, composed of the correlated and associated notional items collected up to a given time; but it is variable to this extent, that it is continually forming new bonds and adding new notional items to its mechanism in a healthy state. Consciousness is merely a single designation for that state in which this addition is being made. It involves, in the first place, the healthy memory of the past, that is, not a detailed memory of the entire past at the given moment, but that summarized sense of identity—the *ego*-consciousness which is as it were an abstract of the chief memories of the entire past; and secondly, the functional disposition to add to these memories and to incorporate them with the continuous *ego*.

So complex a mechanism as the *ego*, is, corresponding to its complexity, readily deranged, and it is its disturbance in insanity that constitutes the most essential feature of that disorder, the one whose analysis from a medical point of view is most important, and the one without which no medico-legal study of insanity can be reasonably attempted.

Self-consciousness may be disturbed in any one of its factors. It is always materially influenced by disturbances of the memory; and no grave disorder of the memory is supposable without a corresponding disturbance of the *ego*, for it deprives the latter of important component elements. But the intrinsically important disturbances of the ego-consciousness are of a different nature: they relate to the failure or the functional indisposition of the *ego* to incorporate the

[36] Ibid., pp. 171–172.

changing outer impressions, and to accommodate itself to them, or its inability to properly correlate these impressions with those already accumulated.

Change of the sense of identity is a result of the latter disability. The individual registering the impressions and conceptions of a given period of life, and combining them in a distinct union, without uniting them to those of the past, there result two *egos*, a present and a past one. Lunatics exhibiting this phenomenon may recognize in a shadowy way the conflict between the old ego and the spurious one; they then complain that they have been changed, and have become other individuals, in which case they will often speak of their former selves in the third person. More frequently the patient's spurious *ego* overwhelms the *ego* of the past, a complete change in sentiments and conceptions occurs, and a person previously a prosperous mechanic may so identify himself with the false character construed on a delusional basis, that it remains his supposed nature for life; he continues to his death to believe himself a king, a religious reformer, or a cheated inventor.

It has been occasionally observed where the patient has a divided identity that the conceptions of either the normal ego or the spurious one rise to the surface in the shape of hallucinations, and under these circumstances asylum inmates can occasionally be found sustaining dialogues between their older and their newer and morbid selves.[37]

Prince (1885)

Morton Prince, who later achieved fame for his work on the multiple personalities of some women, early in his career expressed skepticism about the concept of an executive ego.

> We know by direct consciousness that our thoughts can be determined in this or that direction, according to certain previous desires. But I know of no consciousness which directly informs us of the manner in which this is done, and still less of an extra Ego over and above our states of consciousness, which plays with our thoughts . . .[38]

I know of no evidence for it, and still less for an extra independent Ego. In my judgment, the only way in which we can ascertain the mechanism by which this self-determination is accomplished is to study and analyze that feeling of personality commonly called the Ego, which each individual has. . . . But in questions of this kind involving the deeper strata of human knowledge, it is not only not superfluous, but absolutely essential to define exactly what is meant by every term used, when susceptible of different interpretations. Now there are several conceptions which may be formed of the Ego. There is the idea of an

---

[37] E. C. Spitzka, *Insanity: Its Classification, Diagnosis and Treatment* (New York: Bermingham and Co., 1883), pp. 59-61.

[38] M. Prince, *The Nature of Mind and Human Automatism* (Philadelphia: J. B. Lippencott Co., 1885), p. 133.

"agent distinct from the thinking brain," which directs our processes of thought and bodily actions, and to which a sort of ownership is given over all the individual portions of the body, and the mental faculties. For any such agent as this there is no evidence whatsoever. It is merely an abstract notion, the result of an artifice of thought, and has no existence. Therefore, under such a conception, the phrase "we have a self-determining power" is philosophically empty of meaning.

Another idea of the Ego comprehends the body and the mind united together into a whole. No particular state of mind is thought of as differentiated from the rest, but all possible states of mind united as an abstract notion to a body. This is much like the conception we form of another person's personality, a sort of objective Ego. We have a notion of his body, and we imagine an abstract mind, similar to our own, connected with it. We have in our thoughts no particular state of mind, as an agent, acting on the individual's body, but an abstract mind.

Another similar but less comprehensive notion of this personality is mind as a whole in distinction from the body. Both of these conceptions of the Ego are too abstract to serve the purposes of this inquiry.[39]

REMARKS ON THE ID AND THE SUPEREGO

The idea that the ego might have components or divisions evidently grew out of ancient and medieval notions about the soul. Believing in the holiness of triads[40] philosophers and theologians had defined the soul as a triple or three-part organism. Physicians—perhaps because they were mostly atheists, as Tertullian had pointed out—limited the number of parts to two, at least for a time.

Willis (1680)

Thomas Willis believed that man has two main souls, a corporeal and a rational, the first having vital animal and genital components. About the writing of his book Willis stated, "this difficult task, when at first denied leisure and retirement, it could not be performed; after the Death of my Dear Wife, being lonely, with frequent and unseasonable Studies that I might think the less on my Grief, I have at last finished this, according to my slender Capacity."

I assert a Man to be indued with many distinct Souls, and design sometimes a legitimate subordination of them, and sometimes wicked Combinations,

---

[39] Ibid., pp. 134-135.

[40] See M. D. Altschule, "Only God Can Make a Trio," in *The Roots of Modern Psychiatry*, (rev. ed., New York: Grune and Stratton, Inc., 1965).

For example, Sir Thomas Browne states that "A trinity of souls . . . so united as to make one soul and substance" is present in each of us. Others depreciated the concept. Moore insisted (1846) that the soul "is never practically divisible into three parts, animal, moral, and intellectual, for all our conscious voluntary acts involve all three." The modern id, ego, and super-ego might be regarded as Galen's three souls brought up to date.

troublesome Contests, and more than civil wars.[41] . . . These, I say, some not only Philosophers, but Theologists perhaps may find fault with.[42]

I shall attempt to Philosophise concerning that Soul at least, which is Common to Brute Animals with Man, and which seems to depend altogether on the Body, to be born and dye with it, to actuate its Parts, to be extended thorow them, and to be plainly Corporeal; and that chiefly, because, by the Nature, Subsistence, Parts, and affections of this Corporeal Soul rightly unfolded, the Ingenuity, Temperament, and Manners of every man may be thence the better known . . . then secondly, because the ends and bounds of the aforesaid Corporeal Soul being defined, the Rational Soul, Superior and Immaterial, may be sufficiently differenced from it . . .[43]

. . . the Corporeal Soul does not so easily obey the Rational in all things, not so in things to be desired, as in things to be known: for indeed, she being nearer to the body, and so bearing a more intimate Kindness or Affinity towards the Flesh, is tied wholly to look to its Profit and Conservation: to the Sedulous Care of which Office, it is very much allured, by various Complacences, exhibited through the Objects of every Sense: Hence she being busied about the Care of the Body, and apt by that pretext, its natural Inclination, and indulging pleasures, most often grows deaf to Reason, persuading the contrary. Further, the lower Soul, growing weary of the yoak of the Other, if occasion serves, frees itself from its Bounds, affecting a License or Dominion; and then there may plainly be seen the Twinns striving in the same Womb, or rather a Man clearly distracted or drawn several ways, by a double Army planted within himself. . . . This kind of Intestine Strife, does not truly cease, till this or the Champion becoming Superior, leads the other way clearly Captive.[44]

It is interesting that Willis should express the conflict between the two souls in terms of sibling rivalry.

The ancient idea that instinctive forces, usually carnal, affected human behavior, was repeated by many eighteenth- and nineteenth-century psychiatrists. With the rise of ego-psychiatry some described two separate egos. Massias, for example, spoke of the "le moi logique" and "le moi instinctif."[45] The idea that there were

---

[41] It is evident that Willis's account of the warring souls was based on an ancient mode which years before had received strong expression in such diverse systems as the Manichaean heresy and some ideas of Renaissance philosophers. Erasmus and others held that the human soul was a battlefield, with God and the devil fighting for its control. (See P. D. Green, "Suicide, Martyrdom, and Thomas More," *Studies in the Renaissance,* 1972, *19,* 145.)

[42] T. Willis, *Two Discourses concerning the Soul of Brutes Which Is That of the Vital and Sensitive of Man,* S. Pordage, trans. (London: T. Dring, 1683), p. 2 of dedication to Gilbert, Archbishop of Canterbury.

[43] Ibid., p. 1.

[44] Ibid., p. 43.

[45] Massias, N., *Traité de philosophie psycho-physiologique* (Paris: A. F. Didot, 1830).

always two personalities in everyone became widespread in the mid-nineteenth century and more definite acceptance in the works of Janet (see page 79). Through syncretism the idea soon developed that one of these personalities was made up of instinctive forces. Around 1890 embryologists began to use the word *id* and various compounds of it in their writings. This material was summarized by Weismann[46] and later by Wilson.[47] As then used *id* meant chromatin granule, *idant* meant chromosome, and *idioplasm* meant germ plasm.

Freud, who at that time was still a neuropathologist, must certainly have read some of the embryologic writings of the 1890s that used these terms. With the breezy indifference of his contemporaries in German psychiatry to the established meanings of words he appropriated the word *id* to mean ancestral instinctive forces. Fortunately the use of *id* for chromatin died out; if it had not, serious confusion would have resulted.

The concept of the superego also grew out of ancient modes. The idea of a separate and all-powerful ethical entity within the individual has been eternal and keeps recurring. The presumed relation between the ego and the superego was described by Oliver Wendell Holmes, for example, in his Phi Beta Kappa oration of 1870.[48] He said that questions of right and wrong were resolved within ourselves in a committee of the whole, "the great Me presiding, with Conscience in the chair." This is reminiscent of the phrase of Hildebert of Le Mans (eleventh century): "Myself accuser, and myself accused."

THE PERSISTENCE OF THE EGO CONCEPT

Except in the minds of Griesinger and his followers, the ego concept evoked either indifference or skepticism among nineteenth- and early twentieth-century psychiatrists. It remained a matter of discussion among philosophical psychologists of the twentieth century, but their ego concept was too unsubstantial to be accepted by psychiatrists and has no relation to the ego concept that became the cornerstone of American psychiatry in the mid-twentieth century. The curious dominance of the latter concept, which only now is beginning to recede, involved an almost total rejection of classical psychiatry and the developments of experimental psychology. Its acceptance by influential clinicians resembles the acceptance a century earlier of that other Viennese export, the phrenologic superstition. Whatever happens to the ego concept in clinical psychiatry, it will probably remain a boon to American literature and drama.

[46] Weismann, *Polar Bodies and Their Significance in Essays on Heredity and Kindred Biological Problems,* E. B. Poulton, S. Schonland, and A. E. Shipley, eds. (Oxford: Clarendon Press, 1891).

[47] E. B. Wilson, *The Cell in Development and Inheritance* (New York: The Macmillan Co., 1896).

[48] O. W. Holmes, *Mechanisms in Thought and Morals* (Boston: J. R. Osgood and Co., 1872), p. 56.

Multiple Personalities

5

Contrasting with but more or less related to the concept that the ego has parts is the concept of multiple personalities. This idea goes back to antiquity and the generally accepted notion of possession by one or more demons. A more rational appreciation of the problem of multiple personalities became widespread in the seventeenth and eighteenth centuries, largely due to the writings of John Locke in 1686.

Locke (1690)

For to be happy or miserable without being conscious of it, seems to me utterly inconsistent and impossible. Or if it be possible that the soul can, while the body is sleeping, have its thinking, enjoyments and concerns, its pleasures or pain, apart which the man is not conscious of nor partakes in; it is certain that Socrates asleep and Socrates awake are two persons; since waking Socrates has no knowledge of or concernment for the happiness or misery of his soul which it enjoys alone by itself whilst he sleeps, without perceiving any thing of it; any more than he has for the happiness or misery of a man in the Indies, whom he knows not. . . .

If a sleeping man thinks without knowing it, the sleeping and waking man are two persons.[1]

Wigan (1884)

With the rise of the phrenologic superstition that each part of the cerebral cortex contributed something to thinking, some authors concluded that since there were

[1] J. Locke, *An Essay concerning Human Understanding* (19th ed., London: T. Longman and others, 1793), Vol. 1, pp. 83-84.

two hemispheres on the brain, there must be two minds. Wigan was the most vocal exponent of this view.

I believe myself then able to prove—

1. That each cerebrum is a distinct and perfect whole, as an organ of thought.
2. That a separate and distinct process of thinking or ratiocination may be carried on in each cerebrum simultaneously.
3. That each cerebrum is capable of a distinct and separate volition, and that these are very often opposing volitions.
4. That, in the healthy brain, one of the cerebra is almost always superior in power to the other, and capable of exercising control over the volitions of its fellow, and of preventing them from passing into acts, or from being manifested to others.
5. That when one of these cerebra becomes the subject of functional disorder, or of positive change of structure, of such a kind as to vitiate mind or induce insanity, the healthy organ can still, up to a certain point, control the morbid volitions of its fellow.
6. That this point depends partly on the extent of the disease or disorder, and partly on the degree of cultivation of the general brain in the art of self-government.
7. That when the disease or disorder of one cerebrum becomes sufficiently aggravated to defy the control of the other, the case is then one of the commonest forms of mental derangement or insanity; and that a lesser degree of discrepancy between the functions of the two cerebra constitutes the state of conscious delusion.
8. That in the insane, it is almost always possible to trace the intermixture of two synchronous trains of thought, and that it is the irregularly alternate utternace of portions of these two trains of thought which constitutes incoherence.
9. That of the two distinct simultaneous trains of thought, one may be rational and the other irrational, or both may be irrational; but that, in either case, the effect is the same, to deprive the discourse of coherence or congruity.

Even in furious mania, this double process may be generally perceived; often it takes the form of a colloquy between the diseased mind and the healthy one, and sometimes even resembles the steady continuous argument or narrative of a sane man, more or less frequently interrupted by a madman; but persevering with tenacity of purpose in the endeavour to overpower the intruder.

10. That when both cerebra are the subjects of disease, which is not of remittant periodicity, there are no lucid intervals, no attempt at self-control, and no means of promoting the cure; and that a spontaneous cure is rarely to be expected in such cases.

11. That however, where such mental derangement depends on inflammation, fever, gout, impoverished or diseased blood, or manifest bodily disease, it may often be cured by curing the malady which gave rise to it.

12. That in cases of insanity, not depending on structural injury, in which the patients retain the partial use of reason (from one of the cerebra remaining healthy or only slightly affected), the only mode in which the medical art can promote the cure beyond the means alluded to is by presenting motives of encouragement to the sound brain to exercise and strengthen its control over the unsound brain.

13. That the power of the higher organs of the intellect to coerce the mere instincts and propensities, as well as the power of one cerebrum to control the volitions of the other, may be indefinitely increased by exercise and moral cultivation; may be partially or wholly lost by desuetude or neglect; or, from depraved habits and criminal indulgence in childhood, and a general vicious education in a polluted moral atmosphere, may never have been acquired.

14. That one cerebrum may be entirely destroyed by disease, cancer, softening, atrophy, or absorption; may be *annihilated,* and in its place a yawning chasm; yet the mind remain complete and capable of exercising its functions in the same manner and to the same extent that one eye is capable of exercising the faculty of vision when its fellow is injured or destroyed; although there are some exercises of the brain, as of the eye, which are better performed with two organs than one. In the case of vision, the power of measuring distances for example, and in the case of the brain, the power of concentrating the thoughts upon one subject, deep consideration, hard study; but in this latter case, it is difficult to decide how far the diminished power depends on diminution of general vigour from formidable and necessarily fatal disease.

15. That a lesion or injury of both cerebra is incompatible with such an exercise of the intellectual functions, as the common sense of mankind would designate *sound mind.*

16. That from the apparent division of each cerebrum into three lobes, it is a natural and reasonable presumption that the three portions have distinct offices, and highly probable that the three great divisions of the mental functions laid down by phrenologists, are founded in nature; whether these distinctions correspond with the natural divisions is a different question, but the fact of different portions of the brain executing different functions, is too well established to admit of denial from any physiologist.

17. That it is an error to suppose the two sides of the cranium to be always alike, that on the contrary, it is rarely found that the two halves of the exterior surface exactly correspond; that indeed, in the insane, there is often a notable difference—still more frequent in idiots, and especially in congenital idiots.

18. That the object and effect of a well-managed education are to establish and confirm the power of concentrating the energies of both brains on the same subject at the same time; that is, to make both cerebra carry on the same train of thought together, as the object of moral discipline is to strengthen the power of self-control; not merely the power of both intellectual organs to govern the animal propensities and passions, but the intellectual antagonism of the two brains, each (so to speak) a sentinel and security for the other while both are healthy; and the healthy one to correct and control the erroneous judgments of its fellow when disordered.

19. That it is the exercise of this power of compelling the combined attention of both brains to the same object, till it becomes easy and habitual, that constitutes the great superiority of the disciplined scholar over the self-educated man; the latter may perhaps possess a greater stock of useful knowledge, but set him to study a new subject, and he is soon outstripped by the other, who has acquired the very difficult accomplishment of *thinking of only one thing at a time;* that is, of concentrating the action of both brains on the same subject.

20. That every man is, in his own person, conscious of two volitions, and very often conflicting volitions, quite distinct from the government of the passions by the intellect; a consciousness so universal, that it enters into all figurative language on the moral feelings and sentiments, has been enlisted into the service of every religion, and forms the basis of some of them, as the Manichaean.[2]

The want of harmony in the action of the two brains produces a feeling of intense distress, of which pervigilium is only an aggravated degree. Short of incipient madness, which in excess it very much resembles, there is no malady which excites a more acute misery.[3]

Folly seems to reside generally in one brain only, and to be perfectly compatible with the possession of another brain of ordinary vigour and perfection. When the weaker brain becomes exhausted by its incessant exercise, perhaps through the day, and by the excitement of events, it will at night, in silence and solitude, remain passive, while the sounder organ takes a calm review of the follies it has been unable to prevent; a feeling akin to remorse will arise, with strong resolutions of better conduct in future; and if the *then* thoughts be committed to prayer, we are surprised how so silly a person can write so sensibly. This I imagine must have come to the knowledge of every one. I know that it formerly gave me the conviction that the person thus acting foolishly and writing wisely

[2] A. L. Wigan, *The Duality of the Mind, Proved by the Structure, Functions, and Diseases of the Brain, and by the Phenomena of Mental Derangement* (London: Longman, Brown, Green, and Longmans, 1884), pp. 26–30.

[3] Ibid., p. 153. Within the last decade research has shown that when the connection between the two cerebral hemispheres is divided each hemisphere can exhibit different thoughts, perceptions, emotions and skills. The two minds coexist in complete ignorance of each other.

had been aided by others in the latter process; and it was not till after many conclusive proofs of the fact, that I allowed it to remain in my mind as a settled conviction, that *the same person may be exquisitely silly in conversation and in actions, and yet sober and wise in his closet.*[4]

Dendy (1841)

I can find no primary case material that describes psychosis specifically in only half the brain. Dendy refers to others who believed in it.

We are assured by Tiedeman and Gall (opinions of high value) that they have known patients who (smile as you please) were mad only on *one side* of the brain, and perceived their madness with *the other.*[5]

Holland (1852)

Henry Holland, although aware of the two-brain theory, was reluctant to accept it, preferring to regard double consciousness as only that, nothing more.

It has been a familiar remark that in certain states of mental derangement, as well as in some cases of hysteria which border closely upon it, there appear, as it were, two minds; one tending to correct by more just perceptions, feelings, and volitions, the aberrations of the other; and the relative power of these influences varying at different times. Cases of this singular kind cannot fail to be in the recollection of every medical man. I have myself seen many such, in which there occurred great disorder of mind from this sort of double-dealing with itself. In some cases there would seem to be a double series of sensations; the real and unreal objects of sense impressing the individual so far simultaneously that the judgment and acts of mind are disordered by their occurrence. In other instances the congruity is chiefly marked in the moral feelings,—an opposition far more striking than that of incongrous perceptions, and forming one of the most painful studies to the observer of mental disease. We have often occasion to witness acts of personal violence committed by those who have at the very time a keen sense of the wrong, and remorse in committing it; and revolting language used by persons whose natural purity of taste and feeling are shown in the horror they feel and express of the sort of compulsion under which they are labouring.

Admitting the truth of this description, as attested by experience, the fact may be explained in some cases, as we have seen, by the presence to the mind of real and unreal objects of sense, each successively the subject of belief,—this phenomenon itself possibly depending on the doubleness of the brain and of the parts ministering to perception, though we cannot obtain any certain proof that such is the case. But this explanation will not adequately apply to the instances

---

[4] Ibid., pp. 296-297.
[5] W. C. Dendy, *The Philosophy of Mystery* (New York: Harper and Brothers, 1841), p. 107.

where complete trains of thought are perverted and deranged, while others are preserved in sufficiently natural course to become a sort of watch upon the former. Here we have no conjecture to hazard other than that of supposing the two states of mind to be never strictly coincident in time;—a view in some sort sanctioned by what observation tells us of the inconceivable rapidity with which the mind actually shifts its state from one train of thought or feeling to another. In a former chapter I have treated at large on this subject, and shown our inability to measure by time these momentary passages of mental existence; crowding upon each other, and withal so interwoven into one chain, that consciousness, while it makes us aware of unceasing change, tells of no breach of continuity.

If the latter explanation be admitted, then the cases just mentioned come under the description of what has been termed *double consciousness;* where the mind passes by alternation from one state to another, each having the perception of external impressions and appropriate trains of thought, but not linked together by the ordinary gradations, or by mutual memory. I have seen one or two singular examples of this kind, but none so extraordinary as have been recorded by other authors. Their relations to the phenomena of sleep, of somnambulism, reverie, and insanity, abound in conclusions, of the deepest interest to every part of the mental history of man.

Even admitting, however, that these curiously contrasted states of mind are never strictly simultaneous, it is still a question whence their close concurrence is derived. And, in the absence of any certainty on this very obscure subject, we may reasonably, perhaps, look to that part of our constitution in which manifest provision is made for unity of result from parts double in structure and function. This provison we know in many cases to be disturbed by accident, disease, or other less obvious cause; and though we cannot so well show this in regard to the higher faculties of mind, as in the instance of the senses and voluntary power, yet it is conceivable that there are cases where the two sides of the brain minister differently to these functions, so as to produce incongruity, where there should be identity or individuality of result.[6]

Spitzka (1883)

Spitzka's reference to the rarity of double or alternating consciousness, and to its occurrence only with menstruation and periodical insanity, makes one wonder whether he was in fact referring to what later came to be called "periodische Undämmerungen in der Pubertät" (period "twilight," i.e., confusional states in puberty) or to periodic psychoses in women postpartum.

A very curious disturbance of the memory is manifested in the condition known as *double* or *alternating consciousness*. It is exceedingly rare, and appears

[6]H. Holland, *Chapters on Mental Physiology* (London: Longman, Brown, Green, and Longmans, 1852), pp. 185–188.

to be limited to the mental disturbances of menstruation and to periodical insanity.[7]

Janet (1888)

After a number of authors began to have an inkling of the overriding role of double personalities in hysterics, Pierre Janet clearly defined the phenomenon. His brother Jules discussed the matter in general terms.

My principal wish, in publishing this article, is to make common a notion which, glimpsed by several authors, MM. Azam, Liebault, Bourru and Burot, Ch. Richet, Myers and Gurney, was clearly brought to light by my brother, Pierre Janet, of Havre.

This notion, which springs from the observation of *successive conscious states* of hysterics in hypnotic wakefulness and sleep, seems to me to be quite useful to possess in order to grasp the different phenomena of hysteria and of hypnosis.[8]

This dissociation of psychological phenomena into two groups, one conscious, the other unconscious, is perhaps not peculiar to hysterics; it is possible that it also exists in individuals exempt from hysteria.

What is, in fact, the principal character of the second personality? It is being ignorant of the first. Are there not in the normal man acts, even series of acts, which are executed unconsciously? Who could execute them, if not an unknown personality of the conscious personality? In our natural sleep, without being noctambulists, we have dreams, we execute movements of which we have no memory upon awakening. In certain pathological states of the nonhysterical man, these acts become even clearer: In drunkenness the conscious personality is annihilated by alcohol, and the drunken man walks around during a night without knowing, when he has sobered up, the acts which he has accomplished during this lapse of time; it is the same with chloroform.

With psychotic people, this dissociation is exaggerated even more, and the memory of actions commonly disappears entirely after the attacks in which they were carried out. Who acts in all of these cases, if not an unknown personality of the conscious personality?

There seems to be with the normal man, or more exactly with the man exempt from hysteria, as with the hysteric, two personalities, one conscious and one unknown.

But the nonhysterical man differs from the hysteric in that, with him, the two personalities are of equal value, one as vigorous as the other; the first state is as complete as the second; the first or conscious personality has lost none of its

---

[7] E. C. Spitzka, *Insanity: Its Classification, Diagnosis and Treatment* (New York: Bermingham and Co., 1883), p. 59.

[8] J. Janet, "L'Hystérie et l'hypnotisme, d'après la théorie de la double personalité," *Revue Scientifique*, 1888, *1*, 616.

properties. We could then represent the schema of the nonhysterical man as joining each psychological phenomenon to both the first and second personalities.

In summary, every man presents two personalities, one conscious and one unknown; with the normal man they are equal, both of them complete, balanced; with the hysteric they are unbalanced. One of the two personalities, generally the first, is incomplete, the other remains perfect. It can happen that the first personality can be complete and that the imperfections, that is to say the incomplete state, bear on the second personality. This case is rare, but I will show at the end of this article that one can encounter hysterics of this nature. The hysterical condition of the subject is therefore very difficult to recognize, but it does exist nonetheless. We are in the presence of a larval hysteria.

Let us organize these phenomena even more, let us give a form to these two entities constituted by the two successive consciousness, let us represent them with two individuals, one following the other. Individual 1, who walks ahead, knows himself but has no notion of individual 2, who follows him and shuts him in. In contrast individual 2 knows not only himself but also individual 1, whom he sees walking ahead of him.

With the normal man these two individuals are both vigorous and of equal size; the second is not able to bring down the first, to expose himself to all the attention. To show himself in full light he will have to await a temporary weakness of individual 1, when felled by fatigue, as in natural sleep, or by alcohol as in inebriation. Sometimes, as with the insane person for example, he can annihilate individual 1 and substitute himself because though not incomplete, individual 1 is debilitated. Profiting from the weakness of his companion, individual 2 overthrows him, tramples him under foot and, proud of this exploit, he takes the train for London where he will commit some crime: This is the case of unconscious voyages and impulsive acts of some neurotics.

Hypnotism consists, we have seen, in putting us in touch with the second personality; but for that it is necessary to annihilate the first personality. With the normal man the latter is solid, resistant, does not let itself be beaten; this is why in this case hypnotism is so difficult to induce.

With an hysteric, on the contrary, the equilibrium is broken. The two individuals who follow each other are quite unequal in strength. The first is weak, belittled, degraded; he barely stands erect. In contrast the second is vigorous and of normal size; he can easily expose himself to stares. In fact, by and by he takes advantage of the natural sleep of the first individual and goes walking in the gutters: It is noctambulism. Next, less discreet, in full daylight, he defeats the weak individual who precedes him and rolls on the ground, giving way to disordered muscular gymnastics: a convulsion.

At other times individual 2 destroys individual 1 in detail; he renders him even more incomplete than he was and deprives him, for example, of a part of his mobility. He takes off his leg, and in the space left empty by this member he shows his own leg to all eyes. If he wants to leave it limp and without movement, we are witnessing a paralysis; if it pleases him on the other hand to contract it, following his fantastic habits, we are witnessing a hysterical contraction.

What conclusion can we draw from this conception? It is that, the first individual being weak, it will be easy for us, too, to annihilate him and after that to face the second individual. This is why hypnotism is so easy to induce in hysterics, and why it is even easier to understand that these hysterics are more seriously injured.[9]

THREE OR MORE PERSONALITIES

The number of co-existing personalities (the term which eventually gained dominance) was believed to remain at two for many years. At the turn of the century, however, Morton Prince, according to newspaper accounts of the period, lectured about women with three, four, five, and six distinct personalities. In more recent times a book called *The Three Faces of Eve,* a detailed description of a hysteric, became a great financial success.

[9] Ibid., pp. 620 ff.

Primary Mechanisms and Symptoms

6

The psychology of every era influences the contemporary psychiatry and vice versa. Psychiatric theory developed its own psychology, or else borrowed what was already in existence, in order to describe or explain psychiatric symptoms. Some mechanisms, processes, and nonspecific symptoms considered in the past have come down to the present, often with little or no change except in the language.

HALLUCINATIONS, ILLUSIONS, AND DELUSIONS

Disorders of perception and interpretation have long been recognized as symptoms of mental disease. Nevertheless the basic issue underlying all of them, the nature of reality, has been totally ignored by psychiatrists. Nature has never been an objective reality for man, and the human mind organizes reality for its own purpose. The most that psychiatrists have done is to state that patients' delusions are logical if one grants the psychotic premises. These premises, however, are part of a reality which differs from that accepted by persons deemed nonpsychotic.

The definition of hallucinations became established in the eighteenth century. The great nosologists of that period, de Sauvages, Sagar, Linnaeus, Vogel, and Cullen, discussed the meaning of the word and agreed on it, but their assessment of other disorders varied greatly. Cullen separated hallucinations from what appear to be dissociated feelings.

Cullen (1791)

The Nosologists, Sauvages and Sagar, in a class of diseases under the title of Vesaniae, have comprehended the two orders, of Hallucinationes or false perceptions, and of Morositates or erroneous appetites and passions, and, in like manner, Linnaeus in his class of Mentales, corresponding to the Vesaniae of

Sauvages, has comprehended the two orders of Imaginarii and Pathetici, nearly the same with the Hallucinationes and Morositates of that author. This, however, from several considerations, appears to me improper; and I have therefore formed a class of Vesaniae nearly the same with the Paranoiae of Vogel, excluding from it the Hallucinationes and Morositates, which I have referred to the Morbi Locales. Mr. Vogel has done the like, in separating from the Paranoiae the false perceptions and erroneous appetites; and has thrown these into another class, to which he has given the title of Hyperaestheses.

It is indeed true, that certain hallucinationes and morositates are frequently combined with what I propose to consider as strictly a vesania or an erroneous judgement; and sometimes the hallucinationes seem to lay the foundation of, and to form almost entirely, the vesania. But as most part of the hallucinationes enumerated by the nosologists are affections purely topical, and induce no other error of judgement beside that which relates to the single object of the sense or a particular organ affected; so these are certainly to be separated from the diseases which consist in a more general affection of the judgement. Even when the hallucinationes constantly accompany or seem to induce the vesania, yet being such as arise from internal causes, and may be presumed to arise from the same cause as the more general affection of the judgement, they are therefore to be considered as symptoms of this only.

In like manner I judge with respect to the morositates, or erroneous passions, that accompany vesania; which, as consequences of a false judgement, must be considered as arising from the same causes, and as symptoms only, of the more general affection. . . .

Another circumstance, commonly attending delirium, is a very unusual association of ideas. As, with respect to most of the affairs of common life, the ideas laid up in the memory are, in most men, associated in the same manner; so a very unusual association, in any individual must prevent his forming the ordinary judgement of those relations which are the most common foundation of association in the memory: and therefore this unusual and commonly hurried association of ideas, usually is, and may be considered as, as part of delirium. In particular it may be considered as a certain mark of a general morbid affection of the intellectual organs, it being an interruption or perversion of the ordinary operations of memory, the common and necessary foundation of the exercise of judgement.

A third circumstance attending delirium, is an emotion or passion, sometimes of the angry, sometimes of the timid kind; and from whatever cause in the perception of judgement, it is not proportioned to such cause, either in the manner formerly customary to the person himself, or in the manner usual with the generality of other men.

Delirium, then, may be more shortly defined,—In a person awake, a false judgement arising from perceptions of imagination, or from false recollection, and commonly producing disproportionate emotions.

Such delirium is to two kinds; as it is combined with pyrexia and comatose affections; or, as it is entirely without any such combination. It is the latter case that we name Insanity. . . .

Insanity may perhaps be properly considered as a genus comprehending many different species, each of which may deserve our attention. . . .

The limitation, therefore, of the class of Vesaniae to the lesions of our judging faculty, seems from every consideration to be proper.

The particular diseases to be comprehended under this class, may be distinguished according as they affect persons in the time of waking or sleeping. Those which affect men awake, may again be considered, as they consist in an erroneous judgement, to which I shall give the appellation of Delirium; or as they consist in a weakness or imperfection of judgement, which I shall name Fatuity. I begin with consideration of Delirium.

As men differ greatly in the soundness and force of their judgement, so it may be proper here to ascertain more precisely what error or imperfection of our judging faculty is to be considered in morbis, and to admit of the appelations of Delirium and Fatuity. In doing this, I shall first consider the morbid errors of judgement under the general appellation of Delirium, which has been commonly employed to denote every mode of such error.

As our judgement is chiefly exercised in discerning and judging of the several relations of things, I apprehend that delirium may be defined to be,—in a person awake, a false or mistaken judgement of those relations of things, which as occurring most frequently in life, are those about which the generality of men from the same judgement; and particularly when the judgement is very different from what the person himself had before usually formed.

With this mistaken judgement of relations there is frequently joined some false perception of external objects, without any evident fault in the organs of sense, and which seems therefore to depend upon an internal cause; that is, upon the imagination arising from a condition in the brain presenting objects which are not actually present. Such false perceptions must necessarily occasion a delirium, or an erroneous judgement, which is to be considered as the disease.[1]

Crichton (1798)

Crichton, less interested in nosology than his more famous predecessors, adhered to clinical observation and almost automatically separated hallucinations and delusions.

The diseased notions which delirious people entertain, are of two kinds:

1st. They are diseased perceptions, referred by the patient to some object of external sense; as when he believes he sees, hears, tastes, and smells things which

[1] W. Cullen, *First Lines of the Practice of Physic* (Edinburgh: Bell and Bradfute and William Creech; London: G. G. J. & J. Robinsons and J. Murray, 1791), pp. 117–125.

have no real existence; as when he imagines he sees holes in the wall, through which monsters of various kinds appear in a menacing, or terrifying manner; or when he supposes himself surrounded by dangerous beasts, and serpents.

2dly. They are diseased abstract notions, referrable to the qualities and conditions of persons and things, and his relation to them; as when he imagines that his friends have conspired to kill him; that he is reduced to beggary; that he is forsaken by God, &c.[2]

Haslam (1809)

Haslam revived an ancient discussion about similarities between dreaming and insanity. He added the item of hypnagogic hallucinations in normal persons.

By some persons, madness has been considered as a state of mind analogous to dreaming: but an inference of this kind supposes us fully acquainted with the actual state, or condition of the mind in dreaming, and in madness. The whole question hinges on a knowledge of this *state of mind,* which I fear is still involved in obscurity. As it is not the object of the present work to discuss this curious question, the reader is referred to the fifth section of the first part of Mr. Dugald Stewart's Elements of the Philosophy of the Human Mind, and to the note, o, at the end; he will also find the subject treated with considerable ingenuity in the eleventh section of Mr. Brown's Observations on Zoonomia.

There is, however, a circumstance, which to my knowledge, has not been noticed by those who have treated on this subject, and which appears to establish a marked distinction between madness and dreaming. In madness, the delusion we experience is most frequently conveyed through the ear; in dreaming, the deception is commonly optical; we see much, and hear little; indeed dreaming, at least with myself, seems to be a species of intelligible pantomime, that does not require the aid of language to explain it. It is true, that some who have perfectly recovered from this disease, and who are persons of good understanding and liberal education, describe the state they were in, as resembling a dream: and when they have been told how long they were disordered, have been astonished that the time passed so rapidly away. But this only refers to that consciousness of delusion, which is admitted by the patient on his return to reason; in the same manner as the man awake, smiles at the incongruous images, and abrupt transitions of the preceding night. In neither condition, does the consciousness of delusion, establish any thing explanatory of the *state* of the mind.[3]

[2] A. Crichton, *An Inquiry into the Nature and Origin of Mental Derangement* (London: T. Cadell, Junior, and W. Davies, 1798), Vol. 1, pp. 140–141.
[3] J. Haslam, *Observations on Madness and Melancholy* (London: J. Callow, 1809), pp. 75–77.

Esquirol (1838)

Esquirol refined the concept of hallucination, separating illusion from it.[4]

From all that we can gather from the annals of the infirmities and diseases of the human mind, we may conclude that there exists a certain form of insanity in which individuals believe that they perceive, sometimes by one sense, sometimes by another, and sometimes by several at once, while no external object is present to excite any sensation whatever. Thus, a man in a state of delirium hears persons address him, asks questions, replies, holds a continued conversation; distinguishes very clearly reproaches, abuse, threats and commands which are addressed to him,—discusses questions, is vexed, and falls into a passion. He hears also celestial harmonies; the songs of birds, a concert of voices, and this, when no voice is near, and silence reigns around. Another sees pictures most varied in character, and most animated in expression. Heaven opens, and he contemplates God face to face, takes part in exercises of the Sabbath, and rejoices at the sight of a beautiful painting, of a fine exhibition, and on beholding a friend. He is frightened at the sight of a precipice, of flames ready to consume him, of enemies armed to assassinate him and of serpents who would devour him. . . . One laboring under a hallucination desires that certain odors which annoy him should be removed, or else he smells those of the sweetest character, while there is not at hand any odoriferous body. . . .

In general, these individuals believe that both persons and things are present with them, which can have no real existence, except in their own imaginations. The evidence of the senses, passes for nothing in this form of delirium. This class of patients have to contest every thing with the external world. They are in a state of hallucination. Such are the hallucinated. Notions relative to the qualities and properties of things, and of persons, are imperfectly perceived, and judgment in respect to them consequently incorrect. The insane man mistakes a windmill for a man; a hole for a precipice; and clouds for a body of cavalry. In the last case the perceptions are incomplete; hence an error. The ideas and actual sensations are but imperfectly connected. In hallucinations, sensation and perception no more exist than in reveries and somnambulism, since external objects do not act upon the senses. A thousand hallucinations sport with and mislead the mind. In fact, hallucinations is a cerebral or mental phenomenon, which is produced independently of the senses.

The most rational man, if he will observe carefully the operations of his mind, will sometimes perceive images and ideas the most extravagant, or associated in the strangest manner. The ordinary occupations of life, the labors of the mind and reason, divert the attention from those ideas, images and phantoms. But he who is insane, unable to command his attention, can neither direct it nor turn it

---

[4] Esquirol first made this distinction, albeit very briefly, in his *Aliénation mentale: Des illusions chez les aliénés*. (Paris: Crochard, 1832). This was translated by W. Liddell as *Observations on the Illusions of the Insane* (London: Renshaw and Rush, 1833, pp. 2-3).

aside from these imaginary objects. He remains the slave of his hallucinations and reveries. The habit of always associating the sensation with the external object that solicits and usually calls it into exercise, lends a reality to the productions of the imagination or memory, and persuades the subject of hallucinations that what he actually experiences could never occur, wihout the presence of external bodies. The false sensations of the hallucinated, are the images and ideas reproduced by the memory, associated by the imagination,— and personified by habit. Man then gives a form to the offspring of his mind. He dreams, while fully awake. In a case of a dream, the ideas of the waking hours continue during sleep; whilst he who is in a complete delirium is in a dream, though awake. Dreams, like hallucinations, always reproduce former sensations and ideas. As in a dream, the series of images and ideas in hallucinations is sometimes regular; but more frequently they are reproduced in the greatest confusion and present the strangest associations. The hallucinated are sometimes conscious, as is the case also in a dream, that they are in a disturbed mental state, without the power to disengage the mind. He who is in a dream, as well as he who has hallucinations, is never astonished nor surprised at the ideas or images which occupy his mind, whilst they would have excited the greatest wonder had the patient been fully aroused, or had he not been mentally disturbed. The thinking faculty is altogether absorbed by these objects. The difference between the hallucinated and somnambulists consists in this; that in the greater number of cases the former recall whatever has preoccupied or troubled their mind, while the latter remember nothing. Hallucinations differ from ecstasy in this only, that the latter condition is always produced by a powerful effort of the attention, fixed upon a single object, towards which the imagination of the person affected constantly tends. In ecstasy, the concentration of innervations is so strong, that it absorbs all the powers of life, and the exercise of all the functions is suspended, except that of the imagination.

In hallucinations, on the contrary, a violent effort of attention is not necessary. All the functions are performed with more or less freedom; the man lives amid his hallucinations as he would have done in a world of realities. The conviction of the hallucinated is so entire and sincere, that they reason, judge and decide with reference to their hallucinations. They also arrange, with reference to this psychological phenomenon, their thoughts, desires, will and actions. I have known persons who had been cured of their hallucinations, who were accustomed to remark, "I saw and heard, when laboring under this delusion, as distinctly as you see and hear." Many give an account of their visions, with a coolness that belongs only to the most entire conviction. Hence results the most singular language and actions; for hallucinations, like actual sensations, produce among the insane either pleasure or pain, love or hatred. Thus, one rejoices, laughs aloud, and finds himself the happiest of men. Soothed by so lively and distinct an impression of good fortune is he, that, incapable of indulging in any foreign thought, he sees no limit to his felicity, and believes that it can never end. Another grieves, laments, and is in a state of complete despair; overcome by the frightful hallucinations that engulf him.

But hallucinations have not always the character of a fixed idea, or of a prevailing passion. Some times they extend successively to the recollections of objects, which have made impressions upon the senses, and give to the delirium a character of versatility, which is remarked both in their feelings and actions. This happens in certain forms of mania and febrile delirium. Thus, there are patients whose hallucinations from time to time are found to change their object.

Hallucinations are therefore neither false sensations, nor illusions of the senses; neither erroneous perceptions, nor errors resulting from bodily sensibility, as is the case in hypochondria. We may confound hallucinations with illusions of the senses, or with the false perceptions of hypochondriacs. . . .

Hallucinations relate usually to the occupations, whether mental or physical, to which the person suffering from them has been accustomed, or else they ally themselves to the nature of the cause that has kindled up the excitement of the brain. . . .

Hallucinations take place among men who have never been psychotic, but they constitute one of the elements of insanity which are most frequently found in mania, lypemania, monomania, ecstasy, catalepsy, hysteria and febrile delirium. Among a hundred insane persons, eighty at least have hallucinations. Sometimes this symptom appears a long time before psychosis becomes apparent to those who reside with the patients. They often struggle against their hallucinations before manifesting or complaining of them, and before committing any impropriety either of speech or act. Sometimes at the commencement of the disorder, the hallucinations are fugitive and confused. With the progress of it, they become as distinct and complete as the actual sensations, and are continued and permanent. They not unfrequently persist, though the psychosis may have ceased. During the most general delirium, or a very animated conversation, the insane man suddenly checks himself, to contemplate an object which he believes strikes his eye, or to listen and reply to persons whom he thinks he hears. This symptom may be observed among almost all those who have psychosis. Nevertheless individuals, who, before their illness were controlled by a passion, or subject to strong conflicts of mind, are more exposed to it than others, especially if they have previously applied themselves to speculative and abstract studies. If hallucinations are most frequently the lot of feeble minds, men the most remarkable for their strength of understanding, the depth of their reason, and their vigor of thought, are not always free from this symptom. . . .

Hallucinations depending upon impressions perceived by the senses of taste and smell, are reproduced, particularly at the commencement of insanity. But those which appertain to sight and hearing, are more frequent during all periods of the malady. Hallucinations of sight, reproducing objects which occasion the most general interest, and make the strongest impression upon the multitude, have been denominated visions. This name is suited to a single form of hallucination. Who would dare to say, visions of hearing, visions of taste, visions of smell? and yet, the images, ideas and notions, which seem to belong to the functional alterations of these three senses, present to the mind the same characters, have the same seat, that is to say, the brain, are produced by the same causes, and are manifest in the same maladies as hallucinations of sight,—as visions. A generic term is wanting. I have proposed the word hallucination, as having no determinate signification, and as adapted consequently, to all the varieties of mental disease. As they are only a symptom of mental disease, and may exist in many diseases of the mind, either acute or chronic, they do not require a particular treatment. They ought nevertheless, to have great weight in the intellectual and moral management of the insane, and the therapeutic views which the physician may propose. . . .

. . . In illusions on the other hand, the function of the sensory mechanism is altered: it is super-normal, enfeebled, or distorted. The senses are active and the actual impressions solicit the reaction of the brain. The effects of this reaction being submitted to the influence of the ideas and passions which control the reason of the insane, they deceive themselves in respect both to the nature and cause of their actual sensations.

Illusions are not rare in a state of health, but reason dissipates them. Hypochondriacs have illusions, which spring from internal sensations. These persons deceive themselves, and have an illusion respecting the intensity of their sufferings, and the danger of losing their life. But they never attribute their misfortunes to causes that are repugnant to reason. . . .

The passions, the source of so many illusions among men of sound minds, modifying also the impressions, and giving a wrong direction to the reaction of the brain, are the cause of a thousand illusions among the insane. The understanding and the passions concur with the senses in the illusions of the insane; and the sentiment extremities are the true points of departure of the illusions. There is always an actual impression upon the senses of external objects.[5]

Griesinger (1845)

The idea that hallucinations arose through projection was brought forward by Griesinger.

But the most general and most important sensitive anomalies in states of mental disease are the hallucinations and illusions. By hallucinations we understand subjective sensorial images, which, however, are projected outwards, and thereby become, apparently, objects and realities.[6]

[5] E. Esquirol, *Mental Maladies: A Treatise on Insanity* [1838], E. K. Hunt, trans. (Philadelphia: Lea and Blanchard, 1845), pp. 105-113.

[6] W. Griesinger, *Mental Pathology and Therapeutics,* from the 2nd German ed., C. L. Robertson and J. Rutherford, trans. (London: The New Sydenham Society, 1867), p. 84.

Maudsley (1867)

Maudsley also noted that hallucinations might be normal, as when a person is just awakening.

No one who has observed himself attentively when suddenly awaking out of sleep but must have noticed that he has had at times hallucinations both visual and auditory. He has heard a voice, which no one else could hear, distinctly say something, and on reflection only is convinced that the words were subjective; or he has waked up in the night and seen around him the objects of his dream, and been positively unable for a time to discriminate between the real and the unreal,—has perhaps laid down and gone to sleep again without successfully doing so. When the integrity of nervous element has been damaged, whether by reason of continued intemperance or from some other cause, these half-waking hallucinations acquire a vivid reality, and leave behind them a painful feeling in the mind. If we could imagine this temporary condition to last some time, and our actions to be in accordance with our hallucinations, then we should get a conception of that which is the state of things in sensorial insanity.[7]

Spitzka (1883)

Spitzka's discussion of delusions deserves special note for both its depth and its breadth. It represents the highest type of clinical psychiatric writing.

Delusions may be divided into the *genuine* and the *spurious*. The former group consists of those delusions which have been mainly created by the patient himself; the latter, of those which have been altogether adopted from others. The former alone are of intrinsic importance to the alienist; the latter have only a relative bearing to such extent as it may be necessary to consider the possibility of their existence as a factor in differential diagnosis. They are found in weak-minded patients as evidences of an imitative tendency.

The genuine delusions of the insane, when classified according to their synthesis, naturally fall into two great groups. We find that certain delusions have a complex logical organization—*the systematized delusions;* while others are devoid of such an organization, are not as plausibly based, as elaborately expressed, and as skilfully defended—*the unsystematized delusions.*

The various forms of delusion ordinarily admitted fall under both of these heads. That is, we may have either delusions of grandeur or depressive delusions of the systematized as well as of the unsystematized type, and the same applies to their sub-varieties. In order to fully characterize a given delusion, it hence becomes necessary to incorporate all these elements. If, for example, a medical student, as in a reported case, believes that he is suffering from spinal disease,

[7]H. Maudsley, *The Physiology and Pathology of the Mind* (New York: D. Appleton and Co., 1867), p. 264.

and bases this delusion on alleged symptoms which might justify the belief, if they were not due to illusional misinterpretations and hallucinatory visions of his spinal cord, he is suffering from a *systematized hypochondriacal delusion.* But a person who is unable to give connected reasons for such beliefs as that his body is decaying, that his heart is turned to ice, and that his intestines are stopped up, is afflicted with an *unsystematized hypochondriacal delusion.* In like manner the patient who claims that he is pursued by enemies, because he imagines that people are looking at him in a peculiar way, dogging his footsteps, putting poison in his food, calling out his name at night; and that they do all this to prevent him from making good his claims to a throne, an authorship, or an invention, is a sufferer from *systematized delusions of persecution.* While he who alleges that he is pursued by voices and by persons, although he does this on the strength of similar hallucinations, and can assign no other ground than a subjective feeling of worthlessness or criminality, exhibits the *unsystematized delusion of persecution.*

To answer the question as to whether a given delusion is systematized or unsystematized, is of vastly greater importance than to determine its more superficial features. Take a persecutory delusion, for example! If it is systematized, it may be assumed that we have to deal with that chronic primary insanity, the *Verruecktheit* of the Germans, the *Monomanie* of the French, the *Monomania* of some English authors. If, on the other hand, it is unsystematized, we know with equal certainty that the patient's disorder is a melancholia, unless other evidences point to the existence of senile and secondary insanity, or of paretic dementia in its first stage.

When we proceed, a little later on, to analyze the mechanism of the principal varieties of systematized expansive delusions, namely, the *simple,* or those relating to social and political ambitions; the *erotic,* or those involving sexual relations, and the *religious,* we will find, that while they all indicate a certain degree of logical enfeeblement, that this enfeeblement is more pronounced in the case of the two latter varieties than of the former. The highest general mental activity is found with those lunatics who cherish systematized delusions of social ambition; the patients who are the political reformers, claimants to thrones, inventors of flying machines, or the *perpetuum mobile,* and panaceas for all earthly ills, the poets, the military and the diplomatic geniuses of asylums. The patient here acts consistently with his assumed character, and the continued existence of a certain amount of mental ability and energy is shown by the formation of projects which, whatever their ultimate feasibility—and they sometimes are feasible—are undertaken with some attention to the patient's actual circumstances and to detail. Sometimes, especially with patients of high previous culture, the systematized expansive delusion is not of such a character as to lead to an error in the patient's sense of identity, but limited to his self-esteem in the abstract. He writes doggerel or mediocre verse, for example, and imagines himself as great a poet as Byron; or he invents some unimportant mechanical contrivance, and lays claim to the gratitude of a nation or a king. Not infrequently he commits plagiarism in a *quasi*-unconscious manner.

Systematized delusions of an erotic character are found as the leading symptoms of the so-called "Erotomania." This perversion is not necessarily accompanied by animal sexual desire, and the adjective erotic is here used in its classical sense. The patient, noted in his adolescence for his romantic tendencies, construes an ideal of the other sex in his day-dreams, and subsequently discovers the incorporation of this ideal is some actual or imaginary personage, usually in a more exalted social circle than his own. He then spins out a perfect romance with the adored personage as its subject, and according as the external circumstances appear to him momentarily favorable or unfavorable, expansive or depressive delusions are added to and incorporated with the erotic ones. As a rule the affection for the adored object remains as chaste and pure as it begins; a sort of distant, romantic worship, insane for the reason that unimportant occurrences, accidental resemblances, facts which have no natural connection with the individual or his or her real or imaginary contemplated partner, and hallucinations are woven into the delusive conception, which consequently assumes such a predominating position in the patient's mental horizon as to entirely overshadow it.

Systematized delusions of a religious character are usually rooted in an early developing devotional tendency, and brought to full bloom by incidental circumstances, either actual or in the shape of hallucinations. It is not uncommon to find such patients designated as cases of religious melancholia, because, supposing themselves assailed by inimical or diabolical forces, or commanded to fast for a long period, or forever, they become sad and anxious or refuse food. But to call a patient who, aside from these actions, which are consistently regulated by the false ideas, believes himself or herself to be God, the Christ, a saint, the Messiah, a religious reformer, or the Virgin Mary, and who, perhaps, the very next day passes into visionary or ecstatic states, all the time systematizing his or her acts and notions—a melancholic, is to involve one's self in a profound contradiction with the established use of that term.

Among the systematized delusions of a depressive character, the antitheses of all the preceding forms are found. This is well exemplified in cases where the subjects develop delusions of persecution overwhelming the ambitious notions previously dominating the mental sphere. How very unessential the line of demarkation between the depressive and expansive delusion really is, is made apparent by the fact that an expansive religious, erotic, or socially ambitious delusion may within a few days become depressive through the development of persecutory ideas; just as the reverse is occasionally observed. In fact, such expansive and depressive delusions often are entertained by the patient at one and the same time.

When an individual, without any manifest disturbance of his emotional or affective state, in full possession of the memories accumulated in the receptive sphere, and able to carry out most or all of the duties of his particular position in life, as some of the sufferers are, is found to cherish such a gross error as an insane delusion, firmly believing in the reality of that which from his education and surroundings he would be expected to recognize as absurd, the observer is naturally puzzled to account for the phenomenon. The component elements of the systematized delusion are individually the same as those which are combined to form healthy conceptions; they differ in that they are faultily united. In this respect the insane delusion does not differ from the faulty conclusions which constitute the *error* of the sane. But while the error of the sane person is based on faulty and not on perverted perceptions, on imperfect or vicious training, and on lack of experience, and disappears before the corrected evidence of the senses, improved educational methods, and broader experience; the sufferer from the insane delusion is unable, for the time being, to correct that delusion by a similar process. His logical apparatus stands powerless before the controlling conception. There is a fundamental weakening of those logical inhibitions or checks which the collateral elements of the *ego* constitute for the day-dreams and speculations of a sane person. What is a wish or fear of the sane mind becomes an article of faith with the delusional lunatic; what is a mere possibility in reality becomes a fixed fact in support of that article of faith with the insane; and finally the perceptions themselves are perverted and enslaved to add new building material to the faulty mental structure. It is because the physiological *ego* is weakened that the morbid *ego* is permitted to arise out of the small beginnings which a healthy *ego* could have held in check, and for this reason the following legal definition of the insane delusion—that it is *a faulty belief, out of which the subject cannot be reasoned by adequate methods for the time being*—is a sound one.

Notwithstanding the fact that the delusions of the systematized variety are correlated with the patient's surroundings, in contradistinction to the unsystem-atized delusions, which are not correlated at all, they are *faultily associated*. While there is a chain of reasoning connecting the items of the systematized delusion into an organized whole, which is absent in the unsystematized delusion, yet after all that reasoning is only *pseudo-logical*. The systematized delusion is more similar to a sane conception than the unsystematized delusion; yet this similarity does not pass beyond the degree of an analogy.

As illustrating the readiness with which systematic delusionists utilize casual occurrences in the construction and defence of their delusions, it is but necessary to refer to the common case where such subjects detect a connection between their delusive hopes or fears and an advertisement or a bill-poster containing their initials; that others sustain the allegation of a royal descent by a fancied resemblance to some member of a reigning family; and that still others lay claim to an important office on the strength of a friendly interview with some little great man of the day. The case of a lady whom the writer treated several years ago illustrates this readiness with which trifling matters are framed into delusions, very aptly. From the facts that the irides of her child changed color (which was an occurrence corroborated by the grandmother and others), and that it had greatly altered in appearance owing to an exhausting illness, she concluded that it was not her own child. Her nursery maid and one of a neighboring familiy had been together a great deal, and she claimed, what was in itself not impossible, that her child had been exchanged. Although the observant relatives were able to prove the identity of the child by a number of circumstances which would have been held satisfactory in any court of law, and which would have convinced any sane person, she only interpreted the remonstrances made as attempts to make the best of the case; and because her husband affected to treat her suspicions with indifference she reasoned that he was becoming neglectful of his family. A few ordinary civilities exchanged by him with several ladies belonging to the same church convinced her that from being indifferent to his child he was becoming unfaithful to his wife. One night a large negro looked over the garden wall, and the watchdog did not, as was his wont, bark at him. Several robberies occurring in the neighborhood about the same time, she inferred, ready as she was to believe anything that was bad of her husband, that the negro, who must have been one of the robbers, had not been barked at by the dog, because the latter recognized in him one of his master's confederates. Those who defended her husband or attempted to explain his actions in the face of "such evidence" could only do so in the hypothesis that they had joined the conspiracy against her. Her cousins were members of the conspiracy because a package of chemises put up by them, which ought to have contained a dozen contained a lesser number; and when removed from her native place to New York for treatment she found that the custom-house officers had joined the ranks of her enemies, because after their examination of the contents of her trunk other articles were missing or ruined.

The absurdity of a delusion is not so much a test of the absolute mental rank and the form of insanity of a patient, as is its organization. A very absurd delusive conclusion may be reached by an elaborate and plausibly delivered ratiocination, and a less absurd delusion may be formulated on a very crude process of reasoning.

While the most important factors determining the nature of a delusion are the form of insanity of which it is a symptom and the manner in which it affects the cerebral mechanism, other elements must be admitted to have some influence in tinging it. The general disposition of the patient, whether it be sanguine or suspicious, will often determine the expansive or persecutory character of a given delusion. If the physical state is poor and the visceral functions are disordered, hypochondriacal delusions are more apt to arise than with a robust or fair state of health. The age in which the patient lives and his social circumstances have no inconsiderable influence in the moulding of his morbid ideas. With the development of republics and constitutional monarchies, the growth of the sciences, the arts, the press, and the emancipation of mankind from superstitious creeds; the kings, emperors, prophets, ambassadors from the planets, Holy Virgins and Gods have become less common in the asylum corridor than they once were. They have given way to insane inventors and communistic, journalistic, educational, musical, and scientific delusional project-makers.

The *unsystematized delusions* are found with the acute insanities and the chronic deteriorations. They may be ranged in two great classes according as they are due to the subjective misinterpretations arising from an emotional disturbance, or the result of a destruction of the logical associating force. The delusions of true melancholia are instances of the first type, those of paretic dementia of the second.

When the emotional state of the melancholiac has overwhelmed the mental apparatus, and the logical faculty is thrown in the background by the predominant painful depression, the patient may, in his endeavor to account to himself for his painful feelings, in a vague way conclude that he is a bad person. Since he is a bad person, it must be because he has committed the unpardonable sin; but he cannot tell when nor why nor how he has committed it, nor very often what the unpardonable sin is. Or, again, such a patient feels that he is despised, that he is despised because he is hated, and hallucinatory whispers from all sides drive him to seek relief from a danger which was never clear in his own mind, in suicide. The great distinction between the systematized delusion of persecution and the unsystematized delusion of a depressive nature is, that while the former is distinct and fixed, the latter is vague and changeable; while the former incorporates every present circumstance in a pseudo-logical chain, the latter jumps over the gap; and while such logical power as the patient ever had, is utilized in the assertion and defence of the systematized, it is in abeyance, in part or in whole, with reference to the announcement and defence of the unsystematized delusions.

The unsystematized delusion of grandeur differs in a similar way from the systematized expansive delusion. In the former case—for example, in paretic dementia—the patient may assert that he is a king or president, or that he has a million dollars; because it is a desirable thing for the sanguine patient to be a king, a president, and to have money. But he will make no attempt to explain how he can be a king and yet be named Dennis Maginnis; how he can be Ulysses S. Grant and Samuel Silberstein at one and the same time; and why it is that he has a hundred thousand acres of land to-day, when he only had ten houses and lots yesterday. Such a delusion is never as consistent nor expressed with that firm conviction that characterizes the systematized variety. A systematic delusionist would, if challenged to explain why he answers to the name of a private citizen, when he claims to be a king, say that the name in question is that of the menial child with which he was "exchanged while in the cradle," or that it is the designation which he has adopted to put his persecutors, "the agents of the usurper," on a false track. Again, a systematized delusional lunatic, if claiming great personal attractions, which is rare, fortifies his claim by letters received, containing a "hidden meaning" and by poems and advertisements "referring to him." In paretic dementia, with which affection this delusion is common, the patient will content himself with the vague announcement of the assertion that he is handsome, boast that the women are enraptured with him; but if called on to specify he will hesitate, and then invent his grounds as he goes along—if able—and forget them on the next occasion. Another paretic dement will allege that he is five thousand three hundred and seventy-two feet high, his actual height being rather under five feet (actual observation). If placed side by side with a taller man, and asked to estimate his size, he correctly assigns, six feet. If asked whether he has to look up or down to measure his neighbor he unhesitatingly admits that he has to look up. But on being confronted with his inconsistency, how it is possible that a man over five thousand feet higher than the tallest giant can possibly look up to an ordinary-sized mortal, he simply reiterates that he is so many thousand feet higher than the interlocutor or any other man. A third person claims that he is General Grant, the week before he claimed to be Rothschild the banker, but abandoned that idea when told that the latter was dead. He is unable to say when the war began, what his business was before he became a general, what battles he fought in, and finally what land he is president of. A systematic delusional Ulysses Grant would, in marked contrast with the paretic, be a walking history of the war and of Ulysses Grant; he would very probably content himself too, with the more plausible delusion that he was a brother or intimate friend, or a subaltern of the general, to whom the latter owed his "inspiration" and success.

While, on the whole, the organization of a delusion reflects the essential type of the insanity of which it is a manifestation, it must be admitted that there are special delusions or groups of delusions, in which the formal contents and the superficial guise of these conceptions have a diagnostic value which is lacking with others. The delusions of marital infidelity and sexual mutilation, when combined, suggest the existence of alcoholic insanity. The combination of unsystematized sexual with religious delusions of a hallucinatory tinge is characteristic of certain forms of epileptic insanity.[8]

DRUG-INDUCED MODEL PSYCHOSIS

Foderé[9] stated that drug intoxications might take the form of epidemics of psychosis and mentioned such epidemics among young draftees and children. He also wrote at some length on how to distinguish mental abberations due to drugs from the endogenous types.

A whole book on hallucinations, spontaneous and drug induced, was compiled by Michéa in 1846.[10] He quoted with approval, from Cousin's Cours de la histoire

[8] E. C. Spitzka, Insanity: Its Classification, Diagnosis and Treatment (New York: Bermingham and Co., 1883), pp. 25-33.

[9] R. E. Foderé, Traité du délire, appliqué à la médecine, à la morale et à la législation (Paris: Croullebois, 1817).

[10] C. F. Michéa, Du délire des sensations (Paris: Labé, 1846). Another book also published in France in the 1840s is L. R. Szafkowski, Recherches sur les hallucinations au point de vue de la psychologie, de l'histoire et de la médecine légale (Montpellier: L. Castel; Bordeaux: Lawalle; Paris: G. Baillière; Lyon: Savy, 1849).

de la philosophie, the words "the study of medicine is an excellent preparation for metaphysics."

Moreau (de Tours) wrote a remarkable book entirely about hashish in 1845.[11] His words have a strikingly modern sound. He identified two patterns now current in psychotopharmacology by pointing out that the drug-induced psychosis provides a model for the better understanding of endogenous psychoses and, in his first sentence, that "Curiosity alone initially led me to experiment with the effects of hashish on myself."

Rückert (1854)

The idea that drugs might produce what is today called "model psychoses" was evidently fairly widespread, as shown by Peters translation of Rückert's work. The psychiatry of drug effects comprises a vast, specialized field that deserves separate consideration.

_____ [The] action [of Cannabis-indica] throws much light upon mental derangement in general. A marked correspondence may be traced between the phenomena of insanity and those which are induced by the introduction of Alcohol, Opium, Cannabis-indica, Nitrous-oxide, or laughing gas, Agaricus-muscarius, Belladonna, Stramonium, &c., into the system and blood. There can be no doubt that the properties of the blood may be perverted by unnatural changes going on within the system, as well as by the direct introduction of poisonous substances from without. Schoenlein, we believe, was the first to suggest that absolutely narcotic substances were sometimes formed *de novo* in the blood and system; prussic-acid always exists in the saliva; the narcotic properties of Urea are well known; the drowsiness, heaviness, and low spirits produced by bile circulating in the system are familiar. Hence mental derangement is often a blood disease—the presence of a minute portion of any of these substances circulating in the blood, which is passing through the capillaries of the brain, may excite delirium, illusions, fury, or melancholy, &c., &c.,[12]

CONVERSION

Conversion is a word much used in the twentieth century in connection with the development of bodily symptoms in hysteria. The concept, however, is at least as old as the Hippocratic corpus, and the term itself goes back almost two centuries. As used in the past, conversion referred to a change in the patient from any mental to any physical disorder or vice versa. It also referred to a change from one physical disease to another.

[11] J. Moreau, *Du hachisch et de l'aliénation mentale* (Paris: Fortin, Masson et Cie., 1845).

[12] J. C. Peters, *A Treatise on Nervous Derangements and Mental Disorders,* based on T. J. Rückerts, *Clinical Experience in Homoeopathy* (New York: William Raddie, Philadelphia: Rademacher and Sheek; Boston: Otis Clapp; Manchester: Henry Turner, London: J. Epps, 1854), p. 27.

Burrows (1828)

_____ The conversion, like the relation of diseases, is a neglected part of pathology. Ferriar remarks, that Hippocrates, and his annotators, Baglivi and Castro, were the only medical writers who had attended to this subject. Parry, however, since Ferriar, has added many pertinent observations upon it; and fully shews how highly essential a knowledge of such conversions is in a review of the causes of mental derangement.

Most diseases are susceptible of conversion. Heberden suggests, that madness, like gout, absorbs other distempers, and turns them perfectly to its own nature. Ferriar and Parry adduce many examples of conversion. . . .

Insanity may be completely converted into another disease; in which case it performs a radical cure of the mental affection. . . .

There is no doubt that insanity would be still more frequent, were it not for the intervention of other diseases, through which the labouring system finds relief; so, on the other hand, it is often induced when it would not have been developed, had not the course of a disease been injudiciously or accidentally interrupted and changed.[13]

REGRESSION

Psychologic regression was early recognized as occurring in mental disease, but unfortunately the pejorative term _degeneration_ was sometimes applied. In the minds of some authors regression was not distinguished from the manifestations of degenerative brain disease, which in those days was usually syphilis or senility. This led to the designation of a psychotic person as "a degenerate" and reinforced the prejudice toward such patients which had originated in the notion, by then abandoned, that demonic possession caused mental disease.

Haslam (1809)

It remained for Haslam, echoing the words of Locke, to emphasize the psychologic origin of regression. Later writers adopted these views.

_____ Insane people, who have been good scholars, after a long confinement, lose, in a wonderful degree, the correctness of orthography: when they write, above half the words are frequently mis-spelt, they are written according to the pronunciation. It shews how treacherous the memory is without reinforcement. The same necessity of a constant recruit, and frequent review of our ideas, satisfactorily explains, why a number of patients lapse nearly into a state of ideotism. These have, for some years, been the silent and gloomy inhabitants of the hospital, who have avoided conversation, and courted solitude; consequently

[13] G. M. Burrows, _Commentaries on the Causes, Forms, Symptoms, and Treatment, Moral and Medical, of Insanity_ (London: T. and G. Underwood, 1828), pp. 216-217.

have acquired no new ideas, and time has effaced the impression of those, formerly stamped on the mind. Mr. Locke, well observes, although he speaks figuratively, "that there seems to be a constant decay of all our ideas, even of those which are struck deepest, and in minds the most retentive; so that, if they be not sometimes renewed by repeated exercise of the senses, or reflection on those kind of objects, which at first occasioned them, the print wears out, and at last there remains nothing to be seen."[14]

Griesinger (1845)

Griesinger made what was among the more definitive statements concerning regression.

It is not at all unusual, although hitherto it has been very little attended to, to observe a mental state characterised by moderate weakness occasionally ensue after apparent recovery from other forms, and to remain persistent. In individuals who have recovered in this way, the sentiments regain their former calm; they can also again think and judge in a formally correct manner—the memory is little or not at all disturbed—their conversation is quite coherent and rational. But they are no longer the same persons; it seems as if their mental individuality had been deprived of its best and most valuable qualities, the more delicate moral and aesthetic sentiments, interest in the higher mental aims of life, which form the beauty and the nobleness of human nature. Their thoughts and efforts move henceforth within a limited circle, in the sphere of the immediate wants and requirements; and while they conduct themselves rationally, perhaps with a degree of activity in this circle, all the spiritual and ideal concerns of life, all consideration or desire of them, are foreign to them. These persons might be regarded as perfectly sane—since there are many individuals who are all along of this disposition—if we had not been acquainted with their former life, and if, in many cases, in the physiognomy and whole demeanour, a marked change to idiotic, even animal-like expressions, was not recognised. They are further capable of simple mechanical employments, in the performance of which they show care and intelligence; for themselves they desire nothing more than suffices to satisfy simply material wants. Should such individuals be permitted to leave the asylum and return to ordinary life, they run a great risk of new and severe attacks of insanity, or of gradually passing into confirmed mental weakness. In the asylum they often for years enjoy a life of relative health, calm, and useful employment.

Such states may be regarded as the mildest forms of dementia. In all *higher degrees* the patient ceases to present any appearances of convalescence, and the increasing mental dulness is not restricted to the finer and more delicate faculties. Sometimes the whole mental life again assumes the character it had in

---

[14] J. Haslam, *Observations on Madness and Melancholy* (London: J. Callow, 1809), pp. 62–64.

childhood, in which most strikingly the capacity of abstract thought is lost.[15]

Maudsley (1867)

Maudsley also emphasized the psychologic origin and nature of regression, but unfortunately used the term *degeneration* as a synonym.

Furthermore, it is plain that the degree of development which the mind has reached must determine in no slight measure the features of its disorder; the more cultivated the mind the more various and complex must be the symptoms of its derangement; while it is not possible that the undeveloped mind of the child immediately after birth should exhibit ideational disorder of any kind. Consider what an infinitely complex development the cultivated mind has been shown to be, and what a long series of processes and what a variety of interworkings of so-called faculties even its simpler conceptions imply; it will then be easily understood how great and varied may be the confusion and disorder of its morbid action. The different forms of insanity represent different phases of mental degeneration; and in this disorganisation, degeneration, or retrograde metamorphosis of the mental organization—call the retrograde change what we will—there will be exhibited the wreck of culture. The morbid mental phenomena of an insane Australian savage will of necessity be different from the morbid mental phenomena of an insane European, just as the ruins of a palace must be vaster and more varied than the ruins of a log hut. For the same reason the insanity of early life always has more or less of the character of imbecility or idiocy about it: as is the height so is the depth, as is the development so is the degeneration. The development of the sexual system at puberty, and the great revolution which is thereby effected in the mental life, must needs often give a colour to the phenomena of insanity occurring after puberty. During the energy of mental function in active manhood mania is the form of degeneration which appears most frequently to occur, while as age advances and energy declines melancholia becomes more common.

Because no two people are exactly alike in mental character and development, therefore no two cases of mental degeneration are exactly alike. The brain is different in the matter of its development from other organs of the body; for while the development and function of other organs are nearly alike in different individuals, and the diseases of them accordingly have a general resemblance, the real development of the brain as the organ of mental life only takes place after birth, and, presenting every variety of individual function in health, presents also every variety of morbid function: consequently, two cases of insanity may resemble one another in the general features of exaltation or depression, or in

[15] W. Griesinger, *Mental Pathology and Therapeutics,* from the 2nd German ed., C. L. Robertson and J. Rutherford, trans. (London: The New Sydenham Society, 1867), pp. 322-323.

the character of the delusion, but will still have their special features. Insanity is not any fixed morbid entity; every instance of it is an example of individual degeneration, and represents individual mental life under other conditions than those which we agree to regard as normal or typical. No more useful work could be undertaken in psychology than an exact study of *individual* minds, sound and unsound.

Weigh carefully the manner of its causation, and it will appear that mental derangement must be a matter of degree. There may be every variety (*a*) of deficient original capacity, (*b*) of deficient development of the mental organization after birth, and (*c*) of degree of degeneration. Between the extremest cases of madness, therefore, and the highest level of mental soundness, there will be infinite varieties shading insensibly one into another; so that no man will be able to say positively where sanity ends and insanity begins, or to determine with certainty in every case whether a particular person is insane or not. The question of an individual's responsibility must then plainly be a most difficult one: there are insane persons who are certainly responsible for what they do, and, on the other hand, there are sane people who under certain circumstances are as plainly not responsible for their actions. A madman is notably capable of great self-control when his interest specially demands it; in the majority of cases he knows full well the difference between right and wrong; but, knowing the right, he is instigated by the impulses of his morbid nature to do the wrong, and is not held in check by those motives which suffice to restrain the sane portion of the community.[16]

DISSOCIATION

The concept of dissociation, now regarded as a modern invention, was actually advanced more than a century and a half ago. Benjamin Rush, that sulky, irascible genius, chose one of the several psychological disorders attached to dementia by Pinel and coined a term for it. His term was solipsistic, however, and since he was only a Colonial his contribution was not widely recognized. Actually no American psychiatrist received much attention until the meteoric but short-lived fame of James Beard (see page 288). Dissociation itself, of course led to the invention of the word *schizophrenia* a century later, at a time when the suffix *-phrenia* was at the height of its popularity.

Rush (1812)

──── Related to intellectual madness is that disease of the mind, which has received from Mr. Pinel the name of *demence*. The subjects of it in Scotland are said to "have a bee in their bonnets." In the United States, we say they are "flighty," or

[16] H. Maudsley, *The Physiology and Pathology of the Mind* (New York: D. Appleton and Co., 1867), pp. 250–252.

"hair-brained," and, sometimes, a "little cracked." I have preferred naming it, from its principal symptom, *dissociation*. It consists not in false perceptions, like the worst grade of madness, but of an association of unrelated perceptions, or ideas, from the inability of the mind to perform the operations of judgment and reason. The perceptions are generally excited by sensible objects; but ideas, collected together without order, frequently constitute a paroxysm of the disease. It is always accompanied with great volubility of speech, or with bodily gestures, performed with a kind of convulsive rapidity. We rarely meet with this disease in hospitals; but there is scarcely a city, a village, or a country place, that does not furnish one or more instances of it. Persons who are afflicted with it are good tempered and quarrelsome, malicious and kind, generous and miserly, all in the course of the same day. In a word, the mind in this disease may be considered as floating in a balloon, and at the mercy of every object and thought that acts upon it. It is constant in some people, but it occurs more frequently in paroxysms, and is sometimes succeeded by low spirits.[17]

THOUGHT DISORDERS

Haslam (1798)

Haslam was the first to emphasize the distinctive features of thought disorders, including their association with strong feelings.

Insanity may, in my opinion, be defined to be an incorrect association of familiar ideas, which is independent of the prejudices of education, and is always accompanied with implicit belief, and generally with either violent or depressing passions. It appears to me necessary that the ideas incorrectly associated should be familiar, because we can hardly be said to have our ideas deranged upon subjects, concerning which we have little or no information.[18]

Griesinger (1845)

Griesinger analyzed thought disorders further and stressed the importance of the speed of thinking processes and the psychologic factors that control it.

Within the sphere of distinct perception, of opinion and conclusion, we can readily distinguish two varieties of abnormal states. First, there is an abnormal relation of perception in the abstract; secondly, abnormal views in relation to its (false) objects. These states are intimately related, inasmuch as certain formal modifications, for example, too rapid succession of the ideas, extreme slowness

---

[17] B. Rush, *Medical Inquiries and Observations upon the Diseases of the Mind* (Philadelphia: J. Richardson, 1812), pp. 259-260.
[18] J. Haslam, *Observations on Insanity: With Practical Remarks on the Disease and an Account of the Morbid Appearences on Dissection.* (London: F. and C. Rivington, 1798), p. 10.

in the course of thought, or disorder of the feelings which necessarily accompany them, excite or promote certain morbid ideas; for example, the moderate excitation of perception, where the combinations proceed with increased facility, is frequently accompanied by false judgments, which result from the feeling of mental liberty and mental well-being.

a. Formal Deviations

Extreme sluggishness of thought depends either on suppression arising from violent mental pain, which entirely occupies the mind and permits nothing else to approach it, or on real weakness, especially loss of memory. In both cases, however different they may be as to their internal causes, there is observed poverty and sameness of thought, the train of thought appears to stand still; single words, modes of expression, movements, repeated for hours, show the continued presence of the same perceptions. There is often observed a hesitation of the speech, great uncertainty in the connection of the thoughts, and timidity in judging. This condition is found principally in melancholia and in dementia.

This insufficient interchange of the perceptions is a very important element in many mental diseases. The patient can no more thoroughly divest himself of certain perceptions, he is no longer free, he is continually exposed to their tormenting influences and impulses; he feels how, gradually, in spite of his opposition, his *I*, the oneness of his person, is being snatched from him. Similar states may be observed even in dreaming; many repugnant ideas by their constant recurrence induce a state of despondency. As will be found on minute consideration, sleeplessness often arises from the continued influence of a group of ideas; whenever these disperse sleep returns.

An increased production and accelerated flow of the thoughts in some degree facilitates mental combinations; therefore we sometimes observe individuals who at other times are even intellectually dull become acute and witty, especially in the happy expression of raillery against individuals present, versification, &c. On that account we hear little wisdom from the insane. Then, even in these states where abundant material is offered to the cultivated imagination, generally disorder and incoherence very soon appear. Particularly when great numbers of perceptions originate in the brain, and their course is accelerated, are they succeeded by long series of ideas; and frequently long-forgotten images and events, words, songs, and so forth, are renewed with the freshness of first impressions; but, inasmuch as the perceptions so rapidly succeed each other that they cannot enter into the necessary combinations, and inasmuch as the multiplicity of thoughts is attended by corresponding changes in the sentiments, the only result is extreme agitation and tumult of ideas. All is hurried along in the most confused succession, and it is a chance if here and there in this turmoil the elements of a quaint idea meet together which is in the least more rational than what surrounds it.

The latter states appear principally in mania. There is often apparently great mental vivacity, especially at their commencement, and we have known cases where it was the invariable symptom of an approaching attack when the patient became witty.

Incoherence of the ideas does not, however, solely originate in this way, namely, through over-fulness of the consciousness. There is also incoherence of through and speech corresponding to projections of the thoughts and of the emotions, as anger, and still another which proceeds from complete abolition and deep destruction of the mental processes. The psychological mechanism of this last condition is still very obscure in its details; it appears that the incoherence frequently depends on the fact that the perceptions are called forth, not only according to their (similar or contrasting) contents, but especially according to external similarity of sound in the words. Perhaps deficient reciprocal action of the two halves of the brain may have some influence in producing incoherence. Incoherence is frequent at the commencement of mental diseases, where there is violent disturbance of the emotions, and here it is no more an evil indication than it is in the delirium of fever or in dreams. On the other hand, the incoherence which first appears after a long continuance of melancholia and mania, or at the commencement of chronic insanity, is significant of a transition to the incurable forms of dementia.

Two marked examples of temporary incoherence from transient disturbance of the brain in otherwise healthy persons, with a clear description of the progress of the symptoms, by Spalding and Gädike, may be seen in Jessen, 'Versuch einer wissenschaftlichen Begrundung,' &c., 1855, p. 180.

To the morbid states of thought described in this paragraph there are found many psychological analogies, partly in the determined persistence with which disagreeable ideas often follow us, in intimidation of the judgment by an adverse occurrence, also in so-called sulkiness and in confusion of the ideas owing to fright. To the second series in loquaciousness without ideas, in the internal confusion which originates from abundant simultaneous reception of ideas which have no common characteristic or leading direction, or in the incoherence of images in dreams.

Memory in particular is very variously affected in mental disease. Sometimes it is unimpaired as regards the events of the former life as well as the occurrences during the disease. In the preceding paragraph we have spoken of its morbid increase. It is more frequent, however, to observe enfeeblement of the memory in various modes. Dementia in particular is characterised by feebleness of such a kind that events happening at the present time are quickly, even instantaneously, forgotten, while there is distinct recollection of events that took place in former periods of life, which may even be the subject of tolerably well-ordered conversation. At other times the contents of the previous life are either (seldom) completely effaced from the tablets of the memory, or (more frequently) are so far removed that they become so vague and so strange to the individual that they can scarcely be recognised as events in his own history. Here the actual individual existence is dated from the commencement of the disease, and the entire former life is either attributed to a strange personality or at least to a former quite different state, to an imaginary life. This estrangement, this complete falling away of the former *I*, depends, not only upon weakness of memory, but ordinarly it is produced and rendered persistent by special sensitive anomalies; but the disappearance of whole masses of former perceptions is especially favorable to the consequent internal production of such a delirium.

An individual who has recovered from insanity generally remembers what occurred to him during his disease, and can often narrate with remarkable truth and precision the most trifling incidents in the outer world and the minute details of his motives and sentiments during the disease. He can often interpret every glance, word, and change of expression of his visitor—circumstances which suggest an incidental caution to those who have to do with the insane, to be constantly on their guard as to how they conduct themselves, to be just and mild, if indeed such an exhortation be required! This kind of intelligence is especially observable in those who have recovered from melancholia and moderate states of mania, less frequently after monomania, of which the patient generally retains very confused ideas. The statement of one who has recovered that he has no knowledge of anything that occurred during his disease is to be received with caution, since the patient often conceals what he clearly remembers through deceit.

With the anomalies of form which have been described there are frequently connected changes in speech and the modes of expression. Many are dumb owing to a cessation of perception, or even where numerous perceptions are present, because no reflex action occurs in the apparatus of speech. Others speak incessantly, their narratives are endless, or, without communicating anything precise to a listener, the continuous reflex action in the organs of speech proceeds as incessant prattle (logomania proper, generally with incoherence). Frequently it is rather the formation of sentences and the mode of expression that is altered; they are more fluent or interrupted, disconnected, affected, &c. In other cases, which are the most interesting, there appear in the language of the insane newly formed words, and old ones are employed with new significations; in short, the patient forms for himself a new language. It would appear that occasionally ordinary language is not sufficient to express completely new and strange contents of sensation and perception, and therefore new words are formed, or that in the abnormal cerebral state the conventional images of sound (words) directly stir up and allude to other perceptions, or that frequently the hallucinations of hearing immediately necessitate the formation of new combinations of syllables, which are then retained and held fast (in dreaming also there is thus formed new words). All these changes appear most highly developed in chronic mania more transiently in mania. . . .

b. Perversions of Thought—Delirious Ideas

Mental disease does not necessarily imply the existence of delirious perceptions. Marked changes in the character and in the sentiments, morbid dispositions and emotions, blunting of the sentiments, total or partial relaxation of the mental powers, can exist without truly insane ideas, as acute and chronic morbid states of the mind. A number of such cases may be comprehended under the class of moral insanity (*Gemüthswahnsinn*). But experience teaches that, in the great majority of cases, the mental derangement does not cease here, that special insane ideas are developed, and that these false opinions which can no longer be regulated are accompanied by true delirium, the mental affection, which at the commencement was only an insanity of the feelings and emotions, becomes also *insanity of the intellect*. The pressure of the morbid uneasiness tends rapidly to incorrect perception and interpretation of objective relations, but at first only of such as relate to the patient himself or to his immediate surroundings. The false contents of the thoughts, *i.e.* which are not in harmony with the external world and with the events of the former life, at first generally happen in such a way that the patient attempts to account for his dispositions and morbid emotions by the law of causality. The most varied external causes and events, and the innumerable recollections of his individual existence, afford abundant material for this attempt at explanation, and circumstances, education, and the views of life, have here the most decided influence. . . .

All hallucinations have a special influence, as well on the formation of such insane ideas as on their special objects; they are so frequent, present materials for explanation so lively, obtrusive, and often so constant, that in our experience we must find them to be a common source of insane ideas. . .[19]

BOREDOM

The idea that boredom is a potent motivating force has, of course, been emphasized in countless novels and plays. The idea has also been discussed by philosophers. Kierkegaard, with typical exaggeration, wrote: "Adam was bored alone, then Adam and Eve were bored together; then Adam and Eve and Cain and Abel were bored en famille; then the population of the world increased, and people were bored en masse. To divert themselves they conceived the idea of constructing a tower high enough to reach the heavens. The idea itself is as boring as the tower was high, and constitutes a terrible proof of how boredom had gained the upper hand"—with Kierkegaard, at least. The corrosive effect of boredom was emphasized by Sir Horace Vere, who replied to a question concerning his brother's death, "He died of having nothing to do."

The idea that boredom, or the need to avoid it, is man's prime motivating force has been presented elsewhere.[20] Experimental psychologists have also discussed

[19] W. Griesinger, *Mental Pathology and Therapeutics*, from the 2nd German ed., C. L. Robertson and J. Rutherford, trans. (London: The New Sydenham Society, 1867), pp. 66–70.

[20] See M. D. Altschule, "Invalidity of the diagnosis 'anxiety neurosis': Notes on curiosity and boredom as motivating forces," *New York State Journal of Medicine*, 1959, 59, 3812–3822.

boredom as a drive in animals.[21] It has, however, received little systematic discussion in today's psychiatric texts.

Older authors considered boredom highly important and indicated that it might cause anxiety.

Crichton (1798)

When mental representations and ideas succeed each other slowly, an irksomeness of mind takes place, which the French call ennui. The slowness hinted at is necessarily relative to the nature of the ideas. New ideas please much better when they succeed each other with a certain degree of slowness, than when quickly presented to the mind; but when a person is confined to the house, and is deprived of society, and has no opportunity of seeing a succession of new objects, and is not under the influence of any desire, or passions, which can give rise to a flow of thoughts, he necessarily falls into this distressing state, from the too slow succession of old or accustomed thoughts. If we have no means of escaping from a dull, ignorant, and prolix companion, whose whole conversation is about commonplace topics, and whose thoughts have no association with any of our pursuits, or inclinations, we fall into a state of ennui. This tormenter of human happiness often occasions a degree of inquietude which is productive of the most alarming and fatal consequences; for the desire of relief becomes, in some cases, so great as totally to destroy all judgment, and consequently hurries the person on to the most criminal violence against nature. It is in this way that ennui, like melancholy, may terminate in suicide. In a lesser degree, it produces a number of well-known, but no less remarkable phenomena; a restlessness, and sense of weariness, spread themselves over the whole frame. . . .

It is a favorite opinion with Helvetius, and many other philosophers, that ennui is one of the most powerful motives in the mind of man which stimulates him to great actions. There can be no doubt of the general truth of this fact, only it is not quite accurately expressed; for it is the desire of relief from pain, and not the languor from which the actions spring.[22]

Conolly (1830)

In such inactivity, the intellect stagnates, and the very affections run to waste. Many who have retired from the bustle of the world, to enjoy, as they believed, the felicity of retirement, have found by sad experience, that the government of themselves was more difficult in solitude than in society; and have discredited,

---

[21] See A. D. Myers and N. E. Miller, "Failure to find a learned drive based on hunger; evidence for learning motivated by exploration," *Journal of Comparative and Physiological Psychology*, 1954, 47, 428–434.

[22] A. Crichton, *An Inquiry into the Nature and Origin of Mental Derangement* (London: T. Cadell, Junior, and W. Davis, 1798), Vol. 1, pp. 321–324.

by the weakness and follies of their latter years, the better actions and aspirations of their youth and manhood.

Even amidst the excitement of the capital, the want of those continual motives to industry which arise from a profession, or from some regular pursuit in life, or from the necessity of making some provision for others, or from any of those privations and difficulties of which the operation is always beneficial, though seldom duly appreciated, is most fatal to mental ease. A condition which most men would choose, because apparently including every blessing of nature and fortune, has been known to become tormenting and intolerable. The possession of wealth and rank, a liberal education, great literary acquirements, many accomplishments, correctness of life, elegance of manners, and extra-ordinary powers of conversation, together with the frequent enjoyment of a society in which all these particulars are fully estimated, present a combination of advantages which very few possess, and to which none can be indifferent: if any thing could promise worldly happiness, such a combination of natural and acquired endowments would seem to do so. They were never perhaps more happily united than in the instance of Mr. Topham Beauclerk, the friend and frequent companion of Johnson, by whom, as indeed by all the great men of a time in which great men abounded, he was not only admired but beloved. Yet we are told that the activity or the restlessness of his mind required something more; and that, sometimes unsatisfactorily engaged in desultory studies, and sometimes in dissipation, and sometimes in play, he was too often a martyr to misanthropy, and querulousness, and ennui. At such times, it cannot be doubted that there was an approach to disease of mind. The impressions made by certain circumstances were disproportionate; due consideration was not, or could not be, given to them; they could not be attended to and compared; and therefore the strong impression was allowed to induce all those uncomfortable and discontented feelings which the exercise of the judgment would have kept away, and which in happier moods of mind it was able to disperse. So long as such fits continued, there was a tendency to madness: if they had not been interrupted, the mind would not long have remained sane.

In such examples, the mind is unable to maintain its vigour in the absence of particular stimuli. Restore the stimulus, and the power will be found to remain; at least until years of indolence have brought the mind into a state of imbecility, and nearer to actual disease. In each stage of its declension, it approaches to such imbecility, and may become unable to bear any unexpected shock; the fortitude of the character being thus lost with the mental activity. But it will be only when circumstances make such a strong impression, or the mind has become too enfeebled to be directed in attention, or exercised in the comparison of things, that the man will begin to be insane. In many such instances, no result ensues from these inequalities of mind, except the temporary unhappiness of the individual; an unhappiness however which, whilst it lasts, makes his lot less desirable than that of him who gains his daily bread by daily labour. But a succession of mental disturbances, or some supervening corporeal disease, now and then completes the mental disorder, and hurries the mind to absolute insanity. Some morbid sensation, some imagined wrong, bids defiance to the test of true comparison: the judgment is abused, the actions become first eccentric, then more decidedly irrational, and without prompt and skilful aid the governance of reason is eventually lost.

The man in the Spectator, who hanged himself to avoid the intolerable annoyance of having to tie his garters every day of his life, is but a satire on the misery of many, who, having no useful occupation, find the flight of time marked only by the swift repetition of petty troubles.[23]

ANTISOCIAL BEHAVIOR

A belief widely held in this country is that antisocial behavior is a psychiatric disorder. It is also believed that this is a new idea, and that those who adhere to it have a special understanding of the problem. Actually these ideas are far from new.

In the past some writers attempted to formulate theories that would explain antisocial behavior, and in so doing they categorized all criminal behavior as a form of mental illness. For several centuries some psychiatrists (including phrenologists) have insisted that they not only understood the cause but also could define the cure of the tendency to commit criminal acts. The phrenologists carried the matter still further and claimed that one part of the skull or another indicated some type of inherent moral turpitude. In England they demanded that all criminals have a phrenologic examination before being sentenced. Brodie's ironic discussion of this approach included a hypothetical bump on the skull that indicated "a proclivity for defacing milestones."

There is a vast literature on the psychiatric aspects of crime which should have separate and detailed study. In most of these works, however, criminal acts are seen as manifestations of mental disease only in specific cases, and they will not be quoted here. A number of nineteenth-century authors included various types of assaultive or destructive behavior in their classifications and usually regarded these behavioral patterns as "clear insanity" or "insanity with no disturbance of intellectual function." Other authors of the period entered into detailed discussions of the legal aspects of antisocial acts committed by the mentally deranged, and these will not be included here either. The few authors quoted in this section are presented because they were interested in the specific psychiatric character and significance of antisocial acts; they based their opinions on their own case material.

Pinel (1806)

Pinel was an early commentator on the occurrence of antisocial acts during periods of psychosis.

---

[23] J. Conolly, *An Inquiry concerning the Indications of Insanity* (London: J. Taylor, 1830), pp. 184–187.

A man, rendered insane by events connected with the revolution, repelled with rudeness, a child whom at other times he most tenderly caressed. I have, likewise, seen a young man that was much attached to his father, commit acts of outrage, and even attempt to strike at him, when under the influence of this unfortunate disease.

I could mention several instances of maniacs, of known integrity and honesty during their intervals of calmness, who had an irresistible propensity to cheat and to steal upon the accession of their maniacal paroxysms.

Another maniac, who was naturally of a very mild and pacific disposition, appeared to be inspired by the demon of malice and mischief during the whole period of his attack. His time and faculties were then employed in the most mischievous activity; shutting up his companions in their own rooms, and seeking every means of insulting and quarrelling with them. Some are actuated by an instinctive propensity to commit to the flames every thing of a combustible nature; a propensity which, in most instances, must no doubt be ascribed to an error of the imagination. A madman tore and destroyed the furniture of his bed, (bed-clothes and straw,) under the apprehension that they were heaps of adders and coils of writhing serpents. But, amongst madmen of this description, there are some whose imaginations are in no degree affected, but who feel a blind and ferocious propensity to imbrue their hands in human blood. I mention this circumstance upon the authority of one of my patients, in whose veracity I had the utmost confidence, and who during one of his lucid intervals confided to me the fatal acknowledgement.

To complete this account of automatic atrocity, I shall just mention the instance of a madman who directed his fury towards himself as well as against other people. He had taken off his own hand with a chopping knife, previous to his admission into the hospital; and, notwithstanding his close confinement he made constant efforts to mangle his own thighs with his teeth. This unfortunate man put an end to his existence in one of his fits.[24]

Rush (1812)

One early account by Rush indicates that the pursuit of happiness is not new. Rush considered the disorder a form of partial insanity, one not likely to be curable.

> The symptoms of this third and last form of general madness are, taciturnity, downcast looks, a total neglect of dress and person, long nails and beard, dishevelled or matted hair, indifference to all surrounding objects, insensibility to heat and cold. . . . A fixed position of the body sometimes attends this form of madness. . . .

[24] P. Pinel, *A Treatise on Insanity, in Which Are Contained the Principles of a New and More Practical Nosology of Maniacal Disorders,* D. D. Davis, trans. (Sheffield: W. Dodd, 1806), pp. 20–22.

A strong attachment to tobacco is common in the patients who have been previously in the habit of using it. They frequently ask strangers for it, or for a few cents to buy it.

These are the usual symptoms of manalgia in hospitals, but when persons who are affected with it possess their liberty, they rather seek for, than shun human society. They are often admitted by private families to pass nights in their kitchens, garrets, or barns. Sometimes they wander through neighbourhoods in the capacity of beggars. . . .

There are some instances in which the moral faculties are impaired in manalgic patients, in which case they are mischievous and vicious, but they are more generally inoffensive, and disposed to be kind, and even useful, in hospitals and families. In some of them, the sense of Deity is not only unimpaired, but in an elevated state.[25]

Rush also remarked that hatred for the physician or for a parent might be the last symptom to go during recovery.

A Mrs. D——, whom I supposed, for several months, had recovered from madness, under my care, said to me one day, in passing by her in our hospital, upon my asking her how she was, "that she was perfectly well, and that she was sure this was the case, for that she had at last ceased to hate me."

A similar instance of a perfect recovery succeeding the revival of domestic respect and affection occurred in a Miss H. L. who was confined in our hospital in the year 1800. For several weeks she discovered every mark of a sound mind, except one. She hated her father. On a certain day she acknowledged, with pleasure, a return of her filial attachment and affection for him; soon after she was discharged cured.[26]

Matthey (1816)

Matthey differed from some of his nosological contemporaries. Although his published classification was based entirely on traditional sources, he added an extra heading entitled *Genre Nouveau,* which he defined as "Pathomanie—perversion of the will and the natural tendencies, with no apparent defects in intellectual functions." This included well-known syndromes, together with several of his own invention, all dealing with antisocial behavior.

1. Fureur sans délire. An internal compulsion that leads one to commit acts of ferocity or passion, without confusion and with no participation of the will.

   Variety 1: Tigrodomanie. An unconquerable compulsion that leads one to commit acts of ferocity or passion, without confusion and with no participation of the will.

[25] B. Rush, *Medical Inquiries and Observations upon the Diseases of the Mind* (Philadelphia: J. Richardson, 1812), pp. 216-217.

[26] Ibid., pp. 255-256.

Variety 2: Fury directed entirely toward inanimate objects.
2. Uiophobie. Insurmountable aversion or antipathy toward one's own children.
3. Klopemanie. Compulsion to steal without need and without being led to it by the pressing need of misery, following troubled events or a disordered life.
4. Suicidal melancholia. Disposition toward suicide, with no confusion.

Variety 1: Suicidal melancholy through ennui with life, without manifest changes in organic functions, without emotional cause (English melancholy).

Variety 2: Acute suicidal melancholy. Sudden determination to commit suicide, through the effect of a strong unexpected emotion of the soul.

Variety 3: Suicidal melancholy complicated by hypochondria; consequent to an obvious visceral disorder, without confusion.[27]

It is obvious that the whole gamut of antisocial behavior patterns cannot be given individual names, nor can antisocial behavior be regarded as the same everywhere.[28]

Griesinger (1845)

Although many authors down through the ages had discussed suicide as a phenomenon of depression, it remained for Griesinger to broaden the approach and show that many crimes of violence may also be manifestations of depression. This idea seems to have been rediscovered at intervals and is now very popular among social psychologists.

Directly and immediately connected with the suicidal impulse, is the morbid tendency to injure and destroy other persons or inanimate objects. Not only do these tendencies frequently occur together—not only have these acts of violence towards others, inasmuch as they are often perpetrated upon those most loved and cherished by the patient, fundamentally the same essential character as the tendency to self-injury and self-mutilation—but, in general, both depend upon the same fundamental state of morbid negative emotion, and in both there may be also observed certain differences in the immediate morbid cause.

As to the psychical motives which give rise to these acts of violence in persons *already labouring under melancholia,* these impulses would seem to be due, in part at least, to an actual delirium of the intelligence or of the sensorial perception. To this class belong those cases in which the patients imagine that they are persecuted, or generally injured by others,—where they attribute to

---

[27] A. Matthey, *Nouvelles Recherches sur les maladies de l'esprit, précédées de considerations sur les difficultés de l'art de guérir* (Paris: Paschoud, 1816), pp. 146–147.

[28] Compare this with other examples of similar behavior noted even earlier. See M. D. Altschule, "Beyond good and evil—or how to create the dark in which to whistle," *West Georgia College Studies in the Social Sciences,* 1971, *10,* 16–34.

certain persons insulting and injurious expressions which they hear in their hallucinations of hearing, and consequently actually commit deeds of vengeance upon them. To these are very closely associated those violent deeds which are suggested under the idea, evidently melancholic, that everything in this world is bad, that everything is abandoned and lost; that, for example, the innocent children may be best delivered from the misery of this world by an early (violent) death; or the patient, without the slightest ground for any such fear, imagines that there is now left to him no possible means of existence, and that soon he will perish of hunger and misery, &c. These ideas, more or less obscure, not unfrequently discover themselves in hallucinations, in which the patient is directly commanded to kill, it may be children or wife; and falling under nearly the same category, are those hallucinations of hearing which partake of religious fanaticism (voice of God or of angels), in which the patient hears the command to go and follow the example of Abraham, and such like. Such acts spring from vague ideas of the necessity of sacrificing some person, other than but closely connected with the patient, in expiation of some terrible but imaginary crime; while in other cases the patient, regarding himself as a felon shunned by all, commits some dreadful deed in order to draw down upon himself the well-deserved punishment of death.

In regard to a great many of these cases . . . there is a most important and characteristic circumstance which we have already adverted to in speaking of suicide, viz., the freeing of the patient from his painful emotions and frightful thoughts by the fact that the deed committed has become objective to him; the ease and calm which the patient gains by the manifestation of his disposition, by the accomplishment of the deed—a circumstance which gives to these acts what has been termed a critical significance. . . . There may be . . . various modifications of such mental disburdening; something similar is frequently observed after the actual accomplishment of deeds of murder depending on melancholic motives. . . .

We frequently see in subjects who, up to that moment, have been in the actual, or at least apparent, enjoyment of perfect health, just as in some of those cases in which there is developed a suicidal tendency, attacks of most violent anxiety with obscuring of consciousness suddenly show themselves, accompanied with frightful hallucinations, during which the patient, in the blindness of his fury, seeks to massacre and slay all who come in his way. These cases, which, judged by their symptoms, appertain more, it is true, to mania, but which, in their psychological relations, represent violent fits of melancholic anxiety, and especially morbid negative emotions, possess, in their want of any actual moral cause, a great analogy to those sudden fits of profound anxiety and severe mental suffering which have sometimes been witnessed as precursors of *epileptic* attacks.

Almost as obscure, in so far as the motives which dictate them are concerned, and yet of the greatest importance in a medico-legal point of view, are those cases where individuals hitherto perfectly sane, and in the full possession of their intellects, are suddenly, and without any assignable cause, seized with the most anxious and painful emotions, and with a homicidal impulse as inexplicable to themselves as to others. In such cases there are two categories into which they must be carefully arranged and distinguished.

Under the first fall those cases in which those homicidal impulses, suddenly and without external motive, arise in persons who have been hitherto of a lively, joyous, and loving disposition, and incessantly intrude themselves upon their thoughts. Most generally, there arises a profound and mournful division of the consciousness, an internal struggle and storm of the most painful nature with these new and fearful ideas, against which the whole former contents of the *I* resist with all their power, which of course varies in different individuals. Frequently, during the combat, the individual is only able to prevent the total discomfiture and defeat of the *I* by retiring from the struggle and betaking himself to a solitary neighbourhood where the impulse which thus besets him no longer finds an object. Then, after a certain time, these thoughts may again disappear as quickly as they sprang into existence, and the individual is again as he used to be. He scarcely knows how he fell into this painful, terrible dream, and with a feeling of intense relief he breathes again with the knowledge that it has terminated so happily. At other times, however—and fortunately this is rarer—the *I* is compelled to succumb, and the unfortunate one perpetrates the deed, and that too without affording him any advantage, with the certain prospect of a life of shame and misery—indeed, with the certain expectation of the disgraceful death which the last penalty of the law inflicts. This, however, appears to him as a relief, and an actual benefit, as compared with the perpetual anxiety and tormenting struggle in his soul, which he feels he must end at any cost. . . .

As to these sanguinary impulses, the production of ideas according to the law of contrast is, it is true, almost the only point of connection between them and the normal phenomena of mental life; although there exists a very great difference between the simple fact, that in the fortunate, ideas of want and misery may easily arise—in the lover, ideas of faithlessness—and in him who stands on the brink of a precipice, ideas of a headlong plunge may be suggested, and the actual fulfilment of those ideas which lead to actions, and continually and persistently urge towards their outward expression.

Somewhat more distinct in their psychological motives are those cases which come under the second category, in which such impulses originate in those who have been long overwhelmed with grief, concentrated in self, and have become actual misanthropes. The more an individual gives himself over to habitual morbid brooding upon his own condition, with a negative disposition of the feelings, the more does he retire upon himself, and withdraw from that interchange of friendly and benevolent sentiments which knit man to man; and gradually he arrives at that point where he feels himself excluded from all intercourse with his fellows, and all that interests mankind at large. In such cases we often see developed a feeling of bitter animosity towards the world, which becomes to such individuals perfectly hateful, gloomy, and fearful; and there frequently arise impulses to commit these indeterminate acts, by which the individual thinks to repay the world, in some splendid crime, for all these griefs and imaginary evils, as well as all those painful impressions, the cause of which he is ever seeking, not in himself, but in the outer world. At times, the persons who are most frequently with the patient draw upon themselves his most intense hatred, and become the victims of these impulses which the patient suddenly discovers. More frequently, however, it is neutral persons whom he attacks, as if the feeling of hostility which animates him recognised in them representatives of a race which he detests. Frequently it is the innocent play of a child which irritates him, or the beauty of a woman which incites in him this murderous disposition. . . .

Closely related to those impulses which have just been examined, stand those morbid inclinations which we see also discovered by melancholics, which impel them to the destruction of inanimate objects, and which may be directed against anything or everything that surrounds the patient. Thus, there are some who have a constant desire to tear their clothes and beds, to make *charpie* of them, &c. Most interesting, however, are those cases in which the deed consists of fire-raising, which has been erected into a special monomania, and described under the name of Pyromania—a classification purely artificial, but which possesses at least the advantage of previously settling the object of discussion.

If from the observations which have been published upon this subject we exclude all those cases where egotistical motives have evidently guided the hand of the incendiary, there still remains a certain number in which this crime of arson has been committed by patients labouring under a well-marked melancholia (particularly of nostalgia passing into mania)—a state which is often accompanied by important derangements in the general health, and frequently in the sexual organs. The morbid impulse developes itself precisely in the same manner as does the homicidal impulse which we have just been studying. The feeling of mental anxiety and the general disturbance which arises from the morbid condition of the faculties do not, as has been said (Masius), impel the individual to seek to stifle this anxiety by the sight of a great flame, but merely to relieve by an outward act, however negative and destructive in character, the profound discord and uneasiness which rules within, and thereby to obtain peace and tranquility. The particular direction which this morbid impulse takes, viz. incendiarism, may arise from the fact that to those persons in whom this tendency has been most accurately observed—namely, young people, particularly young maid-servants—fire, with which they in the performance of their duties have much to do, is always ready at hand, and presents itself as the readiest means by which they can satisfy the morbid craving which torments them—a means which is easily employed, and which requires neither great energy of action nor violent determination to make use of.[29]

[29] W. Griesinger, *Mental Pathology and Therapeutics,* from the 2nd German ed., C. L. Robertson and J. Rutherford, trans. (London: The New Sydenham Society, 1867), pp. 261 ff.

Maudsley (1867, 1883)

An early idea, that children were angels and were degraded by life, did not appeal to Maudsley. (He differed from St. Hilary of Poitiers, who, fearing that his daughter might be defiled when she became pubescent, prayed that she might die, which she did.) Maudsley regarded man as basically vile, but capable of improvement by education.

To talk about the purity and innocency of a child's mind is a part of that poetical idealism and willing hypocrisy by which man ignores realities and delights to walk in a vain show. The purity and innocence of the child's mind, in so far as they exist, testify to the absence of mind: and the impulses which actually move it are the selfish impulse of passion. . . . By nature sinful above everything, and desperately wicked, man acquires a knowledge of good through evil; his passions are refined and developed through wider considerations of interest and foresight; the history of mental development begins with the lowest passions, which circulate as an undercurrent in every life, and frequently come to the surface in a very turbulent way in many lives. . . .

When insanity is met with in the young child, we observe what we do in the adult under the same circumstances—passion in all its naked deformity and in all its exaggerated exhibition. The instincts, appetites, or passions, call them as we may, manifest themselves in unblushing, extreme, and perverted action; the veil of any control which discipline may have fashioned is rent; the child is as the animal, and reveals its animal nature with as little shamefacedness as the monkey indulges its passions in the face of all the world. As in the child of three or four years old there is as a rule only the instinct of gratifying itself, involved in which is the effort to reject or destroy what is not agreeable, its disease, if it become insane, will be exhibited in a perverse and unceasing appropriation of whatever it sees, and in destructive attacks upon whatever it can destory. Refuse it what it grasps at, and it will scream, bite, and kick with a frantic energy: give it the object which it is striving for, and it will smash it if it can: it is a destructive little machine which, being out of order, lays hold of what is suitable and what is unsuitable, and subjects both alike to its desperate action. . . .

The most striking manifestation of the destructive impulse which sometimes reaches such an extreme degree in the madness of childhood is afforded by the instance of homicidal impulse.[30]

Maudsley also showed that the psychopathology of nations resembled that of individuals.

The study of the progress or regress of the human mind, as exhibited in *history*, most difficult as the task is, cannot be neglected by one who wishes to be thoroughly equipped for the arduous work of constructing a positive mental

[30] H. Maudsley, *The Physiology and Pathology of the Mind* (New York: D. Appleton and Co., 1867), pp. 282–283.

science. The unhappy tendencies which lead to individual error and degeneration are those which on a national scale conduct peoples to destruction; and the *nisus* of an epoch is summed up in the biography of its great man. Freed from the many disturbing conditions which interfere so much with his observation of the individual, the philosopher may perhaps in history discover the laws of human progress in their generality and simplicity, as Newton discovered in the motions of the heavenly bodies the law which he would in vain have looked for had he watched the fall of every apple in Europe.[31]

Experience proves that the customs and religions of different nations differ most widely; what one nation views as crime, another praises as virtue; what one nation glorifies in as a legitimate pleasure, another reprobates as a shameful vice: there is scarcely a single crime or vice that has not been exalted into a religious observance by one nation or other at one period or other of the world's history. How much, then, is the moral feeling or conscience dependent upon the due educational development of the mind![32]

Maudsley made a great contribution—now almost totally ignored—when he pointed out that criminal tendencies may be the result and the sole remaining residue of a psychotic attack.

The next examples of moral degeneracy to claim notice are those that are met with often at the commencement of mental alienation, before the person is so far deranged as to be deemed positively insane. Almost every kind of mental disorder begins with a moral alienation, not very marked perhaps at the outset, but so thorough after a time in some cases that a person may seem the opposite of what he was in feeling and conduct. Then the hidden potentialities of his nature reveal themselves in a sad and startling development. In place of diffidence and self-restraint we see exhibited a bold and presumptuous address; in place of refined manners and modest conversation, coarse behaviour and indelicate allusions; in place of chaste and decent conduct, indecency and even open lasciviousness; in place of prudence in business, foolhardiness in speculation; in place of candour and honourable dealing, duplicity, guile, and even vicious and criminal tendencies:—these are the transformations that are witnessed in different cases. Moreover, this moral alienation, which is manifest before there is positive intellectual derangement, accompanies the latter throughout its course, and may last for a while after all disorder of intelligence has gone; it is the truer and deeper derangement, being a derangement of character; and therefore it is notoriously not safe to count the recovery of a person sure and stable until he has returned to the sentiments and affections of his natural character.

Here then we perceive plainly that when the mind undergoes degeneration the moral feeling is the first to show it, as it is the last to be restored when the disorder passes away.[33]

[31] Ibid., p. 28.
[32] Ibid., p. 138.
[33] H. Maudsley, *Body and Will* (London: Kegan, Paul, Trench and Co., 1883), pp. 265–266.

ANXIETY

Anxiety is mentioned as a symptom by medical writers of every century since Hippocrates. The synonymous words *inquietude*, often used in the Latin (*inquietudo*), and the medieval English *angor* are commonly encountered. Later authors used the word *uneasiness*. For the most part early writers regarded anxiety as a primary manifestation of depression.

Arnold (1782)

Thomas Arnold quoted a long list of physicians from Hippocrates to those of his own time, who recognized persistent fear, anguish, and distress as a part of melancholia. He emphasized the impossibility of distracting patients' minds from depressive anxiety, which he called "habitual," and stressed its delusional nature.

Fear, anxiety, and conceits, are such as best indicate an irrational and insane *imbecility of mind.*[34]

Locke (1690)

A broader approach to the problem of anxiety was actually begun by Locke and later taken up by the psychiatrist Battie. According to their view any discomfort or want is anxiety.

What is it that determines the will in regard to our actions? And that, upon second thoughts, I am apt to imagine is not, as is generally supposed, the greater good in view: but some (and for the most part the most pressing) uneasiness a man is at present under. This is that which successively determines the will, and sets us upon those actions we perform. This uneasiness we may call, as it is, desire; which is an uneasiness of the mind for want of some absent good. All pain of the body, of what sort soever, and disquiet of the mind is uneasiness. . . .

The greatest present uneasiness is the spur of action that is constantly felt, and for the most part, determines the will in its choice of the next action.[35]

Battie (1758)

Battie not only adapted Locke's views for use in psychiatry but also generalized the occurrence of the symptom, denying that it was specific for madness. In addition he expressed the concept of anxiety in terms of a hyperalert state, as do some neurophysiologists today.

[34] T. Arnold, *Observations on the Nature, Kinds, Causes and Prevention of Insanity, Lunacy, or Madness* (Leicester: G. Ireland for G. Robinson and T. Cadell, 1782), Vol. 1, p. 221.

[35] J. Locke, *An Essay concerning Human Understanding* (19th ed., London: T. Longman and others, 1793). Vol. 1, pp. 237–238, 244.

First then, though too great and too lively a perception of objects that really exist creates an uneasiness not felt by the generality of men, and therefore discovers a praeternatural state in the instruments of Sensation, and tho' such uneasiness frequently accompanies Madness, and is therefore sometimes mistaken for it; nevertheless Anxiety is no more essentially annexed to Madness, so as to make part of our complex idea, than Fever, Head-ach, Gout, or Leprosy. Witness the many instances of happy Mad-men, who are perfectly easy under what is esteemed by every one but themselves the greatest misfortune human nature is liable to.[36]

For uneasiness is so interwoven in the very frame of mortals, that even the greatest present satisfaction implies the removing or stifling the greatest uneasiness which before disquieted. And a sense of future pleasure, as it excites desire, in that very desire implies a present uneasiness adequate to the supposed enjoyment of the pleasure in expectation. By which present uneasiness, according to Mr. *Locke's* just observation, the will is determined.

However paradoxical therefore it may seem, nothing is more true than that Anxiety, a real evil, is nevertheless productive of real good; and, tho' seemingly disagreeable to Nature, is absolutely necessary to our preservation, in such a manner, that without its severe but useful admonitions the several species of animals would speedily be destroyed.

For first, are not hunger and thirst very salutary Anxieties?[37]

There follows an eight-page chapter entitled "The Causes and Effects of Anxiety and Insensibility, Two species of Sensation disordered tho' not delusive." Battie also indicated that anxiety might precede madness as well as accompany it.

Anxiety frequently precedes madness like its cause or accompanies it like its symptom.[38]

Mead (1755)

The idea that normal feelings, if too long maintained, might produce insanity in susceptible persons, is an ancient one. Richard Mead believed that anxiety might lead to melancholia, as did many others before him, but he emphasized individual susceptibility as a main factor.

And it may not be amiss to observe, that inordinate affections, dwelling long on the mind, frequently become tedious diseases according to their respective natures. So anxiety, despair, and grief cause melancholy; and anger ends in fury and madness. But the passions do not act with equal force on all individuals: Their effect varies according to the diversity of constitutions both of mind and

[36] W. Battie, *A Treatise on Madness* (London: J. Whiston and B. White, 1758), pp. 4–5.
[37] Ibid., pp. 27–28.
[38] Ibid., p. 89.

body; and even in the same individual, the disturbances, which they raise, are different at different times. So thoroughly incomprehensible is the construction of our fabric.[39]

Smith (1768)

Smith was vaguely modern when he hinted that anxiety was the result of a threat to the soul. (He thought that the threat arose from a blockage of the flow of animal spirits, which is of course nonsense, but the world knew nothing of neurohumors then).

[In the absence of unpleasant stimuli] the soul receives no disagreeable sensations; believes its tabernacle in safety, and therefore is at ease.[40]

Crichton (1798)

Crichton emphasized that psychiatric symptoms related to fear and apprehension were always anticipatory and hence involved a component of imagination.

Dejection of mind, and melancholy, beget fear and apprehension, and the emotion of these passions being associated with horrid thoughts, the fancy is crowded with pictures of impending danger, for the feelings he experiences are exactly similar to those he has formerly felt from fear or terror.[41]

The painful emotions of apprehension, fear, and dread are never excited in the human beast but through the medium of foresight; for, although they may arise from present calamities, as well as from past events, yet it is not the uneasiness which the calamity itself occasions that we call fear, but that which arises from what we think will follow.

The predisposing cause of fear is to be sought for in the general interest which we take in every thing that regards our own existence; like most of our passions, it may be considered as a modification of self-love: the number of our fears is increased by our experience, and by analogy; and, in this way, knowledge and reason become, at times, the [enemies].[42]

[39] R. Mead, *Medical Precepts and Cautions,* T. Stack, trans. (London: J. Brindley, 1755), p. 271. Mead's influence was unexpectedly wide and touched Mesmer, among others. Mesmer's inaugural dissertation, published after he completed his studies at the Vienna medical school in 1766, was in large part a plagiarism of one of Mead's writings. (See F. A. Pattie, "Mesmer's medical dissertation and its debt to Mead's *De Imperio Solis ac Lunae,*" *Journal of the History of Medicine and Allied Sciences,* 1956, *11,* 275–287.)

[40] W. A. Smith, *A Dissertation upon Nerves* (London: W. Owen, 1768), p. 45. Smith's book is also interesting in that it presents a variant of the triple-soul notion that has dominated one type of psychology since Plato's time. Smith held that the soul has three aspects: vegetable, animal, and spiritual.

[41] A. Crichton, *An Inquiry into the Nature and Origin of Mental Derangement* (London: T. Cadell, Junior, and W. Davies, 1798), Vol. 1, p. 210.

[42] Ibid., Vol. 2, p. 251.

It [anxiety] often also arises in men who have been engaged in an active and lucrative business, and who injudiciously retire from it; for such people, from the nature of their education, having but few resources within themselves, continue to be much occupied about their worldly affairs; and as the constant spending of money is to them the source of many painful thoughts, and, also, as they are deprived of the pleasure they formerly received from the profits of their profession, so this kind of melancholy dread, or apprehension, is very apt to arise in their minds.

A person of a very timorous disposition is almost incessantly exposed to many unavoidable causes of pain; solitude, the darkness of the night, a long journey which must be executed, the common rivalship and enmity of mankind, the causes of anxiety peculiar to the various pursuits of life, are all rich sources of constant apprehension, and hence such people are very apt, at a certain period of their lives, to sink into a state of settled melancholy.[43]

Mayo (1839)

May had the idea that although anxiety might lead to serious mental disorders, it was less potent in this respect than some other feelings.

This condition of the mind is indeed so full of pain, and tends also so strongly to detain it in a single channel of thought, that it may at first sight appear to claim equal importance with regret, despondency, and disappointment. Experience, however, has not authorised me to give it this position, and the conclusions of experience are comfortable to the philosophy of the subject. For the operations of fear are deficient in regard to one condition, which adds powerfully to the influence of regret, despondency, and disappointment. The objects of fear possess nothing attractive; nothing that can keep our associations enthralled, except that which would *repel* us, but for its importance.[44]

Guislain (1852)

Guislain insisted that mental anguish is the basic symptom of mental disease, even when the outward manifestations are those of gaiety.

To suffer and to complain, these are the primordial symptoms of mental disease. A *feeling* of oppression is characteristic of mental pain, a *sensation* of discomfort characterizes physical pain.[45]

These primitive, not quite abortive attempts to relate anxiety to events affecting whatever inner being was then in fashion ignored what every clinician knew, i.e.,

[43] Ibid., Vol. 2, pp. 274–275.
[44] T. Mayo, *Elements of the Pathology of the Human Mind* (Philadelphia: A. Waldie, 1839), p. 9.
[45] J. Guislain, *Leçons orales sur les phrénopathies; ou traité théorique et pratique des maladies mentales* (Gand: L. Hebbelynck; Paris: J. B. Baillière; Bonn: A. Marcus, 1852), p. 20.

that dreadful anxiety was a main feature of severe depression. Griesinger decisively brought the two divergent views together. He was the first to recognize that anxiety usually accompanies all psychotic states, not depression alone. Moreover, he related this anxiety to the ego which was the center of his psychology, both normal and abnormal (see page 46). These ideas were set forth in his first edition (1845) and repeated in subsequent editions during the more than fifty years that his book remained the standard text for German-speaking psychiatrists. Although J was translated into English and French, outside the German-speaking world it was respected only for its clinical perceptiveness and not for its ingenious development of ego psychology as an aspect of psychiatry. Austro-German medical students continued to study Griesinger, however, until the end of the nineteenth century when Krafft-Ebing came to rival him, and then both were supplanted by Kraepelin. Not surprisingly the views of some of these former students, which later came to be widely accepted, appear to have grown out of Griesinger's of 1845.

About mid-century physicians began to note that anxiety might be a main symptom in persons who had no obvious psychiatric illness but were merely reacting to some current psychologic stress. This became especially apparent during the War between the States when a great body of medical data was accumulated on the physical and mental conditions of the young men of the north. According to Baxter,[46] in two years the Boards of Enrollment examined 1,002,070 men (fifty percent of them draftees) and rejected 304,508 of them.

A board in Kentucky reported that "anxiety and fear have been the most prolific causes of disease." From Massachusetts came: "The most remarkable prevalent disability among us was feebleness of constitution. By this I understand permanent disability, whether congenital or induced by manner of living. The ratio of discharges for this disability was 105 per thousand. . . . The New Englander is a restless and excitable being, ever on the drive! The speed of the locomotive and the electric telegraph hardly satisfies him." Vermont contributed: "Heart disease is frequently feigned, and the attempt made to deceive the surgeon by inducing functional derangement of that organ by the excessive use of tobacco and whiskey . . . Of course this produces exaggerated action and fluttering of the heart, which is increased by the exercise in the course of the examination." From other parts of the country came related comments: "Men claiming exemption from heart-disease as their chief ground were mostly suffering from functional derangement. Hysteria simulates all diseases; the heart simulates almost all the symptoms of organic disease. Such cases might be termed 'hysteria of the heart.' The American mode of living deteriorates us physically. . . . Americans indulge in every luxury. Eating destroys more of our people than drinking. Unceasing mental activity generally aids our excessive feeding in prostrating mind and body."

[46] See J. H. Baxter, *On Statistics, Medical and Anthropological, of the Provost-Marshal-General's Bureau Derived from Records of the Examination for Military Service in the Armies of the United States during the Late War of the Rebellion, of over a Million Recruits, Drafted Men, Substitutes and Enrolled Men* (Washington: Government Printing Office, 1875).

The nineteenth century saw an increasing interest in anxiety which was particularly pronounced in philosophic and purely literary writings, such as those of Heidigger and Kafka. So widespread seems the preoccupation with pangs of *angst* that one present-day critic has characterized such nineteenth-century German writings as deriving from "angst in the pangst." The development of the concept of neurasthenia (page 288) stimulated medical interest in anxiety and ultimately led to the new diagnosis of anxiety neurosis (page 289).

Interest in psychosomatic medicine also grew, but more as a systematized superstition than as a body of scientific data. Probably the first formal text on psychosomatic relations was F. C. G. Schneidemantel's *Die Leidenschäften als Heilmittel* (1787), which was followed by a hundred years of highly stereotyped psychosomatic medicine. The physiologic phenomena associated with the feeling of anxiety have actually been known for centuries. The Old Testament mentions cardiac symptoms, and hundreds of authors since have referred to these and other manifestations. By the end of the nineteenth century many authors applied the then new physiologic techniques to the study of anxiety. Binet was among the most famous of these men.

Binet (1897)

Mr. X . . . who was in charge of the supervision of discipline, was subjected to the plethysmographic study, on the day when the student was to come to the laboratory. While the tracing was being made, the bell was heard to sound at the door. Without doubt, it is the student! The professor did not show any external sign of emotion; he remained silent; but he had thoughts of the reproaches to be uttered, he felt stirred up, he experienced a strong feeling of constriction in the epigastrium. The three symptoms . . . are here joined in the large picture: marked vasoconstriction, without pulsations (the pulse as it reappeared lost its dichrotism); enormous increase in heart rate, which changed from 70 beats to 95, acceleration of respiration with marked increase in amplitude, in a word typical emotional respiration. [The appended pulse wave and respiration tracing bears the word "angoisse."] [47]

[47] A. Binet and J. Courtier, "Influence de la vie émotionnelle sur le coeur, la respiration, et la circulation capillaire," *L'Année psychologique*, 1897, *3*, 76.

PART **II**

THE SYNDROMES

Early Symptoms;
Eccentricity

7

The recognition of syndromes is a normal and continuous process among physicians who, from their broad experience, group together patients with clinically similar disorders. However not all syndromes are sufficiently distinctive in their early stages to be recognized. Since this is especially true in psychiatry, a number of the early writers discussed the onset of madness in general terms.

Cox (1813)

The approach of insanity is generally very gradual, at first only observable in a change of habits, disposition, taste, and pursuits, generally succeeded by hurried movements, a rapid succession of ideas, high spirits, acute sensibility, mental irritation, unusual suspicion, listening to fancied whispers or obscure noises, pride, impatience of control, peevishness, restlessness, inordiante mirth or depression, (according to the temperament) occasional abstraction: dreams of the, most grotesque and unnatural description deprive the patient of refreshing slumbers, and frequently whole nights in succession are passed without sleep; in some individuals, the mind is occupied by one impression, in others, agitated by an endless variety, sometimes the judgment is perverted, at others the imagination excited: the body also exhibits various accompanying peculiarities: the face is flushed or pallid, the eyes are prominent and animated, or sunk in the orbit and dull; frequently the features are sharpened, so as to render the expression unnatural: in general, the muscular powers are increased, as is the capability of enduring cold, hunger, fatigue, and long watching; at the same time the natural excretions, and particularly the alvine, become interrupted. The utmost irregularity of appetite and passions usually takes place, and this more or less increases till the disease is established, and there is an absolute necessity for restraining the patient.

Among the varieties of maniacs met with in medical practice there is one which, though by no means rare, has been little noticed by writers on this subject: I refer to those cases in which the individuals perform most of the common duties of life with propriety, and some of them, indeed, with scrupulous exactness, who exhibit no strongly marked features of either temperament, no traits of superior or defective mental endowment, but yet take violent antipathies, harbour unjust suspicions, indulge strong propensities, affect singularity in dress, gait, and phraseology; are proud, conceited and ostentatious; easily excited and with difficulty appeased; dead to sensibility, delicacy and refinement; obstinately riveted to the most absurd opinions; prone to controversy and yet incapable of reasoning; always the hero of their own tale; using hyperbolic high-flown language to express the most simple ideas, accompanied by unnatural gesticulation, inordinate action, and frequently by the most alarming expression of countenance. On some occasions they suspect sinister intentions on the most trivial grounds, on others are a prey to fear and dread from the most ridiculous and imaginary sources; now embracing every opportunity of exhibiting romantic courage and feats of hardihood, then indulging themselves in all manner of excesses.

Persons of this description, to the casual observer, might appear actuated by a bad heart, but the experienced physician knows it is the head which is defective.[1]

Conolly (1830)

Conolly's contribution to the subject revealed him as a man of broad interests with understanding of and sympathy for the human spirit. It is noteworthy that these traits gave him an outstanding ability to evaluate mental aberration but not the means of treating it.

A very eccentric man, therefore, is always a near neighbour to the madman.

Eccentricity may be divided into two species: one, in which the departure from custom is plainly repugnant to reason; the other, in which it is apparently reasonable. . . .

All eccentricity, then, is a departure from sound judgment; it may be a very slight departure, but still it is a departure. It may still be contended, that the man whom I call eccentric, is in fact acting contrary to the dictates of sound judgment. The first person who used an umbrella in London was followed about the streets by the crowd: he departed from the custom of the people. It may be asked if *he* was eccentric, and consequently if his carrying an umbrella was a departure from reason? The answer is, no. The practice was new, and excited surprise: but so plainly reasonable that every body fell into it: insomuch that if a man were now to walk in the rain *without* an umbrella,

[1] J. M. Cox, *Practical Observations on Insanity* (Philadelphia: T. Dobson, 1813), pp. 13–15.

we should justly consider such eccentricity, if voluntary, a proof of a departure from sound judgment. In both cases, then, the general custom of mankind is the rule, the departure from which constitutes eccentricity.[2]

Few men are so happily constituted as not to find, that the imagination is exposed to frequent temporary impairment, when any passion is called into vehement action. Resentment excites the imagination to dress detested objects or persons in odious and extravagant colours: their faults are magnified; and even their good actions are looked upon as faults in disguise. The affections, on the other hand, array every beloved object in the colours of faultless beauty, and the very errors of those we admire seem but the excesses of an amiable and sensitive mind. To feelings so opposite, and to both in quick succession, the imagination lends its power. Friendship which seems as if it would last for ever, is "within an hour" succeeded by coldness, derision, aversion, hatred; and the very circumstances which were the aliment of pleasure and attachment, become the food of disgust. In all these cases, the imagination, roused by an ungoverned or an unhappy passion, is in diseased excess; and the power of exercising just comparison is so nearly destroyed, that we are actually on the limits of insanity, on the subject which engrosses us.—But we are often rather unwilling than unable to make just comparisons, and are conscious of the injustice even of those feelings in which we indulge. It is only when the power of comparing is actually *lost*, that the insanity declares itself, and that the disappointment of a lover, or the fancied wrongs of a neglected favourite, seek gratification or redress in crime.

The Imagination is materially concerned in effecting what is called the Association of Ideas. Its activity causes sounds and images to be brought up in quick succession, whenever any sound or image happens to be present which has the slightest connexion with others; and, where the activity is excessive, matter of association is of course never wanting. It is to this that we are indebted for most of the charm of conversation, as distinguished from prosing; when every subject in turn gains a little attention, and yields to another, which some word or observation of one of the interlocutors recalls to the mind of another. The conversation of an individual commonly shows how far the faculty of association is exercised. One man adheres to his subject, enters fully into detail, supposes his hearers as destitute of imagination as himself, and is never content to make a brief allusion, but must describe every thing; this man belongs to the fearful family of prosers. But there are other branches of the family, in whom the imagination is too active and vagrant: these fly from subject to subject, still contriving "in one weak, washy, everlasting stream," to sustain continuousness of talk; and inflict as much suffering on the hearer, as the heavier plodder who completely exhausts one topic before he removes his sluggish faculties to another. Offenders of this kind would be

[2] J. Conolly, *An Inquiry concerning the Indications of Insanity* (London: J. Taylor, 1830), pp. 136–137.

much surprised to learn, that they really deflect a little from sound mind towards insantiy: but the lunatic asylum shows us the excess of the faults of both, in the wretched man whose dead imagination offers no image to relieve him from the intolerable pressure of one insane idea; and in the happier lunatic, whose words flow on, through every possible variety of subjects, mingling the past and present, without order, system, or sense, from morning until night.

There is in many persons a visible want of imagination, which entails no serious consequences. It deprives them of the power of deriving pleasure from the works of writers of imagination, or of succeeding in any pursuit requiring the exercise of fancy; but as they are generally quite unable to comprehend the pleasures which they are denied, they suffer nothing from their loss. I have sometimes been amused to observe the difficulty with which such persons get through the reading of an ordinary letter, written in a somewhat difficult hand: in their minds, no word, or part of a sentence, seems to suggest the possible nature of those which immediately succeed, and to decypher is to them a task of more difficulty than it would be to others to translate. They unriddle each word by itself, like an hieroglyphic character; not being supplied with instantaneous conjectures concerning the meaning of what follows. A more serious disadvantage arising from the want of imagination is, that it endangers too great an attachment of the attention to one pursuit, or to one idea, which may become a mental disease.[3]

Opposed to this imbecile condition of mind is that of increased susceptibility, which in some is the result of original organization, and in others produced by various accidental causes. The sensations are too acute; the attention vivid, but hurried; the memory and imagination are too active; the affections and passions are intense; and the judgment more rapidly than accurately exercised. Alive to every mental impression, every day brings a change of mental character, and the very countenance varies so much at different times as hardly to appear the same. These are the persons who are distinguished by their irritability. . . .

Like other mental irregularities, this excitement, or this erythismal state, to use a word familiar to medical readers, is a departure from sound mind; and the question of a person's sanity who is so affected, is also a question which turns wholly on the degree of such departure. Is it, in any particular case, so great as to prevent the exercise of just comparisons, and to lead to irrational actions? If it is, the individual is, with respect to those actions, insane. But are the actions merely impetuous follies? or are they dangerous? The propriety of interference depends wholly upon the answer to be given to *these* questions. The direction of such a mind is important, for every stimulus acts upon it, every passion excites it, and whilst in one they lead to generosity and valour, in another they urge to wild ferocity and crime. In the same person, at

[3] Ibid., pp. 150–153.

different periods, or in different circumstances, is thus produced conduct apparently inconsistent, but naturally arising out of a general susceptibility to every feeling. Such individuals are a constant source of uneasiness to those who regard them, and an enigma to those who only see the proofs of their fickleness. They are zealous friends, or even indiscreet, but not capable of steady attachment: and they are revengeful and unscrupulous in their animosities. This inconstancy of character may play within an extensive range without insanity; but the separate actions, by which it is evinced, approach to what is irrational; and the wavering and inconstant mind itself is certainly allied to that which is insane. In its slightest form, and that which is the least possible deviation from sound mind, it has often been described as the female character, "varium et mutabile semper:"

"And variable as the shade,
By the light quivering aspen made;"

and the minds of some women present the most striking illustrations of it. Yet it is not peculiar to the sex. It is seen in the character of many men who are eager in every pursuit, but attached to none; acting under every impulse, and to none constant; rambling from study to study, until their minds resemble those once unvalued manuscripts of ancient authors, which fell into the hands of monks; containing, it may be, some valuable matter, but so crossed and scrawled over with fancies and conceits, as to be with much difficulty legible.[4]

It is not only charitable to believe that many inconsistencies and weaknesses, in the characters of those whom we find it difficult wholly to respect notwithstanding they often act so as to excite our admiration, arise rather from this species of want of perfect moral control over themselves, than from any propensity to vice; but it is also probable that such is often the true explanation. All men are more the creatures of circumstance, than those who most value themselves on the equal tenor of their conduct are willing to allow, or even than they suspect; and the circumstances, which exercise an influence over them, are often such as would at the first view seem inadequate to produce the long train of effects to which they really give rise.

A man accustomed to business, and possessed of an active mind, and who has lived amid the excitements of a large city and a numerous acquaintance, if suddenly removed from such a kind of life to a country house, or to a country town, finds that by far the worst part of the change consists in the removal of an excitement, the effects of which were not fully known to him before. Withdrawn in a great degree from external objects, the attention becomes strongly and almost continually directed inwards; a state which has sometimes been considered as affording opportunity for a review of past

[4] Ibid., pp. 174–177.

conduct and the formation of good resolutions, but in which, in reality, the mind, if not wholly occupied concerning the faults of others, generally dwells on its own movements and its own feelings, until the importance of both becomes exceedingly exaggerated. This state proves to many quite unfavourable to the quiet pursuit of science or literature; the imagination has an irregular exercise; and indolence produces self-reproach and despondency. A suspicion begins to be felt that the mind has not only lost its habit of activity, but also its power to undertake any employment demanding perseverance. The want of external excitement comes at last to be made up for by various sources of mental agitation, which are only rendered important by continuance or frequent succession; and it is found with surprize, that the facility once possessed of profiting by short intervals of leisure is supplanted by an inability to do any thing well when there is nothing to be done. In such a situation, the declension of the mind may be observed, from activity to indolence, and from indolence to that state of apathy which is very little removed from a state of sleep. Even a devotion to the common pleasures of sense is better than such a state of absolute indifference; for if even these give no kind of pleasure, whilst all higher pursuits are neglected, there is danger lest a man become of the same opinion as Dr. Darwin's patient, "that all which life affords is a ride out in the morning, and a warm parlour and a pack of cards in the afternoon;" and like him, finding these pleasures not inexhaustible, should shoot himself because he has nothing better to do.

It fortunately happens, that the majority of those who reside in the country are sufficiently occupied in the care and improvement of their property, in active rural sports, or in various social and public duties which furnish some excitement. Those who have not such cares to occupy them, or who have no pleasure in field sports, or who are not in a station calling for active public duties, often exemplify the great dependence of the mind on external circumstances.—The gallant officer becomes distinguished by the oddity of his attire, and the singularity of his manners; the man of fashion becomes the mere terror of trespassers and vagrants; and many, in an attachment to frivolous modes of destroying time, or even to debasing pleasures, fall into errors of conduct from which the stimulus of busy engagements would have preserved them; for no popular opinion is more incorrect, than that which maintains the favourableness of a country life to the cultivation of virtue. . . .[5]

. . . The diversion of social intercourse, which to other men is necessary to prevent mental torpor, becomes to them a source of irritation, by impeding the workings of the imagination: they find, that when alone, all the nobler aspirations of the soul are free, and images of beauty, and virtue, and wisdom, occupy the mind. Society transforms them into a being they despise, deprives them of all their high and valued thoughts; and it afflicts them to feel what

[5] Ibid., pp. 181–184.

slight circumstances, acting on the man without, may affect the man within. But the pleasures of solitude are transient; their train is closed by baseless fancies, by fears undefined, by griefs unexpressed, and black despondency, from which society can alone relieve. We learn, from observing such effects arising from such causes, the advantage of mixed and varied occupations; suited to a being not made solely for contemplation or for action; and we may gather rules from these observations, the application of which to minds in a morbid state is very direct.

But if all outward circumstances could be kept from change, the mind possesses a singular power of re-acting upon itself, of which the proper effect is very serviceable to us; and the loss of which is often a disadvantage. Habit, the influence of which in weakening the impressions made on the senses, or preventing attention to them, has been already noticed, may deaden this effect, even of its own emotions upon the mind.[6]

Ellis (1838)

Ellis was not only a psychiatrist but also a social critic. He emphasized that drugs and adultery were pursuits of the aristocracy. Today, in this country, both are available to all, which may perhaps be taken as a measure of democracy.

___ Intense abstraction of mind may be considered as the first alteration that is observable in the great majority of patients who become insane from moral causes. The ordinary duties of life are either altogether neglected, or only performed upon the pressing solicitation of friends. After this state has continued for a short time, it becomes necessary, if we wish to arrest the attention of the patient, to speak to him loudly and repeatedly; and when at last he seems conscious of what is said, he appears as if just aroused from a dream, and relapses into the same state of forgetfulness, as soon as the sound of the voice has ceased to vibrate in his ears; his whole air and manner evidently indicate that the inner man is dwelling upon a subject far different from that about which he is being addressed. The general desire to please no longer influences the character, and the dejected looks, and the forlorn dress, sufficiently proclaim that the mind is entirely absorbed in its own contemplations.[7]

One of the most frequent modes in which these mental aberrations exhibit themselves, is by inducing a constant feeling of suspicion. The patient continually fancies that every one is combining against his happiness; his most intimate friends and connexions, probably from being more immediately in contact with him, are the most frequently suspected, and are the subjects of

---

[6] Ibid., pp. 186–187.

[7] W. C. Ellis, *A Treatise on the Nature, Symptoms, Causes, and Treatment of Insanity* (London: S. Holdsworth, 1838), pp. 105–106.

his greatest aversion. In these, as in all other instances of mental delusion, every attempt to convince the patients by reasoning of the extravagance of their notions, is worse than useless.[8]

Another very curious and frequent effect produced in the mind by insanity, is the hypochondriacal supposition of the existence of venereal diseases. So strong is this delusion, that in one instance, although there was no possibility of the disease having existed, the patient fancied she had been infected by it in some unaccountable mode, and could not rest satisfied until put under a course of what she imagined to be mercurial medicines. After having taken these for a time, though nothing more than pills made of bread-crumbs, the patient, from the expectation that they were to produce salivation, spat such a quantity of saliva as to require a vessel constantly by her side for that purpose. After this had continued for some time, she imagined that the medicine had produced its effect; she discontinued the bread pills, and the excessive action of the salivary glands ceased.

Another very frequent symptom of insanity is the patients' entertaining very high notions of their own consequence and ability. It would be an endless and useless task to give the history of all the emperors, kings, queens, and nobles that we have had in our *pauper* establishment; even Omnipotence itself has not wanted a representative. . . .

Some persons are constitutionally so depressed and melancholy in their dispositions, that as the mode in which insanity exhibits itself depends very much on the natural character, the unhealthy action of the brain, occasioned only by some trifling circumstance, which to persons of another temperament would almost pass unheeded, in them increases the feelings of gloom and despondency to such an extent as to lead them to the commission of suicide.[9]

Another circumstance of a very painful character is frequently attendant upon insanity, and, as far as I know, no attempt has yet been made to account for it. I am referring to the change which takes place in the affections towards those to whom the patients have formerly been the most attached. This change generally takes place in those cases where the patients themselves are quite unconscious of the existence of any disease, and where it has come on by slow degrees, and is only very partial in its effects. This unconsciousness, I should observe by the way, is by no means universal in insanity; in many cases the patients themselves are perfectly aware that something is wrong.

When the alteration produced by the insanity has by little and little at length become so marked that even the most affectionate feelings can no longer be blind to the painful reality of its existence, those whom the patient has been in the habit of controlling, are obliged, for the safety of himself and

[8] Ibid., p. 110.
[9] Ibid., pp. 114–115.

others, to apply not only moral but bodily restraint, and to remove him from his home. Not being conscious of the necessity of such measures, they appear to him harsh and unjust, and he thinks that they emanate from a change having gradually taken place in the feelings of those about him; and he is ready at once to exclaim, "You have ceased to love me!" As a proof that these feelings of estrangement are thus produced, it is to be observed that they seldom extend to those individuals of the family who have been at a distance, or who are not associated in the mind as having been accessory to the restraint, first in trifling domestic matters, and subsequently in removal from home, and confinement. I think it may generally be taken for granted, that though every other symptom of the disease may appear to be removed, yet, so long as this feeling of dislike continues towards those formerly loved, and who have really acted in an affectionate manner, throughout all the trying scene, to the unfortunate patient, that some lingering trace of diseased action still continues, and the complaint may be expected to return.[10]

Millingen (1847)

Many authors had written about gonadal function as important in the origin of hysteria. Milligen's writings emphasized the role of puberty in all types of mental disorder.

Mental disorders generally become manifest after the age of puberty. At this period of life a general revolution of the whole system takes place. Our existence, which until then might be called *individual*, now becomes *relative*: in childhood and early youth we have especially lived for ourselves; we now, according to the laws of the creation, exist for others. . . . Instinctive impulses associated with this development of nature, now act both upon his corporeal emotions and his mental faculties. Until this most important epoch of his existence, Nature has only been busied in the growth of the individual, in its physical development: all the mental faculties of the child and the youth are exercised for the purpose of preparing both the body and the mind for their future functions. His passions may be vivid and violent, but they are of an ephemeral nature; in short, his thoughts, his pursuits are childish, his notions puerile. There are to be found precocious exceptions to this rule; but it is because these exceptions are more or less deviations from the laws of nature, that they most frequently disappoint expectations of great mental superiority. . . .

At the age of puberty a new order of functions elicits desires and wants until then unfelt. All nature seems to bear a different aspect. Imagination, on Icarian wings, takes a bold flight to unknown regions—the limits of the universe become unbounded. We feel that we are born to a new life; according to our temperament and our susceptibilities, our passions assume a greater or

[10] Ibid., pp. 127–128.

a less influence over our intellectual power; at this stage of our existence, we may say, arises a conflict between the mind and the body; spirit and matter contend for supremacy, and rarely is the antagonism commensurate in the result. We now *feel*, what we had only *heard of*—an evil principle tends to overthrow the structure of a good education. We had previously been groping in darkness, we now seek the light; but unfortunately the sudden refulgence of its unknown radiance dazzles us, instead of guiding our steps in the pursuit of truth and an imaginary happiness, and we are led into errors as perilous as those that had surrounded us in our former mental blindness. We now endeavour to think for ourselves; we become analytic in all our observations, and therefore sceptical. We trust no longer to the scholastic rules impressed upon our rising understanding—rules—axioms, which the dignitaries of science considered sufficient to direct and limit our faith. Alas! the reign of *prestiges* is over; we belong to a neoteric generation, and we *will* think and we will *act* according to the impulse of our nature; and when reposing in the flowery bowers of love and pleasure, we soon forget the classic shades of *Alma Mater*.

But in this ardent anticipation of life, we shortly find that there are obstacles to encounter on which we never calculated: our pride, our vanity, are crushed—our fondest hopes blasted, ere they were well entertained—our expectations are baffled—our strength set at nought by the stronger—our weakness becomes the theme of ridicule amongst creatures weaker than ourselves—the brain that was once puzzled by a problem of Euclid, is now bewildered by contending and conflicting thoughts, until a temporary delirium ensues. Now all the passions of ambition, love, jealousy, hate, revenge, assume a fatal sway. We no longer seek to emulate our playmates . . . the game of life has commenced—the race to fortune and to fame has begun—we seek to satisfy our lust and our love—to gratify our avarice and our thirst of power. . . .

. . . Emancipated from parental restraint or scholastic discipline, according to his temperament will the youth rush into the vortex of life—he will seek to indulge in every pleasure hitherto forbidden or withheld, or, brooding in ascetic moroseness on visions of future distinction, he will seek for power in cloisters or in camps. . . .

Can we then be surprised when we find that it is after this convulsive period of our life that mental aberrations in their various forms are first observed, sometimes ushered in by maniacal violence, at other times preceded by what are called oddities and eccentricities? It is also at this epoch that the results of a good or a deficient education are observed.[11]

If the period of puberty thus operates a painful revolution in the whole organization of man, woman is equally subject to similar laws; and the nubile maid has perhaps still more arduous obstacles to encounter in this climacteric struggle between instinctive inpulses and her duties—a struggle rendered more

[11] J. A. Millingen, *Mind and Matter* (London: H. Hurst, 1847), pp. 39–42.

difficult in the ratio of the compulsory and artificial concentration of all her intuitive emotions, when nature, in her convulsive throes, is compelled to assume the mask of apathetic calmness. In this revolution, the energies of the brain or of the sensorium of woman are less called upon than the sympathetic system of nerves; and hysteria, in its multiplied and anomalous forms, warns us of the rapidity and the exaltation of the progressive development of all the functional organs of her sex.

It is this important era that ushers in the antagonism between our appetites and our desires, and the duties imposed upon us both by the laws of God and man.[12]

Ray (1873)

Isaac Ray, whose perceptive comments on some general aspects of mental disorders have already been cited (see pages 5-8), also made important contributions to the understanding of the marginal states that require a physician's evaluation.

... For months or even years before the first decided and obvious manifestations of disease, the patient may have evinced something unusual in his conduct or conversation, although engaged in his customary duties, and by the world at large regarded as in the full possession of his reason. In some cases the morbid peculiarities may be sufficiently developed to attract the attention of the world; but, not interfering with the performance of the ordinary duties of life, they are looked upon as a part of the natural character, and take the name of insanity only when accompanied by an extra degree of excitement and violence. In cases like these, who will take upon himself to indicate the precise point when disease began? Who will presume to enter that debatable land which lies between the realms of eccentricity and insanity, and assign to each its respective share of the peculiar manifestations?

The large class of periodical and paroxysmal cases present insuperable difficulties to every attempt to bring them under any general rule. The question of their origin is complicated with that of their recovery, and we are under the same kind of embarrassment in deciding upon the former that we experience with regard to the latter.[13]

---

[12] Ibid., p. 44.
[13] I. Ray, *Contributions to Mental Pathology* (Boston: Little, Brown and Co., 1873), p. 76.

Affective Disorders

8

ORIGIN OF THE TERM MANIC-DEPRESSIVE

Mania and the several types of depression comprise the disorders of affect. The earliest medical writings of the Western world, those of Hippocrates and Areteus, refer to the relation between mania and depression, but this connection was not formalized in terminology until the late seventeenth century. The first hint of a formal connection is found in Théophile Bonet's *Sepulchretum sine anatomia practica ex cadaveribus morbo donatis*. The term *melancholiae mania*, i.e. the mania of melancholy, is used in the 1679 edition and again in the *editio altera* of 1700, revised by Johannes and Jacobus Mangetus.[1] In Bonet's *Medicina septentrionalis* published in 1686 the term *maniaco-melancholicus* refers to the disorder discussed under the heading *Melancholie anniversariae in manium degenerantis admiranda species*.[2] Bonet's use of the term manic-depressive is so casual that it implies common usage, but I have not found it in the sources he mentions.

The types of depression discussed below include psychotic depression or melancholia and neurotic depression or hypochondriasis. Also included in this section are the schizo-affective disorders.

MANIA

Mania was not recognized as a distinct clinical entity by all physicians of ancient times. This stems in part from their practice of labeling as *mania* any

---

[1] T. Bonetus, *Sepulchretum sine anatomia practica ex cadaveribus morbo donatis* (Geneva: L. Chouet, 1679), Bk. I, sec. viii, Obs. 1, p. 176; Rev. ed. by J. J. Mangetus (Lugduni: 1700).

[2] T. Bonetus, *Medicina septentrionalis* (Geneva: L. Chouet, 1686), Bk. I, sec. xix, ch. 11, p. 189.

form of madness without fever and without—or even with—the characteristics of melancholia.

Arnold (1806)

Thomas Arnold, in his meticulous review of ancient ideas, expressed the situation very well.

> In giving the appellation of maniacal to the third species of ideal insanity, I only used the privilege of fixing down to one sense, a term which others, and especially, Hippocrates himself, had used in a variety. The term mania, and its derivatives, as employed by the ancients, as I have shown in the body of the work, are of great latitude, and sometimes mean raving madness, sometimes madness in general, sometimes melancholy, and sometimes that kind of madness to which I have confined it by denominating it maniacal insanity. Not to add, that, so loose were the ancients in the application of terms, that in their writings melancholia is sometimes the appellation of actual, and violent, mania, in the sense in which, mania is most commonly understood by the moderns, and sometimes by the ancients.[3]

Hippocrates (5th century B.C.)

Hippocrates never bothered to define mania, evidently believing that his readers or listeners used the word in the same sense. He did, however, consider mania one of the chief forms of mental disorder.

> The diseases of spring are, maniacal, melancholic, and epileptic disorders . . .[4]

Galen and others following Hippocrates stated that there were three forms of soul diseases, i.e., melancholia, phrenitis (which evidently referred to febrile delirium), and mania.

Aretus (2nd century A.D.)

Since clinical psychiatry commenced with Areteus, it is appropriate to record his views on mania.

> The modes of mania are infinite in species, but one alone in genus. For it is altogether a chronic derangement of the mind, without fever. For if fever at any time should come on, it would not owe its peculiarity to the mania, but to some other incident. Thus wine inflames to delirium in drunkenness; and

[3] T. Arnold, *Observations on the Nature, Kinds, Causes, and Prevention of Insanity, Lunacy, or Madness* (2nd ed., London: R. Phillips, 1806), Vol. 1, p. xxi.

[4] *Hippocrates*, W. H. S. Jones, trans. (Cambridge, Mass.: Harvard University Press; London: W. Heinemann, Ltd., 1948), Aphorisms II, 20.

certain edibles, such as mandragora and hyoscyamus, induce madness: but these affections are never called mania; for, springing from a temporary cause, they quickly subside, but madness has something confirmed in it. To this mania there is no resemblance in the dotage which is the calamity of old age, for it is a torpor of the senses, and a stupefaction of the gnostic and intellectual faculties by coldness of the system. . . .

. . . Mania intermits, and with care ceases altogether. And there may be an imperfect intermission, if it take place in mania when the evil is not thoroughly cured by medicine, or is connected with the temperature of the season. For in certain persons who seemed to be freed from the complaint, either the season of spring, or some error in diet, or some incidental heat of passion, has brought on a relapse.

Those prone to the disease, are such as are naturally passionate, irritable, of active habits, of an easy disposition, joyous, puerile; likewise those whose disposition inclines to the opposite condition, namely, such as are sluggish, sorrowful, slow to learn, but patient in labour, and who when they learn anything, soon forget it; those likewise are more prone to melancholy, who have formerly been in a mad condition. But in those periods of life with which much heat and blood are associated, persons are most given to mania, namely, those about puberty, young men, and such as possess general vigour. . . .

And they with whose madness joy is associated, laugh, play, dance night and day, and sometimes go openly to the market crowned, as if victors in some contest of skill; this form is inoffensive to those around. Others have madness attended with anger; and these sometimes rend their clothes and kill their keepers, and lay violent hands upon themselves. This miserable form of disease is not unattended with danger to those around. . . .

If, therefore, the illness be great, they are of a changeable temper, their senses are acute, they are suspicious, irritable without any cause, and unreasonably desponding when the disease tends to gloom. . . .

At the height of the disease they have impure dreams, and irresistible desire of venery, without any shame and restraint as to sexual intercourse; and if roused to anger by admonition or restraint, they become wholly mad. Wherefore they are affected with madness in various shapes; some run along unrestrainedly, and, not knowing how, return again to the same spot; some, after a long time, come back to their relatives; others roar aloud, bewailing themselves as if they had experienced robbery or violence. Some flee the haunts of men, and going to the wilderness, live by themselves.

If they should attain any relaxation of the evil, they become torpid, dull, sorrowful; for having come to a knowledge of the disease they are saddened with their own calamity.[5]

[5] *The Extant Works of Aretaeus, the Cappadocian*, F. Adams, trans. (London: The New Sydenham Society, 1856), pp. 301–304.

Caelius Aurelianus (5th century A.D.)

Caelius Aurelianus appeared unwilling or unable to limit the meaning of mania to hyperactive states.

In the *Phaedrus* Plato declares that there are two kinds of mania, one involving a mental strain that arises from a bodily cause of origin, the other divine or inspired, with Apollo as the source of the inspiration. This latter kind, he says, is now called 'divination,' but in early times was called 'madness'; that is, the Greeks now call it 'prophetic inspiration' (*mantice*), though in remote antiquity it was called 'mania.' Plato goes on to say that another kind of divine mania is sent by Father Bacchus, that still another, called 'erotic inspiration,' is sent by the god of love, and that a fourth kind comes from the Muses and is called 'protreptic inspiration' because it seems to inspire men to song. The Stoics also say that madness is of two kinds, but they hold that one kind consists in lack of wisdom, so that they consider every imprudent person mad; the other kind, they say, involves a loss of reason and a concomitant bodily affection. The school of Empedocles holds that one form of madness consists in a purification of the soul, and the other in an impairment of the reason resulting from a bodily disease or indisposition.

It is this latter form of madness that we shall now consider. The Greeks call it *mania* because it produces great mental anguish (Greek *ania*); or else because there is excessive relaxing of the soul or mind, the Greek word for 'relaxed' or 'loose' being *manos*; or because the disease defiles the patient, the Greek word 'to defile' being *lymaenein*; or because it makes the patient desirous of being alone and in solitude, the Greek word 'to be bereft' and 'to seek solitude' being *monusthae*; or because the disease holds the body tenaciously and is not easily shaken off, the Greek word for 'persistence' being *monia*; or because it makes the patient hard and enduring (Greek *hypomeneticos*).

Mania is an impairment of reason; it is chronic and without fever and in these respects may be distinguished from phrenitis. For mania is not an acute disease, nor is it observed to occur with fever; or, if fever *is* present in a case of mania, the case may be distinguished from phrenitis by considerations of time, for in mania the madness precedes any supervening fever and the patient does not have a small pulse. . . .

Now when the disease of mania emerges into the open, there is impairment of reason unaccompanied by fever; this impairment of reason in some cases is severe, in others mild; it differs in the various cases in its outward form and appearance, though its nature and character are the same. For, when mania lays hold of the mind, it manifests itself now in anger, now in merriment, now in sadness or futility, and now, as some relate, in an overpowering fear of things which are quite harmless. Thus the patient will be afraid of caves or will be obsessed by the fear of falling into a ditch or will dread other things which may for some reason inspire fear. . . .

. . . Apollonius says that melancholy should be considered a form of mania, but we distinguish melancholy from mania. And mania or madness is sometimes continuous and at other times relieved by intervals of remission.[6]

Willis (1680)

Thomas Willis was evidently writing out of his own experience. He described his patients' behavior but did not attempt to define the disorder.

After Melancholy, Madness is next to be treated of, both which are so much akin, that these distempers often change, and pass from one into the other . . .

It is observed in Madmen, that these three things are almost common to all: First, that their phantasies or imaginations are perpetually busied with a storm or impetuous thoughts, so that night and day they are muttering to themselves various things, or declare them by crying out, or by bauling out aloud. Secondly, that their notions or conceptions are either incongruous, or represented to them under a false or erroneous image. Thirdly, to their delirium is most often joyned audaciousness and fury; contrary to melancholicks, who are always infected with fear and sadness.[7]

Boerhaave (1709)

Boerhaave's description of mania is fragmentary and uninspired compared to his words on melancholy. Nevertheless, he was probably the greatest clinician of his time and his ideas were widely accepted.

If Melancholy increases so far, that from the great Motion of the Liquid of the Brain, the Patient be thrown into a wild Fury, it is called *Madness*.

Which differs only in Degree from the sorrowful kind of Melancholy, is its Offspring, produced from the same Causes, and cured almost by the same Remedies.

In which Disease the Patient generally shews a great Strength of the Muscles, as incredible Wakefulness, a bearing to a wonder of Cold and Hunger, frightful Fancies, Endeavours to bite Men like Wolves, or Dogs, etc.[8]

[6] Caelius Aurelianus, *On Acute Diseases and On Chronic Diseases*, I. E. Drabkin, ed. and trans. (Chicago: The University of Chicago Press, n.d.), pp. 535–539.

[7] T. Willis, *Two Discourses concerning the Soul of Brutes, Which Is That of the Vital and Sensitive of Man* [1680], S. Pordage, trans. (London: T. Dring, 1683), p. 201.

[8] *Boerhaave's Aphorisms: Concerning the Knowledge and Cure of Diseases* [1709], trans. from the last Latin ed., Leyden, 1728 (London: A. Bettesworth and C. Hitch, 1735), pp. 323–324.

Arnold (1782)

Arnold reviewed all the definitions offered by his many predecessors and advanced a distillate of them all.

> Mania is a permanent delirium with fury and audacity, but without fever.[9]
>
> But though Insanity has almost universally been divided into these two kinds [mania and melancholia], which have usually been considered as so perfectly distinct, as to derive their origin from very different and distinct causes... yet they are by no means so absolutely, and universally, distinct and unconnected diseases, as so distinct an origin, and such different symptoms, would lead one to imagine; and indeed it has been observed by Aretaeus Cappadox, Alexander Trallianus, Boerhaave, and perhaps one or two more, that the one is frequently generated by the other.... Mania, however, is not always, as Boerhaave, after Aretaeus and Trallian, asserts, "Melancholia moles"—*the offspring of melancholy*; since it often begins originally, without any preceding melancholy; and is on such occasions, sometimes the parent, instead of being the offspring of that species of delirium.
>
> Even during the course of the same illness, it not infrequently happens that mania and melancholy alternate repeatedly with each other; so that each in its turn generates, and is generated; is, in the language of Boerhaave, both parent and offspring![10]

Cullen (1791)

In his section on mania Cullen attempted to explain the flight of ideas seen in this condition as false associations of ideas and false interpretations of memories.

> There is sometimes a false perception or imagination of things present that are not; but this is not a constant, nor even a frequent, attendant of the disease. The false judgement, is of relations long before laid up in the memory. It very often turns upon one single subject: but more commonly the mind rambles from one subject to another with an equally false judgement concerning the most part of them; and as at the same time there is commonly a false association, this increases the confusion of ideas, and therefore the false judgements. What for the most part more especially distinguishes the disease is a hurry of mind, in pursuing any thing like a train of thought, and in running from one train of thought to another. Maniacal persons are in general very irascible; but what more particularly produces their angry emotions, is, that their false judgements lead to some action which is always pushed with impetuosity and violence; when this is interrupted or restrained,

[9] T. Arnold, *Observations on the Nature, Kinds, Causes, and Prevention of Insanity, Lunacy, or Madness* (Leicester: G. Ireland for G. Robinson and T. Cadell, 1782), Vol. 1, p. 30.
[10] Ibid., pp. 56–58.

they break out into violent anger and furious violence against every person near them, and upon every thing that stands in the way of their impetuous will. The false judgement often turns upon a mistaken opinion of some injury supposed to have been formerly received, or now supposed to be intended: and it is remarkable, that such an opinion is often with respect to their former dearest friends and relations; and therefore their resentment and anger are particularly directed towards these. And although this should not be the case, they commonly soon lose that respect and regard which they formerly had for their friends and relations. With all these circumstances, it will be readily perceived, that the disease must be attended very constantly with that incoherent and absurd speech we call raving.[11]

Haslam (1809)

Haslam traced the development of the disorder, the paranoid thinking, the crowding of ideas, and the final confusion. He too emphasized the delusional nature of the manic thinking and the flight of ideas.

On the approach of mania, they first become uneasy, are incapable of confining their attention, and neglect any employment to which they have been accustomed; they get but little sleep, they are loquacious, and disposed to harangue, and decide promptly, and positively upon every subject that may be started. Soon after, they are divested of all restraint in the declaration of their opinions of those, with whom they are acquainted. Their friendships are expressed with fervency and extravagance; their enmities with intolerance and disgust. They now become impatient of contradiction, and scorn reproof. For supposed injuries, they are inclined to quarrel and fight with those about them. They have all the appearance of persons inebriated, and those who are unacquainted with the symptoms of approaching mania, generally suppose them to be in a state of intoxication. At length suspicion creeps in upon the mind, they are aware of plots, which had never been contrived, and detect motives that were never entertained. At last the succession of ideas is too rapid to be examined; the mind becomes crouded with thoughts, and confusion ensues.[12]

Hill (1814)

To Hill dementia was a frequent sequel of mania, in some cases after an intervening phase of depression.

[11] W. Cullen, *First Lines of the Practice of Physic* (Edinburgh: Bell and Bradfute and William Creech; London: G. G. J. & J. Robinsons and J. Murray, 1791), pp. 148–149.
[12] J. Haslam, *Observations on Madness and Melancholy* (London: J. Callow, 1809), pp. 41–43.

Mania or the sthenic form of insanity very frequently terminates in the opposite form or Melancholia. Chronic incurable derangement or fatuity embraces a large proportion of its subjects.[13]

Jacquelin-Dubuisson (1816)

Jacquelin-Dubuisson enlarged upon the clinical manifestations and emphasized that the condition might be solely a disorder of mood, without any disturbance in thinking.

Although mania has generally been considered a general disturbance of the mind, occasionally one observes a few patients who show no disorder of understanding, but they are dominated by a sort of furious instinct, as if their affective faculties alone were damaged.

This kind of mania (sans délire) is quite rare.[14]

Burrows (1828)

Burrows' writings exemplify the continued development of a detailed appreciation of the symptoms of mania. He also noted the occurrence of anxiety.

At first, general high spirits only mark an alteration from the usual character; new ideas, propensities, and passions, are developed; there is an increased rapidity and expression of ideas; every faculty of the mind is exalted, and new ones are elicited never before remarked—perhaps for poetry, music, or declamation—or the arts, as drawing, painting, or mechanics. Every thing is done by impulse, nothing from reflection. Many things are begun and eagerly pursued, but few are finished. Short reveries suddenly interrupted; restlessness and desire of change; quick and hurried utterance; blustering and authoritative, commanding and countermanding in the same breath; passionate and irascible; laughing immoderately, or singing, or shedding tears, and all equally without cause; scheming, ambitious, and extravagant; taking no note of time; negligent of dress and cleanliness; extreme watchfulness (pervigilium) and suspicion; propensity for drinking, or venery; and general agitation.

As the malady advances, the memory experiences sudden lapses, succeeded by vivid thoughts, sometimes pleasing, sometimes horrific; violent sudden laughter, crying, or shrieking; imaginary noises and whisperings; increased suspicion. All ordinary occupations are executed in a more hurried and less perfect manner, or are wholly forgotten; and there is great confusion of mind, though no positive delusion, hallucination, or delirium, be yet declared. . . .

[13] G. N. HIll, An Essay on the Prevention and Cure of Insanity; with Observations on the Rules for the Detection of Pretenders to Madness (London: J. and J. Haddock, 1814), p. 85.
[14] J. R. Jacquelin-Dubuisson, Des Vésanies, ou maladies mentales (Paris: Pauteur, 1816), p. 176.

The precursory symptoms described may run on for weeks or months before mania explodes; but it occasionally happens suddenly, and sometimes is a rapid change from melancholia. The active stage exhibits all the incipient symptoms, both mental and physical, but much heightened.

The *mental* phenomena present a greater incoherency of ideas and speech; some positive delusion exists; the patient is very loquacious or vociferous, raving incessantly, or with short intervals, during which, perhaps, a transient ray of reason gleams; or he laughs, cries, whistles, shouts, screams, or howls; is restless, full of antics, mischievous, tearing his clothes, and destroying all he can reach; is malicious, swears, prays, perhaps desperately intent on violence to himself or others; is lecherous, obscene, shameless, nasty, and indifferent to the calls of nature. Sometimes he evinces great anxiety, distress, fear or horror, suspicion, and revengeful feelings. Even in this stage of mania, they are cunning, acute, witty, and often capable of writing with correctness and taste, or of executing mechanical arts; and yet the faculty of perception, and sometimes of judgment, or both, are, as to particular objects, lesed. But, in the furious form, all the faculties seem implicated, and there is too much impetuosity, incoherency, and confusion of thought, to be competent to exercise the powers of combination.

The affections are exalted, perverted, or extinguished: occupied by one or a great variety of subjects, the patient's inclinations and actions correspond with that impression which predominates.[15]

Griesinger (1845)

After Burrows a number of authors added to the concept of mania, as seen in the contributions below, though each also gave a general description similar to that of Burrows. Griesinger analyzed the symptoms and described their progression in general psychologic terms. He also related antisocial behavior to the manic state. The relation between mania and depression was again emphasized, as was "acting-out" behavior.

While the pure and simple forms of melancholia represent conditions of depression of the self-sensation and self-confidence, of concentration upon some painful emotion of *morbid self-concentration*, and, in the highest degrees, of even incapacity for making the slightest exertion, we have seen that, in the forms last considered, the emotional disposition is always more and more accompanied by morbid impulses to manifestations of volition. The possibility of exhibiting the emotion by actions, and of thereby obtaining relief, shows that the affective sphere of the mind and the will have become more free; indeed, the stronger and more persistent these impulses are, and the more extended and independent this aspiration to freedom becomes, the

---

[15]G. M. Burrows, *Commentaries on the Causes, Forms, Symptoms, and Treatment, Moral and Medical, of Insanity* (London: T. and G. Underwood, 1828), pp. 344–347.

more there result states of *persistent excitement and exaltation of will*, with which also there is easily united *an increase of the self-sensation and of self-confidence*. Such conditions, which have been appropriately designated in opposition to melancholia, morbid states in which the patients are *out of themselves*, are comprised under the name of mania; and under this head there are included two different forms, which, while they are intimately connected with each other, and not unfrequently pass into each other, occur still more frequently as states or forms fragmentarily mixed together, viz. *mania* and *monomania* (sensu strictiori).

The fundamental affection in the maniacal states consists chiefly in a derangement of the motory side of the soul-life, the effort, and of such a nature, that the latter having become free, unrestrained, and considerably increased, the individual consequently feels impelled to give some outward manifestation of his powers. From this tendency to an exaggerated psychical movement from within outwards, from this augmented energy and more extended range of the efforts, from this extravagance of the will, which constitute the centre-point of maniacal derangement, spring, as from a common source, those two forms which in their nature and mode of manifestation are sometimes so essentially distinct. On the one hand, this necessity for the manifestation of the increased mental activity may manifest itself *directly*, being propagated by a continuous impulse to the organs of motion, and there exploding, as it were; whence there ensues a state of great physical restlessness, the patient keeping his muscles in constant play (speech, gestures, movements of the body generally), and perpetually speaking, shouting, weeping, dancing, leaping, storming, &c.; and thus is constituted the form generally called mania.

Or, on the other hand, the direct result of this more free development of volition may be the development of inordinate vanity, increased self-sensation, and consequently a constant over-estimation of self; and as attempts at explanation of this disposition, delirious conceptions arise which now become dominant over the mind, and take the increased activity of the will into their service. The patient has now no longer to do with mere general manifestation of energy; but this excitation of the motory side of the soul-life is transformed into *extravagant volition in the form of particular delirious conceptions*, for the most part with much greater outward calm. As soon as such a condition, accompanied by delirious conceptions arising from inordinate self-conceit, has in any degree become fixed, there is founded a state of mental derangement infinitely more serious than that of simple mania.[16]

[16] W. Griesinger, *Mental Pathology and Therapeutics*, from the 2nd German ed., C. L. Robertson and J. Rutherford, trans. (London: The New Sydenham Society, 1867), pp. 273–274.

We have more than once had occasion to remark that, in the majority of cases, melancholic states precede the maniacal, and that the latter is engendered by the former. In the more chronic cases we often have the opportunity of following the whole course of the disease, and of seeing in melancholics the mental suffering and anxiety increase from day to day, at first manifesting itself merely by extreme restlessness, but gradually passing into complete mania. In such cases it is undoubtedly the state of mental suffering which induces this convulsive condition—a phenomenon which may appropriately enough be compared on the one hand to those convulsions which are brought on by some particularly severe bodily suffering, and at other times to those involuntary muscular contractions which take place as a sort of instinctive reaction against any acute pain (as setting the teeth, clenching the fist, &c.)

We are not to suppose that, therefore, the nature of mania consists merely in the unregulated and uncurbed manifestation of the negative disposition found in melancholia. For, though often enough this disposition breaks through all barriers, and displays itself in certain acts of convulsive fury or of destruction—conditions which we have already described under the title of *raptus melancholicus*; and although, often enough, during the whole course of the maniacal affection, the melancholia appears behind it as a shady background, and there are even times when it advances to the foreground and may again become dominant; still the mania, when once the motory exaltation has been set free, however short the fit may be, becomes entirely independent of the preceding melancholia, and bursts forth without the necessity of being excited anew by melancholic emotions: indeed, the disposition frequently undergoes a total change, the patient becoming joyful, merry, and over-forward.

At the same time, those deeds of destruction, the savage attempts and ferocious acts committed by maniacs, are far from being always due to a true negative disposition of mind, or to even a momentary hostile intention; much more frequently the acts of these patients are the result of a blind impulse to action, of a necessity to change the external world according to their will. In acts of destruction this desire finds its simplest fulfilment, because this is so much easier than to create anything—for this demands a certain amount of reflection and of care, of which maniacs are wholly incapable. The desire longs to be promptly satisfied, and convulsively hastens, so to speak, to manifest itself without heeding the more slow influence of more orderly thoughts: as he must give vent to his desire in a visible manner, he proceeds at once to the work of demolition; and that which we might be inclined to regard as the object of the deed, is, in fact, merely the termination of his activity. . . .

As we have already remarked, it is rare that mania shows itself without having been preceded by certain symptoms of some other mental affection. In the majority of cases, for some time previous, the desires, the feelings, and habits of the patient have become entirely changed, and generally a tone of melancholy seems to pervade them. This antecedent *stadium melancholium,* which may be of a very gentle and transient nature, is what has been termed the period of incubation of mania. The melancholic gradually becomes very restless, nothing pleases him; he is perpetually wandering about; he strays amongst the fields, or makes excursions to see friends and relatives, frequently to far-distant places, with the vague expectation of obtaining relief. He gives evidence of his distressing delirium, when such exists, by talking in a loud voice, and by his loquaciousness; his voice is stronger on such occasions than usual, and he is generally more active. In particular, his appetite is actually voracious; he frequently complains of disagreeable sensations in the epigastric region, of a feeling of oppression which extremely annoys and torments him. Persons who have once had an attack of mania frequently themselves say that they are going to have a relapse, and beg that they may be watched and removed from their usual neighbourhood. Frequently such persons exhibit a great desire for spirituous liquors; and as they yield to the desire usually in an immoderate degree, it seems as if they would by the alcoholic stimulus perpetuate and increase their state of excitement, which unfortunately they too often succeed in doing. With the increased muscular activity and impulse to exhibit it in actions, new ideas and new sensations arise, which at first plunge the patient into a state of astonishment and fear, but speedily end by gaining the complete mastery. At the commencement he could conceal this state of mind, but soon these new ideas and sensations slip out and display themselves in words and deeds.

Anomalies of the disposition, of the desires, and of the will.—The fundamental disorder in mania, the irritation upon the motory side of the soul-life, exhibits itself, first of all, in this sphere, as a high degree of mental excitement, with restless, impetuous, and violent desires and actions. The desire for ceaseless action and movement, the necessity of immediately exhibiting in action all that passes within the mind, impels him sometimes merely to harmless movements, as in dancing, speaking, singing, shrieking, laughing, weeping, &c.; sometimes to restless, objectless employment, which would attempt, according to the caprice of the moment, suddenly and impatiently to alter everything around, sometimes to destroy everything animate or inanimate—a tendency which may increase to outbreaks of the blindest fury and rage. But while this violent and unbridled impulse attacks all objects, rushes against every impediment, and, totally regardless of consequences, shows itself in eccentric and aimless actions, we nevertheless find in many of these patients a certain cowardice when they are energetically and decidedly resisted, or, more correctly, a state of anxiety still remaining from the primary period of the disease, and which appears not only to have originated the mania, but also to maintain it. In such individuals we can discover no reasonable act, no deed deduced from any rational train of thought, no care either for their own or their family's existence, no possibility of being guided by any rational principle; indifference towards all which does not directly touch upon the point on which they are peculiarly sensitive; entire want of interest in anything going on around; loss of all sense of decency, modesty, and propriety.

The concrete mental acts which show themselves with such violence consist either simply in certain rapidly changing dispositions, or in certain sentiments which have become fixed, and obscure groups of ideas which manifest themselves in some particular determinate impulse. Thus it is, that in consequence of a morbid exaggeration of the sexual sensations, frequently arising from some local cause, as pruritus pudendi or ovarian disease, we see women exhibiting a morbid lasciviousness which they display in the most shameless manner, and seek to gratify by the most brutal means. The desire of possession may show itself as a persistent propensity to collect and accumulate everything, or as a morbid propensity to steal. The pleasure in loud speaking, in the rhythmical form of conversation, in noise-making, in spirituous drinks, in satisfying their appetite, in shedding blood, &c., may show itself in those violent and boisterous ways, and there result fixed or transitory conditions which, according to the predominance of this or that particular desire, are known under the name of nymphomania, kleptomania, logomania, poiematamania, dipsomania, edodomania, homicidal mania, &c. . . .

Sometimes, particularly at the commencement of the disease, the patient himself complains of this necessity to commit violent deeds, and it may be possible in such a case, by reasoning with him, or by some strong mental impression, temporarily to restrain him, and to bring him again to a momentary state of reason; in other cases it seems as if the patient, in a state of semi-consciousness of his condition, gave himself up to the exaltation when it has once begun, and gave the reins to the thoughts which beset him; it seems as if he wished, when his will has thus got loose and is no longer restrained, to revenge himself for that painful restraint to which he has been subjected during the melancholic stadium of his disease.[17]

Melancholia often alternates with attacks of mania; occasionally there is a regular (for example, at certain seasons of the year) alternation of exaltation and depression (*folie circulaire* of the French writers). In these cases the melancholic stage is generally somewhat more prolonged than the maniacal, which consists rather in a state of general excitement and restlessness than in actual mania. At other times we see attacks of mania occur after regular or irregular lucid intervals every one, two, three years, &c.—*periodical mania*, a grave form, a real psychical epilepsy which shares the unfavorable prognosis with ordinary epilepsy which has become habitual.[18]

[17] Ibid., pp. 276–282.
[18] Ibid., p. 290.

Ball (1880)

Ball regarded mania as a syndrome and not as a specific disease.

It is enough to tell you that here it is no more than a symptom, a particular mental state, and not a distinct disease. Mania is found, in effect, in a great number of different diseases.[19]

Spitzka (1883)

Spitzka described the symptoms in excellent detail and explained them as a loosening of inhibitions.

Mania is a form of insanity characterized by an exalted emotional state which is associated with a corresponding exaltation of other mental and nervous functions.

The typical condition of the maniac may be summarized in one phrase: loosening of the inhibitions, or checks, both those of organic and those of mental life. . . .

On the whole the patient in this condition greatly resembles a person slightly intoxicated. But just as the person who while slightly intoxicated is good-natured, generous, careless, mischievous, and perhaps lewd, when more deeply intoxicated becomes irritable, combative, and incoherent; so the maniac as his condition deepens exhibits a tendency to angry rather than to pleasurable excitement. Even in the lighter phases it is noted that he does not bear contradiction well; that trifling causes produce undue emotional reaction; that just as he laughs without cause, so he may become angry at an imaginary affront, at a mere interruption, or cry without due reason. His reproduction of impressions and association of conceptions now attains the rapidity of a delirium. Ideas which were previously followed but not enunciated in words are now not even followed out in thought. The patient is unable to fix his attention long enough on a question to answer it even in his mind; the judgment becomes obtuse, dulled by the myriad of conceptions it is called on to control. Just as the beast came to the surface owing to the removal of the conventional clogs, egotism now asserts itself through the obliteration or weakening of the judgment. The patient believes he is rich, occupies himself with rapidly changing projects, is going to get a high office, or to sue the asylum authorities for a large sum as an equivalent for his "wrongful incarceration." . . .[20]

[19] B. Ball, *Leçons sur les maladies mentales* (Paris: Asselin et Cie., 1880), p. 277.
[20] E. C. Spitzka, *Insanity: Its Classification, Diagnosis and Treatment* (New York: Bermingham and Co., 1883), pp. 131, 133–134.

Krafft-Ebing (1904)

Krafft-Ebing analyzed the symptoms of mania in terms of loss of inhibitions and a change in ego-functions.

The fundamental symptoms of maniacal insanity are a change of self-consciousness characterized by a predominating pleasurable emotional state, and an abnormal ease and rapidity of thought which may become so intense that all control of the psychomotor side of the mind is wanting. In this respect mania is the exact opposite of melancholia. In mania, no more than in melancholia, can the emotional anomalies be exclusively explained by the changed activity of mental processes (here facilitated), though it cannot be denied that a decided increase of pleasurable feeling is found by the patient in the greater ease of thought and the removal of all inhibition.

Both these fundamental phenomena are to be regarded as co-ordinated, and probably their foundation lies functionally in facilitated expenditure of vital forces, and anatomically in a greater supply of blood to the psychic organ. In mania, also, two essential disease-pictures may be distinguished, differing only in degree and frequently passing one into the other. The milder form is maniacal exaltation; the severer form is furious mania.

Maniacal Exaltation

The content of consciousness is pleasure and psychic well-being. It is just as independent of events in the external world as the opposite state of mental pain in melancholics, and therefore can be referred only to inner organic causes. The patient revels in pleasurable feelings, and after recovery states that never in health did he feel so uplifted or so happy as during his disease. This spontaneous pleasure receives powerful stimulation from altered apperception of the external world; from the realization of the facilitated activity of thought and will; from the intense accentuation of ideas with pleasurable feelings; and the comfortable state of general feeling, especially that derived from the muscles (increased muscle-tone). These influences cause the joyful emotion to be intensified temporarily to joyful affects (unrestrained joyousness, wantonness), which find their expression in singing, dancing, jumping, and silly jokes.

Along with the disturbance in content of emotion there is a formal derangement—increased excitability (psychic hyperesthesia), manifest in the fact that sense-perception and reproduced ideas are accompanied, not by mere sentiment, but by affects which, owing to the predominating fundamental emotional state, are principally gay; and they occur with abnormal ease. Necessarily on account of this there is an altered apperception of the external world. Instead of the somber color with which the external world appears to the melancholic as a result of his psychic dysesthesia, to the maniacal it seems warmer, more beautiful and interesting. On this account he cultivates associations, goes into society, travels, in contrast again with the melancholic, who avoids people or even detests them.

The general result of the changed process of apperception of the external world and of self is an increased estimate of self-value which frequently finds its expression in personal adornment.

Though a joyful emotion forms the emotional basis of maniacal insanity, contrary feelings are not therefore excluded. Owing to the unlimited association of ideas and their lively coloring, opposing ideas may be called up. Frequently, however, they arise artificially from restraint of the freedom of the patient, from opposition to his wishes, etc., by which the abnormally intensified feeling of self-valuation is hurt. These painful and choleric states of feeling, however, are only episodic, and, owing to the increased rapidity of thought, are quickly overcome by the pleasurable fundamental emotion. In thought the rapidity of the transformation of psychic energy is expressed in facilitated reproduction, association, and combination of ideas, which necessarily lead to an overfilling of consciousness; they thus stand in striking contrast with the monotony and inhibition of the activity of thought observed in melancholia.

With the facilitation of reproduction and apperception and the warm coloring of thought and apperception, the patient becomes more plastic in his diction and remarks at once the point of the subject, the weaknesses and peculiarities of those about him; he is quicker in his comprehension, and, owing to his facilitated association, is at the same time ready, witty, and humorous, even to irony. The overfilling of consciousness gives him an inexhaustible supply of subjects of conversation, and the greatly increased rapidity of thought, in which long connecting links are manifest only by slight indications without being verbally expressed, makes his train of thought appear interrupted.

The intensified valuation of self causes natural language to be disdained, and the patient tries to express himself in literary language. During the stage of maniacal exaltation of maniacal insanity there may be disturbances in the content of thought that are, for the most part, episodic, and consist of rendering allegorically objective the intensified feeling of self-aggrandizement. Occasionally the patient compares himself with a distinguished personality without identifying himself with the individual.

His consciousness is too little disturbed to permit this. He is always able to exercise critical judgment of his own condition, and describes his state of mind as abnormal, in that he excuses his hasty actions, for want of a better explanation, by saying that he is a fool and that to such an individual everything is permitted.

There may be hallucinations, but at most they are only temporary, and are usually corrected; or at least they are never acted upon. Illusions occur more readily, owing to the greatly increased activity of thought.

On the psychomotor side of mental acitivty the disturbance is first manifest in increased will and impulse; but all motor acts of the patient, in contrast with furious mania, are of psychic origin and take place consciously.

Their causes are affective states or clearly conscious ideas. They are like normal acts, only remarkable in that they are hurried, ill considered, irrelevant, jocular, shocking, or even immoral, without, however, presenting the possibility of characterizing them as absolutely unreasonable. This exaltation of the psychomotor side of mental activity is clinically expressed in desire to wander, frequent saloons, seek out old friends and acquaintances, see notable places, write, make purchases, etc. The absence or too late occurrence of inhibitory controlling ideas causes these acts, which in themselves are not senseless, but only irrelevant and hasty; and since, at the same time, there is an absence of esthetic and ethic inhibitory ideas, they are frequently shocking. The lively coloring of all perceptions by pleasurable emotion causes such patients to be full of desire; and their abnormally intensified feeling of self-aggrandizement renders them troublesome, talkative, and disputative. The transitoriness of their impulses causes them to be inconsistent, incapable of all occupation, and unable to complete whatever they have undertaken.

Not in all of these patients are the general features of the disease developed. In some cases the impulse to talk, in others intensified volition, and in still others pleasant emotion is the most prominent symptom; and in the latter case it may be either a simple exaltation or have an erotic or religious coloring.

It is not worth while to give names to these various clinical varieties. Almost always—and in females, indeed, always—in maniacal exaltation the sexual sphere occupies the foreground of consciousness. The sexual impulse expresses itself here in a superficial disturbance that is still tolerable: in men, by paying attentions to women, hasty promises of marriage, questionable allusions in conversation, visits to brothels; in women, in inclination to self-adornment, to seek male society, to flirt, to talk of scandal, to invent stories of love-intrigues, and in suspicion of other women.

Very frequently in this state of exaltation there is an increased desire for stimulants, satisfied in highly seasoned food, smoking, taking snuff, drinking strong coffee, and especially in the use of alcoholic drinks. Under such circumstances such excesses readily lead to intensification of maniacal exaltation to the height of furious mania.

Disturbance of sleep is here quite constant. The patients sleep but a few hours, get up in the middle of the night, and busy themselves about the house or in the street. There is a feeling of increased physical well-being, of increased power and capability of action. The patient cannot find words enough to describe his maniacal well-being, his infinite good health. There is here no feeling of physical fatigue, not even after forced walking and other kinds of over-exertion.[21]

Furious Mania

Furious mania is a higher stage of development of mania than maniacal exaltation.

The idea of furious mania, originally gained from the external furious conduct of the patient, must be submitted to scientific limitation. Fury is a mere symptom, while furious mania is a distinct pathologic state occurring in the course of mania. The fury of the melancholic due to fear, the fury of the delirious (epileptic, hysteric, alcoholic, febrile), due to frightful hallucinations, is not to be confounded with furious mania. The distinctive characteristic of furious mania is increased rapidity of psychic processes, going even to complete loss of control, in which the ego of the patient has lost all directive power and is no longer able to control the psychic acts. With this there are signs of direct excitation of the organ of consciousness. . . .

Here, too, as in maniacal exaltation, expansive affects predominate; but affects of an opposite nature, especially those of anger, are not excluded. Indeed, there are rare cases in which the affect of anger predominates throughout the whole course of the disease (angry mania). These clinical differences in the disease-picture are partly dependent upon original anomalies (tainted cerebral organization) of a patient naturally choleric and of irritable character, partly artificially produced by restraint, and partly a reactive manifestation dependent upon frightful delusions, hallucinations, and complicating feelings of fear.

If an emotional state of anger be due to any of these factors, owing to the greatly increased excitability, secondary painful reproduction of ideas takes place, which, however, in contrast with agitated melancholia, present the character of the flight of ideas with variations in the train of thought. These then maintain an angry emotional state. Such cases of pure angry mania are the most infrequent. Expansive cases are much more frequent, and the most frequent are those of a mixed form: *i.e.*, those in which, with the great excitement and the rapid change of ideas, together with unlimited association, there is a striking variation in the content of the most varied emotional states (variation of humor). Since the ego is powerless in the face of this excitement, owing to the great increase of all psychic activities and the absence of all inhibition, these affects manifest themselves throughout the entire domain of

---

[21] R. von Krafft-Ebing, *Text-Book of Insanity Based on Clinical Observations for Practitioners and Students of Medicine* [1893 (5th German ed.)], C. G. Chaddock, trans. (Philadelphia: F. A. Davis, 1904), pp. 312–316.

expression and movement. Thus, foolish joy and maniacal exaltation alternate with phases of angry excitement and painful weeping; singing, whistling, shouting, and bawling alternate with angry howling and fury. Often a transitory external impression or some thought suffices to change the emotional state into an opposite one, on account of the psychic hyperesthesia.

The great increase in the rapidity of thought leads to flight of ideas; and since no single thought can be retained in mind, a logical series of ideas is impossible, and the result is incoherence (overfilling of consciousness; association of ideas due only to assonance and alliteration; spontaneous, physiologic production of ideas independently of association).

Thus, necessarily, the logical association of ideas and the grammatic form of speech are lost. Fragments of sentences, disconnected words, and finally mere interjections or cries, indicate the varying degree of the maniacal flight of ideas and incoherence.

Owing to the great rapidity of thought, apperception is imperfect, and therefore illusions are facilitated.

Hallucinations may occur at any time and in any sensory domain. They are very frequent when the course is acute, especially in the visual sphere.

Almost without exception there are delusions. They are, for the most part, connected with errors of the senses, but they may be primordial; least frequently they arise as temporary attempts to explain states of consciousness and sensations. Their content is infinite in variety, but, for the most part, of an expansive nature (grand delusions). Frequently, especially in women, they have a sexual coloring, or its equivalent—a religious tinge. Such delusions are: of being the Virgin Mary; of being overshadowed by the Holy Ghost; of having given birth to Christ. In angry mania, delusions of persecution, especially of a demoniac coloring, may form the nucleus of the emotional state.

These delusions are, owing to the transitoriness of their causes and the rapidity of thought, which allows no reflection, desultory; and only seldom, or in mania that becomes chronic, do they lead to a lasting change of consciousness, with possible termination in secondary delusional insanity.

The psychomotor sphere presents the most important phenomena of the disease-picture, and these have given the disease its name. Aside from the pauses that arise from exhaustion, the patient is in constant activity, and there is no voluntary group of muscles that is not brought into action. The motor acts of the patient are due to various causes. In transition from maniacal exaltation to mania, and during the remissions of mania, there may be formal volitional acts; but, since the underlying ideas, owing to the increasing rapidity of thought and of cloudiness of consciousness, become less and less clear, such voluntary acts take on more and more the character of impulsive acts. At the same time there are psychic reflex acts due to joyous emotion (dancing, singing, etc.), or to fear and anger.

At the height of the disease such psychically conditioned motor acts occur only rarely. They are pushed aside by impulsive movements due to direct irritation of the psychomotor centers; at the same time there are acts due to delusions and errors of the senses.

Very frequently, too, in mania, the sexual instinct is excited, and cases in which this predominates are often called satyriasis in males and nymphomania in females.

The more profound disturbance of consciousness as compared with that of maniacal exaltation allows the sexual impulse to express itself without reserve: in the forms of direct attack on persons of the opposite sex, open onanism, and movements of coitus.[22]

DEPRESSIONS

One current classification of depression divides the syndrome into psychotic and nonpsychotic varieties. A similar classification developed over a thousand years ago out of some words of St. Paul in his Second Epistle to the Corinthians 7:10: "For godly sorrow worketh repentance to salvation not to be repented of, but the sorrow of the world worketh death." The word *sorrow* used in English translations of the Bible stood for the Latin *tristitia*, connoting sadness, sorrow, despondency, depression. Paul's distinction between the two kinds of tristitia, the one "from God" and the other "of the world," led medieval theologians to enlarge on differences between the two kinds of depression.[23]

Snyder contributed an excellent discussion of the ideas of medieval authorities about depression, and most of the following summary is taken from his work.[24]

An early exegetist, the pre-Nicene father Origen, discussed the death of Judas Iscariot in the light of Paul's concepts. As Snyder pointed out, Origen held that, although Judas's sin was not too great for forgiveness, his remorse was excessive. The devil was therefore able to direct him away from the beneficent depression that makes for penitence and toward the depression that leads to death. Other medieval writers, e.g., Bernard of Clairvaux and Hugues de St.-Victor, also referred to the maleficent type of despair as the work of the devil.

The perceptive psychologist John Cassian first gave the discussion a modern psychiatric cast in his guide to the monastic life, *De institutis coenobiorum*, written around A.D. 420. Cassian told how a monk could distinguish the two kinds of depression and described one as rancorous, ineffective, and irrational. His ideas were repeated two centuries later by Isidore of Seville, who contrasted the "disturbed, irrational" type of depression with the beneficent "temperate and rational." Similar comments were made by Bede a century after Isidore. Thus,

[22] Ibid., pp. 319 ff.

[23] M. D. Altschule, "The two kinds of depression according to St. Paul," *British Journal of Psychiatry*, 1967, **113**, 778–783.

[24] S. Snyder, "The left hand of God: Despair in medieval and Renaissance tradition," *Studies in the Renaissance*, 1965, **12**, 18.

from the fifth to the eighth centuries leaders of Christian thought recognized a distinction between rational and irrational depression. Some writers of that period included among the manifestations of irrational depression a desire to "un-be." In *The Vices and Virtues*, Alcuin stated that the despairing one "hateth himself and desireth his owne death." This malignant kind of depression was equated with loss of the hope of salvation. (A different kind of loss, loss of a loved object, is today assumed to cause depression.)

Another medieval belief that presaged modern thought was that irrational depression might be unconscious. Ambrose of Milan, Bede, Bernard of Clairvaux, Gregory the Great, Alcuin, Raymond de Pennaforte, and others stated that *luxuria* and some other vices were caused by unconscious despair.

According to medieval theologians, those with the beneficent type of depression had not only the medieval version of insight, i.e., they recognized and acknowledged their sins, but also the hope, if not the conviction, of relief. (As emphasized by all the authorities, from the earliest to Thomas Aquinas, penitence implied at least a measure of hope. According to this reasoning, those who, like Judas, committed suicide were really impenitent and hence possessed by the devil.) Contemporary psychiatry also makes a good prognosis for depressed patients who have or develop insight and hope.

Even though medieval writers considered despair in connection with the death of Judas and mentioned the desire to "un-be" as a manifestation of despair, they evidently did not consider suicide an important concomitant. Writers from Augustine to Thomas Aquinas discussed the morality of suicide but never mentioned despair as its cause, although they did refer to a desire to punish oneself in connection with suicide. The relation between suicide and despair was clearly recognized by laymen, however. Medieval pictorial or sculptured representations of despair usually portrayed a figure stabbing him- or herself; sometimes despair was personified by Judas with a halter around his neck. In a later period writings such as Timothy Bright's *Treatise of Melancholy* (1586) and Burton's *Anatomy of Melancholy* (1621) did recognize suicide as a manifestation of despair.

It is apparent that many medieval philosophers subscribed to a decidedly modern recognition of both rational and irrational depressions, the latter of which might be unconscious. Well-informed laymen held similar views and like the theologians based them on 2 Corinthians 7:10. For example, Chaucer wrote in the *Persones Tale:*

> Thanne cometh the synne of wordly sorwe, swiche is cleped *tristicia*, that sleeth man, as weith seint Paul. For certes, swich sorwe worketh to the deeth of the soule and of the body also; for thereof comth that a man is anoyed of his owene lif. Wherefore swich sorwe shorteth ful ofte the lif of man, er that his time be come by way of kynde.

One question remains: Was St. Paul's view of depression original or was it derived? It is clear that Paul quoted or paraphrased many Greek poets and philosophers, but the substance of Paul's words has not yet been identified in ancient Greek writings.

Whatever the source, the medieval belief that depression might be either rational or irrational was decidedly a theological and not a medical concept. This is evident in the writings of Isidore,[25] the encyclopedic *Etymologia*, which summarized most of the written knowledge of the time. Included were medical items derived from Plato, Aristotle, Hippocrates, Celsus, Galen, Soranus of Ephesus, and Caelius Aurelianus, both as primary sources and as discussed by Tertullian, Lactantius, Cassiodorus, St. Augustine, and St. Ambrose of Milan. Isidore concurred with the prevailing medical view that all diseases were due solely to a disturbance in the balance of the humors. Although he discussed melancholia in detail in his *Etymologia*, Isidore nowhere related any aspect of this condition to what he had maintained about the feeling of depression.

Without the support of clinical observation the concept of depression developed by medieval Christian philosophers was not absorbed into medical thought. This amalgamation would not take place until the distinction between psychosis and nonpsychosis became clarified. Two thousand years were to pass before the idea of two kinds of depression gained medical confirmation.

Hippocrates (5th century B.C.)

Although Hippocrates mentions both mania and melancholia, he nowhere describes their manifestations, evidently believing that all his readers or listeners would be fully informed about them.

> If a fright or despondency lasts for a long time, it is a melancholic affection.[26]

Galen had little to say about melancholia as a symptom, although he did discuss it as a physiologic state. Renaissance authors believed that Galen had said, "melancholy is an affection which damages the judgement, causes a grave disturbance of the mood and an estrangement from those most closely associated," but this was really from the pseudo-Galenic *On Medical Definitions*.[27]

---

[25] W. D. Sharpe, "Isidore of Seville: The medical writings," *American Philosophical Society*, 1964, n.s. 54, pt. 2.

[26] *Hippocrates*, W. H. S. Jones, trans. (Cambridge, Mass.: Harvard University Press; London: William Heinemann, Ltd., 1948), Aphorisms VI, 23.

[27] Galen, *On the Passions and Errors of the Soul*, P. W. Harkins, trans. (Columbus: Ohio State University Press, 1963). See also R. E. Siegel, *Galen's System of Physiology and Medicine* (Basel and New York: S. Karger, 1968).

Celsus (1st century A.D.)

One of the earliest clinical descriptions is found in the works of Celsus. He was not a physician but an encyclopedist who covered the then current literature carefully if uncritically.

> There is another form of madness which ... goes no further than a sadness. ... The belly is to be kept as soft as possible; terrors are to be dispersed, and rather good hopes are to be given. Entertainment must be sought in amusing stories and diversions, such as the person in health used to be most pleased with. If there are any works of his performing, they must be commended, and placed before his eyes. His groundless sorrow is to be mildly reprimanded. Arguments must be offered now and then to persuade him, that in those very things, which disturb him there is more matter for joy than anxiety. ... .[28]

Areteus (2nd century A.D.)

It must be remembered that Areteus had the benefit of material from Aesclepiades, perhaps Themison, and probably others, which are largely lost to us.

> ... It sends rumbling wind downwards, and disturbs the understanding. On this account, in former days, these were called melancholics and flatulent persons. And yet, in certain of these cases, there is neither flatulence nor black bile, but mere anger and grief, and sad dejection of mind; and these were called melancholics. ... The melancholics become such when they are overpowered by this evil.
>
> It is a lowness of spirits from a single phantasy, without fever; and it appears to me that melancholy is the commencement and a part of mania. For in those who are mad, the understanding is turned sometimes to anger and sometimes to joy, but in the melancholics to sorrow and despondency only. But they who are mad are so for the greater part of life, becoming silly, and doing dreadful and disgraceful things; but those affected with melancholy are not every one of them affected according to one particular form; but they are either suspicious of poisoning, or flee to the desert from misanthropy, or turn superstitious, or contract a hatred of life. Or if at any time a relaxation takes place, in most cases hilarity supervenes, but these persons go mad. ...
>
> The characteristic appearances, then, are not obscure; for the patients are dull or stern, dejected or unreasonably torpid, without any manifest cause: such is the commencement of melancholy. And they also become peevish, dispirited, sleepless, and start up from a disturbed sleep.

[28] A. C. Celsus, *Of Medicine*, J. Grieve, trans. (London: H. Renshaw and others, 1838), p. 133.

Unreasonable fear also seizes them, if the disease tend to increase, when their dreams are true, terrifying, and clear: for whatever, when awake, they have an aversion to, as being an evil, rushes upon their visions in sleep. They are prone to change their mind readily; to become base, mean-spirited, illiberal, and in a little time, perhaps, simple, extravagant, munificent, not from any virtue of the soul, but from the changeableness of the disease. But if the illness become more urgent, hatred, avoidance of the haunts of men, vain lamentations; they complain of life, and desire to die. In many, the understanding so leads to insensibility and fatuousness, that they become ignorant of all things, or forgetful of themselves..[29]

Caelius Aurelianus (5th century A.D.)

Caelius Aurelianus also wrote on melancholia. He disputed the ancient idea that it was caused by black bile. The relation to mania was, according to him, first noted by Themison.

Melancholy derives its name from the fact that the patient often vomits black bile, the Greek word for 'black' being *melas* and for 'bile,' *cholē*. The name is not derived, as many believe, from the notion that black bile is the cause or origin of the disease. For such a notion would be put forward only by those who guess at, rather than observe, truth; and it is, in fact, a false notion, as we have shown elsewhere. Thus Cicero speaks of black bile in the sense of profound anger; and when Hercules is stirred to mighty wrath, Virgil says 'and thereupon the wrath of Hercules burned furiously with black bile', for those suffering from melancholy seem always to be downcast and prone to anger and are practically never cheerful and relaxed. . . .

The signs of approaching melancholy are the same as those of approaching insanity. The signs of melancholy, when it is actually present, are as follows: mental anguish and distress, dejection, silence, animosity toward members of the household, sometimes a desire to live and at other times a longing for death, suspicion on the part of the patient that a plot is being hatched against him, weeping without reason, meaningless muttering. . . .

The followers of Themison, as well as many others, consider melancholy a form of the disease of mania.[30]

Paulus Aegineta (7th century A.D.)

Paulus Aegineta wrote in much the same vein as his Greco-Roman predecessors. His writings are noteworthy, however, in that they contain what seems to have been the first reference to a crackpot.

[29] *The Extant Works of Aretaeus, the Cappadocian*, F. Adams, trans. (London: The New Sydenham Society, 1856), pp. 298–300.

[30] Caelius Aurelianus, *On Acute Diseases and On Chronic Diseases*, I. E. Drabkin, ed. and trans. (Chicago: The University of Chicago Press, n.d.), pp. 561, 563.

Melancholy is a disorder of the intellect without fever, occasioned mostly by a melancholic humour seizing the understanding; sometimes the brain being primarily affected, and sometimes it being altered by sympathy with the rest of the body. And there is a third species called the flatulent and hypochondriac, occasioned by inflammation of the parts in the hypochondria adjoining to the stomach, by which sometimes noxious vapours or aurae are transmitted to the brain, and sometimes part of the substance of the humour. The common symptoms of them all are fear, despondency, and misanthropy; and that they fancy themselves to be, some, brute animals, and imitate their cries; and others, earthen-vessels, and are frightened lest they be broken. Some desire death, and others are afraid of dying; some laugh constantly, and others weep; and some believe themselves impelled by higher powers, and foretell what is to come, as if under divine influence; and these are, therefore, properly called demoniacs, or possessed persons. The peculiar symptoms of melancholy, from sympathy with the general system, are leanness, darkness, and shagginess; the whole appearance melancholic, either by nature, or acquired by anxiety, want of sleep, the administration of noxious food, or stoppage of the hemorrhoidal, or menstrual discharge.[31]

Isidore of Seville (7th century A.D.)

Isidore of Seville, one of the great encyclopedists of the Middle Ages, is included here not for his writings on melancholia, which are without merit, but for his *Synonyma*, subtitled *De lamentatione anima dolentis*. This was a deliberately repetitive, floridly written Ciceronian work which begins "My soul is in anguish" and goes on to describe irregular heart beats, the accumulation of surrounding evils, persecution by (imaginary?) enemies, despair of the future, etc.—in short, all the symptoms of depression. After debating the matter with Reason, the author is persuaded that despair is owing to sinfulness and that relief will come from confession, contrition, and leading a good life thenceforth. The work was a fabricated expression of the symptoms of depression and is important only because it was written to be used by others who had or wished to discuss similar symptoms in anguished detail.[32] St. Isidore's *Synonyma* thus continued a literary and philosophical tradition that began with Cicero's *Tusculan Disputations* and St. Augustine's *Colloquia*, and still shows no signs of atrophy. The idea that depression is caused by one's own sinfulness has been replaced in the present century by the notion that the disorder can be traced to adverse circumstances inevitably experienced by all who have one or more parents.

In this book, here following, which is called *Synonyma*, that is, many words coming together in one meaning, Isidore of blessed memory, archbishop

---

[31] Paulus Aegineta, *The Seven Books*, F. Adams, trans. (London: The New Sydenham Society, 1844), Vol. 1, p. 383.

[32] Thomas Hoccleve's *Complaint* exemplifies this type of plagiarism. See A. G. Rigg, "Hoccleve's *Complaint* and Isidore of Seville," *Speculum*, 1970, 45, 564–574.

of Seville, presents the figure of a man lamenting on the bitterness of the present world, and weeping for himself almost to the point of falling into despair. By a wondrous coincidence, reason meets him, consoles him with gentle soothing, and brings him from the fall of despair to the hope of pardon, and teaches him how he may avoid the pitfall of the fickle world, and lay hold of a way of spiritual life. . . .

Isidore greets the reader.

Lately, a certain book which they call *Synonyma* came into my hands. Its form convinced me to fashion a lament for myself or for the miserable. I imitated therefore, not the wording of this work, but my promise.

Therefore, whoever you are, read this freely, and while you are touched by the adversities of the world, shake yourself loose from its censorious judgment, and immediately you will recognize that whatever sufferings you bear in the world, are brought on you by a most just retribution. The figures of two people are set forth here: that of a weeping man, and that of his advisor Reason.

My soul is in affliction, my spirit is troubled, my heart trembles, distress of soul afflicts me. Distress of the spirit afflicts me, I am surrounded by all evils, encompassed by bitterness, enclosed by mischance, beseiged with misery, covered with unhappiness, weighed down by troubles; I find no reason for such great sorrow, I do not understand how to escape adversity, I cannot find a way to escape grief. I cannot find ways of decreasing my sorrow, every where my unhappiness pursues me, at home or outside, my calamity is always with me.

Wherever I flee, my evils pursue me; wherever I turn, the shadow of my woes accompanies me like the shadow of my body. Hence I cannot flee my own ill luck. I am a man of unknown name, of obscure opinion, of humble lineage, known by myself only. I have harmed no one; I have maligned no one; I have stood against no one; I have brought trouble on no one, and disturbed no one, I have lived among men without any complaint. All gnash and rage against me, drag me to destruction, lead me to danger, attack my safety. No one gives me protection, no one takes on my defense, no one gives me support, no one relieves my woes. I am deserted by all men. Those who look at me either flee, or else they pursue me. They look upon me as an unhappy man, and falsely say I know not what with comforting words. They hide their hidden malice with bland words, and speak one thing with their mouths and intend another in their hearts. By their deeds they destroy what they promised with their mouths. Under the guise of pity they exult over the injured heart.

They cloak malice with the disguise of goodness; they conceal craftiness with false simplicity, they feign friendship by guile; they show in their face what they do not carry in their heart. In whom may you believe? In whom may you put faith? Whom will you consider your neighbor? Where now is faith?

Faith has perished, has been driven away, it is nowhere safe. If nothing is honest, if there is no truth of judgment, if decency is abandoned, if law is not maintained, if justice is denied to all, then laws perish, and chance becomes the judge.

Avarice has grown. The law perishes because of love of greed. Laws have no power; gifts and bribes have taken the strength from the laws. Everywhere money conquers; everywhere judgment is for sale. There is no fear of the law, no dread of judgment. License to live wickedly goes unpunished; no one opposes the sinners, nor is any misdeed punished. All crime remains unavenged: the wicked are saved: the innocent die. The good are needy: the evil are wealthy: criminals are powerful.

The just are in need; wrongdoers are honored; the just are despised. The wrongdoers rejoice; the just are in sorrow and grief. The wicked man prevails against the righteous. The evil condemn the good. The bad man is honored instead of a good man, the good man condemned instead of an evil one; the innocent perish instead of the guilty, and nothing stops it.

For no reason, without complaint, or malice on my part, they accuse me of crime. They heap crime on me: they weave the snares of crime against me. They impute crime and suspicion to me. They lead me into wrongdoing and danger: they cast crime on me, of which I have no knowledge. Nothing was sought for nothing was revealed, no inquiry was made, nothing was found, and yet they continue to contrive evils against me. They ceaselessly prepare false testimonies. My accusers do not stop accusing but the judge does not put it in writing.

I am condemned by the false and malicious opinions of witnesses and judges. By the false testimony of witnesses, I though innocent, am led to death. The witnesses and judges are involved in the same plot, my accusers the same group. They present wicked judges; they bring forth false witnesses, in whose testimony they trust. No one dissents from them, no one disagrees, no one repudiates their counsel. To whom may I speak? Whom may I believe? Whom may I petition? To whom may I go? From whom may I seek counsel? In whose hands shall I place my soul? What protector shall I seek?

I am hateful to all, deserted by the love of all. All have cast me from them, regard me with abomination. All shudder at me, repudiate me, want to desert me. I wish to flee them not but they threaten me. I desire to pray at their footsteps but they flee, turn their backs and hate me. I want to make them favorable with my pleadings but they become all the more annoyed. Meanwhile they approach me with feigned love, not for to give consolation but to tempt me. They speak falsely and if they are silent it is not a sincere silence. They seek for something to accuse me with, something to hear, something to bring out, to seek causes for deception.

But I, with hanging head, cast-down visage and lowered face, am silent, am dumb, and remain in ashamed silence. I set a guard and a seal on my mouth. I restrained my voice from speaking, I held back my tongue from talking. Even when asked about good I am silent, for I preferred to remain silent to evil folk, rather than to answer. But they were not quiet: they raged all the more. They persecute me, already shaken even more. They attack me more and more, they cry out in rage against me. They aggressively deliver accusations with voice, gesture and shouting.

They leap forth onto me, with a public outcry. They hurl contumely and reproaches at me, and they all encouraged by another, rush toward me, and turn their weapons on me. They all rage at me, they strive for my destruction, they ready their hands for my death. Therefore, in such great fear, terror and fright, wretched, I melted, grew pale, and became bloodless. My heart fainted, I am agitated with fear, I melt with the terror of my fright. Fear and trembling have shaken my soul.

Thus I am thrust into and condemned to exile, thus I suffer the penalty of exile, thus I groan because of the condemnation of exile, led in the chain of slavery, crushed by the burden of my condition, enslaved with menial work, in chill weather, in snow, in cold, in raging storms, forced into every task, in every danger. After the condemning of my goods, after the loss of all my possessions, I am made poor and needy. I lack, I beg unhappily, I publicly implore alms. No one stretches out his hand to the needy, no one helps the poor. I am not considered worthy of anyone's pity, I am deprived of everyone's mercy. There is no one who will have pity.

All scorn the beggar, and do not restore the needy with their crumbs. No one pours a refreshing drop into the mouth of the thirsty. No one offers me even a moderate dew-drop of water, for I am made hateful to all. Whenever anyone looks upon me, all despise me as if I were covered with sores, reject me as full of sores, shudder to touch me as if I were a leper. My body is restrained by irons, held by chains, bound by fetters, confined by bonds. The torture, the torments, the punishment do not cease for me. Their fierceness is cruel to me continually.

The butchers rend me with new bodily torture, they tear my insides and limbs with unheard-of kinds of punishment, they invent whatever cruelty they can against me. I do not die a simple death, but am tortured by a thousand pains, a thousand tortures, a thousand punishments. My flesh has festered, slashed with wounds. My half-burned sides pour out pus, my torn limbs drip with stench, blood flows in my tears, and gore in my weeping. It is not only a weeping of tears, but of wounds.

I am wretched, I am consumed with sorrow, my soul is anguish, and my body fails. Finally my mind is conquered, my soul is shackled by sorrow. I have experienced much that is unbearable, bitter and heavy. So serious and cruel a wound I have never received. I am burdened with an unthinkable wound, I am threatened with death every moment. An unexpected calamity crushed me unaware, sudden destructions and misfortunes fell on me.

Unhappy that I am, why was I born? Why was I thrust into this miserable life? Why did I, a pitiable man, ever see the light of day? Why did the beginning of this life happen to me? Would that I might depart more swiftly from this world than I entered it. With good reason now would I go! But alas! Longed-for death comes slowly to the wretched. Let the one who desires to die succumb. For I am weary of living. I desire to die, death alone pleases me. O death, how soothing you are to the wretched! O death, how sweet you are to those who live in bitterness! How cheering you are, O death, to the sorrowful and grieving! Therefore let the great solace of death follow the great evil of life: let the end of life be the finish of such great evils: let the repose of the sepulchre bring an end to misery: and if life will not, let death at least begin to have pity. Death brings an end to all evils, affords a conclusion to calamity, destroys all misfortune. Or, surely death helps the wretched. It is better to die well than to live wretchedly; it is better not to exist than to exist unhappily. This is clear from the magnitude of my sorrows. I bewail that I am stricken, I weep at my calamity, I grieve because of the inseparable pain of my misery. Wretched, I cannot be consoled; my sorrow is unremitting, my grief is endless. My wound is not bound up; there is no moderating of my tears, no end to my sorrows. Now there is no hope of soul. Now the soul cannot endure. Now the soul falls, overcome with miseries.[33]

Bright (1586)

Timothy Bright's work on melancholia was a landmark. He described the feelings of patients in much more detail than had previous authors. Moreover, Bright differed from the scholastics and theological philosophers of the Middle Ages in stating that melancholia was not merely "conscience of sin" although it had some of the same manifestations. And of course he mentioned crackpot.

> *Howe diverslie the word Melancholie is taken.* It signifieth in all, either a certayne fearefull disposition of the mind altered from reason, or else an humour of the body . . . We doe see by experience certaine persons which enjoy all the comfortes of this life whatsoever wealth can procure, and whatsoever friendship offereth of kindnes, and whatsoever security may assure them: yet to be overwhelmed with heavines, and dismaide with such feare, as they can neither receive consolation, nor hope of assurance, notwithstanding there be neither matter of feare, or discontentment, nor yet cause of daunger but contrarily of great comfort, and gratulation. This passion being not moved

[33] St. Isidore, Archbishop of Seville, *Synonyma; or On the Lamentation of the Sinful Soul*, in J. P. Migne, *Patrologiae cursus completus*, Series Latiniae (Paris: Migne, 1844), Vol. 83, cols. 827–834.

by any adversity present of imminent, is attributed to melancholie ... By that hath bene before declared it may easily appeare the affliction of soule through conscience of sinne is quite another thing then melancholy: but yet to the end it may lie most cleare, I wil lay them together, so shall their distinct natures thus compared bewray the error of some, and the prophanes of othersome, who either accompt the cause naturall, melancholy, or madnes, or else having some farther insighte, with a Stoicall prophanes of Atheisme, skoffe at that kinde of affliction, against which they themselves labour to shut up their hard heartes. ... let them consider that this is a sorrow and feare upon cause, & that the greatest cause that worketh misery unto man: the other contrarily a meere fancy & hath no ground of true and just object, but is only raised upon disorder of humour in the fancy, and rashly delivered to the heart, which upon naturall credulity faireth in passion, as if that were in deede wherof the fancy giveth a false larume. In this the body standeth oft times in firme state of health, perfect in complexion, and perfect in shape, & al symmetrie of his partes, the humours in quantitie and quality not exceeding nor wanting their naturall proportion. In the other, the complexion is depraved, obstructions hinder the free course of spirits & humours, the blood is over grosse, thick, & impure, & nature so disordered, that diverse melancholicke persons have judged themselves some earthie pitchers, othersome cockes, other some to have wanted their heades &c, as if they had ben transported by the evill quality of the humour into straunge natures: here the senses are oft times perfect both outward & inward, the imagination sound, the heart well compact & resolute, & this excepted, want no courage. In the other, the inward sense and outward so feebled, the fancy overtaken with gastly fumes of melancholy, and the whole force of the spirite closed up in the dungion of melancholy darkenes, imagineth all darke, blacke and full of feare, their heartes are either overtender and rare, & so easily admitte the passion, or over closse of nature serve more easily to imprison, the chearefull spirites the causes of comforte to the rest of the bodie: whereby they are not in one respect only fainte harted, and full of discourage: but everie smal occasion, yea though none be, they are driven with tide of that humour to feare, even in the middest of security. Here it first proceedeth from the mindes apprehension: there from the humour, which deluding the organicall actions, abuseth the minde, and draweth it into erronious judgement, through false testimony of the outward reporte.[34]

Willis (1683)

Thomas Willis was, as usual, remarkably perceptive in discussing melancholia. Among other symptoms exhibited by patients he referred to their rumination

---

[34] T. Bright, *A Treatise of Melancholie* (London: T. Vautrollier, 1586), pp. 1, 90, 184–187.

and the contraction of their interests. He emphasized that delusional reasoning need not occur in all phases of a patient's thinking and noted the relation to mania. Not only did Willis point out that melancholia was sometimes a precursor of what would today be called schizophrenia but he also recognized that a loss may lead to depression—today popularly regarded as a "new" discovery.

Melancholy is commonly defined to be, a raving without a Feavour or fury, joined with fear and sadness. From whence follows, that it is a complicated Distemper of the Brain and Heart: For as Melancholick people talk idly, it proceeds from the vice or fault of the Brain, and the inordination of the Animal Spirits dwelling in it; but as they become very sad and fearful, this is deservedly attributed to the Passion of the Heart.

It would be a prodigious work, and almost an endless task to rehearse the diverse manner of ravings of Melancholy persons; and there are great Volumes already of Histories and examples of this sort; and more new and admirable observations and examples daily happen. Fabulous antiquity scarce ever thought of so many metamorphoses of men, which some have not believed really of themselves; whilst some have believed themselves to be Dogs or Wolves, and have imitated their ways and kind by barking or howling; others have thought themselves dead, desiring presently to be buried; others imagining that their bodies were made of glass, were afraid to be touched lest they should be broke to pieces. There are extant manifold and various kinds of the Imagination so depraved, concerning which may be commonly observed; That the distemper'd are Delirious as to all things, or at least as to most; so that they judge truly almost of no subject; or else they imagine amiss in one or two particular cases, but for the most part in other things, they have their notions not very incongruous. We shall first inquire into this more universal Distemper, for that the Imagination is prevaricated concerning very many things; to wit, by what causes, and with what difference of Symptoms, this is wont to come to pass; afterwards we shall speak of the special raving or idle talking.

Although the universal Distemper of Melancholy contains manifold Delirious Symptoms, yet they chiefly consist in these three; 1. That the distemper'd are almost continually buried in thinking, that their Phantasie is scarce ever idle or at quiet. 2. In their thinking they comprehend in their mind fewer things than before they were wont, that oftentimes they roll about in their mind day and night the same thing, never thinking of other things that are sometimes of far greater moment. 3. The Ideas of objects or conceptions appear often deformed, and like hobgoblins, but are still represented in a larger kind or form; so that all small things seem to them great and difficult.[35]

---

[35] T. Willis, Two Discourses concerning the Soul of Brutes, Which Is That of the Vital and Sensitive of Man [1680], S. Pordage, trans. (London: T. Dring, 1683), p. 188.

Melancholy, being a long time protracted, passes oftentimes into Stupidity, or Foolishness, and sometimes into madness.[36]

Thus much concerning universal *Melancholy*, by which the sick are affected almost indifferently by any object, so that they are intangled in every place, and by any accidents and circumstances; with a multitude of thoughts continually, with raving, fear, and sadness. We have largely enough handled the *Symptoms* of this Disease being manifold, and the reasons of them, partly in this Chapter, and partly in another Tract.

It is called special *Melancholy*, when the sick respect a certain particular thing, or some kinds of things, of which they think almost without ceasing; and by reason all the powers and affections of the soul being continually imployed about this one thing, they live still careful and sad; moreover, they have absurd and incongruous notions, not only about that object, but also concerning many other accidents and subjects. In this Distemper, the Corporeal Soul, bending from its proper kind, assumes a certain new one, but not being comfortable, either to the Rational Soul, or to the Body, or to it self, it enters into a certain *Metamorphosis*.

This kind of Distemper, is produced by many ways, and on various occasions; for vehement passions, desire, fear, anger, pleasure, yea all other passions both of the *concupiscible* and *irascible* Appetite, being long continued, and carried forth to the height, are wont to excite the same. But there are two general occasions, from which special *Melancholy* chiefly and most frequently doth arise; to wit, first, when there lyes a most heavy pressure on the mind of some present evil, or an evil just at hand, whether it be true or imaginary: or secondly, if the loss or privation of some good before obtained, or desparing of something wished for or desired, happen.[37]

Blackmore (1726)

Although the title of Blackmore's book refers only to hypochondriacal and hysterical disorders, he actually wrote an excellent description of depression which contrasts in detail psychotic depression (melancholia) and neurotic depression (hypochondria).

___ The Symptoms of this Disease are numerous, that either affect the Organs of the Body, or the Exercise of the intellectual Faculties. In the Brain it is accompanied with great Disturbance of the Imagination and Fancy, a continued and uninterrupted Flux or Train of Thoughts fixed upon one sad Object, from which the Patient is unable to call them off, and transfer them to another; and therefore this is not what is called Contemplation, Study, or Deliberation, but unguided and restless Musing; and the Difference between

[36] Ibid., p. 193.
[37] Ibid., p. 199.

them is this, that when a Man studies or meditates, he commands his Faculty of Thinking, and turns it from one thing to another; but in Musing, Man is governed by his own Thoughts, and unable to restrain or divert them to other Matters, but they are obstinately employed in poreing on and revolving the same Images, sometimes in a more regular, and sometimes in a disorderly and incoherent Train, which return and are presented to the Imagination in a constant Rotation, like the Pictures painted on Cloth or Paper, and turned round by a Wheel, which Strollers carry as Shows from Town to Town, and expose for the Entertainment and Diversion of the meaner People. But it must be observed, that all the Images formed by a melancholy Imagination, are sad, dark, and frightful; while gay and delightful Objects are always shut out, or very seldom admitted to the Fancy and lighter Faculties of the Mind; for in regard to such Ideas, the Mind is under a total and lasting Eclipse.

By this, Melancholy is distinguished from Hypocondriac Affections; for Patients obnoxious to the last Distemper, though sometimes sad and pensive, yet have frequent lucid Intervals; and are not only in a chearful, facetious, and pleasant Humour, but are often carried on to so profuse a Pitch of Mirth and Gaity, that by their too great Waste and Expence of Spirits, they soon after sink to a low, dull, and uncomfortable Temper. They differ likewise in this, that Hypocondriack Persons, though sometimes for a Season they are unfit for intense Studies, Contemplation or Business, while the Exercise of their Reason and Imagination is disabled and suspended, during some odd and whimsical Circumstances, when they start aside, and deviate from their usual regular Way of Thinking; yet for the most part, when their Disease is abstracted from all Complications of a melancholy Disposition, they discover great Abilities and Endowments of Mind; as a moderate Degree of the Gout, when free from all Conjunction of other Infirmities and Diseases, is often accompanied with superior Understanding, and a great Measure of Bodily Health. So if the Spleen is taken with the Limitations I have mentioned, one would not wish to be deliver'd from this any more than from the other, since the Benefits arising from them over-balance all the Sufferings and Inconveniences that attend them.

As the Thoughts of melancholy Persons usually dwell upon sad and gloomy Objects, so they generally pore and muse upon such as have been the ordinary Entertainment of their Minds before they fell into this distempered State; and therefore when the Imaginations of religious Persons receive a melancholy Turn, they are always taken up about the important Affairs that concern the Performance of their Duty here, and their Happiness hereafter; hence their Diffidence, Scruples and Fears concerning the Sincerity of their Faith and Repentance, and their everlasting State, are by their Distemper increased, even sometimes to so deep a Despondence and Self-condemnation, as borders on Despair. This the Atheist, Infidel, and loose Libertine, foolishly call superstitious Madness; and then offering violence to Reason, and indulging a petulant, flagitious Humour, they reproach Religion as the Cause of this

Effect, treating the Persons that profess and practise it, in Raillery and Ridicule: hence all pious and devout Men are by such accounted only Hypocondriacal Enthusiasts, or whimsical Visionaries. But let these Contemners of Heaven, who are fond of all Occasions of bringing Dishonour and Contempt upon Religion, reflect, that as many Men express Zeal for Piety and Vertue, who however are entirely delivered from the Symptoms of this Disease, and have not in their Constitutions the least Infusion of Spleen and Vapours; so in Multitudes that fall under the Dominion of Melancholy, the Distemper does not always operate in this manner, nor turn their Thoughts and anxious Cares to religious Objects: but this chiefly, if not only, happens when the Patient, seized with these Disorders, was accustomed to divine Thoughts and spiritual Ideas before; and then it is but natural that a disturbed Imagination should chiefly entertain such Images, as were before well known, and had been long familiar to the Mind. And this falls out in almost all Instances of great Melancholy (while the unhappy Sufferers are more to be pitied than derided and exposed) and the Patients themselves and their Relations should be convinced, that such religious Melancholy is as much a bodily Desease, as any of another Class and a different Nature; and they must more depend upon the Art of the Physician, and the Force of Medicine, than the Skill and Reasonings of the Casuist, for their Recovery: for so fluctuating and unstable are their Minds, that though at this time they seem sedate and calm, yet in a few Hours the Clouds gather again; the Brain is overcast with Darkness, and the same Anxiety, Scruples, Fears and Terrors return, and repossess the Mind. But perhaps I have pursued this Subject too far, though the Nature and Design of this Discourse led me to it.

This continual musing and turning of the Thoughts upon a Series of Sad and afflictive Objects, as well as the lubricous, inconstant, and changeable Disposition of these Persons, must be accounted for from the continual Rotation of their restless and unquiet Spirits; which though poor and weak, are still in a Hurry and perpetual Motion, though that Motion is confined to a narrow Compass. And as the Reason and Judgment of melancholy Persons are much subverted and disabled, who are not receptive of the Force and Light of the clearest and most convincing Arguments against their pre-conceived Opinions, but with an inflexible Obstinacy hold fast their erroneous Conclusions; or if they yield them up one Hour, yet resume them the next, and continually relapse into their former way of Thinking; so their Imagination is much injured and disturbed: and as I have said before, the Scenes they form and represent, are all mournful and uncomfortable, composed only of severe, sullen, and unpleasant Figures. Besides, it is observable to all, that they often entertain the most idle, absurd, and ridiculous Fancies; one believes he is unable to move Hand or Foot, and lies as if deprived of all Motive Power; another thinks his Nose is swollen to a prodigious Dimension; and though at great Distance, he believes it reaches to the Door, and hinders others from entering the Room. One Man has living Frogs in his Stomach, which he perceives, as he thinks, from their crawling and croaking there; another is as much disturbed with a Brood of young Chickens in his Belly, which he is persuaded are really there, by an Opinion that he hears their peculiar Noise, and feels their Motions. Some will by no means be convinced, but that they are entirely formed of Glass, and that by the next Knock or Jog on any solid Objects, they shall break all to pieces; while others are as much concerned to avoid coming near the Fire, for fear of being melted, being fully assured that they are made of Butter. One has believed himself to be Millet-Seed, another a Goose, or a Goose-Pye. And once a Man filled with Strong Drink, feared to render it by Urine, lest he should drown the World by a Deluge. And several Examples there have been of melancholy Persons, who have believed themselves to be actually dying, and imagined they were cold half way the Body; and of others, that took themselves to be really dead, and desired to be laid out, in order to their Funerals: and many of these incredible Examples of Melancholy I have my self seen, and the others are related by credible Authors.

But the History of these fanciful Persons is various and endless; and there is scarce anything so extravagant and ridiculous, even to the greatest Admiration, that may not be found among the various Classes of these everlasting, but absurd and impertinent Thinkers, whose animal Spirits, vitiated and perverted, become unapt Instruments for the Operations of the Mind and Imagination.

As a melancholy Constitution of the Spirits is fruitful of a surprizing and copious Diversity of odd and ridiculous Phantasms, and fills the Imagination with a thousand uncouth Figures, monstrous Appearances, and troublesome Illusions; so it is no less in producing disquieting and restless Passions, while they affect the Heart with Anxiety, Sadness, Fear and Terror; which Perturbations, no less than those of the Mind and Imagination, seem the inseparable and distinguishing Concomitants of this Distemper: for notwithstanding in some very few brighter Seasons, when the dark and melancholy Clouds that overcast the Brain, are dispersed, these Patients may break out into short, extraordinary Fits of Mirth and Alacrity; however this seldom happens, and then too when there is a Mixture and Complication of a Hypocondriack or Hysterick Temperament with that, which is properly Melancholy; as when these Patients, through great Despondency and unsufferable Inquietude, discover Marks of a Design upon their own Lives, their Distemper exceeds its proper Nature and Extent, and has contracted a Degree of Lunacy. And indeed the Limits and Partitions that bound and discriminate the highest Hypocondriack and Hysterick Disorders, and Melancholy, Lunacy, and Phrenzy, are so nice, that it is not easy to distinguish them, and set the Boundaries where one ends, and the other begins: however, continual Thoughtfulness upon the same Set of Objects always returning to the Mind, accompanied with the Passions of Sadness, Dejection, and Fear, seems to be the genuine and discriminating Idea of proper Melancholy.

Now this Assertion, that a previous poor, and vappid Disposition of Blood, that cannot afford by the Mediation of the Strainers of the Brain a sufficient Stock of generous and volatile Spirits, is the antecedent Cause of this Disease, is likewise confirmed by this Observation that the most succesful Remedies in this case, are those that animate and invigorate the Mass of Blood, and inspire it with new enlivening Ferments; by which means the superior, active Principles are more exalted, and the passive prevented from being disproportioned and predominant; whence a greater Plenty of bright, swift, and vigorous Spirits, are imparted to the Brain, such as are capable of being proper Servants of the Mind, and suitable Instruments of the animal Powers; whence they are enabled to perform their Operations in a regular manner: and these are chiefly Steel by it self, or variously prepared by Art, or dissolved by Nature in Waters issuing from Springs and Fountains; though other auxiliary Remedies may be taken in and joined with them, to strengthen them and increase their Force. If, as it often happens, these Diseases, founded in a disorderly and defective Constitution of the Nerves and Spirits, are blended with the Principles of one or more of the other Distempers before named, and accordingly participate of their Properties, and have various Symptoms in common with them. then it is a mixed and complicated Case, though the Denomination is given to the superior and predominant Power. Thus, as Hypocondriack or Hysterick Persons have often an Adhesion or Tincture of proper Melancholy, and sometimes of Distraction, and sometimes of both, and the Effects of these Mixtures are evidently discerned in them; so melancholy Patients are often diversified from one another, by a subordinate Measure of Lunacy, or the Spleen and Vapours combined with their original Principles. And true it is, there is often such an Absence of Mind, such Excursions and Starts from right Reason, and such an absurd, incoherent, and ridiculous Train of Thoughts and Actions, discernible in Men afflicted with this Disease, that all high Degrees of it seem to have more than a Touch of Lunacy adhering to it; and it is notorious, that many celebrated Men of Wit, that derive their superior Genius from an Hypocondriacal Constitution, have sometimes Spirits elevated to a degree above the Standard of sober and uninfected Reason; whence proceeds that known Expression, "nullum magnum Ingenium sine mixtura dementia"; for the bright and active Disposition of animal Spirits, requisite to refined and elevated Parts, borders so close upon the Dominions of Lunacy, that an Excursion or Transition from the first to the last is by no means difficult, since one Heat of the Brain more might have beat down the Inclosures, and laid their Territories in common, as before observed.[38]

---

[38] R. Blackmore, *A Treatise of the Spleen and Vapours; or Hypocondriacal and Hysterical Affections* (London: J. Pemberton, 1726), pp. 155–166.

Boerhaave (1709)

Boerhaave's brief comment is important for only one reason: It was repeated verbatim by eighteenth-century authors. It was not only too brief to be useful but also too rigid to be clinically acceptable.

> Physicians call that Disease a Melancholy, in which the Patient is long and obstinately delirious without a Fever, and always intent upon one and the same thought.
> ... a lessen'd Appetite; a Leanness; Sorrowfulness; Love of Solitude; all the Affections of the Mind violent and lasting; and Indifferency to all other Matters; a Laziness as to Motion; and yet a very great and earnest Application to any sort of Study or Labour.[39]

Mead (1755)

Mead saw mania and depression as facets of a single disease, in part because patients alternated from one to the other. He also noted that the disorders had features in common.

> Medical writers distinguish two kinds of madness, and describe them both as a constant disorder of the mind without any considerable fever; but with this difference, that the one is attended with audaciousness and fury, the other with sadness and fear: and that they call mania, this melancholy. But these generally differ in degree only. For melancholy very frequently changes, sooner or later, into maniacal madness; and, when the fury is abated, the sadness generally returns heavier than before: hence all maniacal people are fearful and cowardly; which is an observation of great use in practice.[40]

Cullen (1791)

Cullen emphasized the extreme variability of melancholia, the possibility of undeluded thinking in some areas, and the common occurrence of anxiety. He also related the psychosis to pre-existing personality characteristics.

> The disease which I name Melancholia is very often a partial insanity only. But as in many instances, though the false imagination or judgement seems to be with respect to one subject only; yet it seldom happens that this does not produce much inconsistency in the other intellectual operations. And as, between a very general and a very partial insanity, there are all the possible

---

[39] *Boerhaave's Aphorisms: Concerning the Knowledge and Cure of Diseases* [1709], trans. from the last Latin ed., Leyden, 1728 (London: A. Bettesworth and C. Hitch, 1735), pp. 312, 314.
[40] R. Mead, *Medical Precepts and Cautions*, T. Stack, trans. (London: J. Brindley, 1755), p. 79.

intermediate degrees; so it will be often difficult, or perhaps improper, to distinguish melancholia by the character of partial insanity alone. If I mistake not, it must be chiefly distinguished by its occurring in persons of a melancholic temperament, and by its being always attended with some seemingly groundless, but very anxious, fear.

To explain the cause of this, I must observe, that persons of a melancholic temperament are for the most part of a serious thoughtful disposition, and disposed to fear and caution, rather than to hope and temerity. Persons of this cast are less moveable than others by any impressions; and are therefore capable of a closer or more continued attention to one particular object, or train of thinking. They are even ready to be engaged in a constant application to one subject; and are remarkably tenacious of whatever emotions they happen to be affected with.

These circumstances of the melancholic character, seem clearly to show, that persons strongly affected with it may be readily seized with an anxious fear; and that this, when much indulged, as is natural to such persons, may easily grow into a partial insanity.[41]

Haslam (1798)

Haslam's brief comment was extremely important. He pointed out that delusional thinking characterized both depression and mania and that the two conditions differed only in the feelings which the patients experienced.

As the terms Mania, and Melancholy, are in general use, and serve to distinguish the forms under which Insanity is exhibited, there can be no objection to retain them; but I would strongly oppose their being considered as opposite diseases. In both, the association of ideas is equally incorrect, and they appear to differ only, from the different passions which accompany them.[42]

Pinel (1801)

Pinel's writings on melancholia were for the most part pedestrian, except for his comments on the influence of some melancholics on the people around them, and on the melancholic pre-psychotic personality. He also mentioned the fact that some melancholics perform crimes in order to attract punishment.

The symptoms generally comprehended by the term melancholia are taciturnity, a thoughtful pensive air, gloomy suspicions, and a love of solitude. Those traits, indeed, apear to distinguish the characters of some men otherwise in good health, and frequently in prosperous circumstances.

---

[41] W. Cullen, *First Lines of the Practice of Physic* (Edinburgh: Bell and Bradfute and William Creech; London: G. G. J. & J. Robinsons and J. Murray, 1791), pp. 177–178.

[42] J. Haslam, *Observations on Insanity* (London: F. and C. Rivington, 1798), pp. 12–13.

Nothing, however, can be more hideous than the figure of a melancholic, brooding over his imaginary misfortunes. If moreover possessed of power, and endowed with a perverse disposition and a sanguinary heart, the image is rendered still more repulsive.[43]

The biography of persons of distinguished talents and reputation, affords many instances of melancholics ... who were remarkable for their ardent enthusiasm, sublime conceptions, and other great and magnanimous qualities. Others, occupying a less exalted station, charm society by the ardour of their affections, and give energy to its movements by their own impassioned turbulence and restlessness. Melancholics of this class are remarkably skilful in tormenting themselves and their neighbours, by imagining offences which were never intended and indulging in groundless suspicions. It is very common for physicians to be consulted by persons of this temperament for nervous palpitations or aneurism of the heart. Some fancy themselves under the influence of hydrophobic madness. Others believe that they have all the diseases which they read of in medical books. I have known many who had had the venereal disease, torment themselves, upon the appearance of the least indisposition, with the belief that the virus of siphilis was still operating; and they have gone for advice to every empyric that flattered their credulity.
Profound melancholia is frequently succeeded by actual derangement of the intellect.[44]

Melancholics are frequently absorbed by one exclusive idea, to which they perpetually recur in their conversation, and which appears to engage their whole attention. At other times, they observe the most obstinate silence for many years, and friendship and affection are refused participation in their secret. On the contrary, there are some who betray no extraordinary gloom, and appear possessed of the soundest judgement, when an unforeseen circumstance happens and suddenly rouses their delirium. . . .
Any cause of fear or terror may produce a habitual susceptibility to those emotions, and, by undermining the constitution, may induce dangerous debility and death. . . .
A certain sourness of disposition, and a surly misanthropy of character, appear to determine some maniacs to shut themselves up in their own chambers, and to treat, with great rudeness and abuse, any person that should offer to molest their solitude. Fanatics, belonging to this class of madmen, often fancy themselves inspired and under divine requisition to perform some sacrificial act or acts of expiation. Those deluded and dangerous beings can commit most barbarous homicides in cold blood.[45]

[43] P. Pinel, *A Treatise on Insanity, in Which Are Contained the Principles of a New and More Practical Nosology of Maniacal Disorders* [1801], D. D. Davis, trans. (Sheffield: W. Dodd, 1806), p. 136.
[44] Ibid., p. 138.
[45] Ibid., pp. 141–142.

A curious phenomenon, illustrative of the tyranny of semantics, arose during the early nineteenth century. Since ancient and renaissance authors had insisted that melancholia was characterized by an intense preoccupation with one delusion. It was concluded that mania, which displayed opposite symptoms, must comprise a multiplicity of delusions. By the mid-nineteenth century this absurd distinction was recognized as invalid. Before that, however, monomania was a common classification for various illnesses, usually but not always those characterized by depression. By chance, monomania came to include psychiatric disorders which are characterized by extreme deviation in one major aspect of behavior, now recognized as a frequent manifestation of depression. Hence the idea that depression was a monomania was reinforced.

Haslam (1809)

Haslam's second book again revealed the subtlety of his comprehension of clinical psychiatry. In addition to giving a good description of the manifestations of melancholia, this work refutes the idea that the number of delusions differs in mania and depression and emphasizes the different speeds of mental associations in the two disorders.

There are patients in Bethlem Hospital, whose lives are divided between furious and melancholic paroxysms, and who, under both forms, retain the same set of ideas. . . .

In speaking of the two forms of this disease, mania and melancholia, there is a circumstance sufficiently obvious, which hitherto does not appear to have been noticed: I mean the rapid or slow succession of the patient's ideas. Probably sound and vigorous mind consists as much in the moderate succession of our ideas, as in any other circumstance. It may be enquired, how we are to ascertain this increased, proportionate, and deficient activity of mind? From language, the medium by which thought is conveyed. The connexion between thought and utterance is so strongly cemented by habit, that the latter becomes the representative of the former.[46]

Burrows (1820)

Burrows made important contributions to the understanding of melancholia. He distinguished grief and despondency from melancholia but showed how the former might lead to the latter. He also noted the development of melancholia without any emotional cause or after a period of mania. The concealed beginnings of melancholia are well described in his writings.

Dejection of mind and constant sadness being always a precursor of this malady, it is apt to be imputed to grief; and if no occasion be known for it,

---

[46] J. Haslam, *Observations on Madness and Melancholy* (London: J. Callow, 1809), pp. 33–34.

then to some secret or other depressing cause. Grief certainly is a frequent moral cause of melancholia; but where it is so, it is often owing to an hereditary predisposition, or the person is of the melancholic temperament. Grief or sorrow, however intense, in most constitutions, by degrees subsides without injury; but if continued a long time, it will produce great disorder both of body and mind, and originate a degree of melancholy which deteriorates vital energy, and brings on gradual decay, though without delirium; and the patient in a few years dies quite exhausted. In others, such a state of abstraction follows grief, that all external impressions which disturb the thought associated with the cause, excite a temporary painful sensation and mental irritation, more insupportable than the cause of grief itself. This alternate state of abstraction and irritation, at length effects a total change in the feelings and mind, and all the incipient symptoms of that mental affection denominated melancholia are gradually unfolded. . . .

Melancholia will arise without reference to any moral cause.

. . . Melancholics are much addicted to biting their nails, picking their fingers, or any pimple or abrasion of the skin, till the parts are often very sore, though the pain attending is unheeded. These habits they are generally most intent upon when conversing or vexed.

While the symptoms are thus gradually developed, the patient appears as if enduring some internal conflict, to suppress the impulse which may betray his mental aberration. He generally entertains a conviction or suspicion of the nature of his malady, which he carefully conceals: a delusion therefore may long be generated before it is exhibited. . . .

In a sudden access of mania there is no disguise: impressed with the reality of the delusion, it is boldly urged and maintained, and the maniac repels with fury and scorn all attempts to convince him that it is an error.

In melancholia the delusion is secretly, perhaps, but not less obstinately, cherished; and opposition to it will often induce violent anger.

. . . By degrees, however, words are dropped, which discover the character of the delusion. At length it is avowed, defended, and persisted in, as the result of deliberate reflection, or conviction, or inspiration; and his conduct and speech are conformable with the impression.

Melancholia sometimes commences with a paroxysm of furious mania; and mania may begin in melancholia. These may interchange or alternate, or either may preserve its pristine character throughout; thus proving their identity and origin from a common stock.[47]

Esquirol (1838)

Esquirol gave a vivid but in no way original account of the symptoms of depression. He coined the unfortunate term *lypemania* to replace *melancholia.*

---

[47]G. M. Burrows, *An Inquiry into Certain Errors relative to Insanity and Their Consequences; Physical, Moral and Civil* (London: T. and G. Underwood, 1820), pp. 352-354.

His positive contributions included a discussion of the extreme intolerance to discomfort exhibited by many patients, the pervasive anxiety, the role of the mood in determining thought content, and a re-emphasis of the fact that murder may be owing to depression.

Melancholy with delirium, or lypemania, presents in its symptoms when taken together two striking differences. Those suffering from this calamity, now exhibit a remarkable susceptibility, attended with extreme mobility. Every thing produces a strong impression; the slightest cause produces the most painful effects. Events, the most simple and common, appear to them to be new and singular phenomena, prepared expressly to torment and injure them. Cold, heat, rain and wind, cause them to shudder with pain and fear. Noise impresses them painfully, and strikes them with terror. Silence causes them to start, and frightens them. If any thing displeases them, they repulse it with rudeness and obstinacy. If their food is not agreeable to them, their repugnance to it is so great, as to produce nausea and vomiting. Have they any ground for fear, they are terrified; they have any regrets, they are in despair; do they experience any reverses, they believe that all is lost. Every thing is forced and exaggerated in their mode of feeling, thinking and acting. This excessive susceptibility causes them to be constantly meeting, in external objects, with new causes of pain. Both day and night their ear is open for hearing and their eye for seeing. They are constantly in motion, in search of their enemies, and the causes of their sufferings. They relate without ceasing, and to every one, the story of their ills, their fears, and despair. . . .

The passions modify the ideas, belief and determinations of the most rational man. The depressing passions produce also a partial lesion of the understanding. The intellectual life of him whom a melancholic delirium controls, is altogether imbued with the character of his passion. The mountaineer cannot support a lengthened absence from the place of his nativity, ceases not to mourn, and at length pines away and dies, if he does not revisit the paternal roof. He who fears the police, or the pursuits of the tribunals, is filled with alarm and dread, and is in constant apprehension of an arrest. He sees every where agents of police, and servants of the magistracy, and that too, among his friends and relatives. . . .

Some lypemaniacs are constantly laboring under fear, and consume their lives, in constantly recurring solicitudes; whilst others are terrified by a vague sentiment, without any motive. *I fear*, say these patients, *I fear*; but wherefore? I know not, *yet I fear*. Their external appearance, their physiognomy, their actions and discourse, all indicate fear the most profound and poignant, from which they can neither relieve themselves, nor secure the ascendency. The delirium takes the character of the moral affection which engaged the mind of the patient before the outbreak of the disease, or preserves that of the cause that produced it; a fact which is especially noticeable when this cause acts promptly, and with great energy. . . .

... The principles of filial piety, love, friendship and gratitude, are sometimes carried to excess, and augment the disquietude and fears of the melancholic, and impel him to such acts as flow from despair. Thus a mother believes she is abandoned by her husband, and desires to slay her children to preserve them from a like misfortune. A vine-dresser slays his children, in order to send them to heaven.[48]

Guislain (1852)

Guislain insisted that all mental disorders were basically depressions and that depression might be the first and the last symptom of any of them. The first concept was largely rejected but the second was given widespread acceptance.

As I have said earlier, mental anguish can be somewhat moderated in its manifestations in impressionable and debilitated subjects above all; it is thus that dementia, catatonia, and deterioration can immediately follow the action of the abnormal cause, without a state of the depression being able to develop. But depression exists fundamentally, and what proves it, is the sadness that does not wait to appear, that reveals itself partly as the disease moves toward convalescence, partly as the general tension or enfeeblement begins to stop. . . .

Zeller, physician director of the insane establishment at Winnenthal, in talking about the origin of mental diseases, states as follows:

"According to our most recent observations, depression is also the basic form of most mental diseases, so that we should consider the case an exception in which one does not encounter it."[49]

Falret (1854)

Falret objected to the statement that all psychoses begin as depressions. He preferred to regard the initial period, which might have some of the features of depression, as one of generalized disturbance.

Can one claim that all mental diseases begin with a depressive psychosis? This assertion appears to us erroneous. Far from being a psychosis, the depressive state, if it occurs, is a true state of generalized trouble, of intellectual confusion, and of spiritual enfeeblement. We believe, in effect, that most psychoses begin with a more or less general state of disturbance of the intellectual and affective functions; it is on the basis of this initial

[48] E. Esquirol, *Mental Maladies: A Treatise on Insanity* [1838], E. K. Hunt, trans. (Philadelphia: Lea and Blanchard, 1845), pp. 205–208.

[49] J. Guislain, *Leçons orales sur les Phrénopathies; ou Traité théorique et pratique des maladies mentales* (Gand: L. Hebbelynck; Paris: J. B. Baillière; Bonn: A. Marcus, 1852), pp. 159, 162.

disturbance of intelligence and feelings that there begins and develops equally the excitement of mania and the fixed ideas of partial insanity.[50]

It was inevitable that someone should recognize the existence of insanity that is continuous but with alternations of mood. Falret coined the term *circular insanity*.

The transformation of mania to melancholia and vice versa has been described, in every era, as an accidental fact, but no one has remarked, or at least no one has said it in a specific manner, that there exists a certain category of psychotics in whom this succession of mania and melancholy manifests itself continuously and in an almost regular manner. This fact has seemed to us important enough to serve as the basis of one particular form of mental disease that we call *la folie circulaire*, because this kind of psychotic revolves in the same circle of disease states that reproduce themselves increasingly, fatally, and that are not divided by a lucid interval, however short. We must point out that the two states whose succession constitutes *la folie circulaire* are, in general, neither mania nor melancholia, properly speaking, with their normal characteristics; this *folie* includes parts of these two kinds of mental disease without their remission. On the one hand, there is no incoherence of ideas, as in mania, but simple manic exaltation, that is to say extreme activity of the faculties with a constant need for movement and strong indications of disordered behavior; on the other hand, there is no subdued disorder of intelligence or the predominence of certain well-defined delusions, as in ordinary melancholy, but physical and mental depression sometimes carried almost to complete suspension of the intellectual and affective faculties. This period of depression in *la folie circulaire* is ordinarily longer than the period of manic excitement. It is remarkable that these two varieties of mania and melancholia, which taken separately are ordinarily more curable than the others, have the greatest seriousness when united to form *la folie circulaire*. Up to now we have seen only remissions, more or less striking, in the course of this disorder; we have never seen complete cure, nor lasting amelioration.[51]

Bucknill and Tuke (1858)

Bucknill and Tuke listed the synonymous diagnostic terms applied to depression.

It corresponds to the *tristimania* of Rush; the *melancolie, phrenalgia, luperophrenie,* of Guislain; the *trübsinn, tiefsinn,* of the Germans; and the *sadness*, and *melancholy*, of English writers.

[50] M. Falret, *Leçons cliniques de médicine mentale* (Paris: J. B. Baillière, 1854), p. 228.
[51] Ibid., pp. 249–250.

Esquirol suggested the word lypemania (λυπεω, to cause sadness, and μανια), in the place of melancholia, but added, that he should employ the two words indifferently.[52]

Morel (1860)

The fact that depression, like mania, is merely a symptom and is found in various types of insanity was stated by Morel.

I have already shown that mania (exaltation) and melancholia (depression) are symptoms that are found in all types of insanity, and that, consequently, they do not constitute essential forms.[53]

Griesinger (1845)

Griesinger provided a massively detailed but highly perceptive description of the symptoms of depression. He observed its vague early manifestations, its role as a precursor of many other forms of mental disease, and its development de novo or as a consequence of despondency. His account of the psychology of the disorder was copied by many others. His emphasis on depression as a cause of antisocial behavior is significant.

The fundamental affection in all these forms of disease consists in the morbid influence of a painful depressing negative affection—in a mentally painful state. This state may, at the outset, in the simplest and the most primitive form of melancholia, continue in the form of a vague feeling of oppression, anxiety, dejection, and gloom; generally, however, this obscure vague feeling of annoyance passes into a single, concrete, painful perception; there arise thoughts and opinions in harmony with the actual disposition of mind, and without external motive (false ideas)—a veritable delirium, revolving constantly upon some tormenting and painful subject, while at the same time the intellect presents some anomalous forms, is restrained in the exercise of its freedom, becomes slow and sluggish, and the thoughts monotonous and vacant. The normal reaction towards the external world is either weakened and blunted (mental anaesthesia, indifference even to actual stupor), or exaggerated in such a manner that all mental impressions are painful (mental hyperaesthesia); and very often these two forms are found in the same patient alternating with each other. Many disorders of the emotion and of the will are moreover associated with this. Their varieties form a basis for the distinction of the several principal forms of melancholia. Sometimes volition is directly

---

[52] J. C. Bucknill and D. H. Tuke, *A Manual of Psychological Medicine: Contains the History, Nosology, Description, Statistics, Diagnosis, Pathology, and Treatment of Insanity* (Philadelphia: Blanchard and Lea, 1858), p. 152.

[53] B. A. Morel, *Traité des maladies mentales* (Paris: V. Masson, 1860), p. 271.

diminished and weakened, at other times it is convulsively restricted (absence of energy and of will); at others there appear certain desires and impulses of will to which material and object are afforded by the morbid mind; or, lastly, a high degree of moral pain excites various impulses of an aimless convulsive character, which manifest themselves in extreme restlessness, the continuance and increase of which cause these forms of melancholia to assume a different character, and to pass into quite another variety of that of mania. . . .

Observation shows that the immense majority of mental diseases commence with a state of profound emotional perversion, of a depressing and sorrowful character. Guislain was the first to elucidate this highly interesting fact, and make it at all serviceable. Of its general correctness there is no doubt, and we can have no hesitation in speaking of the *"stadium melancholicum"* as the initiatory period of mental disease. Of course there are exceptions. Thus, in senile dementia, in periodic mania, in meningitis, in the mental diseases consecutive to typhus fever, pneumonia, cholera, sun-stroke, &c., the outbreak of mania is generally observed without being preceded by melancholia; but the cases are much more frequent in which this *stadium melancholicum* only *appears* to be absent because it was less intense, and was not then recognised as a stage of mental disease. . . .

The melancholia which precedes insanity sometimes appears externally as the direct continuation of some painful emotion dependent upon some objective cause (moral causes of insanity), *e.g.*, grief, jealousy; and it is distinguished from the mental pain experienced by healthy persons by its excessive degree, by its more than oridnary protraction, by its becoming more and more independent of external influences, and by the other accessory affections which accompany it. In other cases the melancholia originates without any moral cause, though most frequently there are such, but it does not originate as their direct continuation, but only shows itself after these affections have wrought considerable disturbances in the functions and nutrition of the nervous system, or have undermined the entire constitution.[54]

Anomalies of self-consciousness, of the desires, and the will.—In many cases, after a period of longer or shorter duration, a state of vague mental and bodily discomfort, often with hypochondriacal perversion, depression and restlessness, sometimes with the dread of becoming insane, passes off, a state of mental pain becomes always more dominant and persistent, but is increased by every external mental impression. This is the essential mental disorder in melancholia, and, so far as the patient himself is concerned, the mental pain consists in a profound feeling of *ill-being*, of inability to do anything, of suppression of the physical powers, of depression and sadness, and of total abasement of self-consciousness. So soon as this condition of the sensorium

---

[54] W. Griesinger, *Mental Pathology and Therapeutics*, from the 2nd German ed., C. L. Robertson and J. Rutherford, trans. (London: The New Sydenham Society, 1867), pp. 209–211.

attains a certain stage, the most important and wide-spread consequences, as regards the demeanour of the patient, result.

The disposition assumes an entirely negative character (that of abhorrence or repulsion). All impressions, even the slightest and formerly most agreeable, excite pain. The patient can no longer rejoice in anything, not even the most pleasing. Everything affects him uncomfortably, and in all that happens around him he finds new sources of pain. Everything has become repulsive to him; he has become irritable and angry. Every trifle puts him out of temper. The result is, either perpetual expressions of discontent, or—and this is more common—he endeavours to escape from all outward mental impressions, by withdrawing himself from the society of men, and, completely idle and unemployed, seeking solitude. This general feeling of aversion and indifference is often expressed by a dislike towards those by whom he is surrounded, his family, friends, and relatives, which often merges into absolute hatred—by a complete and unhappy change in his character.

We may sometimes observe in individuals apparently healthy (particularly among females) a similar though much more chronic state of habitual perversion of sentiment, accompanied by a capricious and morose disposition, with a tendency to contradiction and ill-nature. Nevertheless, it is very rarely that this is regarded as a morbid state, even although it differs widely from similar evil dispositions which we see sometimes displayed in those who are perfectly healthy,—through its frequent origin from palpable diseases, through its frequent remissions, which are explicable by no well-grounded mental motive, and through the fact that at times the patient feels himself constrained to yield to the evil disposition in direct opposition to the dictates of his conscience and his will, and although he is perfectly aware that such conduct is most unwarrantable.

In simple melancholia we frequently find a condition of the sensorium precisely analogous to that which we have described under the head of Hypochondria, in which the objects of the outer world, although they come into consciousness through the medium of the senses, and are indeed properly understood and recognised, still they produce an impression utterly different from what they were wont to do, of which the intelligent and educated sufferers can alone give a true description. "It appears to me," says such a melancholic, "that everything around me is precisely as it used to be, although there must have been changes. Everything around me wears the old aspect, everything appears as it was, and yet there must have been great changes," &c. This confounding by the patient of the subjective change of exterior things, and then objective change, is the commencement of that dreamy state, in which, when it has attained to a tolerably high degree, it appears to the patient as if the real world had actually and completely vanished,—that it has sunk, disappeared, or is dead, and all that now remains to him is an imaginary world, in the midst of which he is perpetually tormented by finding that he has still to live.

At the beginning of this state the patient is perfectly cognisant of the change which has taken place in his moral nature, in all his feelings and affections. Sometimes he seeks to hide it, and the inquiries concerning the cause of his peculiar behaviour weary and annoy him. He feels that his former enjoyment in everything that was honorable and estimable is fast passing into indifference and actual repugnance. He even complains himself that his sensations are no longer natural, that they are perverted; and when his evil genius constrains him to regard the worst side of the world, a new source of pain and sorrow is presented to him, viz., that he can rejoice about nothing, and must oppose everything. The unwonted impressions from the outer world excite his astonishment, grief, and fear. He feels himself excluded from his former intercourse with society; and this feeling of isolation, this exceptional position in which he finds himself, favours, on the one hand, the limitation of all ideas concerning the relation in which he stands to the world, and the relation of external objects to himself. On the other hand, there proceeds from this feeling of isolation, distrust, anxiety, and fear of all possible evils—sometimes a feeling of hatred and revenge towards the world, but more often a powerless, helpless withdrawal from society and concentration in himself.

That which weighs most heavily upon the mind of the patient at the commencement of his trouble, is that feeling of change which has taken place in his own personality, that vagueness and obscurity arising from this undefined feeling of annoyance. Yet at this stage he is sometimes perfectly aware that his fears are absurd, and that those uneasy thoughts which force themselves upon him are utterly false; and he is even conscious of his own actual state. But then, he perceives that it is impossible for him to feel, to think, to act otherwise than he does,—that he cannot resist, and how useless every effort at resistance is; then he receives from this overcoming of the *Ego* the idea of being ruled, of being irresistibly abandoned to some foreign influence, to which, afterwards, ideas of being governed by evil powers, of secret direction of the thoughts, of demoniacal possession, &c., correspond.

The limitation of the will, which is one of the fundamental disorders of melancholia, is manifested by inactivity, cessation of all employment, constant doubt and irresolution, incapacity of decision and absence of will. In the higher degrees, it shows itself in actual torpidity and dulness of feeling, inasmuch as impressions are no longer followed by a reaction of the will; in the more moderate degrees, as slowness, monotony, hesitation in movement and action, feeling of incapacity for the slightest mental exertion, lying in bed, &c.

Frequently there are sensations of intense anxiety, which often appear to spring from the epigastric and cardiac regions, and to mount upwards. "Here," say many of these patients, pointing to the epigastrium—"here it remains like a stone: would that I could get rid of it!" These feelings of anxiety sometimes increase to such an extent as to be almost unbearable; thus driving the patient into a state of despair, which generally passes into an attack of mania. Moreover, these states manifest themselves externally in many various forms, according to the former disposition of the patient, the moral causes, and accompanying physical anomalies, &c.: at times, with the outward signs of grief and care, or as silent melancholy, as self-concentration, or a dull, passionless, reserved bearing; sometimes as loud self-accusation, with weeping, wringing of the hands, and great restlessness; sometimes as morbid peculiarity and intractable obstinacy; or, finally, as a tendency to lay violent hands on self.

There are some melancholics who are always discontented, and whom nothing pleases; others to whom everything is alike indifferent, because their attention is completely absorbed in the contemplation of their own misfortune; and others who maintain that for them "everything is too good, and they cannot understand how it is that people do not despise such miserable creatures as they are."

All these varieties in the disposition of melancholics are at the commencement generally unaccountable, and do not depend on certain definite delirious conceptions; therefore it is that the patient himself is also, at this stage, perfectly incapable of giving any statement which might account for his present condition. "I am afraid," says such a patient; and if asked why, he can only reply, "I don't know, but I am afraid." Hence, we are constrained to come to the conclusion—which, indeed, observation has led us to, and serves only every day to confirm—that exhortations, solicitude, and argument have not the slightest effect upon this state of depression, engendered by some cerebral lesion; that the ideas which conduce to the development of this state must have an internal, subjective origin, and therefore a character of irrefutability, so that they render the patient wholly impervious to anything like argument, and at best only permit him to exchange one mournful train of ideas for another.

Anomalies of the intellect.—The painful concentration of the mind represses the vivacity and the natural course of the thoughts. A few ideas occupy the mind of the patient, and all that he gives utterance to is a few monotonous complaints regarding himself, and of the sad change which has come over him. Or, he continually reverts to certain events which happened about the commencement of his illness, &c. All desire for intellectual intercourse with his friends is generally very much diminished. The patient often sits perfectly mute, or at best speaks timidly, with hesitation, in a low tone, frequently interrupting himself. One melancholic who was under my charge preserved an inviolable silence for several years, and it was only from his physiognomy that we learned his ruling disposition, for it expressed most unequivocally intense anxiety and sadness, while at times he would weep and wring his hands. In other cases the patient bewails himself, heaves deep sighs, and is engaged in prayers and supplications, but always on the same subject; yet, in spite of the extraordinary monotony of his intellectual life, he never becomes a prey to *ennui.*

Together with these formal disorders, there now appear false ideas and judgments, corresponding to the actual disposition of the patient. Thus, for example, he feels that he is in a state of anxiety of mind exactly similar to that which a criminal is likely to experience after the perpetration of some misdeed, and so he believes that he, too, has committed some crime; and from this predominating idea he cannot rid himself. But as in the review of his life he is unable to recall what this crime is, he fixes upon some insignificant event, when he has committed some trivial fault, some petty carelessness (or perhaps he may not even be guilty of that), and this unfortunate occurrence becomes the subject of his delirium. In it he discovers the cause of his present misfortunes, and his fears for the future. Sometimes he feels himself the prey of some undefined torment, and imagines himself encompassed with enemies. Soon he actually considers himself persecuted, surrounded by foes, the subject of mysterious plots, and watched by spies; and as he connects everything with himself, the most insignificant matter tends to nourish his delirium.

Again, the patient who formerly cherished religious ideas feels how profoundly he has changed in regard to this train of thought; how this state of anxiety and uneasiness renders him totally incapable of reflection; how, consequently, he is unable any longer to pray, or at his devotions he is assailed by unhappy negative ideas. He feels that the church and all other external objects give rise in him merely to painful impressions. Thus he seems, in his exceptionable position, like a castaway whom God has given up and abandoned to the devil and to eternal damnation. Soon he comes actually to believe that he has indeed committed grave faults, innumerable sins, and that he has entirely neglected his duties, &c. Hence we see that it often depends upon chance, upon which particular thoughts or ideas the patient attaches so much importance that they recur to him as fixed or partially fixed delusions.

All these melancholic insane ideas have one essential character, that of passive suffering, of being controlled, and overpowered. But we can readily discern how very various must be the special subjects of these ideas, according to the amount of education and the character of each individual, their antecedent history, and the impressions which have been accidentally made. The same feeling of loss of self-control, of being given over to foreign and peculiar sensations and ideas, which awaken in the credulous peasant the idea of being bewitched, may in the better educated call forth the idea that some one is acting upon him by means of electricity, magnetism, or chemistry. To the one it seems as if he had lost all his most cherished goods, his children, his relations, and his fortune. This he firmly believes, and fears that nothing now remains for him and his family but to die of starvation. Another imagines that he has become bankrupt, that his business has gone from him, that he is mixed up in the most serious and criminal offences, and ceases not to bewail that he has reduced his family to the most abject poverty and beggary. At other times it seems to the patient, when he feels the change which has occurred in his whole mode of sensation, and experiences the impossibility of maintaining his ordinary share of worldly duties and employments—imagines that he can no longer be a man—that he is gradually becoming like one of the lower animals, or that he is even already transformed into a beast. As the change in the patient's views of life and morals in general usually gives to the insanity a certain colour and expression, so long as the natural sensations continue the same, and the general relations of love of family, interest, friendship (emotions which in all times most actively bear on the human heart) remain, so also the delirium of the melancholic presents various phases at different epochs. The fundamental disorders of the self-sensation are, however, always the same, whether the melancholic believes, as in the days of old, that Atlas, becoming fatigued with his burden, may at any moment let the arch of heaven drop; or whether he imagines, as in the middle ages, that he is under the power of sorcerers, ghosts, and witches; or, as in our times, that he is sought after by the police, or that he is engaged in the most disastrous speculations, &c.

As to the manner in which this delirium is brought about, we have already several times pointed this out. The patient experiences a feeling of sadness. At first these fits of sadness are only produced under the influence of vexatious causes; but the law of causality demands even here some motive, some cause for this, and before the patient has had time to inquire into the rationale of it, there arise as answers all sorts of mournful thoughts, dark presentiments and apprehensions, over which he broods and ponders until certain ideas have become strong and persistent enough to be, at least for the time, fixed. Thus these delirious conceptions again possess the essential character of *attempts at explanation* of the special state.

At the commencement, and in many cases even during the entire course of the melancholia, there may be no delirium, properly so called. The patients may be able quite correctly to realise their own condition and the things of the external world—to analyse their sensations with precision, and anxiously desire to free themselves from them; but to do this is absolutely beyond their power.

Amongst the most marked cases of melancholia, there is one most important distinction to be made, viz., whether the patients appear to be as it were in a profound *dream*, or whether all their transactions with the outer world are carried on as if they were quite awake. Cases of the first class ordinarily assume a more acute character, and more nearly approach that form known as "melancholia with stupor," the prognosis of which is much more favorable than that of those which fall under the second head; which usually develop themselves slowly, and are much more chronic in their course. The first class of cases may terminate very speedily, as if the patient had suddenly wakened up; the latter never do this.

Anomalies in the sensibility and movement frequently accompany these mental disturbances. These are at times indicated by sensations of emptiness in the head, of deadness in the head, or of some other member, or even of the whole body; sometimes by these annoying sensations experienced over the whole surface of the skin, and suggest to the sufferer the idea that some one is electrifying him; or, finally, by hyperaesthesia of the sight and hearing (trembling, starting at the slightest noise—perhaps a fundamental cause of the so-called panphobia).[55]

An essentially different deportment is presented by movements in that form of melancholia where the inner disquietude is also expressed by physical restlessness (melancholia agitans), in which there usually is a confused tumult of thought. In essentials, however, these are certainly very monotonous and of small variety; and it is through this paucity of ideas, this want of fertility, that this state differs from mania. At other times, the patient keeps up a perpetual motion, often breaks out into fits of weeping, and constantly wrings his hands. Not unfrequently, he manifests a great desire to wander about at liberty, to make long excursions, and to visit his friends and relations (melancholia errabunda). Often while walking he wrings his hands, or, becoming violently agitated, throws his arms into all manner of wild contortions. We may quite correctly recognise in these two different modes of appearance of the morbid mental pain, the analogues to the painful emotions of the healthy: on the one hand, to the immobility consequent on shock or fright; on the other hand, to the physical restlessness and agitation (running about in the open air, &c.) observed in these in this frame of mind.[56]

The Course of the simple forms of melancholia is often very acute: thus, for example, in those cases where a very short period of painful perversion of the feelings, accompanied with profound anxiety, precedes the development of mania, particularly of intermittent mania. Usually, however, the course of melancholia is chronic, with remissions; more rarely with complete intermissions, of variable duration. I have once seen, in a woman attacked with intense melancholia (ideas of complete loss of fortune, of forced starvation, &c.), a complete lucid interval of scarcely a quarter of an hour's duration supervening without any assignable cause, and terminating quite as suddenly. Naturally, the remissions are of more frequent occurrence at the commencement of the melancholia, and also on the approach of convalescence. . . .

A very moderate degree of melancholia with considerable remissions may persist for many years. Such patients very rarely come into asylums, or at least only during an exacerbation or an intercurrent attack of mania. They may generally be maintained in their ordinary relations, and are torments to

---

[55] Ibid., pp. 223–229.
[56] Ibid., p. 231.

those who surround them, and objects of the most varied mistaken speculation on the part both of physicians and of the laity. . . .

We have already seen that melancholia not unfrequently passes into one of the forms of mania; but further, simple melancholia, or melancholia with stupor, may also terminate by leaving the patient in a state of intellectual weakness, a more or less exaggerated state of veritable dementia. This is probably owing to the development of organic alterations within the cranium. Although the patient may have regained his physical vigour, yet the physiognomy wears an expression of heaviness and stupidity. The sadness may have gradually disappeared, but the intellectual faculties have lost their energy. Not unfrequently, there are also developed states of more or less profound partial dementia, where the patient has some fixed delirious conceptions, particularly certain hallucinations, through which he is led to believe that people desire to poison him, that he is the subject of various plots, or that he is constantly electrified, &c.; in which case the patient is almost always incurable. Such patients, labouring under this partial dementia, states of mental weakness, with the remains of melancholia (and mania) and hallucinations, generally with numerous exacerbations, in the form of one or other of the primitive states (apathy alternating with turbulence, a modified sadness with a gaiety equally superficial, &c.), constitute by far the major portion of the chronic cases met with in asylums. We shall enter more into detail on this subject when we come to consider partial dementia and dementia. At first the condition frequently continues for a long time stationary in the form of melancholia, varied only with slight changes for the better, only again to relapse. At this period it is extremely difficult to say anything with certainty as to the curability of such patients; but when this state of melancholic apathy continues for three or four years consecutively without remission, recovery is extremely rare.[57]

The modes of expression of the mental pain experienced in melancholia are so diverse and so multifarious, that, founding upon these principal differences, *certain forms and varieties of melancholia* have been constituted.

In so far as the difference extends merely to the *form* and *subject* of the *delirium*, which often agree with the most salient causes of the mental affection, the classification of such varieties is of minor importance. . . .

It is of more importance to distinguish various forms of melancholia according to the *different relation of the* emotional nature; of the will and of the actions. Thus the conditions which we have just been considering may present important modifications in two different and, in some degree, opposite ways. On the one hand, they may proceed to a state of still deeper self-concentration with complete loss of will, or more usually with convulsive tenacious effort. On the other hand, in these states, new desires and new

[57] Ibid., pp. 234–236.

movements of the will may appear, corresponding to the general negative disposition, which either manifest themselves only in one isolated act of violence, or in a continual outward restlessness and excitement; when the melancholia passes into the form of mania.[58]

Dickson (1874)

Dickson commented on the diurnal variations in the symptoms of depression, and also on the fact that recovery from depression was likely to take a long time.

There is a point in the clinical history of melancholia particularly to be noticed, viz., that the subjects are very often better towards the end of the day, but that there is usually an accession of symptoms about bed-time when they become very restless and often sleepless. The hour of bed-time is too often merely the indicator of the aggravation of the distress. And should the patient succeed in sleeping, the distress seems to be exaggerated still more in the act of waking; fortunately however, the exaggeration generally soon subsides. But the moment of waking is worthy of very special note, as it is the time when the unhappy victim of this black despair often succeeds in accomplishing his suicidal or violent attempt; and as the brain at the waking time is with everyone in a very active condition, so unfortunately when the fixed subjective melancholy impression has become the only one occupying the mind, it often appears in its strongest and most powerful force at that moment. I have already in a former lecture spoken of the hallucinations which frequently occur in the sanest people in waking. . . .

The stage of recovery is usually marked by an improvement in spirits, but, as a rule, the mind of the patient for a long time is very feeble, and it must be brought face to face with the world, and with society and excitement, by degrees only.[59]

Spitzka (1883)

Spitzka pointed out that depression in its mildest form was likely to be regarded as neurosis.

In private practice melancholia, particularly of the lighter grades, is very common; and is not unfrequently treated as "neuraesthenia"—whatever that may or may not be—and dyspepsia, and, thanks to the self-limiting tendency of the lighter forms of the psychosis, it is frequently cured on either theory.[60]

[58] Ibid., p. 240.
[59] J. T. Dickson, *The Science and Practice of Medicine in Relation to Mind: The Pathology of Nerve Centers and the Jurisprudence of Insanity* (New York: D. Appleton and Co., 1874), pp. 189, 233.
[60] E. C. Spitzka, *Insanity: Its Classification, Diagnosis and Treatment* (New York: Bermingham and Co., 1883), p. 148.

Krafft-Ebing (1893)

Krafft-Ebing modernized the clinical description of melancholia, but his debt to Griesinger and some others is evident. Krafft-Ebing evidently had difficulty in distinguishing melancholy with stupor from catatonia, for he mentions "cataleptiform states" as common and *flexibilitas cerea* as occasional in the former.

The fundamental phenomenon in melancholia consists of the painful emotional depression, which has no external, or an insufficient external, cause, and general inhibition of the mental activities, which may be entirely arrested. . . .

The content of the melancholic consciousness is psychic pain, distress, and depression, as the expression of a nutritive disturbance of the psychic organ. This painful depression in its content does not differ from the painful depression due to efficient causes. The solidarity of the psychic activities causes the depression to be total; the psychic organ is incapable of calling up any other than painful psychic activities, so long as the causal abnormal disturbance exists. This organically conditioned state of psychic pain is psychologically augmented by other simultaneous disturbances of the psychic mechanism, largely arising out of the painful depression.

These accessory sources of pain are found in unpleasant apperception of the external world in the mirror of the painfully altered consciousness (psychic dysesthesia); in the feeling of being overwhelmed which the patient experiences in his psychic mechanism; and finally in the consciousness of inhibition which all psychic activities thus undergo (ideation, desires). The most painful thing for the patient at the height of the disease is the absence of both pleasant and unpleasant emotional coloring of ideas and sense-perceptions (psychic anesthesia).

The general result of these painful psychic processes expresses itself clinically in depression and sadness. Psychic dysesthesia causes the patient to be retiring, with desire to avoid people, or to assume a hostile attitude toward the external world; psychic anesthesia causes indifference, even to the most important things of life.

Along with the disturbance of content there is a change (formal) in the sphere of emotional life. This is manifest in the fact that ideas, as well as sense-perceptions, are accompanied with extremely vivid unpleasant feelings, which may attain the degree of affects, while at the same time the threshold of excitability of emotion lies abnormally deep.

Thus it may happen that every mental act, even sense-perceptions, may be accompanied by intense feelings of displeasure (psychic hyperesthesia).

Such states of psychic hyperesthesia, like phenomena observed where nerves are affected with neuralgia, precede those of psychic anesthesia, or they alternate with the latter.

The affective states thus produced express themselves in feelings of displeasure or sadness, which may be intensified to despair; or in feelings of surprise (embarrassment, confusion, astonishment, fright, shame) or emotional states of apprehension (anxiety, oppression, fear). This abnormal excitability expresses itself clinically in irritability, sensitiveness, and moodiness, since hyperesthesia and anesthesia alternate and differ in intensity.

The mental need of quiet in the patient is expressed in retiring from society and seeking isolation; the avoidance of sense-impressions and emotional activities.

Disturbances in the intellectual domain are partly those of form and partly those of content. The former consist of retardation of thought and slowness of the association of ideas.

This retardation is part of the general slowing of psychic activities; in part, too, dependent upon the painful feelings with which every psychic act is colored.

The inhibition of the free course of ideas is an important accessory source of psychic pain. This expresses itself clinically in a feeling of fatigue, of mental vacuity, and of lessened mental energy (stupidity, lack of memory of which so many patients complain). Temporary complete stoppage of thought induces despair. The disturbance in the association of ideas is essentially due to the fact that only such ideas are possible as are in accord with the painful feeling, and thus the sum of the ideas that can possibly be reproduced is limited to those of painful content. Inhibition and disturbed association favor the occurrence of imperative ideas.

Formal disturbances of ideas occur in all melancholics. They may be the only anomalies (melancholia without delusions); frequently, however, there is disturbance in the content of ideas: delusions.

In the great majority of cases these arise psychologically and are an attempt to explain the abnormal state of consciousness; but the delusion is not necessarily the product of a logical conscious operation of thought; it may also be merely the conscious result of an unconscious product of association. Delusions arising out of errors of the senses are infrequent in melancholia, and pure primordial delusions are still more infrequent.

The content of melancholic delusions is extremely varied, for they include all varieties of human trouble, care, and fear. Since they are always created out of the ideas peculiar to the individual, it is natural that they should vary infinitely according to individual endowment, sex, position, education, and age, even though certain constant cares and fears of the human race lend to the delusions of innumerable melancholics of all races and all times certain features and characteristics of content which are alike.

The common character of all melancholic delusions is that of suffering, and, in contrast with the similar delusions of paranoia with delusions of persecution, they are referred to personal guilt.

Errors of the senses are very frequent in the course of the severer forms of melancholia.

Just as the content of the ideas in melancholia are hostile and painful, so, too, are the delusions frightful. In affective states, especially where they are of the nature of an anxious apprehension, errors of the senses are especially intense and frequent.

The peculiar inhibition of the psychic activities in melancholia expresses itself with especial clearness on the psychomotor side of mental life.

The intensification of mental pain by every kind of mental activity causes laziness, avoidance of work, neglect of occupation, and inclination to retire and take to bed. The want of self-confidence makes the attainment of ambition seem impossible and destroys all effort. The inhibited psychic activity in itself, the difficulty of change of ideas and their coloring by unpleasant feelings, the loss of mental interests which incite to act, find their expression in the complaints of the patient that he would like to act, but that he cannot will himself to act.

The painful effect of the concrete idea impelling to a voluntary act, due to contrasting ideas arising out of the greatly diminished sense of self, consciousness of defective power, psychic powerlessness, and the possibility that an idea may be sufficient to prevent success, cause the patient to vacillate between impulses and inactivity, expressed clinically in the vacillation and want of decision that characterize such patients.

The fundamental character of melancholia is that of absence of energy: passiveness. However, in such cases, at least episodically, a very stormy, violent activity, going even to the extent of *furor*, is possible. This is explained by the fact that temporarily the inhibition is overcome by intense emotion. . . .

Melancholic insanity manifests itself clinically in two definite forms, which may be called *simple melancholia* and *melancholia with stupor*, and they demand separate description.

Simple Melancholia

The milder cases of melancholia are those in which the symptoms of mental inhibition are essentially psychic, due to a conscious painful mental process, and not organically induced by arrested activity in the psychomotor nervous paths, shown in its extreme degree by disturbance of muscular innervation (tetany, catalepsy). In these cases, too, there is not deep disturbance of consciousness. The inhibition in the emotional life shows itself in anesthesia with despair; in the intellectual life, as painful obstruction to the processes of thought in all directions; in the will, as distressing incapacity to decide upon an action, reaching even to the extent of complete arrest of voluntary acts. The necessary results is a profound diminution of confidence in self.

Since the consciousness of the patient is a constant source of pain, and since the patient is a martyr to emotions and thoughts of threatening danger, which constantly maintain and intensify the painful state of emotional strain, his position becomes proportionately more painful, since he feels incapable or at least not capable at all times, of performing the act that will deliver or save him.

The funadmental manifestation of the disease-picture is passivity: a distressing arrest of psychic activities. The passivity of melancholics may temporarily reach a degree where there is complete arrest of the psychomotor activities. Not merely acts, but even speech and movements of locomotion then become slower or difficult, and occur only in obedience to intense and repeated external stimuli and necessity. They are later only begun and not completed, until finally every motor act has become impossible (passive melancholia).

These cases, in which evidently the psychic inhibition is increased and complicated by augmented organic (molecular) resistance in the voluntary paths, constitute transitional forms to the severer forms of melancholia with stupor, in which consciousness is also troubled and the patient sinks into a cloudy mental state.

Except when episodically or in the transition to stuporous melancholia such states of complete mental inhibition occur, the consciousness of the patient suffering with simple melancholia is not more profoundly disturbed, even though it be filled by painful images and ideas.

Thought is interfered with and limited, but judgment is possible, in contrast with stuporous melancholia, in which there is a state of delirious dreaming with spontaneous delusions—for example, like those that occur in the delirium of fever or intoxication, and which undergo no further combination and elaboration.

Owing to the fact that the patient suffering from simple melancholia is capable of drawing conclusions, there is the possibility of the creation of delusions, and of their further systematic combination and logical valuation. The passive attitude of the patient may at any time change to a condition in which the patient is continually excited and active, and he obtains relief by expressing his mental pain and state of emotional tension in the most furious way in crying, wringing his hands, constant movement (melancholia errabunda), and even in destructive acts (agitated or active melancholia).

The cause of this state is not to be sought in increased readiness in the transformation of ideas into motor impulse, as is the case in mania, but in the enormous force with which the motor impulse is present in consciousness, which enables it to overcome all inhibition.

The fact that these agitated melancholic states form only the height of the general disease-picture or are episodic phenomena in the course of (passive) melancholia. These affect-like outbursts of despair, which may temporarily overcome the classic inhibition of the melancholic, arise out of the painful mental state, which temporarily may become unbearable, and which depend upon psychic anesthesia, hyperesthesia, inhibition of thought, imperative ideas, lack of energy, and also complicating neuralgias, perversions of bodily feeling in general, precordial distress, frightful hallucinations, and delusions. In such imperative psychic states suicide is near. Analgesia facilitates the act. Frequently, especially under the impelling influence of precordial distress, there are destructive acts directed toward others. Psychic dysesthesia and anesthesia favor them.

During such paroxysms the patient in violent agitation resembles a case of furious mania; indeed, he may surpass the latter in destructiveness. As a rule, by inexperienced observers these cases of depression with continued excitement are diagnosticated as furious mania, although, between the destructive impulse of the maniac and the motor activity of the depressed, dependent upon painful states of consciousness, there is an essential difference.

In active melancholia there may be even the rapidity of ideas called the flight of ideas; but here this phenomenon has entirely a different character from the flight of ideas that occurs in mania, as Richarz has cleverly pointed out. In spite of all possible rapidity in the flow of ideas, the delirium of active melancholia is still monotonous, painful in content, and moves in the narrow circle of melancholic emotions, and is but a constant variation of the same theme.

The power to form a series of ideas with continued and infinite associations is wanting here, in contrast with mania, in which association of ideas is infinitely facilitated.

The ideas of the melancholic are only fragments of chains of thought. He is unable to finish the train of thought commenced, which constantly escapes from him, and he is constantly forced back to begin again. For this reason such patients compalin of the constant painful resultless impulse to think; of the impossibility of continuing a train of thought and carrying it to its logical conclusion; of the emptiness of consciousness in spite of the fact that it seems to be overfilled.

It is therefore with a certain amount of justice that Emminghaus regards this condition as an overpowering imperative idea.

Simple melancholia is decidedly the most frequent form of mental disease. It presents clinically great variety in the grouping of the symptoms and the intensity of the disease. From this standpoint essentially three degrees may be distinguished, for a case may pass through them all or end at any one of them. The mildest form of the disease may be called:—

Melancholia without delusion The disease picture is limited to anomalies of the feelings and will, with disturbance of thought that is merely formal. There are neither delusions nor errors of the senses (hallucinations and illusions). This mild form of melancholia is only exceptionally observed in institutions for the insane, but it is extremely frequent in private practice.

Often it long escapes the observation of the laity, as well as of physicians, for the patient is able to preserve an appearance of calm and reason.

To be sure, the somber character, the irritability, the depression, and the change from the usual manner of thinking and feeling are remarked; but these are explained or attributed to external causes, and the patient who does not wish to appear ill gives all manner of excuses for his carelessness and laziness and his neglect of customary duties. Thus, often for a long time, the true mental condition remains undiscovered until aggravation of the malady, or some act of violence arising out of the unbearable painful state of strain, reveals it. The ordinary medical diagnosis, overlooking the psychic anomaly, is frequently limited to anemia, chlorosis, hysteria, neurasthenia, etc. The disease does very frequently rest upon this physical and neurotic foundation, especially in connection with puberty (homesickness) and also in hypochondriacs, neurasthenics, and constitutional neuropaths. When it is dependent upon this herediatry foundation, it is not infrequently associated with imperative ideas (murder, suicide, fire), and also with somatic, neurotic, and especially sensory functional disturbances (paralgias, neuralgias). In these cases the disease is protracted, of graver prognosis.[61]

Melancholia with delusions and errors of the senses In the course of melancholia delusions and errors of the senses often occur. They develop gradually in the course of *melancholia without delusion,* and represent the acme of the development of the disease, or they occur at an early period after the beginning of the depression. This is the rule in acute and subacute cases. Since in contrast with the delusions of primary hallucinatory insanity and paranoia the false ideas of melancholics are almost always the product of efforts to explain the abnormal state of consciousness, it is usually possible to trace the delusions to their source: *i.e.,* to the fundamental elementary psychologic disturbance.

Thus, the profoundly changed feeling of self in the patient, which depends either upon consciousness of the inhibition of feeling or upon ideas and impulses, and which finds its clinical expression in depression and want of self-confidence, leads to the delusion of being ruined, a beggar, or forced to die of starvation. The psychic dysesthesia causes the external world to appear in a hostile light, and gives rise to ideas of persecution and threatening danger. The feeling of inhibition and of being overpowered, in individuals of limited mental power, leads to the delusion of being under the influence of the powers of darkness—of being bewitched. Psychic anesthesia, which destroys all ethic and humane feelings, leads to the delusion that all human attributes have been lost, and of being changed into an animal. On the religious side, since

[61] R. von Krafft-Ebing, *Text-Book of Insanity Based on Clinical Observations for Practitioners and Students of Medicine* [1893 (5th German ed.)], C. G. Chaddock, trans. (Philadelphia: F. A. Davis, 1904), pp. 286–293.

comfort in prayer is lost and all relation with religion is felt to be destroyed, the delusion of being rejected by God, of having lost eternal happiness, or of being possessed by the devil, easily arises. In the highest degrees of psychic anesthesia, when sensory perceptions no longer have any intensity or emotional coloring, the external world seems to be merely a shadow, which awakens distressing delusions of general and personal destruction.

Precordial distress and anxious emotional states of expectation in general are very important sources of delusions. They give rise to the delusion that some danger actually threatens. This may be individually translated objectively into ideas of imaginary persecution, threatened death, or loss of fortune. At the same time, on account of the loss of confidence in self, the patient easily develops the delusion of being a sinner or a criminal meriting such punishment. As a further motive there may have been previously an actual infraction of the law, or some harmless previous act or neglect, which to the hyperesthetic conscience appears to be a crime.[62]

Roubinovitch and Toulouse (1897)

The mental anguish that characterizes depression was commented on by many. Its intensity, and the variations in its intensity, are nowhere better discussed than in the work of Roubinovitch and Toulouse.

_____ There are other fairly constant characteristics of what we call melancholia, which are especially pathognomonic in their implication, i.e., mental anguish and the slowing of the intellectual functions. German psychiatrists have contributed most to the study of these two essential symptoms of melancholia. Mental anguish, even more than the slowing of the intellectual faculties, is an attribute of the melancholic. It is that which creates constant depression together with transports of overwhelming emotion and crises of anxiety. One can say that melancholia is above all a pathologically sad emotion.[63]

Melancholia is a state of sadness without adequate cause, with a tendency toward despair, a state in which mental anguish is the fundamental symptom. . . .

The mental anguish of the melancholic is a painful chronic emotion, which, in the serious cases, gradually envelopes the entire field of consciousness. Is there a difference between this mental anguish and that which occurs in a normal person under the influence of a reasonable cause? Apparently there is not. In a normal person suffering extreme disappointment, the possibility of receiving agreeable perceptions still persists, and there remains a certain hope

---

[62] Ibid., pp. 298–299.
[63] R. Roubinovitch and E. Toulouse, _La Mélancolie_ (Paris: Masson et Cie., 1897), p. 28.

of escaping from the painful phase he is in. The true melancholic has completely lost the ability to experience the feelings that might turn aside his disappointment; and he is persuaded that he can never free himself of his mental anguish. . . .

The intensity of this suffering is not equalled by any other.[64]

The intensity of this mental anguish is not always the same in the same person. There are fluctuations, and, on a given day, the melancholic can feel more afflicted in the morning than in the evening; sometimes a few days pass with relative calm.

At its extreme, one may see exacerbation of the mental anguish that takes on the proportions of a veritable attack: It is then anxiety, that while it is continuous, constitutes a clinical syndrome. . . . The attack continues for a longer or shorter time, then it vanishes, only to reappear. . . .

At times the sadness is replaced by terror. The patient has a feeling of an imminent and inevitable danger; and this fear can, if it is so intense, plunge the patient into a stupor.[65]

Kraepelin (19th–20th centuries)

Kraepelin offers a special problem because of the changes in his formulations during a short period. His psychiatric text was extremely popular, and, becuase each edition was rapidly sold out, he produced a succession of revised editions over a period of two decades. In the early editions of his *Psychiatrie* he treated depression as did his contemporaries, but with much less feeling for the human spirit than Krafft-Ebing (whom he evidently admired and respected). From the sixth edition on, however, Kraepelin handled endogenous depression as part of the manic-depressive syndrome. Almost all authors since Areteus had mentioned that mania and melancholia often changed from one to the other, and Kraepelin was not alone in treating them as a single entity, though he did so more systematically and rigorously than others. Some of today's less well-informed students refer to him as the discoverer of the manic-depressive psychosis, but even the word *manic-depressive* had been used two hundred years earlier (see page 139).

Types of Melancholia

The subdivisions or varieties of melancholy were defined solipsistically by many Renaissance physicians. De Sauvages collected this anecdotal material and tried to define the essential character of each of fourteen deviations from normal behavior:[66]

---

[64] Ibid., pp. 39–40.

[65] Ibid., p. 42.

[66] F. B. de Sauvages, *Nosologie méthodique* (Paris: Hérissant le fils, 1771), Robert Burton, however, described eighty-eight deviations in his *Anatomy of Melancholy... with All the Kinds, Causes, Symptoms, Prognostics, and Several Cures of it* (Boston: Dana Estes and Co., n.d.).

1. ordinary melancholy
2. lovesickness
3. religious melancholy
4. melancholy with imaginary illnesses
5. extravagant melancholy
6. atonic melancholy (with stupor)
7. vagabondous melancholy
8. dancing melancholy
9. hippotropic melancholy
10. Scythian melancholy
11. English melancholy
12. zoantropic melancholy
13. fanatical melancholy
14. worried melancholy.

It is interesting that de Sauvages omitted homesickness, which later authors included prominently as nostalgia. It is probable that his "atonic melancholy," which he quoted from Bellini's writings, should be considered melancholia with stupor.

Jacquelin-Dubuisson has his own simplified list: demonomaniac, nostalgiac, suicidal, homicidal.[67]

Foderé's list was both similar to and different from the others: misanthropic, amourous, prophetic, superstitious, nostalgic, suicidal.[68]

Ball's classification was based more on feelings than on actions: melancholy with conscience, depressive melancholy, anxious melancholy, perplexed melancholy.[69] It is evident that the last was merely melancholy with stupor, the third agitated depression, the second retarded depression, and the first guilty depression. They all obviously overlap. Thus the urge to subdivide depressions died out.

WITCHCRAFT

The history of witchcraft pertains to the history of psychopathology in many ways. Considered here are the delusions of the purported witches themselves and of those who believed them.

Parrinder wrote a brief but excellent history of witchcraft, which is the source of the following nonmedical historical comments.[70]

Although the pagans, including the Romans, had laws against witches, and the Old Testament recommended killing them, the early Christian church considered belief in witchcraft a delusion. The synod of Paderborn (A.D. 785) decreed that

[67] J. R. Jacquelin-Dubuisson, *Des Vésanies, ou maladies mentales* (Paris: Pauteur, 1816).

[68] R. E. Foderé, *Traité du délire, appliqué à la médecine, à la morale et à la législation* (Paris: Croullebois, 1817).

[69] B. Ball, *Leçons sur les maladies mentales* (Paris: Asselin et Cie., 1880).

[70] G. Parrinder, *Witchcraft* (Baltimore, Md.: Penguin Books, 1958).

"whoever being fooled by the devil maintains in accordance with pagan beliefs, that witches exist and causes them to be burned at the stake shall be punished with death." Charlemagne ordered his bishops to exclude from the Christian community all believers in witchcraft. The Council of Ancyra (A.D. 314) stated that "Thereafter, priests everywhere should teach that they know this [night-flying] to be false and that such phantasms are sent by the evil spirits who delude them in dreams." This became part of canon law. However, the rise of powerful heresies after A.D. 1000 alarmed the church, and heresies and witchcraft were joined together. After the Crusades a renewed and wide acceptance of the existence of witchcraft developed as a result of the great epidemic of drug abuse in western Europe when a host of drug takers reported their delusions as real.[71]

The first witch trial occurred in A.D. 1264. Pope Innocent VIII subsequently issued a bull against witchcraft and started the persecution of suspected witches on a large scale. Years later, after examination of hundreds of records, the inquisitor Salazar Frias could not find a single act of proven witchcraft.

Physicians and others exclaimed against the superstition. Molitor's book[72] is sometimes described as the first work that opposed the belief in witches after Pope Innocent's bull, but it was decidedly lukewarm in this respect and did not reject the belief completely. It remained for Wier to take his strong stand in 1577, followed by Pierre Massé[73] who also wrote against the belief in witchcraft. Reginald Scot, like Wier, insisted that those who admitted being witches were mentally ill. His book was also notable for its spritely style, e.g.:

> You shall read in the legend how in the night time Incubus came to a ladies bed side and made hot love unto hir: whereat she being offended cried out so loud that companie came and found him under hir bed in the likenesse of the holie bishop Sylvanus, which holie man was much defamed therebie, until at the length this infamie was purged by the confession of a devill made at St. Jerom's tombe. Oh excellent piece of witchcraft or cosening wrought by Sylvanus.

A century later Bekker[74] again flatly denied the existence of witchcraft, of possession by the devil, and even of the devil himself. He also reiterated that people believed to be possessed by demons were actually mentally ill. Still later Webster[75] stated on the title page that his book "affirmed that there are many sorts of Deceivers and Imposters, and Divers Persons under a passive Delusion of Melancholy and Fancy."

[71] See B. Barnett, "Drugs and the Devil," *New Scientist* 1965, 27, 222.

[72] Molitor, *De lamus et pythonicus mulieribus* (Cologne: C. de Zierikzee, 1498).

[73] P. Massé, *De l'imposture et tromperie des diables, deuins, et autres* (Paris: J. Ponpy, 1579).

[74] B. Bekker, *Die bezauberte Welt* (Amsterdam: Daklen, 1693).

[75] J. Webster, *The Displaying of Supposed Witchcraft* (London: J. M., 1677).

It is evident that Wier's and Scot's forthright statements (see below) concerning the delusional nature of witchcraft had widespread and lasting effects.

Wier (1577)

The people most likely to be attacked by these follies are those who have a temperament and a constitution which easily give way to forces established by outside causes, or through being affected by the illusions of the devil, or tempted by his false impressions, or becoming a genuine instrument of his will. Such are the melancholics, who through feebleness or for some other reason grow sad gradually. In the words of Chrysostom: great confusion has more power to do harm than have all the acts of the devil; for those whom the devil masters, he does so by means of quarrels and sorrows. . . . They believe that the visions which he represents to them in fantasy are really as they appear and are substantial. . . . He makes internal things to appear external, and these poor deluded people see them not only while they are asleep but also when awake.[76]

I beg you to consider the thoughts of the melancholics, their words, their visions and actions, and you will know that all their senses are depraved by a melancholic humor, accumulated in the brain, which so affects the spirit that some believe they are animals, of which they assume the voice and picture. Some of them imagine they are vessels of clay, and for this reason they draw back from passers-by, for fear that they will be cracked; others fear death. . . . Others imagine that they are guilty of some crime.[77]

Scot (1584)

How melancholie abuseth old women, and of the effects thereof by sundrie examples

If anie man advisedlie marke their words, actions, cogitations, and gestures, he shall perceive that melancholie abounding in their head, and occupieng their braine, hath deprived or rather depraved their judgements, and all their senses: I meane not of cosening witches, but of poore melancholike women, which are themselves deceived. For you shall understand, that the force which melancholie hath, and the effects that it worketh in the bodie of a man, or rather of a woman, are almost incredible. For as some of these melancholike persons imagine, they are witches and by witchcraft can worke woonders, and doo what they list: so doo other, troubled with this disease, imagine manie

---

[76] I. Wier, *Histoires disputés et discours des illusions et impostures des diables, des magiciens infâmes, sorcières et empoisonneurs: des ensorceleursez et démoniaques et de la guérison d'iceux: item de la punition que méritent les magiciens, les empoisonneurs et les sorcières* [1577] (Paris: Aux Bureaux du Progrès Médical, 1885), p. 298.

[77] Ibid., pp. 303–304.

strange, incredible, and impossible things. . . . But if they may imagine, that they can transforme their owne bodies, which neverthelesse remaineth in the former shape: how much more credible is it, that they may falselie suppose they can hurt and infeeble other mens bodies; or which is lesse, hinder the comming of butter? &c. But what is it that they will not imagine, and consequentlie confesse that they can doo; speciallie being so earnestlie persuaded thereunto, so sorelie tormented, so craftilie examined, with such promises of favour, as wherby they imagine, that they shall ever after live in great credit & welth? &c.

If you read the executions doone upon witches, either in times past in other countries, or latelie in this land; you shall see such impossibilities confessed, as none, having his right wits, will beleeve. Among other like confessions, we read that there was a witch confessed at the time of hir death or execution, that she had raised all the tempests, and procured all the frosts and hard weather that happened in the winter 1565: and that manie grave and wise men beleeved hir.

That voluntarie confessions may be untrulie made, to the undooing of the confessors, and of the strange operation of melancholie, prooved by a familiar and late example

But that it may appeere, that even voluntarie confession (in this case) may be untrulie made, though it tend to the destruction of the confessor; and that melancholie may moove imaginations to that effect: I will cite a notable instance concerning this matter, the parties themselves being yet alive and dwelling in the parish of *Sellenge* in *Kent*, and the matter not long sithence in this sort performed.

One *Ade Davie*, the wife of *Simon Davie*, husbandman, being reputed a right honest bodie, and being of good parentage, grew suddenlie (as hir husband infomed mee, and as it is well knowne in these parts) to be somewhat pensive and more sad than in times past. Which thing though it greeved him, yet he was loth to make it so appeere, as either his wife might be troubled or discontented therewith, or his neighbours informed thereof; least ill husbandrie should be laid to his charge (which in these quarters is much abhorred). But when she grew from pensivenes, to some perturbation of mind; so as hir accustomed rest began in the night season to be withdrawne from hir, through sighing and secret lamentation; and that, not without teares, hee could not but demand the cause of hir conceipt and extraordinarie moorning. But although at that time she covered the same, acknowledging nothing to be amisse with hir: soone after notwithstanding she fell downe before him on hir knees, desiring him to forgive hir, for she had greevouslie offended (as she said) both God & him. Hir poore husband being abashed at this hir behaviour, comforted hir, as he could; asking hir the cause of hir trouble & greefe: who told him, that she had, contrarie to Gods lawe, & to the offense of all good christians, to the injurie of him, & speciallie to the losse of hir owne soule, bargained and given hir soule to the divell, to be delivered unto him within short space. Whereunto hir husband answered, saieng; Wife, be of good cheere, this thy bargaine is void and of none effect: for thou hast sold that which is none of thine to sell; sith it belongeth to Christ, who hath bought it, and deerelie paid for it, even with his bloud, which he shed upon the crosse; so as the divell hath no interest in thee. After this, with like submission, teares, and penitence, she said unto him: Oh husband, I have yet committed another fault, and doone you more injurie: for I have bewitched you and your children. Be content (quoth he) by the grace of God, Jesus Christ shall unwitch us: for none evill can happen to them that feare God.[78]

Willis (1680)

Willis was another early physician who regarded the phenomena of witchcraft as basically delusional.

It is wonderful, what ordinarily happens to Witches, or Wise-women; to wit, they, whilst they lye buried in a profound sleep imagine that they are in very far and remote places, and that they have seen the spectacles of seas and lands, and things wholly unknown to them and shall exactly describe them; which without doubt is because the devil brings the ideas of these things before the phantasie, and so strongly impresses them, that they for a certain believe, that they had been in them.[79]

Esquirol (1838)

The spread of psychiatric enlightenment was only one cause—perhaps a minor one—of the disappearance of demonomania. Esquirol offered another reason.

The state of modern society has modified the causes and character of monomania, and this malady now reveals itself under new forms. With the weakening of religious convictions, demonomania, and forms of insanity depending upon superstition, have also disappeared. The influence of religion over the conduct of people being lessened, governments, in order to maintain authority over men, have had recourse to a police. Since that period, it is the police that troubles feeble imaginations, and establishments for the insane are peopled with monomaniacs who, fearing this authority, are delirious respecting the influence which it exercises, and by which they think themselves pursued. This monomaniac, who would formerly have been delirious with respect to magic, sorcery and the infernal regions; is now delirious, thinking himself threatened, pursued, and ready to be incarcerated by the agents of the police. Our political convulsions, in France, have been the occasion of much

---

[78] R. Scot, *The Discoverie of Witchcraft* (London: W. Brome, 1584), pp. 52–56.

[79] T. Willis, *Two Discourses concerning the Soul of Brutes, Which Is That of the Vital and Sensitive of Man* [1680], S. Pordage, trans. (London: T. Dring, 1683), p. 94.

monomania, which has been provoked and characterized by events which have signalized each epoch of our revolution.[80]

SCHIZO-AFFECTIVE DISORDERS

The term *schizo-affective* is of relatively recent origin, but the concept is ancient, though unfortunately not well described, much less defined. One cannot be sure of the concept in all cases, but it was probably first designated, however poorly, by the term *melancholia attonica*, popularized by de Sauvages (page 201). The nineteenth-century use of the term *melancholia with stupor* plainly referred in some instances to what is today called catatonia as well as to severely retarded depressed patients. Furthermore *melancholia with stupor* cannot be equated with *schizo-affective states* because of the fact that manic syndromes with severe schizophrenic admixtures may also occur. All these considerations prevent a clear account of the development of the concept of schizo-affective states. For the present purposes these states will be considered to be made up of depression or mania, plus a significant amount of the thinking disorder today called schizophrenia.

Baillarger was the first to achieve a measure of clarification of the confusion that revolved about the concept. As he pointed out, some of his precursors had been puzzled by the disorder, and a few of them, notably Georget and Esquirol, had fallen into the error of assuming that the patients' muteness indicated cessation of thought.

Georget (1820)

Obtundity (Stupidité)

Eventual absence of the manifestation of thought, such that the patient has no ideas, or cannot express them.

The patients with obtundity appear to be in a state of complete mental annihilation. They are indifferent to all that surrounds them, indifferent to the actions of surrounding things; their appearance conveys a perfect tranquility. Their general sensibility is always feeble; the patients feel nothing; they urinate without being aware of it. It is not until after their cure that one can learn from them what the true mental state was that affected them; the following example will give an idea. A. F., aged thirty-six, entered for the fifth time in six years in the following state: general lack of sensibility; she does not respond in any manner to the questions put to her; she does not appear to understand them either, and she remains in the spot and the position in which she was placed. . . . This state gradually subsided after three months. . . . Her intelligence regained all its ordinary activity. She then gave an account of her situation. She thought of nothing; when spoken to she retained only the

[80] E. Esquirol, *Mental Maladies: A Treatise on Insanity* [1838], E. K. Hunt, trans. (Philadelphia: Lea and Blanchard, 1845), p. 201.

first word of the phrase and did not have the ability to respond; she felt no pain when operated on. . . .

These are the intellectual phenomena that I believe should be grouped in a species of insanity, separating them from mental deficiency and from dementia; it is for the observers to judge whether it is suitable to distinguish this kind of change from the others; if it resembles them superficially, they differ in nature, since there is never intelligence in mental deficiency, and there will never again be in dementia.[81]

Baillarger (1843)

Georget has given the name of obtundity to a particular kind of madness that Pinel confused with idiotism, and that Esquirol had indicated to be a variety of dementia (acute dementia).

The obtundity for Georget is characterized by the eventual absence of signs of thinking, either because the patient has no ideas or because he cannot express them.

The suspension of intelligence, or else the impediment or confusion of ideas, a sort of decaying of the spirit that blocks their organization, these are the symptoms he assigns to this new type of insanity. . . . [These ideas were adopted verbatim by Etoc, Ferrus, and others.]

The observations that I have gathered do not permit me to adopt the opinion of Georget, of M. Etoc and of M. Ferrus, as regards the intellectual state of the patients while the obtundity persists.

Before examining the state of the patients studied and discussing whether or not it can be attached to one of the types of insanity recognized by these authors, I believe I ought to combine the principal symptoms that characterize it.

After a few hours, a few days, of delirium, the patient gradually becomes as dumbfounded. He remains immobile; his eyes are wide open and fixed; his face loses all expression; his indifference toward external objects is complete. He does not reply to questions put to him, and seems at times not to understand them; or his replies are slow, brief, and interrupted by periods of silence. The will seems to be suspended, the patient pays no attention to cleanliness; one gets him up, puts him to bed, makes him eat. He seems insensitive to the strongest stimuli. On seeing his immobility, the fixity of his eyes, one would take him, in some cases, for a cataleptic; but the important symptom of catalepsy does not occur. These are the external signs that the illness presents in its severest form.

Several months pass in this state of torpor; then, all of a sudden, this obtunded facies becomes animated, life returns to those traits that it seemed to have abandoned. The patient begins to respond; his deportment is better;

[81] M. Georget, *De la folie: Considérations sur cette maladie* (Paris: Crevot, 1820), pp. 115–116, 117.

he eats by himself, and presently he consents to do things. But he is as if thunderstruck; he does not give a good account of what went on about him, he looks with a kind of surprise at the place he lived in for several months, the people who have not left him. He seems as if everything was new for him. He asks where he is, for how long he has been there, why did they bring him here. Little by little his memories return, he recognizes who he is, he re-enters the world, his cure is complete. . . .

You understand that thinking did not cease to be active but that the patient has lived in an imaginary world. Everything around him had been transformed. He has not ceased to be in the grip of terrible illusions and hallucinations. . . .

The figures he sees are hideous and menacing; it seems to him that the whole world is intoxicated. . . .

The patient accuses himself of all the sins; he ceaselessly experiences in his soul an idea of a kind of general dissolution; he believes only that he must die to be delivered from his sufferings. . . .

If one analyzes this state, by isolating the principal features, one finds that it is above all characterized:

1. internally, by the loss of the sense of time, place, person; by the existence of the patient in an imaginary world; by numerous illusions and hallucinations; by the suspension of the will; and finally by a psychosis exclusively sad in nature.

2. externally by inertia, immobility, an appearance of obtundity, the loss or diminution of sensibility.

In all the cases I have reported the psychosis is of an exclusively sad nature, and since this is the principal characteristic it is evident that we ought to consider it an example of melancholia.

Nevertheless it is easy to show that these facts differ from ordinary melancholy, as evidenced by many reports, and we ought to distinguish it as a special variety.

Conclusions

1. The psychotics who have been called by the name *obtundity* in most cases have only the appearance of obtundity, and there is in these patients a completely internal psychosis that they tell about after being cured.

2. The psychosis appears to be exclusively sad in nature; it is often accompanied by ideas of suicide.

3. The state of obtunded psychotics is characterized chiefly by disorders of sensation and by numerous illusions that project the patients into an imaginary world.

4. Obtundity does not appear, in most cases, to be anything but the most severe degree of a type of melancholia.

5. The state of obtunded psychotics suggests in the highest degree many analogies with a dream state.[82]

Baillarger did not solve the problem of how to classify hallucinated depressions. This problem remained unsolved in the writings of his successors until the mid-twentieth century, when the decision was made to include them under the heading *schizo-affective*.

Griesinger (1845)

Griesinger's careful description of melancholia with stupor emphasizes the intense but masked mental activity and presents a picture that by today's criteria resembles schizophrenia more than it does the depressed phase of the manic-depressive psychosis.

That form of melancholia in which is represented the highest degree of self-absorption under the outward form of stupor, is not only of the highest theoretical importance on account of the well-marked mental symptoms, and of the very characteristic anatomical lesions in the brain, which exist in some cases; but on account of its being so often and so readily confounded with dementia, which may lead to serious errors both as regards prognosis and treatment.

Really the patients in the higher degree of these states present to appearance the very picture of dementia. They are perfectly dumb, completely passive, they only move when compelled by some strong external motive; their whole bearing is that of stupidity; the expression is that of general profound mental opression, of a veritable annihilation; but the glance of such patients does not indicate the nullity proper to dements—it expresses a painful emotion, sadness, anxiety, or concentrated astonishment. . . .

The voluntary muscles appear at times to be perfectly rigid and on the stretch, sometimes benumbed; it is not uncommon to find such patients in a cataleptic condition, and many of the observations concerning so-called catalepsy belong in reality entirely to this form. The mobility of the members under the control of the will is always very much diminished, occasionally almost suppressed. There is a condition like that of restraint of all the motory functions of the brain.

In such circumstances, the patients have in the majority of cases lost all consciousness of time and place, as well as the appreciation of their bodily necessities: consequently, they are in the highest degree unclean—require to be fed, to be clothed, to be put to bed, &c. Usually they then emaciate rapidly, marasmus speedily comes on, and death is by no means uncommon in this form of melancholia.

In what condition is the intellectual life of the sufferer during the course

[82] J. Baillarger, "De l'état désigné chez les aliénés sous le nom de stupidité," *Ann. Medico-Psychol.*, 1843, 1, 76–103 and 256–280.

of this disease? On this subject certain patients have, after their recovery, given us the most remarkable information. So far from experiencing that total psychical void which is proper to dementia, the mind in the great majority of instances retains its normal activity. But the patient, owing to this abnormal condition of the sensorial perception, unconscious of what goes on around him, lives in an imaginary world. So far as he is concerned, all reality has disappeared, all around him is effaced and transformed. An intense internal anxiety constitutes the fundamental state which torments him almost to suffocation, and from this proceed ideas of being threatened every moment with misfortunes; as, houses going to fall upon him, of the world coming to an end, of total annihilation of everything, as well as certain delusions of having committed some frightful crime, of depravity, &c.

The sufferer is unable to exert his will, and therefore feels the impossibility of freeing himself from the terrors which threaten him on all sides. Very frequently he cannot afterwards tell why he was incapable of the least exercise of will, why he could not reply, why he could not cry out. . . . But this absence of will is most evidently manifested in the utter passiveness, inactivity, and immobility of the patients; as well also by the intercurrent fits of intense activity which sometimes occur, in the same way as many patients may have now and then a short moment of consciousness, and obtain a glimpse of the actual world.

Very often this external insensibility, this suppression of the effort, and the exclusive sad delirium, are accompanied by hallucinations and illusions of the same nature. The patient hears voices which seem to reproach him, to insult him, and to threaten him with death; or a confused noise of bells, trumpets and cannons, &c. He sees witches, funeral processions, subterranean vaults, volcanic craters, which appear to yawn at his very feet. He sees, also, the most cherished of his relations martyred, &c. He fancies himself in a desert, in hell, chained to the galleys; in one word, the entire subjective change which is produced in his sensorial perceptions, and the consequent transformation in all impressions, causes all external objects which he still perceives to appear only in the forms and figures coloured by the predominating sentiment—a state which is also characterised by a considerable degree of confusion of ideas.

In many ways this condition presents the greatest similarity to a state of half-sleep or dream. The production of emotions of ideas and thoughts of a mournful and painful description find an exact analogue in the appearance of peculiar new and disagreeable sensations (formication, pricking, cold) in the deadened sensory nerves; and we shall ses that this comparison is only the more true because in a large proportion of these cases we are able to prove the existence of an evident pressure upon the brain. The patients themselves, when they again commence to become more lively, to feed themselves, and to do a little work—in short, to convalesce—are as astounded as if they were just waking up, and often ask where they are, and only gradually recover themselves. They then compare their actual state to a dreadful dream, and their convalescence to an awakening therefrom.

Still, there is not always present during the course of this form of melancholia such a multiplicity of painful sensations, ideas, and images as have been mentioned. In many cases it is rather a half-sleeping state, without distinct dreams or lively hallucinations—a state of self-absorption, of estrangement from the outer world, in which little else is perceived than the feeling of profound internal disturbance and absence of will; where the intellectual faculties, it is true, seem to be in a state of abeyance, but yet the patient retains the consciousness of his condition. Perhaps, indeed, it may be because the patient cannot give a good account of his state, or at best can only feebly recall it, that psychical anomalies so striking in themselves are so little known.

. . . This form of melancholia, as melancholic stupidity, may, when it lasts for a lengthened period, become transformed into actual persistent weakness of the intellectual faculties, with cessation of the painful emotions, into dementia,—into conditions, therefore, where the intellectual activity is not merely restrained, but actually persistently and most profoundly destroyed. . . .

When melancholia with stupor does not pass into dementia, it is rarely prolonged beyond a few months; many sufferers from it recover, and recover generally quickly as if awaking from a dream.[83]

Luys (1881)

The terrifying hallucinations were given a central role in the writings of Luys on the syndrome.

The depressive state that from its onset is chiefly characterized by a severe anxiety secondary to hallucinatory disorders, sometimes bearing mysterious voices, epithets of subjective origin, imaginary visions, becomes little by little more irregular than at first. The lucid intervals become shorter, and the hallucinatory obsession ends by being complete.

The individual, prey to incessant visions that upset and terrify him, is found in a way fixed in place and maintaining a state of immobility. He looks around him without seeing. One speaks to him but he does not understand, he walks with slow steps like a sleepwalker who walks with care, he murmurs through his lips disjointed phrases, but when one strongly excites him, while trying to gain his attention, he hides himself quickly, walks forcibly and overturns all obstacles. The hallucinatory stupor is therefore not a passive state of the spirit . . . it is an active state of obsession of the conscious personality by stubborn, continuous hallucinatory phenomena, which through their multiple excitations keep the individual in a perpetual state of abnormal irritability and of obsession.[84]

[83] W. Griesinger, Mental Pathology and Therapeutics, from the 2nd German ed., C. L. Robertson and J. Rutherford, trans. (London: The New Sydenham Society, 1867), pp. 247–250.

[84] J. Luys, Traité clinique et pratique des maladies mentales (Paris: A Delahaye and E. Lecrosnier, 1881), pp. 502–503.

The subsequent history of the concept of melancholia with stupor and its ultimate transformation into schizo-affective psychosis can be sketched very briefly. The syndrome was clearly described in the nineteenth century and only its classification remained undecided. Meynert[85] took a different direction by grouping reversible thinking disorders under the unfortunate name *amentia*. Except for the inclusion of delirium tremens and a wide variety of infectious and toxic stupors, Meynert's amentia resembled the older melancholia with stupor. Meynert emphasized its benign course, and his influence persisted. Many years later (1921) Hoch wrote a monograph on what he called "benign stupors."[86] The manic-depressive nature of the syndrome was forever destroyed by Rochlin in 1935.[87] His follow-up study of thirteen of Hoch's forty patients showed that six of them had developed a chronic psychosis with deterioration—a schizophrenic syndrome. This did much to establish melancholia with stupor and related syndromes as schizo-affective psychoses.

HYPOCHONDRIA

Hypochondriasis, hypochondria, and hypochondriac passion are ancient terms for what is best regarded today as a nonpsychotic depression with a strong component of gastrointestinal distress of various types, including the flatulent. The earliest authors stressed the visceral complaints, but in the eighteenth century the psychiatric came to the fore.

Purcell (1707)

Purcell gives one of the earliest of the eighteenth-century accounts and a clear description of the anxious depression and emotional instability that characterize the illness.

> Lastly, we observe that those who have labour'd long under this distemper, are oppressed with a dreadful anguish of mind, and a deep melancholly, always reflecting on what can perplex, terrify, and disorder them most; so that at last they think their recovery impossible, and are very angry with those who pretend there is any hopes of it: the least contradiction to their will calls them into violent passions; they are fickle, wavering, and unconstant, now resolving on one thing, and immediately changing to something else, which they presently quit; and indulging their distemper they decline all diversions.[88]

[85] T. Meynert, *Klinische Vorlesungen über Psychiatrie* (Wien: W. Braunmüller, 1890), p. 33-125.

[86] A. Hoch, *Benign Stupors: A Study of a New Manic-Depressive Reaction* (New York: Macmillan, 1921).

[87] H. L. Rochlin, "A follow-up of Hoch's benign stupor cases," *American Journal of Psychiatry*, 1935, 92, 531-558.

[88] H. Purcell, *A Treatise of Vapours or Hysteric Fits* (London: E. Place, 1707), pp. 13-14.

Cheyne (1733)

Cheyne received worldwide praise for his characterization of the disorder as the "English malady." (He was a Scot.) This term was enthusiastically adopted on the Continent, but some writers in Great Britain went to great lengths to prove the disorder no more common in England than elsewhere.[89]

The Title I have chosen for this Treatise is a Reproach universally thrown on this Island by Foreignors, and all our Neighbors on the Continent by whom nervous Distempers, Spleen, Vapours, and Lowness of Spirits are, in Derision, called the *English malady*. And I wish there were not so good Grounds for this reflection. . . .

The Spleen of Vapours, as the Word is used in England, is of so general and loose a Signification, that it is a common Subterfuge for meer Ignorance of the Nature of Distempers. All Lowness of Spirits, Swelling of the Stomach, frequent Eructation, Noise in the Bowels or Ears, Frequent yawning, Inappetency, Restlessness, Inquietude, Fidgeting, Anxiety, Peevishness, Discontent, Melancholy, Grief, Vexation, Ill-Humour, Inconstancy, lethargick or watchful Disorders, in short, every symptom, not already classed under some particular limited Distemper, is called by the general Name of Spleen and Vapours: of which there are various and different Symptoms.[90]

Burrows (1828)

Burrows pointed out that the hypochondriac can put on a cheerful false front—in fact may be forced to do so—when most miserable. He also stressed the hypochondriac's self-absorption.

Hypochondriasis I have known induced in a healthy but nervous person simply by reading medical books.

The unhappy vapourer, J. J. Rousseau, is a striking illustration of this fact. Having commenced a course of medical reading to cure his own complaints, he became most wretched, fancying himself afflicted with every one of which he read; and at length imagined that the basis of his disease was a polypus of

---

[89] There were many who agreed that the English were particularly susceptible to mental disease. This susceptibility seems to have spread somewhat. After Jonathan Swift established St. Patrick's Hospital for the Insane in Dublin he wrote a few satirical couplets to celebrate the event (H. Williams, ed., *The Poems of Jonathan Swift* [Oxford: Clarendon Press, 1935], Vol. 2, p. 751):

He gave what little wealth he had
To build a house for fools and mad;
And show'd by one satiric touch,
No nation needed it so much.

[90] G. Cheyne, *The English Malady; or a Treatise of Nervous Diseases of all Kinds* (London: G. Strahan and J. Leake, 1733), pp. i, 194.

the heart! But this contagion is not confined to philosophers and the
unlearned in medical science; even physicians, as well as medical sutdents in
attending their first courses of instruction, have self-appropriated diseases, of
which they have been merely reading, or have lately seen. There is no wonder
if such susceptible beings should induce in themselves morbid affections, and
especially hypochondriasis.

Inquietude as to the event of a real ailment, or chagrin at being ill, may be
actual causes of hypochondriasis. The delirium of the hypochondriac is always
that of self-love. His anxieties, fears, and delusions, being always personal, he
flies with eagerness to every remedy suggested for his relief and the
preservation of life. The melancholic, on the contrary, cares little about
himself, and usually is very repugnant to, or obstinately refuses, all aid.
Except as it regards his own imaginary grievances, the judgment of the former
is correct. He can converse rationally and freely when diverted from himself,
or write or compose with his former ability; and is even capable of intellectual
exercises foreign to his taste, if he have resolution to set about them.

Cowper was naturally highly sensitive and melancholic, and his mental
aberrations at times exceeded hypochondriasis. He acknowledged that when he
trifled, it was by necessity; for that a melancholy, which nothing else so
effectually dispersed, engaged him sometimes in the arduous task of being
cheerful by force. Strange as it may appear, his most ludicrous verses were
written in his saddest mood, and but for that sad mood had never been
written at all: the famous ballad of John Gilpin owed its birth to an effort to
beguile the unhappiness of the amiable poet.

Molière, in his *Malade Imaginaire*, gives an appropriate and faithful portrait
of the hypochondriac.[91]

Romberg (1851)

The hypersensibility which is recognized today as a hallmark of neurosis was
discussed with wisdom and perceptive detail by Romberg.

I apply the term *hyperaesthesia psychica* to that frame of mind in which
abnormal sensations are excited and maintained by directing the attention to
impressions; it is commonly called *hypochondriasis*.

To elucidate this position more fully, we may mention that in health the
activity of the nerves of sensation is constant; it does not require to be
produced by irritants, it is merely strengthened and modified by them. There
is always a large stock of sensations at command, among which we may at
will select food for our perceptive or reasoning powers; by directing the
attention to the sensations, or to the details of an impression, we may give
them a definite shape and a permanent character.

[91] G. M. Burrows, *Commentaries on the Causes, Forms, Symptoms, and Treatment, Moral
and Medical, of Insanity* (London: T. and G. Underwood, 1828), pp. 469-470.

The stimuli that influence the sensitive functions are of an objective and subjective, or simply a subjective kind. Among the latter we yield to the stimuli of mental impressions a more extensive sphere of action than is commonly accorded them. Nobody doubts the effect of voluptuous thoughts, but the doctrine that pain may result from reflecting upon pain is objected to; and yet the result of a vivid impression of nausea, horrification, tickling or itching, which we are familiar with, is nothing but an abnormal sensation. . . . The hypochondriac is, so to say, a virtuoso on the sensitive nerves.

In hypochondriasis, doubts and anxiety about his health oppress the patient, and they generally take the shape of a conviction of a malady affecting a special organ. . . .

. . . In Broussais' times, the educated hypochondriac in France imagined himself afflicted with gastritis, and in the same manner the German of forty years since was tortured with atrabiliary follies, to which he was led by diligent contemplation and study of the delineations contained in Kempf's book. But the imagination does not deal exclusively with the hypochondria; the thoracic organs are also visited in a similar manner. The sensation of anxiety and dyspnoea is one which the hypochondriac most frequently induces spontaneously and augments. The motor action at the same time participates; the heart beats and pulsates irregularly. A suspicion of a disease of the heart seizes the patient, until an accidental catarrh directs his attention to the lungs. The distress and palpitation cease, and phthisis becomes the nightmare that absorbs every consideration, and in the same ratio the patient complains of pains in the chest; the cough becomes more and more urgent; and the sputa are carefully preserved and carefully examined. Not alone, however, in the abdomen and chest are the phenomena excited; they are also produced by imagination and reflection in the sensory relations of the head; hyperaesthesiae of the nerves of sense, pains in the cranium and face supervene, there is weight and tension, vertigo, and oppression; an approaching attack of apoplexy tortures the patient; when he suddenly hears of cholera, his head is set at liberty, and the precursors of the mortal malady seize upon his devoted intestines.[92]

Diagnostic errors are frequent from psychical hyperaesthesia being confounded with melancholia and hysteria. The characteristic peculiar to the former, as to insanity generally, consists in an alienation of the feeling of identity and consciousness as regards sensations and impressions, and this in melancholia is combined with a tendency to self-negation (negirendem Affect). In hypochondriasis, on the contrary, the egotistic principle is exalted, and in no ways estranged to some other sensation or impression, so as to render this

[92] M. H. Romberg, *A Manual of the Nervous Diseases of Man*, from the German ed., 1851, E. H. Sieveking, trans. (London: The New Sydenham Society, 1853), Vol. 1, pp. 178–180.

an apparent reality in contradistinction to the essential and true reality. The difference is clearly expressed in all the patient's relations, not excepting his relation to his physician. The hypochondriac looks upon his physician, however often he changes his medical attendant, as his guardian and saviour; while the person labouring under melancholia, treats him as if he were a hostile or ignorant individual, and constantly tries to avoid him.[93]

Griesinger (1845)

To Griesinger the somatic complaints figured prominently in the picture of hypochondria. Nevertheless the mental symptoms were often so marked, he pointed out, as to suggest some degree of insanity.

The hypochondriacal states represent the mildest, most moderate form of insanity, and have many peculiarities which essentially distinguish them from the other forms of melancholia. While they, of course, share with the others the generic character of dejection, sadness, depression of mind, diminution of the activity of the will, and of a delirium which corresponds to this mental disposition, they yet differ from them in this characteristic manner—that in these states the emotional depression proceeds from a strong *feeling* of *bodily illness* which constantly keeps the attention of the patient concentrated upon itself; that, consequently, the false opinions relate almost exclusively to the *state* of *health* of the subject, and the delirium turns constantly upon apprehensions of some grave malady— upon unfounded and curious ideas regarding the nature, the form, and the danger of this his disease. This feeling of bodily illness is sometimes general and vague, sometimes it resolves itself into particular anomalous and disconnected sensations. It often depends on irritation of the nervous centres arising from peripheral disease—often very obscure and concealed—of the viscera. It is also frequently provoked centrally under the direct influence of moral causes—*e.g.*, reading medical books, frequent contact with hypochondriacs.

These morbid sensations are always increased through the direction of the attention to them; and when the disease has attained a caertain degree of development, such may, through direction of the attention to this or that organ, be awakened, displaced, and called forth anew in each organ of the body in succession. As to the part which the intellect plays in this disease, it may be said that, in spite of this emotional disorder and of the false conceptions, the association of ideas is usually unimpaired; the abnormal sensations and ideas are logically connected throughout, and justified by reasons which are still within the bounds of possibility. And just because of this absence of actual derangement of the understanding, hypochondria appears to be essentially a *folie raisonnante mélancholique*, the antithesis of

[93] Ibid., pp. 184–185.

which—the ordinary so-called monomaniacal *folie raisonnante*—we shall find in the states of mental exaltation.

We recommend the thinking and intelligent reader to verify for himself the analogy which results from the comparison of these two forms of the morbid states and feelings. Hypochondria really finds no other suitable place in nosology than among mental diseases, among which Sauvages and Cullen have long ago ranged it, and since then Pinel, Georget, and Falret. It is also the natural consequence of the symptomatology of the affection. It is a perversion of sentiment which may go to the slightest or the most extreme degrees without essentially changing the character. The hypochondriac, it is true, may reason correctly—setting out from false premises; but this does not in the least invalidate the fact that hypochondria is a mental affection, any more than that because hypochondria often accompanies or complicates various chronic diseases seated in different organs, it ought on that account to be identified or confounded with these diseases.

Symptoms.—The disposition of the patient begins to change without any assignable cause. He becomes dejected, peevish, suspicious, exhibiting more extreme sensibility and a disposition to connect everything with himself. Everything wearies him, and he is very easily fatigued. At the commencement, this state experiences many remissions; and the paroxysms assume the form of an irritable, restless, and distrustful disposition, or of a mental apathy, which may go so far as to produce weariness of life, or anxiety which may proceed to despair and loss of self-control. An undefined yet vivid feeling of illness torments and annoys the patient in an obscure sort of manner. All the parts of the sensory nervous system may be the seat of morbid sensations, often very painful (formication, heat and cold, crawling about of a foreign body—as if his head would burst—as if he were empty, dead, pierced, torn in pieces, &c.). And the higher senses also often present an exaggerated sensibility or great bluntness, and actual hallucinations. All these anomalous sensations urge themselves vividly into the consciousness, awaken and maintain an idea which relates to the disease in all its various possible forms and means of cure. All sensations are watched, and seriously commented upon and analysed in the sense of the ruling gloomy and anxious frame of mind. From these the patient concludes that he is the subject of very serious and dangerous diseases; and often he expresses his fears with an exaggeration of which he himself is half aware, and in the most graphic and ludicrous language. The patient who exhibits only the most insignificant symptoms of disease, speaks of apoplexy—asserts that he is half dead, that his heart is dried up or petrified, his nerves are burning coals, his blood is boiling oil, &c. He willingly allows that he is the subject of serious disorders, or of entire new diseases which have never before existed, because the gravity and danger of the disease is in proportion to the intensity of the feeling which annoys him. Whenever the morbid sensations change their situation and nature, the ideas regarding the seat and nature of the disease also change, and the patient believes himself to be successively attacked with all the diseases whose pathology he knows. So much do these ideas constitute a true delirium, so false and purely imaginary are they, and so little do the sensations which serve as their basis seem to be connected with them, that they may be regarded essentially as mere *attempts at explanation.* . . .

The psychical changes, too, which occur in the sphere of the will, are, in the majority of instances, very striking. The patients become dejected, thoughtful, indecisive; in the higher grades volition is altogether absent. "I wish that I could be more determined, that I could persevere longer; but to do this depends no longer upon myself. I feel that if I could will, I might rescue myself from this desperate situation, but I am obliged to yield to my painful sensations. I feel myself incapable of everything, and the smallest obstacle appears to be insurmountable," &c. These are expressions which may frequently be heard in the higher degrees of hypochondria, as well as in all other forms of melancholia. In the more advanced stage of this disease, the *intellect* also suffers not only in the manner of which we have been speaking, but the constant direction of the thoughts to the special state, and the means which might possibly aid him impart likewise to the perception a certain monotony, and in consequence of this ruling preoccupation of the consciousness, everything that does not fall within this circle of ideas is without the slightest interest, of perfect indifference, and is very speedily effaced from the memory. Hence it is that such patients are often in the highest degree absent and forgetful. They are very loquacious upon the one subject of their affection, but are little inclined to speak on any other theme; and those are never severe cases of hypochondria where the patient is still amiable and can be an interesting companion. But the intelligence and acumen which the patient often displays in fine combinations upon his favorite theme may still remain intact as also in regard to objective relations. It is only in the most extreme grades of hypochondria that any actual diminution in the intelligence is observed in a form of dull and morose dementia which renders the sufferer almost incapable of any intellectual exertion.

In the aggregate of these mental disorders which collectively have the character of depression, hypochondria shows itself as a form of melancholia. Although in general, on account of the peculiar nature of these delirious conceptions, and of the much greater command which the patient has over himself, hypochondria may be regarded as to a certain extent specific, yet that ruling tendency which the patient has to connect and to compare everything with himself, the limitation of the perception to the special *I*—this morbid egotism is an essential characteristic corresponding to the concentration in self of the melancholic states in general, and occasionally, at the commencement of the melancholic perversion, it is more by chance that the body and not external objects becomes the object of the morbid mode of thought. The higher degrees of hypochondria, too, gradually pass, partly through increase of the feeling of anxiety, partly through the fixing of certain attempts at explanation, not only into true melancholia, but even complicated with delusions (ideas of being surrounded by an invisible agency, of being the victim of evil machinations, influenced by magnetism, &c.). That considerable degree of self-control also which hypochondriacs still possess, often disappears during each exacerbation. Could the physicians only observe these paroxysms as freely as they can at any time in severe cases in asylums, all doubts concerning the mentally morbid nature of hypochondirasis would very soon disappear.[94]

Krafft-Ebing (1903)

Krafft-Ebing likewise emphasized the interplay between body and mind in this disorder, especially as regards the genesis of delusions.

In many cases of melancholia the attention of the depressed patient is attracted and directed to his own body by disturbances of general sensibility. Then the patient readily finds the reason for his depression in his bodily sensations, though these are only accessory symptoms, and not causes of his melancholic depression. Thus, just as in other varieties of melancholia, delusions arise out of attempts to explain the abnormal processes in consciousness, which, however, in this case are not brought into false relation with the external world, but become delusional conceptions of physical conditions and processes.[95]

PERIODIC PSYCHOSES

The cyclic aspect of the manic-depressive psychosis, first observed centuries ago, received formal recognition when it was given the name *circular insanity* (see page 182). The periodicity of other psychoses were also noted; Foderé, for example, mentioned periodic mania a century and a half ago.

Foderé (1817)

Mania has been divided by most authors into continuous and noncontinuous; the first remains acute, which means that we believe that it will last three months, more or less; and mania that remains chronic, by which we mean mania of the hospitalized, which is always more or less complicated by dementia. The noncontinuous mania is divided into remittent, that is to

[94] W. Griesinger, *Mental Pathology and Therapeutics*, from the 2nd German ed., C. L. Robertson and J. Rutherford, trans. (London: The New Sydenham Society, 1867), pp. 212–215.

[95] R. von Krafft-Ebing, *Text-Book of Insanity Based on Clinical Observations for Practitioners and Students of Medicine*, C. G. Chaddock, trans. (Philadelphia: F. A. Davis, 1903), p. 304.

say in which the exacerbation is replaced by a quiet and calm delirium; into regularly intermittent, that is to say in which the intervals are distinct, and in which the attacks return at fixed intervals; and finally, in irregularly intermittent, in which the periods of the attacks are variable and indeterminate.[96]

Although some nineteenth-century psychiatrists included periodic insanity in their classifications, this approach in general seems artificial and of no clinical value. Periodicity is today recognized as an essential manifestation of manic-depressive psychosis, periodic catatonia, hyperestrogenic cyclic psychosis[97] of the postpartum period, and so-called "periodische Umdämmerungen in der Pubertät" or "periodic dim-wittedness of puberty."[98]

[96] F. E. Foderé, *Traité du délire, appliqué à la médecine, à la morale et à la législation* (Paris: Croullebois, 1817), p. 451.

[97] P. Lingjaerde and R. Bredland, "Hyperestrogenic cyclic psychosis," *Acta Psychiatrica Scandinavica.* 1954, 29, 355.

[98] M. D. Altschule and J. Brem, "Periodic psychosis of puberty," *American Journal of Psychiatry*, 1963, 119, 1176.

Thought Disorders

9

DEMENTIA PRAECOX AND HEBEPHRENIA

Dementia was among the most ancient of the diagnostic categories in psychiatry. The loss of reasoning power distinguished it from amentia, in which this power never developed. Dementia was first subdivided according to the age at which it occurred, rather than in accordance with its clinical features.

Dufour (1770)

Dementia is a kind of incapacity to judge and to reason sanely. It has received different names according to the different ages at which it manifests itself. In infancy one ordinarily calls it *bêtise, niaiserie*; it is called *imbecility* when it accompanies or presents itself at the age of reason; and when it comes in old age, it is known under the name of *dotage* or *second childhood*.[1]

The schizophrenia concept has its roots in dementia praecox, despite Sullivan's belief that the two are distinct disorders.

Willis (1680)

Thomas Willis pointed out that dementia may be a sequel to protracted melancholia. This perceptive observation was repeated, usually without attribution, by a host of nineteenth-century authors.

Melancholy being a long time protracted, passes oftentimes into stupidity, or foolishness, and sometimes also into madness.[2]

---

[1] J. M. Dufour, *Essai sur les opérations de l'entendement humaine et sur les maladies* (Amsterdam: Merlin, 1770), p. 357.

[2] T. Willis, *Two Discourses concerning the Soul of Brutes, Which Is That of the Vital and Sensitive of Man* [1680], S. Pordage, trans. (London: T. Dring, 1683), p. 193.

Crichton (1798)

Hartley's *Essay on Man*, with it's extended exposition of the phenomena of mental association, stimulated the evaluation of psychiatric disorders in relation to these phenomena. A number of eighteenth-century psychiatric writers made comments along these lines (see, e.g., page 35). Crichton was evidently the first to refer to the looseness of associations in dementia.

> —— Fatuitas. Imbecility of all the faculties of the human mind, particularly those concerned in associating and comparing ideas; accompanied with want of language, a stupid look and general bodily weakness.[3]

Pinel (1801)

The essential psychologic disorders of what is today called schizophrenia was defined by Pinel in 1798 under the term *démence* or dementia.

The translation given here differs in a small but highly important detail from that of Davis (1806). I have preferred to translate Pinel's *disparat* as "unfitting" or "unsuitable" rather than as "unequal."[4]

> —— Rapid succession, or rather uninterrupted alternation of isolated ideas and of trifling and unsuitable emotions, disordered movements, and continual extravagant acts, complete loss of memory of all of the previous state, loss of the faculty of recognizing objects through impressions made on the senses, obliteration of judgment, continuous activity without purpose or plan, and a kind of automatic existence.[5]

Haslam (1809)

Haslam offered the first clear picture of a schizophrenic psychosis. He gave the disorder no name, but his description of its onset at puberty and the

---

[3] A. Crichton, *An Inquiry into the Nature and Origin of Mental Derangement* (London: T. Cadell, Junior, and W. Davies, 1798), Vol. 2, p. 344.

[4] Pinel's use of the term *disparat* requires some elucidation. The definition given in French-English dictionaries of Pinel's time is not the modern meaning of "unequal" but rather "unfitting" or "unsuitable." A philological study of *disparat* and related words in the Romance languages circa 1880 would be out of place here, but it is worth noting that in Spanish the root had the implication of folly. It was so used by Goya in his chalk drawing entitled "Gran Disparate" (Prado Museum, Madrid, No. 382). The drawing shows a man holding his own severed head while another pours wine through a funnel into his body, apparently through the exposed esophagus in his neck. Goya also had a series of drawings entitled "Los Disparates," in a similar vein.

[5] P. Pinel, *Traité médico-philosophique sur l'aliénation mentale* (Paris: J. A. Brosson, 1809), p. 180; *A Treatise on Insanity, in Which Are Contained the Principles of a New and More Practical Nosology of Maniacal Disorders*, D. D. Davis, trans. (Sheffield: W. Dodd, 1806), p. 164.

progressive deterioration that follows indicates that he was in fact the first to describe what later came to be called hebephrenia.

Connected with loss of memory, there is a form of insanity which occurs in young persons; and, as far as these cases have been the subject of my observation, they have been more frequently noticed in females. Those whom I have seen, have been distinguished by prompt capacity and lively disposition: and in general have become the favourites of parents and tutors, by their facility in acquiring knowledge, and by a prematurity of attainment. This disorder commences, about, or shortly after, the period of menstruation, and in many instances has been unconnected with hereditary taint; as far as could be ascertained by minute enquiry. The attack is almost imperceptible; some months usually elapse, before it becomes the subject of particular notice; and fond relatives are frequently deceived by the hope that it is only an abatement of excessive vivacity, conducing to a prudent reserve, and steadiness of character. A degree of apparent thoughtfulness and inactivity precede, together with a diminution of the ordinary curiosity, concerning that which is passing before them; and they therefore neglect those objects and pursuits which formerly proved sources of delight and instruction. The sensibility appears to be considerably blunted; they do not bear the same affection towards their parents and relations; they become unfeeling to kindness, and careless of reproof. To their companions they shew a cold civility, but take no interest whatever in their concerns. If they read a book, they are unable to give any account of its contents: sometimes, with steadfast eyes, they will dwell for an hour on one page, and then turn over a number in a few minutes. It is very difficult to persuade them to write, which most readily develops their state of mind: much time is consumed and little produced. The subject is repeatedly begun, but they seldom advance beyond a sentence or two: the orthography becomes puzzling, and by endeavouring to adjust the spelling, the subject vanishes. As their apathy increases they are negligent of their dress, and inattentive to personal cleanliness. Frequently they seem to experience transient impulses of passion, but these have no source in sentiment; the tears, which trickle down at one time, are as unmeaning as the loud laugh which succeeds them; and it often happens that a momentary gust of anger, with its attendant invectives, ceases before the threat can be concluded. As the disorder increases, the urine and faeces are passed without restraint, and from the indolence which accompanies it, they generally become corpulent. Thus in the interval between puberty and manhood, I have painfully witnessed this hopeless and degrading change, which in a short time has transformed the most promising and vigorous intellect into a slavering and bloated ideot.[6]

[6] J. Haslam, *Observations on Madness and Melancholy* (London: J. Callow, 1809), pp. 64–67.

Jacquelin-Dubuisson (1816)

Jacquelin-Dubuisson referred to dementia in what was by then the established manner but with more detail than his predecessors. He made a clinical distinction between acute and chronic dementia in terms of course and outcome and noted that dementia might be a sequel to some other psychoses. He did not, however, distinguish sharply enough the psychologic features of some types such as senile dementia.

> Dementia is a state of debility or ataxia of the intellectual and affective functions, characterized by weak and imperfect sensations, by blurred and false perceptions, by confused and incoherent ideas, by vague and indeterminate reasoning, by indifference in feelings, by irresolution in motivation, and by carelessness toward domestic interests and needs. . . .
>
> *General Symptoms.* Weak sensations and imperfect perception of surrounding objects; confused and isolated ideas that change instantly and succeed each other in an incoherent manner, lack of or errors in judgment, vague and uncertain motivations, fleeting and transitory impressions and feelings, more or less complete absence of the emotions, of desires or of aversions; memory consists mostly in remembrance or recall of things of the past or previous to the illness. . . .
>
> The patients are violent or apathetic, they move restlessly without motive endlessly, or they remain plunged in an indolent immobility; they have automatic practices from which they cannot be dissuaded. . . .
>
> It is not rare to encounter in society persons who, by the confusion and incoherence of their ideas, and the pointlessness and bizarreness of their behavior, show the frequent signs of a derangement of spirit that often degenerates into confirmed insanity. What are they which are called vulgarities, originalities, tics, or manias, if not the isolated acts of a sort of unreason, that fortuitous circumstances can change to dementia?[7]
>
> Dementia also presents, in the development and progression of its symptoms, differences in its duration, its continuity, and its remissions, that can serve to establish the following types: 1) acute dementia, 2) chronic dementia, 3) senile dementia, 4) periodic or intermittent dementia.
>
> [Acute] dementia differs essentially from the other types by its short and sharply defined duration.[8]
>
> The slow and poorly defined progression of [chronic] dementia, as well as the nature of the symptoms, clearly show that his psychosis is due to the debility and enfeeblement of the intellectual and moral faculties. These senseless persons are apathetic, careless, powerless; their faces

---

[7] J. R. Jacquelin-Dubuisson, *Des Vésanies, ou maladies mentales* (Paris: Pauteur, 1816), pp. 249–251.

[8] Ibid., pp. 253–254.

are expressionless. They endure patiently physical sufferings, are little moved by affective feelings and neglect the rule of propriety, they engage ceaselessly in automatic practices they have developed, such as rubbing their hands, grinding their teeth, scratching their heads, or imparting to different parts of the body regular oscillations or other monotonous movements.

This type of dementia either depends on a hereditary disposition, as in certain persons whose parents had been psychotic, and who fall into dementia at the age of forty to fifty without other recognizable cause; or else this dementia is consecutive, that is to say that it follows preceding psychoses. . . .

The symptoms of chronic dementia do not always continue; they sometimes diminish to the point of leaving intervals during which the mental disorders appear obscure or latent, then they manifest themselves anew. This constitutes remittent dementia.[9]

Georget (1820)

Georget was even more emphatic than others in specifying dementia as the terminal state of all incurable psychoses. He mentioned the nonspecificity of dementia's precursors and sequels. He also stressed the hebetude of the patients and noted that this was not necessarily incurable. His observation that shock (e.g., fever) may have a curative effect is interesting.

Dementia terminates all the psychoses that become incurable, provided that the illnesses exist long enough for this transformation to take place.[10]

Burrows (1820)

The clinical description offered by Burrows exemplifies the development of a clinical concept as more detailed observations were recorded. His debt to Pinel is obvious.

Fatuity or demency, however, must not be confounded with imbecility or idiotism: it is materially different from either. The faculties of a person in demency, though perhaps alienated, are not always abolished; they are often only in abeyance; and may revert to a state of sanity, either spontaneously or from judicious treatment; or they may be only partially affected. But assuredly, if the case be misjudged, as it too often is, the patient may pass into perfect idiotcy. . . .

Demency is ever, in extent of mortality the most fatal of all the states of mental disorder. In the French hospitals a greater number of deaths have

---

[9] Ibid., pp. 257–259.
[10] M. Georget, *De la folie: Considérations sur cette maladie* (Paris: Crevot, 1820), p. 119.

ensued from it than from mania and melancholia jointly. Indeed, in those receptacles, a full moiety of the fatuous die.[11]

The condition of the mental faculties designated *moria* or *morosis* by the Greeks, and *amentia* and *dementia* by later authorities, is recognised by nosologists as a distinct genus; but, like mania or melancholia, it is only a variety: it is liable to the same alternations, and is met with both in an active and chronic form.

It is defined to be a defect or hebetude of the understanding, general or partial, confined to individual faculties of the mind, particularly those concerned in associating and comparing ideas; whence proceeds great confusion and incapacity of arranging the thoughts, though they are sometimes very vivid, a partial or total loss of memory, a relish for childish pursuits, with garrulous babble or drawling speech, impotency, and diminution or loss of the powers of volition, and premature senility. . . .

The faculties in demency are not, however, always abolished; they are often in abeyance only, and may revert on the cessation of the morbid action inducing this condition, or on the improvement of the corporeal powers, when they have been impaired by disease or any extenuating cause. . . .

There is a marked difference between demency and imbecility or idiocy. The connate imbecile never had his mental faculties fully developed, and therefore never attains the ordinary standard of adult intelligence. True demency implies a previous possession and exercise of the mental faculties; but one or more of those faculties may, by accident, disease, or age, have become simply deteriorated. The conversation and manners of the latter preserve some traits of the character of the original man; those of the former always retain the impress of childhood. The connate idiot never possessed any intellectual endowment; there is neither sensation, memory, nor judgment. He displays mere animal instincts, and his internal and external conformation indicate the vices of cerebral organisation.

The depravity of the mental faculties which characterises demency is very apt to be confounded with permanent mental alienation, imbecility, or absolute idiocy; in consequence of which many cases have been pronounced irremediable, which might, by judicious treatment, have been restored to reason.

Demency may alternate with mania or melancholia, or it may, which is more usual, be the sequel of either. It may continue several weeks or months, and suddenly cease; and instances have been known of its preserving its pristine form for years, and at length the understanding be restored; or it may degenerate into chronic fatuity or perfect idiocy. . . .

[11] G. M. Burrows, *An Inquiry into Certain Errors relative to Insanity and Their Consequences; Physical, Moral and Civil* (London: T. and G. Underwood, 1820), pp. 164–165.

When this condition of the mental faculties succeeds mechanical injuries of the head, violent evacuations, venery, masturbation, paralysis, epilepsy, or old age, it assumes the chronic form, and is generally a permanent affection.

Demency is often a mere concomitant of other forms of insanity; and then is usually quite temporary. This fact is particularly worthy of remark, because the appearance of fatuity frequently leads to the hasty prognostic, that a patient is sinking into a irremediable chronic state, or that it is the result of excessive depletory practice. It is advisable, when such symptoms appear, to wait; for a few days, perhaps, prove, by the remission of the symptoms, the fallacy of either of these conclusions.

When demency comes on slowly, it is almost impossible to fix the exact date of its origin; but the signs which characterise it soon leave no doubt of its existence: if the patient becomes suddenly furious or agitated, fatuity disappears, and afterwards he will cease his noisy babble, be tranquil, and sleep profoundly.

When reduced to this hopeless state, ideas the most opposite and extravagant succeed, without connexion or motive, and his conversation then becomes quite incoherent. He utters words or sentiments without attaching any precise meaning to them; and talks without the consciousness of what he says. Memory is often sufficiently retentive to remember some stories of past-gone days; but they are repeated, as it were, from an involuntary or automatic impulse, or recollection is revived by fortuitous accordance with objects which actually strike his obtuse senses.

Before insanity thus degenerates, the delirium either remains the same a long while, or varies in character or intensity. In this state it is often very difficult to decide if there still exist a hope of cure, or if the disease be incurable. Should it continue above two years, the ordinary limitation, it is very rarely cured.[12]

Deterioration of the intellectual faculties sometimes arises from a constitutional and inexplicable cause. I have seen instances of youth, in whom more than ordinary abilities have been displayed, and who, up to the period of puberty, have made all due progress in their studies; yet when they have arrived at that epoch at which all the mental faculties are usually developed, have gradually retrograded, till a perfect state of chronic demency, or rather idiocy, has been established.[13]

A perfect and permanent restoration of reason has followed a paroxysm of fever, even where fatuity in its worst form has persisted many years.

Of the effects of fever in cases of fatuity I have quoted several striking examples, when discussing the influence of the circulation on the intellectual powers.

[12] Ibid., pp. 484–487.
[13] Ibid., p. 489.

The ancients in many places, and Thomas Willis in particular, refer to the effect of fever in removing fatuity.

Indeed, so decided is the effect of fever in suspending, and often in curing demency, that could we as readily inoculate fever, and define the limit of its operation, as we do that of variolous infection, it might be applied as a remedy in the treatment of this form of mental derangement.[14]

The diseases which prove most fatal in chronic demency are generally organic; or those attending the cachectic state, and therefore never inflammatory. The majority die of phthisis, or of cerebral affections, such as paralysis. . .[15]

Conolly (1830)

Conolly, as was his wont, described the early subtle changes in personality that might usher in a psychotic episode.

Torpidity becomes a kind of disease. I have occasionally been consulted in cases of this kind, and they are probably not uncommon. A young lady is observed to discontinue her usual occupations; books no longer amuse her; she neglects her music, her drawing, and every kind of feminine work; neglects her correspondents; makes excuses when visiting is proposed to her; can with difficulty be persuaded to take any exercise; and seems to consider it the summit of human happiness to sit by the fire, or at the window, motionless, silent, unoccupied, and abandoned to indolence. Of course, the causes of this state are very various; some misplaced and disappointed attachment; or vanity, or pride, may have been the commencement; but the mental state consists at first of a sluggishness in the faculty of attention, which accounts for all the other phenomena of that class; for as the attention is not exercised, the memory is not exercised, nor the comparison, nor the judgment. It is yet only an impairment of mind. . . . After many attempts to revive the mind, with temporary success, the attempts are found to fail; the attention can no more be roused, nor the memory or comparison exerted; the judgment is impaired: and then we have a form of true insanity. The brain, in such instances, is brought into a state in which the ordinary stimulus of external circumstances, and of the circulating blood, fails to excite its proper actions.[16]

Guislain (1833)

Although Guislain acknowledged that dementia is a disorder of intellectual function, he saw it as basically the result of abnormal affective processes.

[14] Ibid., p. 501.
[15] Ibid., p. 503.
[16] J. Conolly, *An Inquiry concerning the Indications of Insanity* (London: J. Taylor, 1830), pp. 125–127.

Dementia, considered as an adventitious or incidental illness, like dreaming, delirium or other morbid states of the intellectual apparatus, is likewise a consequence of that primary change in affective function that is at the root of mental disturbances.

Dementia arises, in some cases, directly from a painful mental cause: this effect is chiefly found in weak persons, exhausted by previous illnesses or damaged by congenital weakness; in persons in whom the cerebral apparatus, little capable of reacting, succumbs to the slightest mental or physical strain. Or else this disorder follows violent and prolonged mental reactions.[17]

Pritchard (1837)

Pritchard's succinct statement emphasized the weakness of associations in dementia.

A want of sequence, or connexion between the ideas, a failure of that aptitude in the mental constitution by which in the natural state one momentary condition of the mind follows in the train of its antecedent, seems to be the fundamental or essential circumstance in this state of disease; and it not only constitutes the most striking phenomenon of incoherence, but perhaps accounts for all the peculiar features which accompany it.[18]

Esquirol (1838)

Esquirol gave a detailed analysis of the effects of weakened associations and also emphasized the passivity.

Dementia is a cerebral affection, usually chronic and unattended by fever, and characterized by a weakening of the sensibility, understanding and will. Incoherence of ideas, and a want of intellectual and moral spontaneity, are the signs of this affection. Man in a state of dementia, has lost the faculty of perceiving objects correctly, of seizing upon their relations, comparing them and producing a distinct remembrance of them. Hence results the impossibility of reasoning correctly. . . . Individuals in a state of dementia, are incapable of concentrating their attention sufficiently; and being incapable of forming a clear and correct notion of objects, they can neither compare nor associate ideas; nor have they the power of abstraction. Ideas, the most unlike, succeed, independently one of another; and follow without either connection or motive. Their conversation is incoherent, and the patients repeat words and entire sentences, without attaching to them any precise signification. They

---

[17] J. Guislain, *Traité sur les phrénopathies; ou Doctrine nouvelle des maladies mentales* (Brussels: Etablissement Encyclographique, 1833), p. 325.

[18] J. C. Pritchard, *A Treatise on Insanity and Other Disorders Affecting the Mind* (Philadelphia: Haswell, Harrington, and Haswell, 1837), p. 71.

speak as they reason, without a consciousness of what they are saying. It seems that they have sentiments treasured up in their minds, which they repeat in obedience to the force of former habits, or yielding to fortuitous congruities. . . .

. . . Many also are irrational, only because the intermediate ideas do not connect those which precede and follow. We clearly perceive breaks, which it would be necessary to fill up, in order to give to their discourses the arrangement, filiation and perfections, which belong to a connected and complete process of reasoning. The energy of the sensibility and intellectual faculties, which is always in proportion to the activity of the passions, being almost extinct, the latter are null, or almost so, in dementia. The insane, in a state of dementia, have neither desires nor aversions; neither hatred nor tenderness. They entertain the most perfect indifference towards objects that were once most dear. They see their relatives and friends without pleasure, and leave them without regret. They are not uneasy in consequence of the privations that are imposed upon them, and rejoice little at the pleasures which are procured for them. What is passing around them no longer awakens interest; and the events of life are of little account, because they can connect themselves with no remembrances, nor any hope. . . .

. . . Those who are in a state of dementia, are destitute of spontaneity. They no longer determine, but abandon themselves; yielding implicitly to the will of others. Their obedience however is passive, and they have not sufficient energy to be intractable. Notwithstanding, they are irascible, like all feeble beings, and those whose intellectual faculties are weak or limited. Their anger however, is only of a moment's duration. They are so feeble that their fury must necessarily be of short duration, and they can but for a brief period, sustain so great an effort.[19]

Morel (1860)

Early and mid-nineteenth-century authors described the syndrome of primary dementia in the pattern of Pinel, Haslam, and their immediate followers and distinguished primary from secondary dementia. Many instances of the latter undoubtedly represent syphilis of the brain, while the rest are examples of dementia following endogenous mania or melancholia. The discussions of primary dementia followed the example of Haslam in paying little detailed attention to the earlier manifestations.[20] Morel remedied this defect.

[19] E. Esquirol, *Mental Maladies: A Treatise on Insanity* [1838], E. K. Hunt, trans. (Philadelphia: Lea and Blanchard, 1845), pp. 417–418.

[20] M. Georget, in *De la folie: Considérations sur cette maladie* (Paris: Crevot, 1820, p. 353) referred to "la démence prématurée" during the course of general paralysis, a disease whose syphilitic origin was unknown to him.

An unfortunate father consulted me one day about the mental state of his twelve- or fourteen-year-old son, in whom a violent hatred for the originator of his life had suddenly replaced the most tender feelings. This child, who had a well-shaped head and in whom the intellectual faculties exceeded greatly those of his schoolmates, struck me first by a kind of arrested development in his height. He was despondent at being the smallest in his class, despite the fact that he was always first in his compositions, and that without effort and almost without work. It was, so to speak, by intuition that he comprehended things, which he organized in his memory and his intelligence. He gradually lost his cheerfulness, became gloomy, taciturn, and showed a tendency toward solitude.... His mother was psychotic and his grandmother eccentric to an extreme degree.

I ordered the interruption of the child's studies and his confinement in an institution for hydrotherapy.... A most happy change occurred in the bodily state of the child. He grew considerably, but another phenomenon as disquieting as those I have mentioned came to dominate the situation. The young patient progressively forgot everything he had learned; his brilliant intellectual faculties underwent in time a very distressing arrest. A kind of torpor akin to hebetude replaced the earlier activity, and when I saw him again I concluded that the fatal transition to the state of *démence précoce* was about to take place. This dreadful prognosis is ordinarily far from the minds of the parents and also of the physicians who care for these children.

Such is nevertheless, in many cases, the sad termination of hereditary insanity. A sudden paralysis of the faculties, a *démence précoce*, indicate that the patient has reached the end of his intellectual life that he can control.[21]

Morel used the descriptive words not as a diagnostic term (the index of his book does not refer to *démence précoce* or any derivative of it) but so casually that they evidently made no impression on most other psychiatrists or even on himself.[22]

Gauthier (1883)

The first occurrence of *démence précoce* as a diagnostic term is in the title of Gauthier's Paris thesis. His patients' maladies included delusions, hallucinations, paranoia, and catatonia. He nowhere mentions Morel.

We have been struck by the precocity of the dementia in the young patients, who had a hereditary disposition.[23]

[21] B. A. Morel, *Traité des maladies mentales* (Paris: V. Masson, 1860), pp. 565-566.

[22] See M. D. Altschule, "Whichophrenia, or the confused past, ambiguous present, and dubious future of the schizophrenia concept," *Journal of Schizophrenia*, 1967, 1, 8-17.

[23] G. C. Gauthier, *De la démence précoce chez les jeunes aliénés héréditaires.* Unpublished thesis, Université de Paris, 1883, No. 376.

Clouston (1888)

Clouston brought the psychoses of adolescence to the fore, although he preferred the term *secondary dementia* and did not mention dementia praecox. Later Krafft-Ebing showed the same preference.

I answer the question "what is the typical form of insanity?" by saying that the insanity of adolescence is the typical form, because it most frequently ends in typical secondary dementia, without any other function being affected but mentalization, and because in its course we have all the forms of psychosis represented. . . . Almost all pure cases of secondary dementia will be found to have originated in the developmental (pubescent and adolescent) insanities. . . . Undue and unphysiological means through a forcing-house mode of education during adolescence without regard to the heredity capacity and weaknesses of the organism tend toward dementia. The constant changes in each generation of modern civilized life in the adaptation of the human organism to its environment and the special efforts thus rendered necessary by the struggle for existence tend toward dementia through the strain they put on the most delicate of all organized tissues.[24]

Charpentier (1890)

Charpentier muddied the waters when he used the term *dementia praecox* to mean any mental disorder in a young person, designating eleven groups.

1. dementia praecox in normal children
2. in epilepsy
3. in syphilis
4. in alcoholism
5. in pubertal insanity ("We do not wish to say that every hebephrenia is a dementia praecox nor that every dementia praecox that develops at puberty has this cause.")
6. in hereditary degenerative states
7. in psychopathic states (moral insanity)
8. in chronic mania or melancholia
9. in bodily disease—anemia, starvation, paresis
10. in precocious general paralysis
11. in children born to aged parents[25]

[24] T. S. Clouston, Presidential address, delivered at the annual meeting of the Medico-Psychological Association, *Journal of Mental Science*, 1888, 34, 325-348.

[25] Charpentier, "Les démences précoces," *Compte rendu du Congrès Annuel de Médicine Mentale*, Première session, 1890 (Paris: G. Masson, 1891), pp. 247-268.

A short time later A. Pick of Prague published a paper which referred to both Morel and Gauthier.[26] Tuke's *Dictionary* (1892) does not include dementia praecox, however, and other authorities continued to prefer *secondary dementia.*

Dickson (1874)

Among the various discussions of dementia that of Dickson is noteworthy in several respects: It mentioned what may have been autism; it recognized that the term *dementia* needed clarification; and it did not use the term *dementia praecox*. Dickson treated infantile dementia as a separate category, but it is clear from his descriptions that he had grouped together the results of a variety of organic brain syndromes.

The term dementia is very definite, yet, strange to say, there exists much confusion in its use, it has been erroneously applied to every abnormal mental state, from acute mania to idiocy, but as implied from its derivatives *de* out of, and *mens* the mind, it is applicable only to the cases in which there is loss of mind.

It must be distinguished from madness or perversion of mind, as mania or melancholia, and from amentia, as exampled in the condition of idiocy in which the mind has never been developed. An idiot is not the subject of dementia, but of amentia, because his is not a case of the loss of a mind he once had, but an absence of mind, because he never possessed any. Much confusion indeed exists in the common use of the terms imbecile, idiotic, and demental, but they are definite enough and ought not to be used convertibly. . . .

Idiocy is a condition of amentia, or the absence of mind because it was never developed, and it co-exists with undeveloped, though not necessarily unhealthy conditions of brain substance. As a rule the amentia is more or less comparative; a greater or less degree of mind is usually developed in idiots, for those who are absolutely amental commonly die in infancy. . . .

Dementia may be acute or chronic, and there is a third form of the disease to which the adjectival expression "infantile" has been applied, and it is a useful term and sufficiently indicative of its special condition.

The first class, or acute dementia, occurs as a primary disorder. It may, and often does, make its appearance quite suddenly, and sometimes it is irrecoverable.

The second class, or chronic dementia, appears in two distinct varieties. The one, more or less a secondary condition, following either acute dementia or mania or melancholia. The other, a primary disorder, which begins

[26] A. Pick, Über poinäre chronische Demenz (sog. Dementia praecox) im jugendlichen Alter, *Prager medizinische Wochenschrift*, 1891, 16, 312–315.

insidiously and progresses hopelessly, and with it are grouped the cases of dementia which are the legacy of old age, of some cases of epilepsy and other deteriorating nervous disorders.

The third class, or infantile dementia, is very frequently confounded with idiocy and imbecility. But it is a distinct condition. It is a true dementia, having its origin in infancy, and its nosological relationship to imbecility and idiocy is highly important.[27]

The term *hebephrenia* originated in the mid-nineteenth century following the acceptance of *phren* as a prefix or suffix. In 1852, for example, Guislain[28] suggested using *phrenalgia* for depression, *phrenoplexia* for catatonia, *hyperphrenia* for mania, *ideophrenia* for impulsive insanity, and *aphrenia* for dementia. A decade later Kahlbaum[29] suggested *dysphrenia* for secondary insanity and *paraphrenia* for age-related psychoses, the group being further divided into *neophrenia* for infantile brain dysfunctions, *hebephrenia* for pubertal psychoses, and *presbyphrenia* for senility. Some decades later the trend was continued with *schizophrenia*. Of Kahlbaum's list only hebephrenia became widely accepted as a term, largely owing to Hecker's writing on the subject.

Hecker (1871)

Plato stated that if anything has a name it must exist as a real thing. Once Kahlbaum had invented the term it was therefore to be expected that one of his pupils should write about hebephrenia as if it were a distinctive disorder and not a figment of classification. Hecker's detailed presentation of Kahlbaum's concept of hebephrenia was long regarded as the definitive work on the subject.[30]

The clinical observation of mental disturbances teaches us to distinguish at first glance between two main classes which clearly differ from each other by the peculiar nature of their course. Whereas in one class the typical disease picture[31] remains unchanged for the whole duration of the illness once it has been established, the second class is characterized by a number of changing clinical pictures which run in a definite succession through the stages of melancholia, mania, and confusion to dementia. This latter class, which in

[27] J. T. Dickson, *The Science and Practice of Medicine in Relation to Mind: The Pathology of Nerve Centers and the Jurisprudence of Insanity* (New York: D. Appleton and Co., 1874), pp. 290–292.

[28] J. Guislain, *Leçons orales sur les phrénopathies; ou Traité théorique et pratique des maladies mentales* (Gand: L. Hebbelynck; Paris: J. B. Ballière; Bonn: A. Marcus, 1852).

[29] K. Kahlbaum, *Die Gruppierungen der psychischen Krankheiten und die Einteilung der Seelenstorungen* (Danzig: Kafemann, 1863).

[30] E. Hecker, "Die Hebephrenie," *Virchow's Archiv für pathologische Anatomie*, 1871, 52, 394–429. (O. M. Marx, trans.)

[31] Zustandstypus.

turn contains within it a number of diseases[32] in their own right, is the one which the opponents of classification are willing to accept as the only existing form of mental diseases. Nevertheless they cannot refute "general progressive paralysis of the insane" as a special disease form. For these cases take such a peculiar course and have such a great number of striking, stereotyped symptoms and such an exquisitely pronounced prognosis that they undoubtedly provide a clearly definable clinical disease picture. This must be sharply differentiated from the so-called *vesania typica* (Kahlbaum) which, like paralysis, goes through the stages of melancholia, mania, etc. in more or less regular sequence.

Hecker then cites Westphal's description of the early appearance of a progressive mental weakness in general paralysis and credits Kahlbaum with pointing out that this also applies to hebephrenia, an otherwise quite different disease.

Despite the unusual characteristics of mental diseases during puberty, Hecker found the literature on them very scarce. Nearly all forms of mental disease occur in puberty, but they do not take the same course of development. The form of hebephrenia that Hecker describes follows a specific course and shows a succession of specific symptoms. It is not rare. Having studied five-hundred patients in two different institutions during a four-year period, Hecker saw fourteen cases of hebephrenia, some in the course of their development, others only in their final stage. In addition he studied a large number of case histories provided by Kahlbaum. Because hebephrenia rapidly progresses to dementia most patients were seen only at the conclusion of the actual disease, i.e., as mental cripples in the institution. He provides a lengthy case description.

Hebephrenia is a disease which invariably erupts following puberty. In all cases before me where the onset of the disease could be exactly determined, it falls into the eighteenth to the twenty-second year of life. Under normal conditions this is the time when the "psychologic renewal and transformation of the 'I' " (Griesinger) takes place. This psychological process, which is accompanied by a number of especially pronounced symptoms, becomes pathological and permanent in the case of hebephrenia. The manifestations, which are occasionally observed in the transitional stage of puberty, obtrude themselves to a pathologically heightened degree, finally leading to a peculiar final stage which, because of its characteristic properties, we may call hebephrenic dementia.

In the beginning of puberty heretofore unknown sensations arouse in the soul of the youth or the maiden a large number of mental images which come into conflict with the existing mental images and bring about a strange consternation. The new "I" wants to obtrude itself actively into the old, but

---

[32] Krankheitsbilder.

it does not, so to say, find space in the existing forms. Body and mind try to adapt to the new feelings and images. . . . The old ego, still wearing the outgrown shoes of childhood on its feet, does not yet want to be repressed.[33] A battle begins, a peculiar conflict of thoughts and feelings which finds its expression in the total being and behavior of the individual. . . . This is the time when the sharpest unresolved contrasts come into direct contact with each other and come to the fore in close contiguity or sequence. A certain exuberant seriousness, a pleasure in eccentric ideas, and precociously mature talk are combined with a special type of silliness and a pleasure in base or frivolous jokes. Next to the most tender and fondest sensations and feelings there is a certain courseness and roughness of the emotions. Before the form has assumed its new shape and has been consolidated to accept the new content it appears to be formless and hazy. Internally and externally, thought, speech, movement, and action lack the definite and assured form which we find both in the child and the adult. A certain thoughtlessness asserts itself. The tall, grown, lanky, clumsy figure doesn't quite yet know what to do with hands, arms, and legs; movements are jerky and angular. Silly and foolish actions result from an unrestrained drive to activity. Similarly the mind does not seem to have an appropriate use for the new images, sensations, and drives. These are spent for no purpose just as unminted gold may be squandered when its value is not recognized. Only gradually, in the course of the eighteenth to the nineteenth year, a certain composure and concentration sets in and the form of the "I" begins to take shape, yet for the time being it remains thin and fragile.

In that period we find the mental disturbance which we call hebephrenia. Aside from other aspects of its course, its principal effect is the destruction of the crystallizing form, leading to a renewed dispersion of the mental content which is still so easily dissolved. The result is that the most precious part of this content is lost. The disease process sets a limit to further mental development. It brings out a peculiar form of mental deficiency which contains only the dead elements of the phase of development that has just transpired. The battle has come to an end, but the warring elements are frozen in their positions as if they would continue to quarrel.

The end result of the disease process [is thus foreshadowed by] the first stages. Besides the specific form of the resulting dementia its early appearance is typical for hebephrenia.

In most cases the disease apparently begins as a sequel to a profound alteration in emotions with decidedly melancholic symptoms. The melancholia expresses itself first in an indefinite nameless sadness and depression of mood and only gradually consolidates into definite but changing delusions. Nearly all aspects of emotional life can become a part of the melancholic disorder which will then express itself in contrite self-accusations, indolent reverie, or ecstasy

---

[33] verdrängen.

of love, ending in a silent, brooding persecutory mania or a delusion of injury. A marked shallowness of affect soon appears in conjunction with the melancholia whose clinical picture is therefore quite different from the abject misery seen, for example, in genuine dysthymia. Frequently it appears as if the patients were playing or willfully flirting with their melancholic feelings as a contrasting joyful mood appears in the early phases. Side by side with morbid lamentations of his terrible misery, his misfortune, the sins he committed, the persecutions to which he is exposed, the patient frequently cannot suppress an impulse to laughter and silly jokes. At the same time a heightened and frequently bizarre drive to action asserts itself, which may be exacerbated to a fully developed expansive frenzy. This drive expresses itself most frequently in aimless, purposeless, silly actions and in a tendency to vagrancy and tramping. Such individuals can roam about the world for a long time without being considered ill. Because of the peculiar nature of the dementia they are frequently in danger of being thought to simulate. For, indeed, one frequently gains the impression that they purposely and consciously indulge in silly talk and action. This form of mental illness is therefore of great importance in forensic psychiatry. In one such case, to be published elsewhere, five contradictory medical opinions were given, and though undoubtedly hebephrenic the defendant was at first declared healthy and sentenced. Only after the penitentiary initiated a second process of evaluation in which Kahlbaum participated was he declared mentally deficient. The difficulty in evaluating such cases is due to the fact that most of the disturbances are of a formal nature. Definite delusions can only seldom be proven. There are all kinds of bizarre ideas. But these are transient and have the quality of being purposely affected, thereby differing from true delusions (fixed ideas). Our patient, for example, said that he had been married for fifty years. The manner in which he says it rather gives the impression of a silly idea, invented to entertain or dupe others, or conveys a childish pleasure in willful creations of the imagination (confabulation, according to Kahlbaum). In some cases remnants of the melancholic stage appear in the form of rudimentary elements of a persecutory delusion. Most frequently, however, the subject matter expressed relates to objective circumstances and shows a certain demented, uncritical, childish conception of them. This is in strange contrast to a frequently pronounced inclination to pursue popular scientific subjects and arguments. Silly, precocious chit-chat, is engaged in, obviously made up of fragments of earlier acquired half-knowledge combined with a tendency to generalize singular or totally individual experiences most uncritically. Consequently these patients prefer the pronoun "one" to "I." (This is also frequently observed for the same reason in other uneducated people.)

Of special importance are the disturbances of form which come to light in the speech of hebephrenics and which can be more readily observed in their writing. I therefore chose only case histories which contained letters from the patients. These gain in value because of their objectively reportable nature. The disturbances of form can be basically characterized as follows: First there is a peculiar deviation from logical sentence formation. Without losing the correct thread of the thought processes, the speaker or the writer changes the construction several times in the course of the long sentences he preferably uses. With this appears a typical sloppiness in connecting the sentences one to another and an inability to conclude a thought in briefer form. Without definite structuring, without punctuation, the thought process is spun off for some time, and there occur these peculiar periods which have the greatest similarity to the way in which Carlchen Miesnick writes in *Kladderadatsch*.[34] This way of writing basically differs from that of other demented patients (e.g., paralytics in the stage of dementia) in that significant disturbances and intervals in association and thought process can be proven only exceptionally. Furthermore the patient neither lacks a wealth of ideas nor does he suffer from flight of ideas; he shows a noticeable tendency to remain stuck on a topic once he has taken it up, and he flogs certain idioms and forms to death. At the same time he is not able to suppress or present in a certain order those thoughts which come to him directly from external impressions or from bizarre jumps in the thought process. . . . Besides the great sloppiness in the formation of syntax, there is a strong devotion to a completely unrefined mode of expression, and a broad provincial dialect even in writing is very typical—a dialect the patient did not speak at all in health, or far less noticeably, and certainly never wrote. There is altogether a very noticeable inclination to deviate from the natural mode of writing and speaking, to disguise speech, to speak and to write in strange jargons. In our reported observations we find, for instance, examples of imitation of Jewish jargon, of "the jargon of officers," a mixture of various languages, and so on. This frequently is connected with a preference for foreign words which are incorrectly used or peculiarly mutilated, at times in distinct contrast to the education the patient enjoyed. I want to emphasize emphatically once again that in all the cases reported by me here, the patients came from the educated classes, and as some of their positions in life prove, in healthy days they were far from demonstrating the anomalies of writing and speech mentioned. Otherwise one could attribute some of them to a lack of education. Even more surprising in our patients is the emergence of a pleasure in the use of coarse, obscene words not permissible in educated language. Yet these are not produced by affect. On the one hand the mode of speech and expression of the patient sinks well below his previous level of education. In conjunction with this, on the other hand, we see a propensity to gush, a preference for sentimental descriptions, a seemingly poetic diction, and, consequently, an overflow of empty, misshapen phrases. In all letters reported below we will be able to prove these anomalies in writing in their most essential characteristics,

[34] Satirical journal.

and frequently one can make the diagnosis of this disease from the letters of the hebephrenics.

In the over-all picture of hebephrenia, it is self-evident that not all cases display the enumerated symptoms totally or to the same extent. Despite the differences among individual cases, the always demonstrable peculiarity of their course and, before all else, the early appearance of the unmistakable silly dementia provide a definite delimitation of the total form of the disease. The typical configuration of hebephrenic dementia is more or less pronounced depending upon the greater or lesser development of single symptoms. In some cases the silly character and bearing is kept in bounds by a more serious but quite peculiar precocious gravity. In others it is suppressed and concealed by a more severe degree of dementia which is close to idiocy. Although on the whole we do not find in our patients the severest grades of dementia and zero mental states (as we do, for instance, in paralysis), we frequently find an enduring intermediate stage of mental decomposition that appears to be more characteristic. Intermittent attacks of excitement which can increase to pronounced frenzy frequently occur in the stage of dementia. The reason is often found in external causes, e.g., sexual excitement (through onanism or at the time of menstruation) and any irritation of peripheral centripetal nerves (e.g., toothache). Sometimes they are related to periodically appearing hallucinations (namely, auditory delusions). Hallucinations, a frequent symptom of mental disturbances, are not rare in hebephrenia and frequently give a definite coloration to the disease picture without having further pathognomonic meaning.

Hecker presents more lengthy case descriptions, invariably including written projections because of their pathognomonic importance. He then summarizes once more the essential characteristics of hebephrenia: its onset following puberty, the successive or alternating appearance of the various syndromes (melancholia, mania, and confusion), and its very rapid development to terminal dementia.

Regarding the etiology of hebephrenia the first striking fact is that we are mostly (although not always) dealing with individuals who have been slightly retarded in their physical and in their mental development from early on, through known or unknown circumstances (frequent physical illnesses, especially head injuries, onanism, etc.). A certain weakness of intellect, laziness, and inability to do mental work is already noticed in childhood, but this is not as extreme or as noticeable as in idiotism. The mental development of these individuals is not prevented from reaching the point where they can at least approach doing justice to the demands made upon them, depending on their age. [A discussion of the specific cases follows.]

The mental weakness is only the predisposing cause of our disease. The immediate reason for its eruption we frequently find given as mental alterations, anger, worry, and so on. We cannot attach any great value to this.

In somatic pathology as in hebephrenia, etiology is one of the darkest areas; only extensive statistics will be able to throw some light on the question.

The final proof that hebephrenia can be justified as a uniform mental disease can of course only be brought by pathological anatomic facts. But with the uncertainty still exhibited by anatomical pathology of the brain we shall have to do without this proof for a long time to come, especially because as a rule our patients reach advanced age, and cases will seldom come fresh to autopsy. In the first place I consider my task done if I succeeded in demonstrating from clinical observations that the reported cases (I could easily multiply their number if I did not know that every psychiatrist could provide extensive material from his own observations) can be combined into a uniform clinical disease picture.[35] The conclusion that such uniform symptoms, with a definite, exactly predictable course, would have a common cause is not quite correct but nevertheless frequently applied and unobjectionable in the rest of medicine. The definition of disease forms such as cholera, typhoid, Basedow's disease, and so on, are a proof of this.

An autopsy report without striking findings in brain or spinal cord follows. Hecker did not feel justified in speculating on it. Addressing the question of prognosis, he considers hebephrenia incurable. Despite a single diagnosed case which was reportedly released cured, he shares the doubts of his colleague who questioned the actual cure of the patient. In treatment he objects to all measures which induce nutritional deficiencies because hebephrenia usually develops in anemic conditions. For that reason he also objects to bleeding, cathartics, and other modes of deprivation. Only potassium bromate seemed to be helpful in manic attacks. He closes with comments of forensic importance, saying that it is probably very difficult to simulate hebephrenia because the disturbances are of a formal nature.

If my research has made it easier to recognize the disease and helped one or another unlucky hebephrenic from the danger of being sentenced by a judge, that will give me much satisfaction. Perhaps I may indulge in the hope that my work represents a not unwelcome contribution to the clinical elaboration of psychiatry.

CATATONIA

Catatonia received its name late in the nineteenth century, but it had been recognized a century before. Its earliest mention was merely in passing, in clinical accounts that described its occasional occurrence in what was then called melancholia attonica (see page 206). Guislain defined the syndrome and gave it the name *ecstasy*.

---

[35] einheitlichen klinischen Krankheitsbilde.

Guislain (1833)

It shows itself by a propensity toward immobility. The patient is always seated on a chair, leaning against a wall, or lying on his bed. By his immobility, by his fixed gaze, one believes he is looking at a statue. *By a state of muscular rigidity.* On pinching his skin, the patient does not withdraw the irritated part at all, or he withdraws it slowly. . . . Carried to its highest degree, this disease constitutes catalepsy: The patient remains in the position in which he has been placed.

Some confuse ecstasy with dementia. However in dementia there is enfeeblement of the intellectual functions; in ecstasy their suspension indicates some active disorder of the central nervous system. . . .

Although inactivity, immobility, rigidity, catalepsy, and the absence of all signs of ideation constitute the characteristics of the ecstatic reaction, nevertheless it does not always manifest itself with this cluster of phenomena. It is sometimes a simple inactivity, some retarded responses, in an occasional case a state of semi-rigidity or contracture of the face muscles.[36]

Gooch (1859)

A remarkable early account of the entire course of a catatonic attack is to be found in the writings of Gooch, a specialist in diseases of women.

[She] was much depressed in spirits; one evening she told her husband that she had never discharged the duties of a wife as she ought to do, and that her death would be a happy release both to him and her; the next morning she made an unsuccessful attempt to cut her throat. I now saw her in consultation with Dr. Sutherland; she was put under the care of a regular attendant, and was at times so violent that it was necessary to confine her with a waistcoat.

A few days after our first visit we were summoned to observe a remarkable change in her symptoms; the attendants said she was dying, or in a trance; she was lying in bed motionless, and apparently senseless; it had been said that the pupils were dilated and motionless, and some apprehensions of effusion on the brain had been entertained, but on coming to examine them closely, it was found that they readily contracted when the light fell upon them; her eyes were open, but no rising of the chest, no movement of the nostril, no appearance of respiration could be seen; the only signs of life were her warmth and pulse; the latter was, as we had hitherto observed it, weak, and about 120; her faeces and urine were voided in bed.

The trunk of the body was now lifted so as to form rather an obtuse angle with the limbs (a most uncomfortable posture), and there left with nothing to

[36] J. Guislain, *Traité sur les phrénopathies; ou Doctrine nouvelle des maladies mentales* (Brussels: Etablissement Encyclographique, 1833), pp. 258–260.

support it; there she continued sitting while we were asking questions and conversing, so that many minutes must have passed.

One arm was now raised, then the other, and where they were left, there they remained; it was now a curious sight to see her, sitting up in bed, her eyes open, staring lifelessly, her arms outstretched, yet without any visible sign of animation; she was very thin and pallid, and looked like a corpse that had been propped up, and had stiffened in this attitude. We now took her out of bed, placed her upright, and endeavoured to rouse her by calling loudly in her ears, but in vain; she stood up, but as inanimate as a statue; the slightest push put her off her balance; no exertion was made to regain it; she would have fallen if I had not caught her.

She went into this state three several times; the first time it lasted fourteen hours, the second time twelve hours, and the third time nine hours, with waking intervals of two days after the first fit and one day after the second. After this the disease resumed the ordinary form of melancholia, and three months from the time of her delivery she was well enough to resume her domestic duties.[37]

Griesinger (1845)

Griesinger's general description followed that of Guislain, but it was more detailed as regards the mental state.

In Ecstacy, together with much diminished, or almost, or completely suppressed, external sensations, there exists a strong internal concentration on certain feelings, circles of ideas, images, &c., with great elevation and tension of the entire mental activity. This state is manifested by a very highly emotional expression of the countenance, in which there is depicted astonishment, rapture, pain, according to the nature of the emotions. It is generally accompanied by complete loss of speech, immobility of the limbs, and often by a cataleptic state of the muscles. The patients appear to be quite absorbed in their emotions, they generally refuse nourishment, and particularly does volition appear to be entirely prostrate. These states are not very frequent; they sometimes come on primarily after a violent shock, in hysterical insanity, in onauists, also in epileptics, and, now and then, in alternation with violent attacks of mania. Fasting, causes of weakness of any kind, want of sleep, appear to favour their origin. In the religious ecstacies of bygone times, of which we have reliable information, these causes appear also to have played an important part.

The diminished external sensibility combined with immobility of the body, sometimes even with abolition of hearing, cause this condition closely to

[37] R. Gooch, *The Most Important Diseases Peculiar to Women* (London: The New Sydenham Society, 1859), pp. 58–59.

resemble sleep; nevertheless, it is truly a state of wakefulness, with complete concentration on certain powerful domineering circles of ideas or sensations.[38]

Kahlbaum (1874, 1884)

Catatonia is sometimes called Kahlbaum's syndrome. Although earlier authors had clearly referred to the physical manifestations of the disorder, he was the first to define its psychopathology. He emphasized its cyclic nature, the occurrence of manic, melancholic, and paranoid symptoms during its course, and the terminal development of dementia in some cases. In this he must be considered the forerunner of Kraepelin, who defined catatonia as a syndrome of dementia praecox. Nevertheless Kahlbaum maintained that negativism, both psychologic and somatic, was the unique basic process.[39]

If we first observe the total mental picture in catatonia, we note that the course of its development the whole gamut of mental states can occur—usually in the sequence of melancholia, mania, stupor (atony), confusion, and dementia. The duration of the various conditions can vary, and not infrequently there is a repeated alternation of depression and exultation. To say anything more precise at this point is not of interest. The most important fact to accept and recognize is that not only melancholia but also mania, confusion, and dementia may make up the general mental picture of this type of disease just as with the mental disturbance of paralysis. One may therefore find the disease in either one of the two old diagnostic categories of melancholia or mania. Nevertheless we have to admit that a melancholic mood seems to predominate and to continue for a long time before the cases terminate in dementia. Yet mania also occurs and has been observed in the course of tension psychosis; in fact at times such cases are diagnosed as mania. See for instance Burrows (*Commentaries,* 1829), Kelp (*Correspondenzblatt für Psychiatrie,* 1864, p. 322), Baillarger (*Annales med. psych.,* 1853, p. 262), and so on. In the second edition of his handbook Griesinger says that melancholia with dementia develops only "occasionally," but may also follow epileptic attacks or mania and may alternate with it.

Because of the great variety of symptoms contained in mental syndromes[40] it is important to preface the description of individual symptoms by a discussion of the sequence of syndromes, i.e., describe the clinical course of the diseases.

Among somatic diseases those which are cyclical and undergo certain changes with some regularity, leading to a definite final stage, are

[38] W. Griesinger, *Mental Pathology and Therapeutics,* from the 2nd German ed., C. L. Robertson and J. Rutherford, trans. (London: The New Sydenham Society, 1867), p. 83.
[39] K. Kahlbaum, *Die Katatonie oder das Spannungsirresein: Eine klinische Form psychischer Krankheit* (Berlin: A. Hirschwald, 1874), ch. 2. (O. M. Marx, trans.)
[40] Zustandsbilder.

differentiated from others with a simpler and more regular course of development. In the same way one can differentiate in the mental sphere between cyclical disease forms and those taking a more regular course. Aside from specific details, we can and inevitably have to assume two main phases in the development of all somatic disease processes: The phase or the period of the beginning and growth of the disease process (*stadium crescendi* and *incrementi*) and the phase of decline and involution (*stadium decrescendi* and *decrementi*). Depending on the number of manifestations of the disease process, these main phases are then subdivided into smaller stages, the prodromal stage, the evolutionary stage, and so on. Recognition of the stage of highest development of the disease process, the acme, is of particular importance. The main phases in mental diseases will be apparent when there are changes in the manifestations of the disease. The appearance of a variety of different mental syndromes in a particular sequence permits the ready appreciation of this scheme. Most cases of mental disease begin with a dejected mood[41] which should be considered melancholic but which is often not initially recognized. This turns into mania in which the extreme degree of mental alteration is recognized. Confusion follows, and with the disappearance of the manic symptoms mental functions deteriorate one after the other, ending with dementia. Thus the disease process itself has come to rest, showing only the defect of the mental organs. It follows that melancholia signifies the *stadium evolutionis*, mania the *stadium akmes*, confusion the *stadium decrementi* and dementia the *stadium defecti.*Whereas somatic diseases take their course in a brief period of time, usually in days or weeks so that the stages are only of short duration, mental diseases continue through much longer periods of time—months and even years. Accordingly each stage is of such duration that it demands attention. As a result the various stages were considered separate disease forms until recently, although it was known since ancient times that there is a frequent transition of one form to another. In more recent times the observation that different forms of mental disease belong together led to the idea that there are no actual forms of mental diseases but only different stages. These stages were differentiated into primary and secondary, depending on whether they were part of the ascending development of the disease process or its subsiding development. Melancholia and mania were therefore preferably called primary, whereas insanity, confusion, and dementia were considered secondary forms. The insufficiency of this particular point of view cannot be discussed here. . . .

The course of catatonia can be readily discussed in conjunction with this scheme. In this disease form we could establish an initial dejection which may at first appear quite motivated, so that it is not yet recognized as an illness. Then, however, follows a succession of abnormalities in feeling and in thought which may be of striking severity and which finally turn into the other

---

[41] Gemüthsverstimmung.

conditions. Only then do other people recognize that there is a mental disturbance. The initial melancholic mood disturbance is therefore appropriately the stadium evolutionis and found in most cases. In a certain number of cases a definitely manic condition of short duration follows, and only after that does the clinical picture appear which has led to the term atonic melancholy. For the time being it cannot be determined whether the atony more frequently follows immediately after the initial melancholia or whether it is more often separated from it by an intervening stage of mania. According to my own notes, cases in which no trace of mania was observed are much rarer than those cases in which mania, frenzy, raving, excitement, or whatever else one wants to call this condition, was noted between melancholia and atony. It is noteworthy that among the cases lacking a stage of manic acme there are several which suffered an attack of so-called mania in earlier years. In very rare cases the total disease process begins with atony. This occurred most frequently after very severe mental or physical insults, e.g., after great fright or, according to the literature, after an attempted hanging. . . .

Case 10*

A 25-year-old strong prisoner hangs himself. Immediately after the body has been taken down there are signs of life. Consciousness returns. The patient very quietly and reasonably gives his life history and his motivations (*tedium vitae*). The next day he is quiet and speaks little. The third day he becomes mute. He has a vacant gaze, injected rolling eyes, spasms of the temporal and masticatory muscles and of the eyes, hands that grasp for his head, and a rigid, lifeless gaze like a statue. No sensory impression appears to be perceived. Only very strong sound causes slight twitchings of the facial muscles. He walks about and eats without expressing his feelings or desires. After three weeks the patient is brought to an institution and a few weeks later he wakes up. He fully remembers the time and the circumstances preceding the hanging and up to the beginning of unconsciousness and describes the vivid battle of his feelings from the time of his decision until its execution and the sensations in the moment of hanging, the ringing in his ears and the flames before his eyes. From this moment on all memory of his personal existence up to the hour of his awakening in the institution has appeared. He was also totally unconscious of the resuscitation after the hanging and of the several hours in which he had gained consciousness.

Like similar cases published since then, this one was classified as dementia and differentiated as primary dementia by Spielmann or acute dementia by and mania is the acme, but the place of atony could be questioned. . . . Atony

*This case is from Spielmann's *Diagnostik* (p. 285), which quoted the case according to Siebenhaar's *Magazin der Staatsarzneikunde* Vol. 1. A similar case is that by König in Nasse's *Zeitschrift für Anthropologie*, 1826. Compare with Albers, *Memoranda der Psychiatrie*, p. 236.

Albers. But what has been gained if cases of reduced or abolished mental performance are simply shelved together on account of their symptomatology regardless of duration or cause? The clinical picture of this case becomes much clearer if we see it in relation to catatonia and view the fleeting phenomena as representative of the significant long-lasting states of other cases. Conversely the pathogenicity of catatonia is thereby illuminated and confirmed! After an insult which comes close to having the significance of an exact cerebral experiment—a transient ligation of the cervical nerve—we see a brief prodrome of quiet and apparently sensible behavior. Then a similarly brief phase of depression of mood is followed by the complete picture of atony, which is initially accompanied by symptoms of irritation of the muscular nerves, usually of the upper half of the body. A few weeks later there is an improvement with the peculiar symptom of intervals of consciousness for the remaining period of the abnormal condition.

Occasionally there is manic excitement after a short period of atony, or once again a condition of definite melancholia which is then immediately followed by atony or mania. This can be viewed as a recrudescence of the disease process. Occasionally, in the course of several weeks or months which are on the whole clearly characterized by mania, atony may occur only transiently on single days. In rarer cases atony alternates with another condition which is designated secondary confusion. Finally, however, if neither cure nor death have already ended the disease process, the atony turns into apathetic obtuseness and mental impoverishment which must be designated terminal dementia.

There are other variations in the development of catatonia: In some cases, which develop from a state of nervous irritability or vague general physical complaints, the initial stage of melancholia is either completely missing or takes a hypochondriac form which is otherwise not typical of mental disease, and the beginning of the mental disturbance seems to be a manic stage. Usually the duration of atony is longer than all preceding stages, partly because the transition from atony to terminal dementia is not clear-cut. Despite the subsequent variations in the development and progression of the disease it is not difficult to prove the cyclical nature of its total course. It is absolutely impossible to speak of different diseases following or changing into each other in cases which go through several phases of development. The cyclical nature of the whole disease process will have to be regarded as the unifying characteristic of catatonia, and the multitude of differences will have to be considered individual and subordinate modifications of the primary scheme. In most cases the disease begins with apparently insignificant symptoms. With an increase in the number and intensity of the various anomalies the disease process rises to a certain height, and after a certain point the intensity and abundance of disease symptoms decreases until it is reduced to the monotony and lack of differentiation of dementia. In this cycle of three phases melancholia is of course the first stage of incrementation must be considered as the beginning of the stadium decrementi and is therefore one of the secondary forms. But it must be decisively separated from dementia with which it was earlier classified.

Kahlbaum then addresses himself to the specific mental symptoms which characterize the various stages of catatonia. The initial stage of melancholia is nonspecific. The actual onset of the disease process was hard to define because it developed gradually from grief, care, sorrow, or other emotional states. Disappointment in love and guilt over secret sexual sins were most frequent; worries over finance and shame second in line. Kahlbaum emphasized the importance of masturbation for the onset of the illness. Hypochondriasis and anger, hypersensitivity, and irritability were third. Other symptoms of melancholy like fear of being poisoned, persecutory ideas, and religious scrupulousness were not infrequent.

The manic stage was likewise nonspecific. A certain pathos was more typical of catatonia in contrast to paralysis in which an egotistical pride and superciliousness were more commonly found.

The third patient reported by Kahlbaum was frequently found in the center of the hallway with fixed gaze, giving nonsensical sermons. Noting the exact words of the patient Kahlbaum comments that at other times the patient could communicate quite well. He inferred that the uninterrupted speech represented a seizure of the nerve or of the cerebral speech center, a symptom he called verbigeration.

Verbigeration is a psychopathic manifestation in which the patient repeatedly expresses meaningless or unconnected words and sentences in the form of an apparent speech. The words are either taken from everyday life or from a chance occurrence. They may also derive from a particular area of human interest, frequently from the religious sphere. At times they are created quite willfully, according to the character of some language, and they are frequently repeated. The characteristics of a speech, that is, speaking to others for a particular purpose or out of a particular mood, are apparent in certain parts of what is said and in the fervor which the speaker demonstrates by his mien and his behavior. Nevertheless one frequently sees exactly the same speeches given without anyone being there. When someone is present the speaker in no way adjusts himself to the impression which his words make upon the listener, and will not permit interruptions. In some respects this symptom is similar the the process of memorizing part of a speech; single sentences or fragments or even single words are frequently repeated, so that one who perchance listens to such memorizing may not be able to understand the content or the connection of what he hears. Verbigeration is readily differentiated by its content from the trivial twaddle and chatter of the confused or mentally deficient, although the content of verbigeration does not have to be particularly meaningful. Similarly it must be differentiated from the simple symptom of speech mania which is meaningful. Its content understandably emanates from the patient's mood. The so-called flight of ideas can also be compared with verbigeration but differs in that there is sequence to the content of what is said, aside from other characteristics demonstrated by the patient at the time. Confabulation differs from verbigeration by its subject matter, which is the product of fantasy. Occasionally in the course of the disease process verbigeration may turn into one of these other symptoms.

The above-mentioned symptom is all the more striking and peculiar as in the same disease form and in the same cases we have a symptom which is its exact opposite. I mean the much talked-about taciturnity, the chief symptom of the state of atony. The taciturnity (*mutacism* of the French) is either complete and absolute or relative, partial, and intermittent. In the latter case the patient speaks in a very low voice, hardly audible, frequently only moving his lips; or he speaks only a few brief words when pressed with questions but never speaks of his own accord. Most questions he leaves unanswered and tries to circumvent answering by simple gesticulation. At the other extreme there is an absolute mutism, frequently for months or even years. The patient cannot be motivated to speak even by the most severe pain.

Here Kahlbaum gives the case history of a 22-year-old catatonic who, after having been intermittently mute for about two years and completely mute for five, responded to the application of galvanic current.

The patient was shown the induction apparatus, and it was indicated to him that when the rheophores were held to his body he would experience a sensation of current through his body which would also touch his speech nerves and would enable him to speak again, either immediately or gradually. One morning electrodes were put on his upper and lower right-arm muscles, and the current was gradually increased so that the muscles contracted and his face became distorted with pain. He held out steadfastly and expressed a certain feeling of satisfaction. The same day he spontaneously addressed the physician on afternoon rounds. Galvanization was continued for some time. Each time he came to the sessions with evidently great pleasure and exercised his redeemed ability to speak with apparent satisfaction. Since then he has not lost his speech, although the symptom of unmotivated silence, gesticulatory speech, and speech by the indication of words continued frequently. . . .

In some cases patients who, as it were, awoke from silent atony indicate that they did not speak because a voice (an inner one or one that they could hear loudly, hence an hallucinated one) ordered them not to speak, whereas in other instances the patients speak about a lack of any thought and an inability to pay attention. In still other cases they could not comment on the situation. In the case of the first response one could look upon the mutism as willful, whereas in the others one could think of a kind of paralysis within the nervous tracts serving speech. . . . It is therefore permissible to think in both instances of a convulsive condition which through a secondary reflex upon the acoustic nerve arouses hallucinations. With this concept both symptoms—the mania to speak as well as mutism—would be attributed to one and the same alteration in innervation. The speaking mania and verbigeration would then be comparable to the clonic and mutism comparable to the tinic seizure.

All symptoms especially considered so far are formal disturbances. In this group the symptom of so-called flight of ideas deserves further mention. It occurs in the manic stage of catatonia and is not essentially different from that occurring in the mania of other mental disease forms. Further there is the symptomatic peculiarity of frequent use of the diminutive form. . . . Finally, a subjective lack of ideas or a standing-still of ideas is to be mentioned. According to the patients' reports these occur most frequently during the phase of atony.

Kahlbaum goes on to say that there is little in the content, that is, in the disturbance of intelligence itself, that can be differentiated from other disease forms. In addition to other symptoms Kahlbaum frequently found the delusion that the patient was not the actual child of his parents but of noble descent.

In the sphere of action and will, there is early in the course of the disease a noticeable tendency to negation which is most fully developed in and characteristic of the phase of atony. . . . In extreme cases this leads to a refusal of the patient to leave his bed or to take food.

There is probably no case of catatonia in which the symptom of the tendency to negation is not present to some degree, sometimes more actively, sometimes more passively.

After discussing negation at great length, including refusal of food, assignments to other rooms, or getting out of bed, Kahlbaum speaks of peculiar, more or less bizarre habits of body movements, posture, and other pronounced repetitive actions.

Most noticeable are those bizarre, stereotypic movements which are seen in all larger institutions in great numbers. One reaches every few minutes to the tip of his nose; another from time to time swings his arm horizontally around his head and ends with a flinging movement of the hand. A woman makes arm and hand movements while she is sitting which are quite similar to those made spinning at the spinning wheel.

One patient, the sixth case described by Kahlbaum, had the mannerism of walking on the edge of his foot with the medial side elevated and with bent knees. Others grimaced frequently.

Also the immobile posture, the way in which the limbs and parts of the body are held at rest are typical of the catatonic. A woman patient in Allenberg sat many months in her bed with back bent and head forward, after a long time during which she had lain apathetically in bed. . . . One patient, while resting, had the habit of holding his right forearm in front of his chest, covering his face or the right side of it with the right hand, the left hand tightly holding the right elbow, a position frequently assumed to rest the arms or while thinking. But for him this posture became so stereotyped that there were deep impressions where the body parts touched. In this category also belongs the spasmodic forward pressing of the lips (snout spasm) which is very frequent in catatonia. Most frequently these peculiarities of stereotypic postures and mannerisms of movement are described only in those cases which are already in the state of terminal dementia. But they occur much earlier and, aside from the very well-known rigid posture of the patient with completely developed atony, they occur also in the manic stage, especially when states of frenzy alternate with atony. In these early phases of the disease, or at other times during remission and intermission where delusions can no longer be determined, these patients characteristically display a stiff posture of their whole body and can be recognized by the stereotypic quality of their actions and their appearance. For instance, one patient, who during an intermission was completely lucid, always used one specific path in the garden and turned abruptly around at its end. He was still conspicuous because of his swinging movements a long time after no intellectual disturbance in the narrower sense could be observed. Occasionally asked for the reason, he said that on other paths it was sunny, but this was not at all the case. A healthy person would not be likely to cling to the monotony and discomforr of this one short walk, but as the seasons progressed there was no change in his habit.

Let us go on to somatic symptoms. In the last-mentioned manifestations of disturbed actions of the will one is likely to think of a pathological innervation of the motor nerves, and this assumption becomes exceedingly likely when we see that decidedly convulsive states are characteristic symptoms of this disease form. Now it is well known that the convulsive form of flexibilitas cerea is a frequent symptom of the atonic state. As the related cases demonstrate, other forms of seizure occur frequently enough. The patient Adolph K. (first case) had cloreiform convulsions of the face and extremities. The second reported case history mentions the appearance of an epileptiform attack. In the third case history it is said that there were hysterical incidents, actual spasms of the feet, then of the arms and cheeks, whereby a sound like the ticking of a watch could be heard in the mouth; later, crying and laughing spells. In the fourth case I myself observed these attacks and convulsive states in the institution: In the beginning there was convulsion of all muscles of the extremeties (waves of twitchings of single muscle parties) then tetany and trismus. In the sixth case seizures were also observed in the institution. As in the previous case there was first a general convulsiveness, then a true epileptiform attack. In the case of Paul M. (eleventh case) the convulsions appeared for several days, typically along with manic attacks. Single spasms in the upper body were observed in the case of the patient who hung himself. In two cases there was no mention of spasms in the medical reports sent to the institution, but I later heard about attacks of seizures through interrogation of relatives. The literature considers the frequent occurrence of seizures in cases of atonic melancholy. . . . Some of these motor abnormalities could be viewed as something mental, even dependent upon the will, like those manifestations which were earlier described as disturbances in voluntary movement and action. Others will have to be considered cerebrospinal, such as the state of flexibilitas cerea and the contracture-like distorted postures of the limbs. Actual paralyses occur in catatonics so seldom that they do not have to be considered part of the picture of this disease form. Sensory weaknesses including more or less complete anesthesia are very frequent. Especially in cases of atonic melancholy it is frequently reported that very deep needle pricks are tolerated without the slightest expression of pain, and I have made similar observations. But the abolition of the sense of pain is not always present and appears in many cases to depend upon the abolition of the ability to react motorically. Later, when the mental reaction has been freed, the patient immediately shows full sensibility and occasionally the memory of the pain of the pricks has been retained from the atonic period.

Another frequent symptom to be mentioned is hyperesthesia. Catatonics frequently complain about a very severe and continuous occipital headache. While pain in the area of the forehead or the temples or the vertex occurs in other mental disease forms, such pains are practically never observed in catatonics. The occipital pain characteristic of catatonia occurs more rarely in other forms.

Kahlbaum also mentions edema of the lower extremities or of the eyelids as well as oligemia and chlorosis. In addition he mentions halitosis (which he found in catatonia despite the greatest cleanliness), abnormal taste sensations, and anorexia. He found it difficult to determine how much was due to mental processes and how much to processes which can be physically explained, like the reduced intake of food. Finally he discusses the relationship between catatonia and tuberculosis and contrasts it with that between general paresis and tuberculosis. Although in earlier times poor nutrition both within and without institutions led to a high correlation of tuberculosis with all mental illness, Kahlbaum wanted to restrict the high correlation to catatonia. Other disease forms seem to show no particular relationship to catatonia.

Kahlbaum believed that all mental disorders of childhood were best treated by means of special education. He had a school for disturbed children, and some of its clients had catatonia.

It is well known that most mental diseases can appear in youth, especially dysthymia and vesania, which strangely enough are still called melancholia and mania; further, catatonia may occur in the simpler form of so-called atonic melancholy as well as in the more complex form with manic and choreatic symptoms...[42]

Spitzka (1883)

Spitzka wrote about catatonia shortly after Kahlbaum published his own writings. Spitzka followed Kahlbaum closely but with different emphasis and, in one respect, some disagreement.

Katatonia is a form of insanity characterized by a pathetical emotional state and verbigeration, combined with a condition of motor tension.
This well-marked though not generally recognized mental disorder was first demarcated by Kahlbaum of Görlitz about eight years ago. In the course of the writer's study of the pauper insane at Ward's Island he became impressed with the genuineness of the grounds on which Kahlbaum based this classification....

The excited stage presents symptoms of a kind different from those of ordinary melancholia, and constitutes a connecting link, as it were, between the symptoms of an agitated melancholiac and those of a lunatic with fixed delusions. Some of the patients present exaggerated, others diminished, self-esteem; and not rarely does the developing delirium assume an expansive tinge. But all katatonics exhibit a peculiar pathos, either in the direction of declamatory gestures and theatrical behavior, or of an ecstatic religious exaltation. Frequently the patients wander about, imitating great actors or preachers, and often express a desire and take steps to become such preachers and actors. In America, as Kiernan remarks, the chronic stump-speaking tendency is more frequently displayed by these patients, and in a negro suffering from katatonia the conversation in excited periods was noted to present the grandiloquent character which has been so aptly rendered in the minutes of the "lime-kiln club." This patient had, without any prodromal symptoms, fallen down suddenly while at work, his face and arms twitching; a lucid period followed, the patient gradually became depressed, and in the asylum his depression gave way to a maniacal condition, which was followed by another fit of depression, marked by numerous hallucinations. With this he refused food and passed into a cataleptoid condition, from which he suddenly emerged one morning, saying that he was "equal to any white man." Apparent recovery took place, but between 1871 and 1875 he was re-admitted three times. On these occasions he presented mainly alternations between atonic stupor with catalepsy and a peculiar condition which was so characteristic that it first called the writer's attention to the distinctness of

[42] K. Kahlbaum, "Über jungendliche Nerven- un Gemütskranke und ihre pedagogische Behandlung in der Heilanstallt," *Allgemeine Zeitschrift für Psychiatrie*, 1884, **40**, 868–873.

the disorder. On going up to the patient and loudly addressing him, he lifted his ordinarily bowed head in a very consequential way and prefaced the reply to any question by the words "I do not doubt but what." Asked his name, for example, he said, "I do not doubt but what my name is William Henry G— ;" asked his age, "I do not doubt but that I was born in the year 1838, so my mother said;" asked his nativity, "I do not doubt but that I was born in some part of the world;" asked whether he had any desire, "I do not doubt but what I want to *get* out and *go* home and get me *some* work, in order that I may buy me some food, *and* some clothes, and—" here he relapsed into the passive state. Before he answered a most remarkable series of grimaces were gone through, a series of spasms of the oral muscles, which culminated in the explosive enunciation of the first word of his reply. The answers were deliberately and pompously given, something after the fashion of a juvenile actor. . . .

It has seemed to the writer as if there were at times a recognition on the part of the patients that their "verbigeration" is nonsensical, and that they have a silly enjoyment of the "fun." Although this suspicion can be based only on the facial expression of the subjects as shown when they are sharply cross-questioned, it seemed convincingly strong in the two cases referred to.

Kahlbaum has noted the tendency of katatoniacs to use diminutive expressions, a tendency which can be better gratified by German than by Anglo-American patients, and was observed in the case just cited. One of Kahlbaum's patients would say, for example, "Ach ich bin so klein*chen*, und in zwei Minut*chen* bin ich todt*chen*—Ich bin so schwach*chen*—jezt bin ich bisweilen so gross*chen*—Ich muss sterb*chen*, alle menschen todt*chen*, ich muss wein*chen*," etc.[43]

PARANOIA

The word paranoia originally had a meaning different from that given it today; at first it meant nothing but "mentally distraught." According to Professor Renehan of Boston College, the word is found in several places in ancient Greek drama: *Seven against Thebes* by Aeschylus (v. 756) presented in 467 B.C., *Orestes* by Euripides (v. 824) presented in 408 B.C, and *Clouds* by Aristophanes (v. 1976), perhaps the version presented in 423 B.C. or the revised later one. In all cases the word paranoia was used simply to indicate mental disorder. Hippocrates used it in a similar sense.[44]

Vogel is known to have used the word *paranoiae* as the general heading for his group of mental diseases in his works before 1770, but by 1772 he had replaced

[43] E. C. Spitzka, *Insanity: Its Classification, Diagnosis and Treatment* (New York: Bermingham and Co., 1883), pp. 149–152.

[44] *Hippocrates*, W. H. S. Jones, trans. (Cambridge, Mass.: Harvard Univeristy Press; London: W. Heinemann, Ltd., 1948), Vol. 1, p. lix.

it with *morbi mentis.*[45] Heinroth continued to use it as Vogel had, and other German clinicians did likewise. It came to have a new and highly specific meaning when Kahlbaum in 1878 suggested that *paranoia* be reserved for the primary form of systematized delusions to distinguish it from the secondary occurrence of delusions in other psychoses. The confused histories of both the word *paranoia* and the syndromes to which it was or was not attached are described in detail by Séglas, who wrote: "There is perhaps no word in psychiatry that has a wider acceptance or a vaguer definition."[46]

The word paranoia was used as a formal diagnosis in the first edition of Krafft-Ebing's text (1879). Spitzka discussed the condition in his first edition but did not use the name until his second.

Haslam (1810)

Although writers of Haslam's era and before had described delusions of persecution, Haslam's report was the first systematic and detailed account of a patient who seemed normal in all respects but those relating to his systematized delusions.

> Mr. M. insists that in some apartment near London Wall, there is a gang of villains profoundly skilled in Pneumatic Chemistry, who assail him by means of an Air Loom. A description of this formidable instrument will be given hereafter; but he is persuaded that an account of it is to be found in Chambers's Dictionary, edited by Dr. Rees in 1783, under the article *Loom*, and that its figure is to be seen in one of the plates relating to Pneumatics.
>
> It is unnecessary to tell the reader that he will fruitlessly search that work for such information.
>
> The assailing gang consists of seven members, four of whom are men and three women. Of these persons four are commonly resident, and two have never stirred abroad since he has been the subject of their persecution. Of their general habits little is known; occasionally they appear in the streets, and by ordinary persons would be taken to be pick-pockets or private distillers. They leave home to correspond with others of their profession; hire themselves out as spies, and discover the secrets of government to the enemy, or confederate to work events of the most atrocious nature. At home they lie together in promiscuous intercourse and filthy community.[47]

There were more than forty additional pages of similar material. When Mr. M. was examined by two famous physicians, the immortal Clutterbuck and the outstanding Birkbeck, they declared him completely sane.

---

[45] R. A. Vogel, *Academicae praelectiones de cognoscendis et curandis praecipuis corporis humani affectibus* (Gottingen: Vanderhoeck, 1772).

[46] J. Séglas, "La Paranoia," *Archives de Neurologie*, 1887, 13, 62–76.

[47] J. Haslam, *Illustrations of Madness* (London: G. Hayden, 1810), pp. 19–20.

Lasèque (1852)

Lasèque's paper was a highly important contribution to the development of a psychiatric concept and one that has been almost entirely unrecognized. He stated that delusions of persecution are common in all types of psychosis and that they may be the primary manifestation of mental disease, unassociated with other symptoms. Most important of all he held that the basic psychologic process is an intense preoccupation with explaining the delusions logically. The last feature has received only tangential recognition in today's comment that there is nobody so logical as a paranoid. Lasèque's concept of the nature of paranoia fits what is observable about the disorder and hence is more satisfactory than Freud's trivial explanation that it is a manifestation of latent homosexuality.

I will discuss the type of insanity that I designate here under the name of *délire de persécution*, and which I consider a type sufficiently distinct to separate it entirely from other types of mental disease.

The délire de persécution is not the consequence of one type of personality; it occurs in persons very different from each other by their native character, by the nature and degree of their intelligence, and by their social position. . . .

The more or less definite idea of persecution is one of the most frequent manifestations among the insane in the form of an incidental idea. One finds it changeable and startling, accompanied by genuine terror in an attack of delirium tremens; it is equally common in psychoses due to narcotic substances, and it is not a rare occurrence in so-called clear insanities. The mere fact of its frequent occurrence permits us to regard this type of psychotic thinking as an important symptom of insanity; yet, in the case in which it is not destined to become predominant, the belief of persecution is only a transitory phenomenon, about which the patients are not insistent. . . .

When the delusion begins to concentrate on that fixed idea, the patient begins by acting with a certain reserve, he hesitates, he himself expresses his doubt, he asks if, in default of this explanation, one can find him another that takes into account the proofs he has submitted. . . . Little by little the uncertainty vanishes. It is replaced by certainty, and the patient composes in a definitive manner the delusional system in which he becomes fixed. . . .

The patients afflicted with delusions of persecution submit to a pervasive and predominant idea, but again they are forced by the nature of their psychoses to use intellectual processes similar to their disorder, and to move in an unchanging circle.[48]

---

[48] C. Lasèque, "Du délire de persécution," *Archives Générales de Médicine,* 40 Série, 1852, 28, 133–134, 138.

Morel (1860)

What is today called paranoia Morel in 1852 named *folie systématisée* or *manie systématisée*. He was describing the secondary form, however, and it was Lasèque in the same year who defined the primary syndrome and gave it the name *délire de persecution*. Morel later adopted this term for the secondary variety as well.

> The transition [of hypochondriac insanity] to the second variety is recognized by that singular transformation that makes the patients seem to occupy themselves less with interest in their physical health and move with more elevated interests, comprising their honor, their reputation, and all that refers to the most precious circumstances of their existence. Those afflicted with persecution insanity form a numerous class in the table of nosology of the mental diseases, and the gravity of the acts into which they are betrayed is in accord with the painful state which they endure.
>
> It is in persecution insanity that one sees a special variety of suicides and homicides and patients with systematized delusions of the most dangerous sort. One has seen these patients, having every appearance of rationality, commit incredible acts such as robbery, incendiarism, murder, with the sole motive of attracting public attention in order to receive the justice that in their systematized delusions they believed had been refused them.
>
> *Third variety.* At the very end, when the disease moves toward a fatal termination, there will occur an extraordinary transformation in the ideas and feelings of the patient with delusions of persecution. . . . The patients believe themselves called to great destinies and to play a role that most of the time is not in accord with their education, or with the intellectual qualities they formerly had. I have said that these phenomena indicate a fatal termination, but this prognosis is not absolute.[49]

On the Insanity of Ideas and Acts That Is Consequent to Hypochondria

> The patients begin to exhibit great impatience; they become restless, variable, fantastic, imperious, and extremely irritable. . . . At first they are hypochondriacs and occupy themselves solely with matters of physical health. When they develop the belief that their illnesses are poisonings or that other substances cause the sensations that trouble them, when they imagine that they are exposed to the sorcery of occult powers, as they call them, such as electricity, magnetism, and that the police themselves are bent on their ruin, one can be sure that they have entered the phase of this special psychosis that we cannot better designate than under the name of *persecution psychosis.*
>
> It is during the active period of this psychosis that the persecuted hypochondriacs are subject to strange illusions and hallucinations, and the

[49] B. A. Morel, *Traité des maladies mentales* (Paris: V. Masson, 1860), pp. 266–267.

senseless acts they commit have no concordance to the external world.[50]

Transformation of the persecution psychosis; systemization of the psychotic conceptions; transition to the idea of being called to great destinies In the mental hospitals one finds a certain number of patients who have lost all the external signs of melancholia; they appear content, beaming, satisfied; they exhibit the greatest activity, equally for themselves and for others. These are the useful servants whom the physicians are happy to employ willingly to help in treating the infirm patients, to carry out manual labor of all sorts. While these servants obey and submit ordinarily to the most intimate tasks, they consider themselves millionaires, kings, prophets, and in any case persons invested with great power. Unfortunately they are forced to bow, as they say, to superior powers; they attribute to electricity, to magnetism, the dependent state in which one finds their minds, the malignant feelings that they resent. One ordinarily sees these types of patients occupying themselves in writing, in formulating their complaints, composing, in order to place them before the eyes of the authorities, enormous memoirs intended to expose the tricks, the plots, the machinations of their enemies, visible and invisible. They console themselves by twisting for their own justification the events of the external world. I knew one of these systematizers who kept an exact list of the misfortunes that occurred to the persons who had persecuted him, and he attributed their natural deaths to the vengeance of heaven.

During their periods of remission many of these patients, in whom judgment is strangely false, occupy themselves as writers, and many as versifiers.[51]

Ball (1880)

Ball described the manner in which the patient is completely engulfed by his delusions despite the outward lucidity and reasonableness manifested in other areas of mental life.

One cannot conceive of a delirium more general, more profound, and more extreme than that of persecution. By its origins, by its consequences, by the totality of the ideas that characterize it, it engulfs an individual entirely, and one is rightfully astonished that such a delirium can be considered a partial disorder of the intelligence. But many of these patients are men of lucid spirit and elevated culture, who have preserved adequately the free exercise of their faculties. One hesitates accordingly to consider them psychotic, and while one accepts this diagnosis, one is tempted to believe that it constitutes a partial insanity. Nothing could be more wrong than such an idea.

When one goes over the details of their history, most of the patients have presented from their earliest years a certain strangeness of character and spirit. But at the onset of the truly pathologic period one can see a general

---

[50] Ibid., p. 707.
[51] Ibid., p. 714.

depression suddenly appear, a profound sadness that bends all the ideas toward the melancholic, like gray sky that puts a uniform color on everything. However, in the midst of these constant preoccupations, we often see these patients enjoy an active life and sometimes play an important role in society. Their influence is considerable during this period of the illness, and several have left their mark on history. These patients are evidently different from the collapsed depressives. They have a spirit as active and as penetrating as normal. Accustomed to hide their mental illness, one can see them elevate themselves to the highest status, some savants, literary men, and politicians have shown in the plainest fashion the characteristics of the persecution mania.

However, one should not believe that all these patients are cast from the same mold and exhibit the same intellectual caliber. The insanity of some, incoherent and disconnected, testifies to their intellectual poverty, the insanity of others comprises a logical conception in which the various parts occupy a reciprocal bearing. Some are active persecutees who react violently against their enemies; there are passive persecutees who control themselves and accept their misfortune without resistance. . . .

For most of these patients, a mysterious power, a general conspiracy, menaces and dominates their entire existence. It is an impersonal power that originates from no named person.[52]

THE DEMENTIA PRAECOX CONCEPT

Kraepelin (1904)

Kraepelin needed a new term which he hoped would unite the entire group of endogenous psychoses of the young. He chose *dementia praecox* which he considered particularly apt because of the high incidence of mental deterioration in the patients.

Kraepelin is currently derogated because he emphasized deterioration. It is clear from his writings, however, that what he considered deterioration is today, at least in this country, regarded as remission of the active psychosis and a return to a state of merely inadequate personality. Although deterioration would in many cases include loss of the most florid psychotic manifestations, calling a patient cured rather than deteriorated cannot but have a favorable effect on the statistics.

Dementia praecox is the name first applied by A. Pick, in 1891, to a group of cases including the hebephrenia of Hecker and Kahlbaum, characterized by maniacal symptoms followed by melancholia and rapid deterioration.

[52] B. Ball, *Leçons sur les maladies mentales* (Paris: Asselin et Cie., 1880), pp. 238–239, 240.

Since then the meaning of the term has been extended so as to include a larger group of cases appearing in earlier life, characterized by a progressively chronic course with certain fundamental symptoms, of which progressive mental deterioration is the most prominent. Some psychiatrists, especially the Italian, use the name *primary dementia*, because it enables them to include a few cases characterized by similar symptoms which appear in patients long past the period of pubescence. The group of cases as understood by us is a large one, and includes, besides hebephrenia, the catatonia of Kahlbaum and certain forms of paranoia which undergo early deterioration.... A number of patients present mental peculiarities from youth up, such as seclusiveness, precocious piety, impulsive actions and great susceptibility to alcohol, and at least seven per cent have always been weak-minded. ...

Symptomatology.—The disease picture appears so varied that upon superficial observation the fundamental symptoms are not recognized. These symptoms, however, permit of an early recognition of the disease process and become more and more marked as the disease progresses.

In the field of *apprehension* there is usually very little disturbance. External impressions are correctly perceived, the patients being able to recognize their environment and to comprehend most of what takes place about them. This explains the fact that they remain quite well oriented, as to time, place, and person. During the acute or subacute onset of the disease, apprehension is affected, and there is some disorientation. This may also appear during transitory stupor or excitement; but even in these conditions, and especially in the apparent stupidity and indifference which characterize the later stages of the disease, it is surprising to see how many things in the environment are perceived. It is not unusual to find that they notice changes in the physician's apparel, in the furniture, or in the landscape. Nevertheless, as the disease advances and deterioration appears, apprehension, as well as other mental phenomena, becomes perceptibly impaired.

Occasionally delusions entertained by the patient lead to a misinterpretation of some of their surroundings. They may be days or years ahead of the correct time, their nurses may be called by fictitious names, or the hospital may be regarded as a nunnery, while in other respects the orientation is correct.

Apprehension is always more or less distorted by *hallucinations*, especially in acute and subacute development of the disease. These usually disappear later in the course of the disease, but may persist into the end stages. Hallucinations of hearing are most prominent, next come hallucinations of sight, and at rare intervals we find those of touch. Hallucinations at first are distressing, resulting in fear; but later in the course of the disease they do not excite much interest, and the patients when questioned are unable to give much information about them. Some patients seem to take pleasure in listening to the voices, whose communications are both incoherent and silly.

During exacerbations of the disease the hallucinations may induce the former fear and distress.

Consciousness is usually clear, but in conditions of excitement and stupor there is always some clouding of consciousness. It is, however, much less marked than one would judge from superficial observation, as the patients later are able to give some details of things that happened in the interval.

On the other hand, there is pronounced impairment of voluntary *attention*, which is one of the most fundamental symptoms. The controlling force of interest is altogether lacking, so that the presentation which happens to be the clearest and most distinct at any given moment is an accident of passing attention, never persistent enough to occasion connected activity. In spite of the fact that the patients perceive objects about them correctly, they do not observe them closely or attempt to understand them. In deep stupor and in the stage of deterioration it is absolutely impossible to attract the attention in any way. In the catatonic form of dementia praecox the presence of negativism inhibits all active attention. This becomes evident as the negativism gradually disappears. The patients emerging from this condition are caught stealthily peeping about when unobserved, looking out of open doors or windows, and following the movements of the physician, but when an object is held before them for observation they stare vacantly about or close their eyes tightly.

There is a characteristic and progressive, but not profound, impairment of *memory* from the onset of the disease. Memory images formed before the onset of the disease are retained with remarkable persistence,—retention is good. Though their reproduction is increasingly more difficult, unusual stimulation or excitement may occasion the recollection of events long since supposed to be effaced by the advance of deterioration,—recollection is not free. The formation of new memory images is increasingly difficult with the advance of the disease. Memory for recent events is poor. Events previous to the onset, especially school knowledge, may be recalled after the patients show advanced deterioration. . . .

In the earlier stages of the disease *thought* shows a characteristic *incoherence and looseness.* One finds even in the mild cases some distractibility, a rapid transition from one thought to another without an evident association, and interpolation of high-sounding phrases. In severe cases there is genuine confusion of thought with great incoherence and the production of new words. In cases of the catatonic form especially, we meet with evidences of stereotypy; the patients cling to one idea, which they repeat over and over again. Besides, there is occasionally noticed a tendency to rhyme or to repeat senseless sounds.

In *judgment* there appears from the onset a progressive defect. While patients are able to get along without difficulty under familiar circumstances, they fail to adapt themselves to new conditions. Owing to their inability to grasp the meaning of their surroundings, their actions are irrational. This condition of defective judgment becomes the basis for the development of delusions. The patients believe that they are the objects of persecution, and they may have delusions of reference and self-accusation. The lack of judgment becomes still more apparent in the silliness of their delusions. At first the delusions may be rather stable, but later they tend to change their content frequently, adding new elements suggested by the environment. Even relatively persistent delusions are constantly taking on new meanings. Furthermore, the delusions, which at first are of a depressive nature, later may become expansive and grandiose. In most cases the wealth of delusions so apparent at first gradually disappears. A few delusions may be retained with further elaboration from time to time, but they are usually expressed only at random. During exacerbations the former delusions, whether depressive or expansive, may again come to the foreground. In the paranoid forms, however, there persists from the beginning a great wealth of delusions, but these become more and more incoherent.

The disturbance of the *emotional field* is another of the characteristic and fundamental symptoms. There is a progressive, more or less high-grade, deterioration of the emotional life. The lack of interest in the surroundings already spoken of in connection with the attention may be regarded as one phase of the general emotional deterioration. Very often it is this symptom which first calls attention to the approaching disease. Parents and friends notice that there is a change in the disposition, a laxity in morals, a disregard for formerly cherished ideas, a lack of affection towards relatives and friends, an absence of their accustomed sympathy, and above all an unnatural satisfaction with their own ideas and behavior. They fail to exhibit the usual pleasure in their employment.

As the disease progresses the absence of emotion becomes more marked. The patients express neither joy nor sorrow, have neither desires nor fears, but live from one day to another quite unconcerned and apathetic, sometimes silently gazing into the distance, at others regarding their surroundings with a vacant stare. They are indifferent as to their personal appearance, submit stupidly to uncomfortable positions, and even prodding with a needle may not excite a reaction. Food, however, continues to attract them until deterioration is far advanced. Indeed, it is not unusual to see these patients go through the pockets and bundles of their friends for goodies, without expressing a sign of recognition. This condition of stupid indifference may be interrupted by short periods of irritability.

Early in the disease, and especially during an acute and subacute development, the emotional attitude may be one of depression and anxiety. This may later give way to moderate elation and happiness. The latter, however, in a few instances prevails from the onset. Yet emotional deterioration remains a fundamental symptom.

Parallel with the emotional disturbances are found disturbances of *conduct*, of which the most fundamental is the progressive *disappearance of voluntary activity.* One of the first symptoms of the disease may be the loss of that activity which is peculiar to the patient. He may neglect his duties and sit unoccupied for the greater part of the day, though capable of doing good work if persistently encouraged. Besides this characteristic inactivity, there may appear a tendency to impulsive acts. The patients break out window lights, tear their clothing into strips, leap into the water, break furniture, throw dishes on the floor, or injure fellow-patients, all of which seems done without a definite motive. These states usually pass off very quickly, though in some this tendency may be more marked for a period of a few days.

The inability to control the impulses is also present in the stuporous conditions, and especially in the catatonic form of dementia praecox. Here each natural impulse is seemingly met and overcome by an opposing impulse, giving rise to actions directly opposite to the ones desired. In this condition, which is called *negativism*, the patients resist everything that is done for them, such as dressing and undressing, they refuse to eat when food is placed before them, to open their mouth or eyes when requested, or to move in any direction. In extreme conditions there may even be retention of urine and faeces. This condition varies considerably in intensity at different times. It is not unusual to see the patients suddenly relieved of it, assume their former activity, talking freely and attending to their own needs, and again after an interval of a few hours or days relapse gradually into the negativistic state.

Still another condition is produced by the repeated recurrence of the same impulse, giving rise to a great variety of *stereotyped movements and expressions.* The verbigerations and mannerisms of the catatonic are explained in this way. The patients repeat for hours similar expressions, utter monotonous grunts, tread the floor in the same spot, dress, undress, and eat in a peculiar and constrained manner. While these symptoms vary considerably in individual cases, it is unusual not to find at least some of them present in every case.

The *capacity for employment* is seriously impaired. The patients may be trained to do a certain amount of routine work, but they utterly fail when given something new. A few patients display artistic abilities, as, for instance, in drawing or in music, but their efforts are characterized by eccentricities. They may show some technical skill, but their productions exhibit the absence of the finer aesthetic feelings.[53]

Hebephrenic Form (Hebephrenia)

The *onset* of the psychosis in this form varies. In a few cases it is so insidious in origin that the relatives are unable to place the date of the appearance of the first symptom. Usually the patients complain first of

---

[53] E. Kraepelin, *Clinical Psychiatry,* from *Lehrbuch der Psychiatrie,* 6th ed. [1899], A. R. Defendorff, ed. and trans. (New York: Macmillan Co., 1904), pp. 152–160.

headache and insomnia, then a gradual change of disposition comes over them. They lose their accustomed activity and energy, becoming self-absorbed, shy, sullen, and seclusive, or perhaps irritable, obstinate, and careless. They may become rude and assertive, or they may be perfectly indifferent. They are careless of their obligations, are thoughtless and unbalanced. They accomplish nothing, but rather sit about unemployed, apparently brooding or engaging in useless conversation, or they leave their work to go to bed, lying there for weeks without evident reason. Others, instead of this inaction, exhibit a marked restlessness, and continuous effort is impossible. They leave their work, stroll about or ride wheels from place to place, especially at night. Others, with increased sexual passion, indulge in illicit and promiscuous intercourse.

During this period, which may extend through several months, there are apt to be remissions, when for a short time the patients improve greatly and may even appear natural. Women show premonitions of the disease during the menses.

More often the onset is characterized by a period of depression, when the symptoms appear more rapidly and are more pronounced. Here the patients become more apprehensive, dejected, sad, and sometimes suspicious. They are troubled with thoughts of death, life seems to have lost its charms, and friends appear indifferent. Their mental condition at this time often leads to suicidal attempts. *Hallucinations*, especially of hearing, and less often of sight, appear at this period. The patients are annoyed at strange noises, unintelligible voices, unfavorable comments upon their personal appearance; they hear threats and imprecations, music and singing, telephone messages, and commands from God. They may also see heavenly visions, crosses on the wall, dead relatives, frightful accidents, and deathbed scenes. Occasionally they smell various odors, especially illuminating gas and sulphur. A patient may experience various hyperaesthesias which lead him to believe that his head is double, that the throat or nose is occluded, that the genitals are being consumed, or that the bowels are all bound together.

Preceding the appearance of the hallucinations, and accompanying them, there develops a tendency to the formation of *delusions*, which are almost always of a depressive character. The patients believe themselves guilty of some crime, accuse themselves of being murderers, claim that they are lost, are damned, are unfit to live, have practised self-abuse, and can never recover from its ill effects. They suspect their surroundings, detect poison in the food, are being worked upon by others, their thoughts are not their own, friends have turned against them and are trying to do them harm, some one is watching them constantly, and they are being harassed by various agencies. Women are followed by men who would ravish them. Later in the course of the disease, and occasionally from the onset, the delusions are expansive; the patients regard themselves as prominent individuals, the President, the Son of God, the Creator, the possessor of the universe, they converse with God, are the Saviour of men, ahve all knowledge imparted to them or can stop all wars by lifting their hands. Some of these patients are controlled by sexual ideas. They fancy that they are betrothed to prominent individuals of the opposite sex. Men believe themselves possessed of many wives, or regard themselves as the centre of attraction for all women.

These delusions may be augmented by numerous *fabrications*; the patients claiming that they have been President for a century, chief commandant in various engagements, have been knighted, that they have been in heaven, have possessed the key of hell, have just returned from a visit to Mars, where there is eternal war. These fabrications, together with delusions, gradually recede to the background. At first they become fewer, less fantastic, then incoherent, and still more scanty, until finally in the advanced stages of the disease there remain only incoherent residuals, which may never be expressed except as the result of questioning or during excitement.

Some *insight* into their condition is often expressed at first by the patients. They are conscious that a change has come over them, and often complain that the head feels strange, benumbed, and empty. These may be expressed in connection with somatic delusions, the patients saying that the brain is rotting, the memory is failing, that they are different in every way and are very much confused. Even this scanty insight gradually disappears as the disease progresses.

In those forms of the disease which develop slowly there is at first neither *clouding of consciousness* nor marked disturbance of orientation. In the acute or subacute onset cloudiness and general disorientation may unite in the clinical picture with pronounced hallucinations and delusions, anxiety and restlessness and incoherence of thought. The patients mistake persons, do not appreciate where they are, and are unable to record passing events. The physicians are regarded as enemies, trying to kill them, working upon them with electricity, etc. They are confined in a prison for some grave offence, or are among the heavenly hosts, surrounded by saints. A patient, although he recognized the physician, still believed that both the physician and himself had been entrapped in a prison and that they must hasten to escape.

The *association of ideas* is at first very little disturbed, the content of speech being both coherent and relevant, but later in the disease with progressive deterioration thought suffers profoundly. The ideas become disconnected and incoherent. Questions fail to elicit anything more than monosyllables, or entirely irrelevant remarks.

The *memory* from the onset presents a progressive deterioration, at first mostly for recent and passing events. The memory of earlier life and the chronological order of events is well retained for a long time. Some of the patients are able to tell with surprising accuracy the exact definitions in geography and many historical events almost word for word, as committed to memory years before. The events dating from the onset of the psychosis, with notable exceptions, such as time of admission to hospital, etc., are not remembered, or at best only imperfectly.

The patients may be able to control their *attention*, but they do not try to do it. There is a total lack of interest. Without this there is no incentive for observation and thought, and they fail to observe what is going on about them. As the disease progresses, there is increasing limitation of thought. For this same reason their past experiences are seldom recalled, and so finally fade from their memory; though it is not unusual for them, in reaction to unusual stimulation, to recall events that seemed to have entirely passed from them..

The defect in *judgment* appears early, develops rapidly, and becomes profound. This may not be so evident while the patient is confined at home, or during the early part of his residence in an institution, as long as his thought is employed with familiar facts and his range for action limited. It becomes apparent, however, when he leaves the trodden path and attempts to adapt himself to new circumstances. He is unable to reason, to perform mental work, to recognize contradiction, or to overcome obstacles. The defect can also be seen in his tendency to formulate and hold to senseless, incoherent delusions.

In *emotional attitude* the most prominent and permanent feature is that of emotional dulness and indifference. Whenever we do find emotional activity it is increasingly self-centred. At first there is usually more or less depression, with anxiety, peevishness, and often irritability. Exaggerated expressions of religious feelings are apt to be prominent, the patients being devout, praying frequently, reading their testaments, at first apparently in the spirit of penitence, but later because they are led by God or ordained to do some special work. The sexual feelings very often play a prominent role, particularly in those who have been addicted to the habit of masturbation. Thought may centre about sexual matters; they enjoy obscene literature, write long letters to acquaintances, giving expression to their lascivious feelings, they masturbate and solicit intercourse. The female patients are more apt to associate with their own sex. In both sexes these feelings are apt to disappear later in the course of the disease. Later in the disease the delusions, both expansive and hypochondriacal, are expressed without display of emotion. They fail to express emotion at the loss of friends, at the visits of relatives, or at an unusual supply of food, fruit, or candies. They live a very empty life, devoid of any cares or anxieties, and without thought for the future.

In *conduct* and *behavior*, the most characteristic symptom is that of childish silliness and senseless laughter. The voluntary activity is inconsistent and lacks independence. At one moment they are increasingly headstrong, at the next as supremely tractable. They neglect their personal appearance, perform all sorts of outlandish and foolish deeds, such as prowling about all night, setting fire to buildings, throwing stones to break windows, travelling about without evident purpose. They may even run away and secrete themselves, or as unexpectedly demand some one in marriage, forget their obligations, and finally are completely incapable of continued and comprehensive employment. . . .

The patients are very often seen to converse with themselves, sometimes aloud, while associated with this there is almost always silly laughter. This silly laughter is a very prominent and characteristic symptom. It is unrestrained, appears on all occasions without the least provocation, and is altogether without emotional significance. Besides these actions, mannerisms, such as peculiarities of speech and movements, eating and walking, are often present. A few of the mannerisms characteristic of the catatonic may prevail: echolalia, echopraxia, stereotyped expressions and movements.

Their speech presents peculiarities indicative of looseness of thought and confusion of ideas. Their remarks may be artifical, containing many stilted phrases, stale witticisms, foreign expressions, and obsolete words. The incoherence of thought becomes most evident in their long drawn out sentences, in which there is total disregard for grammatical structure. The structure changes frequently, and there are many senseless interpolations. All this becomes even more apparent in their letters, which are verbose with frequent repetitions, while the handwriting is characterized by a marked lack or a superfluity of punctuation marks, shading of letters, and copious underlining.[54]

Course.—The course of disease in this form is *progressive*, leading to characteristic states of mental deterioration of different grades, except in a very small percentage of cases. The course is marked by short periods during which the patients show great motor restlessness, irritability, sexual excitement, silly aggressiveness, and great show of emotion; there may be a clouding of consciousness with great impulsiveness, increased incoherence of thought, singing, dancing, and insubordination. These states of deterioration are usually reached within two years of the onset. In some cases, where the development of the disease has been very rapid, the deterioration appears in six months; in other cases it may not be evident for a few years. The degree of mental defect increases from year to year, more especially following the transitory periods of excitement.

Of the cases that are admitted to insane institutions, about *seventy-five per cent. reach a profound degree of deterioration.* These patients are dull, indolent, apathetic, anergic, sluggish, and fail to apprehend the surroundings. They remain seated for hours wherever placed, are incapable of caring for themselves, are untidy, have to be dressed and undressed, and led to meals. At table they are slovenly, spattering and smearing themselves with food. They give but little evidence of voluntary activity. They seldom speak, are unproductive and mute; occasionally they may be seen to laugh sillily or repeat to themselves some unintelligible word or syllable.

Their attention is attracted with difficulty and held only for a short time. External objects usually fail to make an impression upon them. Questions are apparently uncomprehended, seldom exciting intelligible answers. These are

[54] Ibid., pp. 162–167.

usually monosyllabic and irrelevant. Simple directions, however, may be correctly carried out. Relatives and acquaintances may not be recognized. Bits of former knowledge are retained in many cases for a long time, such as historical and geographical facts and the ability to solve problems in arithmetic. In this respect the patient often surprises one. One of my patients was able to name the islands of the Pacific and give the names of their sovereignties. Another, who for two years had been mute, unable to care for himself, untidy, sitting through the day with bowed head, entirely unmindful of his surroundings, recognized a college mate, straightened up with an air of dignity, and laughed at some college jokes. In the course of time even such relics of former mental activity disappear, and we have nothing left but the unproductive vegetative organism. A few patients retain some remnants of mental activity, but they are quite unbalanced, silly, and present the residuals of hallucinations and delusions. Instead of the extreme stupidity and indolence some patients continue restless and talkative, producing an incoherent babble with silly laughter. During the periods of transitory excitement these patients are very apt to be aggressive, breaking windows and attacking fellow-patients, to masturbate shamelessly, pull out their hair, and frequenlty show homicidal tendencies.

In about *seventeen per cent. of the cases the degree of deterioration is not as far advanced.* These patients, after the subsidence of the more acute symptoms, show a certain amount of mental activity and are capable of some employment under supervision. They are oriented and have a certain amount of insight into their mental incapacity, but lack mental energy and the power of application. They have little interest in the surroundings, no care for their own livelihood, and no thought for the future, but are contented to live and be cared for. In conduct they are apt to present many mannerisms.

The judgment is weak and memory defective. Important events may be retained, together with school knowledge, but memory for events subsequent to the onset of the psychosis is very poor, while they are quite incapable of acquiring additional knowledge. The hallucinations and delusions of the various stages of the disease for the most part entirely disappear. While retained in a few cases, they are of little importance to the patients, rarely influencing their behavior. As in the other grades of dementia, so here, there is a tendency for the deterioration to increase as the patients advance in age. This is especially noticeable following short periods of excitement, which are apt to be coincident with menstruation. At these times the patients show motor restlessness, with great irritability and sometimes violence, with a reappearance of former delusions and hallucinations, talkativeness, silly behavior, and incapacity for employment. The delusions are more apt to be expansive, changeable and incoherent, but at times there may be verbigeration and repetition of single phrases. The actions are usually purposeless.

A *few cases leave the institution apparently recovered,* but upon reaching home the patients fail to employ themselves profitably. They spend much time in reading, evolving impractical schemes, pondering over abstract and useless questions. Or, if employed they show a lack of interest, are unbalanced, and unable to advance in their profession or occupation. Later their field of thought becomes more circumscribed and their relations with the outside world correspondingly meagre. They become seclusive and so much disinterested in intellectual work that they pass their time in purely machine-like action, engaged in gardening or transcribing.

Finally in about *eight per cent. of the cases the symptoms of the disease entirely disappear, leaving the patients apparently in their normal condition.* Not all of these cases should be regarded as perfect recoveries, because in some instances there have been recurrences in later life, followed by deterioration. In still other cases there has been a stunting of mental development. The patients have been unable to realize their ambition. Young men and women whose academic or collegiate courses have been interrupted by the psychosis find themselves unable to enter into active business or professional life. These patients are able to care for a farm or a small business where there is little demand for intellectual work. In this way we lose sight of the mental shipwreck following dementia praecox, because enough mental capacity is retained to permit them to maintain the battle of life in their chosen narrow field.

Catatonic Form

The catatonic symptom-complex, first described by Kahlbaum in 1874, and which by several psychiatrists is regarded as a separate disease process, is by us considered a form of dementia praecox.

This form is characterized by *a peculiar condition of stupor, with negativism, automatism, and muscular tension; excitement with stereotypy, verbigerations, and echolalia, leading in most cases, with or without remissions, to a condition of mental deterioration. . . .*

The *onset* of the psychosis is usually subacute, with a condition of mental depression. The patients for several weeks before the onset may have appeared unusually quiet, serious, or even anxious, complaining of difficulty of thought, of headache, or of peculiar sensations in the head. Besides this, they may have suffered from insomnia and loss of appetite, and have left their work because of nervousness and general ill health. Gradually the patients show great anxiety, and express fear of impending danger. Their religious emotions become more prominent, and *hallucinations* and delusions appear. A voice from heaven directs them to do all sorts of things. One patient is commanded to spit to the right, and another to convert sinners. There is a vision of Christ on the cross, the Virgin Mary appears, faces are seen at the window and pictures on the wall, spirits hover about, some one speaks from the radiator, and there is music in the next room. He hears his children cry for help. Some one calls his name, and he hears his own thoughts. Little birds speak to him. Specks of poison are detected in the food, sulphur fumes are set free about him, some one pulls at his hair, injects water into his limbs, or applies electricity to him.

The *delusions* are usually of a religious nature, are incoherent and changeable from day to day. The patient is persecuted for his sins, a priest has come to anoint him before he dies. God has transferred him to heaven, where he is surrounded by angels. He no longer needs food, as Christ has forbidden him to eat. He is eternally lost, is possessed of the devil, has caused destruction of the whole world; all are dead, he is surrounded by spirits, battles are being fought outside, his children are lost, the wife false, his body has been transformed, his head replaced by that of a horse, his feet transformed into mules' hoofs, his hands into claws, his brain has been drawn off, and while hung to a cross, his limbs and body have run away like molten metal. The delusions usually become expansive later, though they are occasionally expansive from the onset. The patient then believes himself transformed into Christ, has all power, can create worlds, has lived for thousands of years, has waged many wars, possesses all knowledge, can instruct physicians in medicine, can cast out evil spirits, has pleaded in the highest courts, is a millionaire, and possesses railroads, ocean steamers, etc.

During the earlier stages of the disease some peculiarities of movement and action appear, of which *constraint* is the most prominent. This may increase to a state of muscular tension. The patients assume constrained attitudes, holding the arms in awkward positions, as in the form of a cross, etc., standing or walking in an awkward manner, all of which may be symbolical of their ideas. One patient stood for hours with hands behind him and head thrown back, staring fixedly at the ceiling, and another lay in the form of a cross upon the floor. In some there is a tendency to execute rhythmical movements, such as rolling the head from side to side, or expectorating at stated intervals in a fixed direction.

In this period of depression the *consciousness* is somewhat clouded, orientation is slightly disturbed, and the patients do not apprehend clearly what goes on about them. They may know that they are at home or in an institution, but they fail to appreciate the mental condition of their fellow-patients, mistake those about them for friends and acquaintances, or they claim that everything is changed and that they cannot understand the mysterious occurrences. Some believe themselves translated to heaven, that they are in a cloister or in a foreign city.

Thought is much disturbed, being incoherent and disconnected. The patients are quite unable to reason. When questioned about their ideas they make all sorts of contradictory and irrelevant remarks. The memory, on the other hand, is good except for events since the onset of the psychosis. The attention can be maintained only for short periods.

The *emotional attitude* is at first quite in accord with the delusions and hallucinations. The patients are sad, dejected, anxious, complaining, irritable, distrustful, and sometimes threatening; when interfered with, they are very apt to become violent. Occasionally sexual excitement leads to masturbation and obscenity. Later they lose their early anxiety, become indifferent or contented with their environment, and the delusions are expressed without emotion. Some patients are even cheerful and happy, or ecstatic.

Following this period of depression the more characteristic catatonic symptoms appear, namely: the *catatonic stupor* and the *catatonic excitement*. In at least one-third of the cases these symptoms appear at the very onset of the desease without the prodromal period of depression.

The symptom most characteristic of the catatonic stupor is *negativism*. In negativism the voluntary impulses seem to be overcome by counter impulses. The patients may begin an act readily, but immediately a counter impulse checks and finally overcomes the former, producing an action contrary to the desired one. These adverse impulses may suddenly disappear, when the actions of the patient again become perfectly free. Negativism usually occurs first as mutism, when the patients refuse to speak. They begin by speaking low, breaking off in the midst of a sentence or answering in monosyllables, then they may whisper unintelligibly, and finally refuse to speak altogether. Some patients in this condition may be persuaded to write or sing answers to questions. When addressed they remain with closed eyes or staring fixedly at some distant object, apparently paying absolutely no attention to the physician. Even shaking patients, pinching them, or prodding them with a needle fails to elicit a response, except when in pain, then the lips may become more closely pressed together or the patients may move away indifferently.

Further evidence of negativism is seen in the obstinate and persistent resistance which the patients make to every attempt at handling them. They resist being put to bed and being taken out, dressing or undressing, moving forward or backward, opening the eyes or closing them. The active resistance is well demonstrated by suddenly withdrawing the hand which has been placed against the patient's forehead, when it springs forward with a jerk. The physical origin of this resistance becomes more apparent in those cases in which the desired action is only elicited by commanding the patient contrawise. One may get a patient to open his eyes by urging him to close them tightly, to lower the hand by telling him to lift it, etc.

Even the most natural impulses are resisted, as seen in their stubborn refusal to wear shoes or stockings, in the tendency to sit on the floor rather than in a chair, or to sleep under the bed and not in it, and go to the closet by the longest route. They prefer to eat another's food, and some persist in crawling into the beds of others. Finally the refusal of food and the retention of urine and feces are evidences of more extreme negativism. The former may last for months. The absence of food for a week will not overcome this disinclination to take food voluntarily. It is not unusual for this form of negativism, as well as the others, to appear and disappear suddenly. Sometimes the patients will begin to eat if transferred to another building or to speak if placed in another ward, or will remain in bed if given a different bed. The urine and feces may be retained until there is marked distention. . . .

... The *muscular tension*, though exhibited in several ways, is most marked in the extraordinary uniformity of position maintained by the body or its various parts. In this condition patients maintain the same position for weeks and even months. The usual position is on the back with limbs stretched out, the eyelids closed with the eyeballs rolled upward and inward, or with the eyes open, staring fixedly in the distance, the face mask-like with the lips slightly closed and at the same time protruded, producing what the Germans call Snautzkrampf. The hands are very often clenched, as if there were permanent contractures, the fingers producing pressure marks on the palms. ... Others lie rolled up like a ball, with head thrown forward and knees drawn to the chin. In the extreme condition these patients may be rolled about or lifted and laid across some object without movement, as rigid as a piece of wood.

Where muscular tension is less pronounced, the limbs may be moulded into any position, which condition is called "cerea flexibilitas." ... Muscular tension is not evenly distributed, but is most frequently seen in the hands, arms, face, and lower limbs. The gait is often influenced by this condition, some patients being unable to move at all, falling rigidly to the floor when raised to their feet; others walk stiffly, with unbent knees, on tiptoes, or on the outer side of the feet with the body bent forward or backward. The movements are usually slow and constrained. Sometimes the counter impulses seem to be suddenly overcome and the movements become rapid.

A condition which seems to be directly the opposite of negativism is occasionally met during the stupor. Instead of increased resistance to every impulse, there is *greater susceptibility to suggestion, producing echolalia and echopraxia.* The patients repeat quite mechanically that which is said to them or done before them. Questions asked are only repeated, the songs of another are sung over after them, and the actions of another patient or of the physician are repeated, such as limping or offering the hand to be shaken, and rolling the head about after the stereotyped fashion of another patient.

These opposite states pass directly from one to another during the stage of stupor. Absolute silence suddenly gives way to loud and unrestrained shouting or to incessant prattle, the patients awake from the stupor and talk as if nothing had happened, and again in a few hours relapse into their former stuporous state.

Interrupting the stupor or following it, and sometimes even preceding it, we have the *catatonic excitement*, which is characterized by *impulsive actions* and *stereotyped movements.* The condition of excitement usually makes its appearance rapidly. The patients suddenly leap from bed, tear their clothing, break the furniture, race about the room, shouting or singing, throw themselves upon the floor, rotating the head from side to side, breathing rapidly, churning saliva in the mouth, making a peculiar blowing sound, or rotating and pronating the forearm. They may run about the house for hours at a time, striking the bed or the wall in a certain place. While lying in bed the body may be swayed regularly back and forth, or the bed tapped at a certain place at regular intervals. In walking they are apt to assume peculiar attitudes. One patient stood for hours against the wall in the form of a cross repeating, "the Father, the Son and the Holy Ghost," another holding his nose tightly with his hands uttered a monotonous grunt for hours at a time. These movements may be less constrained and regular when the patients jump about from one object to another, pounding themselves, knocking their heads against the wall, wringing their hands, jumping up and down on the bed and stamping on the floor. All of these most varied movements are carried out with great strength and recklessness, without regard for the surroundings or themselves, and are for the most part purposeless and impulsive. In the midst of their ceaseless tramping about the room they may suddenly grab at the clothing of the physician or assault a fellow-patient. During this excitement the patients are very untidy and filthy, expectorating in the food, smearing with feces and food, urinating in the bed and clothing, and even washing themselves with the urine. Sexual excitement often accompanies this condition.

Another prominent symptom of this stage of the disease is the *mannerisms* in facial expression and speech. Accompanying speech there is a peculiar gesticulation, winking of the eyes, senseless shaking and nodding of the head, and drawing of the muscles of expression. The voice assumes a peculiar intonation or may quiver. The manner of speech may be scanning, rhythmical, or explosive. The content of speech is often quite characteristic, consisting of a series of senseless syllables repeated in a fixed measure or rhyme. Words or short sentences are likewise repeated; the words may be clipped or the last syllable drawn out. Usually these expressions bear no relation to the trend of conversation. One patient, when asked how he felt, repeated for three minutes, "I see you, I see you." The formation of new words often accompanies the senseless repetition of syllables, making a childish babble which the patients may repeat for hours. Verbigeration is especially noticeable in the letters. The excessive underlining, shading, and addition of symbols are clearly manifestations of the tendency to mannerisms. . . .

The conditions of catatonic stupor and catatonic excitement succeed each other during the entire course of the disease, and often quite suddenly. The degree of stupor and excitement varies considerably in individual cases.

As in the depressive stage, so also during the catatonic stupor and excitement, the *consciousness* is somewhat clouded, but the patients seldom lose their orientation completely. In spite of the fact that they seem quite unconscious of and unable to comprehend their surroundings, the patients awake from this condition and give the names of those about them, telling the day and the month, and showing surprising knowledge of what has happened within their limited range of observation.

At first there is occasionally some *insight* into the mental disturbance, the patient remarking during the depression that his head is not right, and later, during the excitement, that many of his constrained and peculiar acts are foolish, but that he cannot help doing them. Others explain them by saying that they are commanded to do so by God. On the other hand patients are quite unable to appreciate the necessity for their confinement or for the care of a physician. The *emotional attitude* after the marked dejection at the onset is quite in accord with the delusions. Occasionally there is noticed childish petulancy or irritability. . . .

Course.—The usual course in the catatonic form is depression, followed by excitement, passing into deterioration. In a few cases the stupor is immediately followed by dementia without the intervention of the characteristic excitement. Occasionally the excitement precedes the stupor and may even appear at the very onset of the disease.

A prominent feature in the course of the disease, which rarely appears in other forms of dementia praecox, is the *remissions*. Remissions for a few days or a few hours occur in almost all of the cases. The consciousness of the patient becomes perfectly clear, they apprehend and remember events, are quiet and rational and often express a feeling of illness. At these times close observation discloses a certain restraint in manner and actions, a distorted emotional attitude, and a lack of full appreciation of their previous condition. In at least one-third of all the cases the remissions are long enough for the patients to seem to have completely recovered. It may last from five to fifteen years. In these cases one often detects certain peculiarities, indicating that recovery is not complete, such as irritability, seclusiveness, and forced, affected or constrained manners. These remissions more frequently appear after stupor and are followed by excitement.

The outcome in *eighty-six per cent.* of the cases is ultimately *mental deterioration, which in thirty-nine per cent. becomes extreme.* In these cases usually within two years the stupor and excitement disappear and the hallucinations and delusions become less prominent, but the patients remain sluggish and indifferent, without mental energy. They are able to comprehend simple questions, but they lack mental initiative. The memory is defective, the judgment poor, and they are unable to acquire new knowledge. They have no regard for themselves, their personal appearance, or their future. They remain contented wherever they happen to be, never expressing desires. They are wholly unfit for intellectual employment, as they have no idea of how to work. Upon questioning, and voluntarily in a few cases, delusions and hallucinations are expressed; the former are usually expansive but quite incoherent and without effect upon the bearing of the patient.

Some of the patients are very inactive, remaining stupidly in one place most of the time, sometimes muttering to themselves, but taking no interest in their surroundings. Other patients are active, restless, and unbalanced. In both of these groups, and especially in the latter, we find mannerisms which are the residuals of former stereotypy. The movements lack freedom, are constrained and peculiar; the patients walk on tiptoe, along cracks, or with bent limbs, with head thrown forward and with cramped hands. The head is usually held in peculiar positions. When sitting they always assume fixed positions, shaking or nodding the head at regular intervals, making a blowing noise with the lips or grunting. They pass to meals only through certain doors, or perhaps backwards. The mannerisms are especially marked in dressing and at table.

They may eat with great rapidity, filling the mouth to its fullest extent before swallowing. Others eat very deliberately, waiting a certain interval between mouthfuls, perhaps counting three, each bit of food being prepared and carried to the mouth in a certain definite manner. Many patients eat with their hands, others hold the knife and fork in some peculiar fashion. One of my patients refused to eat unless he had been allowed to stand on his head and crawl under the table. Similar mannerisms are evident in speech and writing. In speech there may also be a tendency to form new words, especially during the transitory periods of excitement, when the patients produce a genuine word-jumble.

The deterioration gradually deepens, and especially following short periods of excitement, which appear in almost all cases. At these times the patients are restless, irritable, and threatening, expressing delusions of persecution; in speech the confusion becomes marked, with shouting and laughing. There is a great tendency to perform impulsive acts, breaking furniture, attacking individuals, and even becoming homicidal.

In twenty-seven per cent. of the cases the dementia is of a lighter grade. Here the patients return to clear consciousness, are quiet and orderly, are able to return home, and in a few cases resume their former occupations. But a profound change in the character is noticed; their former mental vigor does not return, they are listless, dull, lack energy and endurance. Their judgment is defective. They are cleanly and except for a few catatonic mannerisms might be regarded as well. Some of these patients are very quiet, seclusive, distrustful, or over-conscientious; while others are somewhat childish and silly.

In about thirteen per cent. of the cases patients seem to recover. Some of these patients manifest some peculiarities in conduct and a change in character which is apparent only to those associated closely with them. A certain number of these cases after five to fifteen years suffer from another attack which leads to deterioration.

As yet there are no means of judging which cases will recover, have long remissions, or lead to different degrees of deterioration. This much can be said, however, that those with rapid and more acute development are more apt to have a remission than those with a gradual onset. Clearing of consciousness without proportionate improvement in the emotional attitude, with persistence of mannerisms and the appearance of short periods of excitement, point to deterioration. The mere presence of prolonged stupor does not necessarily indicate deterioration, as patients have remained in stupor from three to five years. . . .

Paranoid Forms

The paranoid forms of dementia praecox, which include *two groups of cases, are characterized by the great prominence and persistence of delusions and hallucinations for several years, in spite of progressing mental deterioration.* While there are many delusions and hallucinations in the hebephrenic and catatonic forms of dementia praecox, they are never very prominent and usually disappear as deterioration progresses. The cases grouped under this term are by many psychiatrists considered as forms of paranoia, a view which in our minds is untenable, because of the comparatively rapid appearance of mental deterioration, and also becuase of the occasional acute onset and the frequent occurrence of single catatonic symptoms, such as stuporous states, mannerisms, and neologisms.

The First Group of cases is characterized by many incoherent and ever changing delusions of persecution and grandeur, and a light grade of motor excitement, with retention of clear consciousness for a considerable time and rapid appearance of mental deterioration.

The onset of the disease is gradual, following a period of headache, malaise, and insomnia with a rapid loss of energy and often irritability. The patients act peculiarly, are unusually devout, seem depressed and anxious, and remain alone. In a short time they divulge a host of *delusions*, almost entirely of persecution; people are watching them, intriguing against them, they are not wanted at home, former friends are talking about them and trying to injure their reputation. These delusions are changeable and soon become fantastic. The patients claim that some extreme punishment has been inflicted upon them, they have been shot down into the earth, have been transformed into spirits and must undergo all sorts of torture. Their intestines have been removed by enemies and are being replaced a little at a time; their own heads have been removed, their throats occluded and the blood no longer circulates. They are transformed into stones, their countenances completely altered, they cannot talk, eat, or walk like other men, etc. *Hallucinations*, especially of hearing, are very prominent during this stage; fellow-men jeer at them, call them bastards, threaten them, accuse them of awful crimes. Messages over the telephone are overheard mentioning that they are about to be sent to prison. Occasionally faces and forms are seen at night, or a crowd of men throwing stones at the window. Foul vapors may be thrown into their bedding. Patients during this time are anxious, agitated, restless, and emotional. They mistrust the surroundings, at times becoming aggressive and violent. In a paroxysm of fear they may even attempt suicide.

The *consciousness* usually remains unclouded. The emotional attitude before long loses the sad and anxious tinge, being replaced by a certain cheerfulness and exaltation. At the same time the delusions become less depressive and more expansive and fantastic. The patient in spite of persecution is happy and contented, extravagant and talkative, and boasts that he has been transformed into the Christ; a female is pregnant by the Holy Ghost; others will ascend to heaven, have lived many lives, have visited other worlds, and have journeyed over the whole universe. They have the talent of poets, can surpass famous war correspondents, have been nominated for president, and have represented governments at foreign courts. These delusions may become most florid, foolish, and ridiculous. A patient will say that he is a star, that all light and darkness emanate from him; he possesses all knowledge, is an artist, the greatest inventor ever born, can create mountains, is endowed with all the attributes of God, can prophesy for coming ages, can talk to the people in Mars; indeed, is unlike anything that has ever existed.

Associated with these variegated and ever changing expansive delusions are delusions of persecution, almost as absurd and extreme, but expressed without corresponding emotion. While laughing they may complain that they have been deprived of their limbs, are wrecks of a dreadful struggle with enemies, having been pierced with thousands of bullets and been thrown into hell, where they were exposed to furnace flames. Suggestions for many of these delusions may arise from pictures on the wall or from reading.

These patients are usually talkative, expressing freely their many delusions. Some of them fill hundreds of sheets of paper trying to describe them. At first they are quite coherent, but later there is such a wealth of ideas loosely expressed that it is difficult to find any system in them. They wander aimlessly about from one delusion to another, showing frequent repetitions of the same ideas. Questions, however, are answered in a coherent and relevant manner. Later in the course of the disease the speech becomes more and more difficult of comprehension, because of the number of peculiar phrases and expressions to which they attach special significance and freely repeat. The writings likewise become more and more unintelligible.

The patients rarely possess *insight* into their condition. The consciousness becomes somewhat clouded later in the disease. Orientation as to place is least disturbed, but people are soon mistaken, often designated as celebrated personages, and all conception of time is lost. They recognize relatives, and can give a fairly clear statement as to where they are. They may recall some past knowledge, but they soon become unable to use it in reasoning. They cannot apply themselves to any mental work. The patients show an exaltation of the ego with heightened feelings, they are self-conscious, with an important bearing, and demand special attention. In emotional attitude they are almost always exalted, rarely depressed, although a few patients show restlessness, some irritability and occasionally some passion, often in connection with the menses. Many of the patients are able to perform some mechanical work, but need supervision because of their lack of application.

The Second Group of paranoid cases is characterized by hallucinations and fantastic delusions of persecution and of grandeur, which are mostly coherent, and are adhered to for a number of years, when they disappear, leaving the patient in a state of moderate deterioration.

The first symptoms to appear are those of despondency with some self-accusation. The patients are troubled with thoughts of death and religious doubts; they are unusually devout, and seek religious advice. They fear that they have done wrong, have committed some crime, or are suffering the penalty of self-abuse. Coherent *delusions of persecution* develop gradually; people watch them, peculiar actions are noticed, acquaintances are less friendly, and children on the street jeer and laugh at them, perhaps mimicking their manners. Passers on the street who are entirely unknown to them turn and stare. In public places, in the cars and at the church, remarks are made which refer to them. They are libeled in newspapers. All these incidents have a hidden meaning, which however, is fully understood by the patients. They are making their own observations and will be ready to expose the offenders and bring them to justice at the proper time. Affairs at home are unsatisfactory: the children are different, and the husband or wife is unfaithful.

Hallucinations, especially of hearing, rarely of sight, are prominent at this time, aiding in the elaboration of the delusions. Enemies take advantage of their confinement by standing below the window calling them all sorts of names, announcing that they are to be imprisoned, that they have committed murder, and are to be put to the rack. Voices are heard from the walls and from under the floor stating that they are wretches and outcasts of society. Very often the noises really heard, such as the blowing of whistles and the ringing of bells, are misinterpreted in accord with their delusions. They complain that the food contains poison which they can taste, they suspect phosphorus in the tea and detect kerosene on the clothing.

They notice that their clothing is changed, buttons are missing, there is a rip in the coat and a pocket torn. Objects in their surroundings are changed in order to confuse them. Many somatic sensations, such as twitching of individual muscles, headache, specks before the eyes, pain about the heart, and cramp in the bowels, are all evidences of injuries caused by their enemies. The explanation of these somatic hallucinations often takes fantastic forms. An itching of the foot is sufficient evidence that a poisonous powder has been blown into their shoes, pain in the back indicates that they have been shot there while asleep, a frontal headache is the result of poisonous vapors, which are set free in the room at night in order to destroy their intellect. A tremor of the fingers is produced by means of electric currents sent through the air. Something is placed in their food to create sexual excitement.

The means employed by the persecutors for producing physical discomfort are varied. All known agencies are mentioned, as, magnetism, hypnotism,

X-rays, telepathy, and electricity. These are accountable for the most various sensations in all parts of the body. They are compelled to act contrary to their own will and to say distasteful things. Organs of the body are removed and then replaced out of order, and the intestines are shrunken. It is quite characteristic for the patients to refer to these physical changes by some invented names, such as, ugly duberty, snicking, lobster cracking, etc. Others complain that their minds are influenced, their thoughts are gone, they have no control over their thoughts, which in spite of themselves are always evil. They attribute the origin of such thoughts to others which are forced upon them in spite of themselves.

Ideas of *spirit-possession* are often a prominent feature. Here the enemy enters and takes possession of the body, causing the bones to crack and the head to rattle; obscene remarks proceed from the stomach; their ears are filled by all sorts of noises made by these spirit-possessors. They cause the testicles to fall and the throat to dry up.

Expansive delusions are also present in almost all cases. These are as variegated and fantastic as those of persecution. The patients have been awarded a crown for bravery and now rule over some country, possess beautiful dresses, and are betrothed to the king. They represent the Pope and are to travel all over the world. God daily appears to them and gives them a blessing. They have recently been entrusted with millions which they are to invest in mining. They have consummated immense trusts which they are to manage. All of the many delusions expressed by the patients are at first coherent, and show a tendency to some course of reasoning, but after a few years they become quite incoherent.

The *consciousness* during the development of these delusions, and for a long time afterward, perhaps years, remains clear. The patients are oriented. Thought is coherent, but centres about the delusions. The patients are able at first to offer some basis for the delusions and to refute objections, but later, as deterioration appears gradually in the course of several years, thought becomes cloudy and confused. Then the delusions are incoherent, contradictory, and unstable, and change rapidly. There is rarely insight into the disease. Many patients appreciate that they are not normal, but their defects and ailments are all regarded as the works of their persecutors.

The *emotional attitude* is at first characterized by depression and anxiety, but later this gives way to a certain amount of happiness and cheerfulness, with considerable egoism.

In *conduct* and *manners* the patients may at first be quite orderly; but later, in accord with their delusions, they are suspicious, journeying about to get rid of their enemies, applying to police for protection; or, taking the matter in their own hands, they attack supposed persecutors or attempt to expose them through the papers. Others contrive a sort of armor for themselves, place metals in their shoes or wires in their clothing to divert the electrical currents. In accord with expansive delusions they may decorate themselves in fantastic costumes, adorn themselves with badges, assume a superior air, and use high-flown language.

The course is slowly progressive to mental deterioration. However, one can discern certain stages. At first there is a change of disposition, then a prominence of delusions of persecution, later the appearance of the delusions of grandeur, indicating the onset of deterioration, and finally the fading away and entire collapse of the delusions. Remissions have occurred in a few cases.

The *outcome* is always deterioration. The delusions in the course of several years cease to further develop and gradually fade away, leaving the patient with a certain degree of mental weakness, seen in lack of judgment, and absence of mental energy. Ideation is scanty. In conversation the patients are incoherent and unintelligible, with occasional references to former delusions. In their actions they show many peculiarities, and a lack of appreciation of and conformity to external relations. They are usually capable of employment, and sometimes are even industrious, the former "Pope" becoming a trusted farm-hand, and the "queen" a good seamstress. Finally they reach a stage of apathetic deterioration, when they are incapable of any employment.

Diagnosis of Dementia Praecox.—Acquired neurasthenia is distinguished from the hebephrenic form by the fact that the hypochondriacal ideas are not silly, the judgment is retained, there is no evidence of deterioration, the patients are not stupid, and finally they improve with treatment. The presence of hallucinations is a positive sign of dementia praecox. . . .

The greatest difficulty arises in distinguishing the *depressive form of manic-depressive insanity* from the period of depression which one meets at the onset of the hebephrenic and the catatonic forms. The early appearance of many hallucinations speaks for dementia praecox, as well as an emotional attitude which does not correspond to the depressive character of the delusions. The patients remain quite indifferent during the visit or at the death of a relative, while in manic-depressive depression the feelings are apt to be intensified. The apparently similar conditions of negativism of the catatonic and of retardation of the manic-depressive are at times distinguished only with difficulty. In the former there is uniform, rigid, and stubborn resistance to every passive movement, and if pain is produced by pricking, there is a simple withdrawal without effort at defence; while in retardation the passive movements are permitted and painful contacts are resisted. Voluntary movements in the catatonic stupor are rare, but when executed are carried out without delay, and at times even rapidly, except when these movements are made by request, then there is always delay. In retardation all voluntary movements are carried out very slowly. There is sometimes a certain resistance due to apprehension and fear, but this is active.

The excitement of the catatonic is to be distinguished from the excitement of the *maniacal forms of manic-depressive insanity*. In the catatonic form there is greater disturbance of conduct, the content of speech and emotional attitude, while in the maniac there is greater disturbance of apprehension, orientation, and thought. In the catatonic excitement the clouding of consciousness is less marked than in the maniacal excitement, the patients being partially oriented, even in the greatest excitement, while in the extreme maniacal state there is complete disorientation. On the other hand the speech of the catatonic who has less motor excitement is more senseless and difficult to follow than that of the maniac who has extreme motor excitement. The catatonic speech abounds in verbigerations and stereotyped expressions and is free of comments upon the surroundings, while the speech of the maniac presents the characteristic flight of ideas, and is centred upon or drawn largely from the immediate surroundings. In this condition attention is readily distracted by the surroundings, while the attention of the catatonic cannot be. The attitude of the catatonic is silly, childish, exalted, or irritable. The movements of the catatonic are purposeless, frequently repeated, in contrast to the pressure of activity of the maniac in whom the movements are always purposeful with some relation to the surroundings, dependent upon ideas, impressions, and emotions, and always appearing in new forms. The increased activity of the catatonic is more apt to be limited to one corner of the room or of the bed, while that of the maniac is limited only by his confines.

It is sometimes necessary to differentiate catatonic excitement with epileptiform or hysteroid attacks from *hysterical states.* In the latter one is usually able to detect slyness and method in the contrariness and purpose in the actions, while in the catatonic there is evident senselessness and lack of purpose in movements, and the emotional attitude exhibits more stupidity. Finally, hallucinations and delusions are more exaggerated and prominent in the catatonic.

The distinction between the paranoid forms of dementia praecox and pure *paranoia* depends upon the lack of system, the rapid development of fantastic delusions commencing with prominent hallucinations; while in paranoia the onset is very gradual, sometimes extending over one year with only a few hallucinations. The delusions in dementia praecox are extremely fantastic, changing beyond all reason, with an absence of system and a failure to harmonize them with events of their past life; while in paranoia the delusions are largely confined to morbid interpretations of real events, are woven together into a coherent whole, gradually becoming extended to include even events of recent date, and contradictions and objections are apprehended and explained. In emotional attitude the dementia praecox patient soon shows clear and marked changes;—depression or silly elation, sexual excitement and remissions; while in paranoia the emotional attitude is uniformly natural, the demeanor is almost normal, and the patients are capable of occupation for a long time. In paranoia there may be partial remissions when the patients react less actively to the delusions, but the delusions never disappear.[55]

---

[55] Ibid., pp. 169-199.

SENILE DEMENTIA

Esquirol (1838)

Although Esquirol made no distinction between the psychoses today called endogenous and organic, he did distinguish senile dementia from the other varieties.

Senile dementia results from the progress of age. Man, passing insensibly into the vale of years, loses his sensibility, along with the free exercise of his understanding, before reaching the extreme of decreptitude. This form of mental disease is gradually established. It commences with a weakening of the memory, especially with respect to recent impressions. Sensations are feeble. Attention, which is at first fatiguing, at length becomes impossible. Volition is uncertain, and without impulse; and the movements are slow, or impracticable. However, senile dementia begins not infrequently with a general excitement, which persists for an indefinite period; and is revealed, now, by the increased activity of one function, and now, by that of another. This function is exercised with a new and unusual energy, which deceives the aged subject of it, and imposes upon those around him. Thus, there are persons who, before sinking into dementia, become exceedingly susceptible, and are irritated by the most trifling matters. They are exceedingly active; desiring to understand and do, everything. Others experience venereal desires, which have long been extinct, and which urge them to acts which are contrary to their habits of continence. Others still who are naturally temperate, experience an irregular desire for spiced and highly seasoned food; for wine and liquors. To this inordinate excitement, dementia is not slow to succeed. These symptoms of general excitement indeed, are the first indications of senile dementia. The transition from excitement to dementia is sudden, especially when the aged are opposed in their unreasonable desires, or placed where it is impossible to gratify them. We shall not confound this excitement with the mania which bursts forth at a very advanced age, in strong, robust, and well-sustained persons. Mania, attended even with fury, bursts forth after the age of eighty; and is sometimes cured. This study of illustrative cases ought to suffice, to render our diagnosis sure. Country air, moderate exercise, and a tonic regimen, may retard the progress of senile dementia, and suspend, to some extent, its termination.[56]

[56] E. Esquirol, *Mental Maladies: A Treatise on Insanity* [1838], E. K. Hunt, trans. (Philadelphia: Lea and Blanchard, 1845), pp. 434–435.

Nervous Disorders

10

NEURASTHENIA AND SO-CALLED ANXIETY NEUROSIS

Earlier in this work anxiety was discussed as a symptom in general (pages 119–124) and as a manifestation of depression (pages 160–200). Now the origin of the currently popular though seemingly invalid diagnosis of anxiety neurosis or anxiety state will be considered.

Whytt (1765)

Whytt's discussion of the symptoms of nervous disorders is a landmark. The occurrence of "an uneasiness not to be described," the somatic complaints, and the mood changes were all noted. The basic hypersensibility was also described, as was its similarity to the functional state of a child's nervous system.

A giddiness, especially after rising up hastily; pains in the head, sometimes returning periodically; a violent pain in a small part of the head; not larger than a shilling, as if a nail was driven into it; a ringing in the ears; a dimness of sight, and appearance of a thick mist, without any visible fault in the eyes. Objects are sometimes seen double, and unusual smells are perceived; obstinate watchings, attended sometimes with an uneasiness, which is not to be described, but which is lessened by getting out of bed; disturbed sleep, frightful dreams, the night-mare; sometimes a drowsiness, and too great inclination to sleep; fear, peevishness, sadness, despair, at other times high spirits; wandering thoughts, impaired memory, ridiculous fancies; strange persuasions of their labouring under diseases of which they are quite free; and imagining their complaints to be as dangerous as they find them troublesome;

they are often angry with those who would convince them of their mistake.[1]

The hypochondriac and hysteric diseases are generally considered by physicians as the same; only in women, such disorders have got the name of hysteric, from the antient opinion of their seat being solely in the womb; while in men, they were called hypochondriac, upon the supposition, that in them they proceeded from some fault in those viscera which ly under the cartilages of the ribs. . . .

But whether these two distempers be considered as the same or distinct, since the symptoms of both are so much akin, we shall consider them under the general character of Nervous; and begin with inquiring into the causes from which they most commonly[2] proceed.

All children, when compared with adults, have their nervous system very sensible and easily moved, and are in this respect something like those grown people, who are most subject to the highest nervous or hysteric symptoms. . . .

A delicate or easily irritable nervous system must expose a person to various ailments, from causes, affecting either the body or mind, too slight to make any remarkable impression upon those of firmer and less sensible nerves.[3]

Women, in whom the nervous system is generally more moveable than in men, are more subject to nervous complaints, and have them in a higher degree. On the other hand, old people, in whom the nerves have become less sensible, are little afflicted with those disorders.[4]

Trotter (1807)

Trotter's book was a classic in its description of the symptoms, their relation to social conditions, and the involvement of the sympathetic nervous system.

The last century has been remarkable for the increase of a class of diseases, but little known in former times, and what had slightly engaged the study of physicians prior to that period. They have been designated in common language, by the terms, Nervous; Spasmodic; Bilious; Indigestion; Stomach Complaints; Low Spirits; Vapours, &c. A generic definition of them, from their protean shape and multiform appearance is almost impracticable. They vary in every constitution; and assume in the same person, at different times of life, an inconstant assemblage of symptoms.

---

[1] R. Whytt, *Observations on the Nature, Causes, and Cure of Those Disorders Which Have Been Commonly Called Nervous Hypochondriac, or Hysteric, to Which Are Prefixed Some Remarks on the Sympathy of the Nerves* (Edinburgh: J. Balfour; London: T. Becket and P. Du Hondt, 1765), pp. 101–102.

[2] Ibid., pp. 104, 107.

[3] Ibid., pp. 114–115.

[4] Ibid., p. 118.

In another work, when cursorily treating of these diseases, I have attempted to give a general character of them, and for want of a better, I shall insert it here.

"Nervous feelings, nervous affections, or weak nerves, though scarcely to be resolved into technical language, or reduced to a generic definition, are in the present day, terms much employed by medical people, as well as patients; because the expression is known to comprehend what cannot be so well explained. An inaptitude to muscular action, or some pain in exerting it; an irksomeness, or dislike to attend to business and common affairs of life; a selfish desire of engrossing the sympathy and attention of others to the narration of their own sufferings; with fickleness and insteadiness of temper, even to irrascibility; and accompanied more or less with dyspeptic symptoms, are the leading characteristics of nervous disorders; to be referred in general, to debility, increased sensibility, or torpor of the alimentary canal."

In the present day, this class of diseases, forms by far the largest proportion of the whole, which come under the treatment of the physician.[5]

[These disorders] are so far to be classed among mental disorders, that a *disposition of mind*, not easily to be defined, attends every degree and stage of them; beginning with uncommon sensibility to all impressions; peevishness of temper; irresolution of conduct; sudden transitions from sadness to joy, and the contrary; silent or loquacious; officially busy, or extremely indolent; irrascible; false perceptions; wavering judgement; melancholy; madness: exhibiting in the whole, signs of deranged sensation.

These diseases receive a stronger tincture from the manners of the age, than any others to which the human frame is liable: and when they appear in great numbers, as in the present day, they form an epoch in the physical and moral history of society; so wide is their range, so important their influence on the state and condition of mankind. . . .

The causes which produce nervous diseases, may be divided into two kinds, namely, those which arise from the mind; and those which arise from the body. Of the first kind, are all the disorders of the passions: of the second kind, all those causes which affect particular organs of the body, that by their office, are intimately connected with the nervous system.[6]

It is evident, from the history of these diseases, that where the nervous temperament prevails, all the causes which operate upon it, bring forth motions and sensations very different from what is found in a healthful structure of nerves, in persons who are without the predisposition. This is more exemplified in what may be called the mental causes, than in the corporeal. The moral evils of life are very much of a relative nature; their

[5] T. Trotter, *View of the Nervous Temperament* (London: E. Walker, 1807), pp. xv–xvii.
[6] Ibid., pp. 195–196.

effects depend, in a great measure, on our capacity of feeling, for receiving them; or the fortitude which we are able to oppose to them. Thus, one man is condemned for sinking under adversity, as a proof of deficient virtue and spirit; while another is extolled for his courage, as a token that he possessed nobleness of mind. Yet the physical train of their temperaments, will best decide with impartiality on their respective merits. . . .

The living body possesses the faculty, if I may so call it, of receiving impressions, and retaining them, even to the hazard of its destruction. All predispositions are of this kind.[7]

We know so little of the nature of the nervous power, that we can only judge of the moral causes of nervous indisposition, from their effects. Some of the passions have received the name of exciting, and others that of depressing; but their effects on the nervous temperament, seem much alike. The chief of the passions, such as anger, joy, grief, fear, &c. destroy appetite, disturb digestion, prevent sleep, make the breast labour, and the heart palpitate; render the mind fickle, timid, incapable of judging accurately, &c. Here is no proof that any of these passions weaken the nervous system; they only dissever that combination, or association of ideas, which impresses the mind with pleasing objects; and which disseverment to the mind is painful, and throws all the more sensible organs of the body into immediate disorder.[8]

But however afflicting the condition to which the body is often brought by nervous infirmity, the mental indisposition is the cause of greater misery. . . .

The temper of mind with nervous people, renders them very prone to what is called reverie. In the sunshine of their sensations, much of the time passes in contemplating imaginary pleasure; or what in common language is called, building castles in the air. And when they are roused from this fool's paradise, they are very apt to fall into the other extreme of low spirits and apprehensions. So certainly does a corresponding train of thought follow every odd feeling, in these whimsical disorders.[9]

On the whole it is fair to conclude, that the pathology of these diseases is to be sought in the deranged sensations, and inverted sympathies of the great sympathetic nerve; and in the irregular action of all those organs to which it is distributed. The causes therefore, whether moral or physical, exert their influence on this portion of the nervous system; whose office directs the most important operations in the animal economy; and binds together in one great circle of feeling, actions and motions both distant and opposite. Hence a concourse of symptoms of the most extraordinary kind, that invert the usual functions of so many viscera; suspend their powers, or give to them new movements: by which means a train of false perceptions occupies the mind;

[7] Ibid., pp. 198-199.
[8] Ibid., pp. 209-210.
[9] Ibid., pp. 218-220.

and ideas the most monstrous and incongruous, supplant for a while, all rational thought. In this reciprocal action between body and mind, in whatever part of the circle disease commences, it is quickly communicated to all the others. For as bowel complaints speedily affect the mind and depress the spirits; so all violent emotions, in their turn, induce affections of the chylopoietic viscera, and raise such commotion throughout the sensitive system, as to bestow the nervous character on these diseases.[10]

Wilson (1843)

Wilson made the remarkable observation that anxiety precedes the langorous, idle state of young people.

Languor is especially frequent in the early years of adult life; when, at this, the ripe age of bodily energy, habits of physical exertion are superseded by those of imagination and mental study. It is the scholar's great affliction; and is bred, with thought, beneath the brow that never sweats. Scarcely a morning passes, of which, in "chambers," or the counting-house, certain hours are not in this way rendered useless to their tenants. On the student lawyer, as on the imprisoned merchant, languor, irresistible as spasm, will often, and suddenly, steal; arresting every purpose,—chaining up the faculties as by a spell,—and bringing the further penalty of self-reproach for a supposed moral inefficiency, which is, in truth, the result of physical illness. Very much of real bodily suffering, of suffering which might, by remedial means, be lessened or removed, is thus hopelessly endured by those who are ashamed to complain.

Languor seems especially to affect persons, of what is termed an excitable and nervous temperament,—whose sense is fine in nature,—the thin rather than the fat, and the young more frequently than the aged. With those liable to this distressing influence, the exact moment of its commencement can often be determined, by peculiar feelings of disquiet and oppression; by a sense, as it were, of misgiving.[11]

Millingen (1847)

Millingen's account emphasized the abnormal personality of persons with nervous temperament.

The *nervous temperament*, as I have already observed, may be considered of a complex character. In this constitution the sentient system predominates, and one might say that the frame is *all sensation*; a vivid susceptibility to all external impressions prevails. The limbs are feeble, and the muscles flaccid and

[10] Ibid., pp. 228-229.
[11] J. A. Wilson, *On Spasm, Languor, Palsy, and Other Disorders, Termed Nervous* (London: J. W. Parker, 1843), p. 146.

small, the skin pale and dry, the features restless and uneasy, the pulse small and quick, respiration hurried, digestion weak, and appetite capricious, the nights restless and perturbed with anxious dreams. They are constantly seeking sensual enjoyments and novel excitement. Love, or what they fancy to be love, is to such individuals a necessary *pabulum*. For a while their attachment is ardent and enthusiastic; but as selfishness and fickleness are the attributes of this temperament, their affections are changeable, and rarely of long duration; and their vanity once offended, they can hate as fiercely as they adored the former idol of their worship. Their great irritability, both in their moral and physical faculties, will sometimes render such persons miserable; for they are jealous, suspicious, and impatient, and ever seeking to ameliorate their condition, they must be subject to frequent disheartening disappointments. Thus, miserable themselves, while in the vain pursuit of an imaginary happiness, they involve in their sufferings those who have had the weakness to rely on their professions, or attach themselves to their checquered destinies, unless they are of a similar temperament, and seek fresh emotions to replace past enjoyments and revive faded pleasures. Females of this constitution are subject to constant hysterical and convulsive affections, that often render them a plague to others and a nuisance to themselves. Their ideas are as romantic as their partialities are whimsical and unaccountable; vivid emotions constitute their life. They must breathe an atmosphere of excitement, or linger and pine away in self-inflicted consumption, or what they fancy "a broken heart."[12]

Beard (1871, 1881)

The term *neurasthemia* was coined by G. M. Beard in 1869 and announced in a book by him and Rockwell.

The morbid condition or state expressed by this term has long been recognized, and to a certain degree, understood, but the special name *neurasthemia* is new, we believe, for the first time presented to the profession.... Among the special exciting causes of neurasthemia may be mentioned the pressure of bereavement, business and family cares, parturition and abortion, sexual excesses, the abuse of stimulants and narcotics, sudden retirement from business, and civilized starvation, such as is sometimes observed even among the wealthy orders of society. *The disease is most frequently found in the United States among the brain-working classes of our large cities.*[13]

[12] J. A. Millingen, *Mind and Matter* (London: H. Hurst, 1847) pp. 86–87.
[13] G. M. Beard and A. D. Rockwell, *A Practical Treatise on the Medical and Surgical Uses of Electricity* (New York: W. Wood and Co., 1871), pp. 294, 298–299.

Beard's *Practical Treatise on Nervous Exhaustion (Neurasthemia)* included the word in the title but added nothing new.[14] His *American Nervousness* added little except the notion that Americanization was ruining Europe.

> While modern nervousness is not peculiar to America, yet there are special expressions of this nervousness that are found here only; and the relative quantity of nervousness and of nervous diseases that spring out of nervousness, are far greater here than in any other nation in history and it has a special quality. . . . The nervousness of America is extending over Europe, which, in certain countries at least, is becoming rapidly Americanized. . . . The cause of the increase of nervous diseases is that the conventionalities of society require the emotions to be repressed.[15]

His *Sexual Neurasthemia* (1884) has an engaging title but nothing more.

Although Beard's clinical comments oscillated between the merely superficial and the utterly trivial, the term he coined became the object of learned comment, particularly in Europe. If his writings on psychopathology have any value at all it is that they stimulated such men as Janet and Freud to try to place neurasthemia somewhere in the scheme of things. Beard himself was a highly original but far from profound thinker. He should perhaps be known for his electroshock therapy of mental disease a century ago, and for his having discovered the Hertzian waves in partnership with Thomas Edison many years before Hertz himself did.

After Beard introduced "neurasthemia" into the medical vocabulary, his word, if not his concept, rapidly became popular. (Actually his concept was so vaguely stated that it is difficult to see how anyone could have adopted it.) Within only a few years anxiety was widely recognized as an important symptom of the disorder. Ewald Hecker[16] was perhaps the first to emphasize this, but for him the anxiety was highly specific, taking the form of one phobia or another. Löwenfeld,[17] a prolific and influential writer held similar views, and his words carried much weight. Less prominent was Hanns Kaan[18] who also discussed

---

[14] New York: A. P. Putnam's Sons, 1880.

[15] G. M. Beard, *American Nervousness, Its Causes and Consequences: A Supplement to Nervous Exhaustion (Neurasthemia)* (New York: G. P. Putnam's Sons, 1881), pp. 13–14, 120.

The year after Beard's book was published, Herbert Spencer, during a visit to America, gave a lecture which used many of the ideas and some of the specific language of Beard's writings but without mention of their source. In 1883 Beard published his *Herbert Spencer on American Nervousness: A Scientific Coincidence.*

[16] E. Hecker, "Zur Behandlung der neurasthenischen Angstzustande," *Berliner klinische Wochenschrift,* 1892, 29, 1195–1197; "Uber larvirte und abortive Angstzustande bei Neurasthenie," *Centralblatt für Nervenheilkunde,* 1893, 4, 565–572.

[17] L. Löwenfeld, *Pathologie und Therapie der Neuresthenie und Hysterie* (Wiesbaden: J. F. Bergmann, 1894).

[18] H. Kann, *Der neurasthenische Angstaffect bei Zwangsvorstellungen und der primordiale Grübelzwang* (Wien: F. Dietricke, 1892).

anxiety but somewhat more broadly. To all these authors anxiety was only one symptom, albeit highly important in some cases, of what they called neurasthemia and is today known as neurosis. Freud gave the anxiety much more importance and labeled the syndrome *anxiety neurosis*, despite the lack of any evidence that such an entity exists.[19]

Freud (1895)

I call this syndrome 'anxiety neurosis', because all its components can be grouped round the chief symptom of anxiety, because each one of them has a definite relationship to anxiety. I thought that this view of the symptoms of anxiety neurosis had originated with me, until an interesting paper by E. Hecker (1893) came into my hands, in which I found the same interpretation expounded with all the clarity and completeness that could be desired. Nevertheless, although Hecker recognizes certain symptoms as equivalents or rudiments of an anxiety attack, he does not separate them from the domain of neurasthenia, as I propose to do. But this is evidently due to his not having taken into account the difference between the aetiological determinants in the two cases. When this latter difference is recognized there is no longer any necessity for designating anxiety symptoms by the same name as genuine neurasthenic ones; for the principal purpose of giving what is otherwise an arbitrary name is to make it easier to lay down general statements. . . .

What I call 'anxiety neurosis' may be observed in a completely developed form or in a rudimentary one, in solation or combined with other neuroses. It is of course the cases which are in some degree complete and at the same time isolated which give particular support to the impression that anxiety neurosis is a clinical entity. In other cases, where the syndrome corresponds to a 'mixed neurosis', we are faced with the task of picking out and separating those symptoms which belong, not to neurasthenia or hysteria, and so on, but to anxiety neurosis.

The clinical picture of anxiety neurosis comprises the following symptoms:

(1) *General irritability.* This is a common nervous symptom and as such belongs to many *status nervosi*. I mention it here because it invariably appears in anxiety neurosis and is important theoretically. Increased irritability always points to an accumulation of excitation or an inability to tolerate such an accumulation—that is, to an *absolute* or a *relative* accumulation of excitation. One manifestation of this increased irritability seems to me to deserve special mention; I refer to *auditory hyperaesthesia*, to an oversensitiveness to noise—a symptom which is undoubtedly to be explained by the innate intimate relationship between auditory impressions and fright. Auditory hyperaesthesia

[19] See M. D. Altschule, "Invalidity of the diagnosis 'anxiety neurosis': Notes on curiosity and boredom as motivating forces," *New York State Journal of Medicine*, 1959, **59**, 3812–3822.

frequently turns out to be a cause of sleeplessness, of which more than one form belongs to anxiety neurosis.

(2) *Anxious expectation.* I cannot better describe the condition I have in mind than by this name and by adding a few examples. A woman, for instance, who suffers from anxious expectation will think of influenzal pneumonia every time her husband coughs when he has a cold, and, in her mind's eye, will see his funeral go past; if, when she is coming towards the house, she sees two people standing by her front door, she cannot avoid thinking that one of her children has fallen out of the window; when she hears the bell ring, it is someone bringing news of a death, and so on—while on all these occasions there has been no particular ground for exaggerating a mere possibility.

Anxious expectation, of course, shades off imperceptibly into normal anxiety, comprising all that is ordinarily spoken of as anxiousness—or a tendency to take a pessimistic view of things; but at every opportunity it goes beyond a plausible anxiousness of this kind, and it is frequently recognized by the patient himself as a kind of compulsion. For one form of anxious expectation—that relating to the subject's own health—we may reserve the old term *hypochondria.* The height reached by the hypochondria is not always parallel with the general anxious expectation; it requires as a precondition the existence of paraesthesias and distressing bodily sensations. Thus hypochondria is the form favoured by genuine neurasthenics when, as often happens, they fall victims to anxiety neurosis.

A further expression of anxious expectation is no doubt to be found in the inclination to *moral anxiety*, to scrupulousness and pedantry—an inclination which is so often present in people with more than the usual amount of moral sensitiveness and which likewise varies from the normal to an exaggerated form in *doubting mania.*

Anxious expectation is the nuclear symptom of the neurosis. It openly reveals, too, a portion of the theory of the neurosis. We may perhaps say that here a *quantum of anxiety in a freely floating state* is present, which, where there is expectation, controls the choice of ideas and is always ready to link itself with any suitable ideational content.

(3) But anxiousness—which, though mostly latent as regards consciousness, is constantly lurking in the background—has other means of finding expression besides this. It can suddenly break through into consciousness without being aroused by a train of ideas, and thus provoke an anxiety attack. An anxiety attack of this sort may consist of the feeling of anxiety, alone, without any associated idea, or accompanied by the interpretation that is nearest to hand, such as ideas of the extinction of life, or of a stroke, or of a threat of madness; or else some kind of paraesthesia (similar to the hysterical aura) may be combined with the feeling of anxiety, or, finally, the feeling of anxiety may have linked to it a disturbance of one or more of the bodily functions—such as respiration, heart action, vasomotor innervation or glandular

activity. From this combination the patient picks out in particular now one, now another, factor. He complains of 'spasms of the heart', 'difficulty in breathing', 'outbreaks of sweating', 'ravenous hunger', and such like; and, in his description, the feeling of anxiety often recedes into the background or is referred to quite unrecognizably as 'being unwell', 'feeling uncomfortable', and so on.

(4) Now it is an interesting fact, and an important one from a diagnostic point of view, that the proportion in which these elements are mixed in an anxiety attack varies to a remarkable degree, and that almost every accompanying symptom alone can constitute the attack just as well as can the anxiety itself. There are consequently *rudimentary anxiety attacks* and *equivalents of anxiety attacks*, all probably having the same significance, which exhibit a great wealth of forms that has as yet been little appreciated. A closer study of these larval anxiety-states (as Hecker [1893] calls them) and their diagnostic differentiation from other attacks should soon become a necessary task for neuropathologists.[20]

On the basis of chronic anxiousness (anxious expectation) on the one hand, and a tendency to anxiety attacks accompanied by vertigo on the other, two groups of typical phobias develop, the first relating to general physiological dangers, the second relating to locomotion. To the first group belong fear of snakes, thunderstorms, darkness, vermin, and so on, as well as the typical moral over-scrupulousness and forms of doubting mania. Here the available anxiety is simply employed to reinforce aversions which are instinctively implanted in everyone. But as a rule a phobia which acts in an obsessional manner is only formed if there is added to this the recollection of an experience in which the anxiety was able to find expression—as, for instance, after the patient has experienced a thunderstorm in the open. It is a mistake to try to explain such cases as being simply a persistence of strong impressions; what makes these experiences significant and the memory of them lasting is, after all, only the anxiety which was able to emerge at the time [of the experience] and which can similarly emerge now. In other words, such impressions remain powerful only in people with 'anxious expectation'.

The other group includes *agoraphobia* with all its accessory forms, the whole of them characterized by their relation to locomotion. We frequently find that this phobia is based on an attack of vertigo that has preceded it; but I do not think that one can postulate such an attack in every case. Occasionally we see that after a first attack of vertigo without anxiety, locomotion, although henceforward constantly accompanied by a sensation of vertigo, still continues to be possible without restriction; but that, under certain conditions—such as being alone or in a narrow street—when once

---

[20]S. Freud, "Über die Berechtigung, von der Neurasthenie einen bestimmten Symptomen-complex als 'Angstneurose' abzutrennen," *Neurologische Centralblatt*, 1895, 14, 50-66. In *The Complete Psychological Works of Sigmund Freud*, J. Strachey, ed. (London: Hogarth Press, 1962), pp. 91-94.

anxiety is added to the attack of vertigo, locomotion breaks down.

The relation of these phobias to the phobias of obsessional neurosis, whose mechanism I made clear in an earlier paper in this periodical, is of the following kind. What they have in common is that in both an idea becomes obsessional as a result of being attached to an available affect. The mechanism of *transposition of affect* thus holds good for both kinds of phobia. But in the phobias of anxiety neurosis (1) this affect always has the same colour, which is that of anxiety; and (2) the affect does not originate in a repressed idea, but turns out to be *not further reducible by psychological analysis, nor amenable to psychotherapy.* The mechanism of *substitution*, therefore, does not hold good for the phobias of anxiety neurosis.

Both kinds of phobias (and also obsessions) often appear side by side; although the *atypical* phobias, which are based on obsessions, need not necessarily spring from the soil of anxiety neurosis. A very frequent and apparently complicated mechanism makes its appearance if, in what was originally a simple phobia belonging to an anxiety neurosis, the content of the phobia is replaced by another idea, so that the substitute is *subsequent* to the phobia. What are most often employed as substitutes are the '*protective measures*' that were originally used to combat the phobia. Thus, for instance, 'brooding mania' arises from the subject's endeavours to disprove that he is mad, as his hypochondriacal phobia maintains; the hesitations and doubt, and still more the repetitions, of *folie du doute* [doubting mania] arise from a justifiable doubt about the certainty of one's own train of thought, since one is conscious of its persistent disturbance by ideas of an obsessional sort, and so on. We can therefore assert that many syndromes, too, of obsessional neurosis, such as *folie du doute* and the like, are also to be reckoned clinically if not conceptually, as belonging to anxiety neurosis.[21]

P. Janet (1903)

The word *neurasthenia* was so popular (probably because it was both meaningless and euphonious) that it encouraged the invention of similar words. For example, P. Janet used the word *psychasthenia* in a remarkably thorough discussion of what are today called anxiety neurosis and compulsive-obsessive neurosis. His book is clearly the source of all subsequent descriptive writings on these subjects. Significantly, Janet considered as "highly speculative" Freud's attempts to relate all the symptoms of these disorders to underlying anxiety.

Part I. Analysis of Symptoms . . .

Chapter III. The Psychasthenic Stigmata

First Section. Feelings of Inadequacy

1. Feelings of inadequacy in action
    1. The feeling of difficulty

[21] Ibid., pp. 96–97.

2. The feeling of incapacity
3. The feeling of indecision
4. The feeling of constraint in action
5. The feeling of automatism
6. The feeling of being dominated
7. The feeling of discontent
8. The feeling of being intimidated
9. The feeling of revolt

2. Feelings of inadequacy in intellectual processes
   1. The feeling of difficulty in thinking
   2. The feeling of incomplete perception
   3. The feeling of unreal conceptions
   4. The feeling of disappearance of time
   5. The feeling of unintelligence
   6. The feeling of doubt

3. Feelings of inadequacy in the emotions
   1. The feeling of indifference
   2. The feeling of uneasiness
   3. The need for stimulation; ambition

4. Feelings of inadequacy in perception of personality
   1. The feeling of estrangement of the ego
   2. The feeling of splitting in two
   3. The feeling of complete depersonalization

Second Section. Psychologic Insufficiencies . . .

2. Problems of the will
   1. Indolence
   2. Irresolution
   3. Slowness in performance
   4. Delays
   5. Weakness of effort
   6. Fatigue
   7. Disorganization of actions
   8. Inachievement
   9. Absence of firmness
   10. Misoneisme
   11. Social inadequacy; timidity
   12. Professional inadequacy
   13. Lack of will and inhibition
   14. Insurmountable fatigue
   15. Inertia

3. Problems of intelligence
   1. Amnesias
   2. Failure to learn

HYSTERIA

According to an ancient superstition, the first coherent account of which is to be found in Plato, the uterus, when in an unsatisfied (nonpregnant) state, wandered about the body, pressing on different organs and causing palpitation of the heart, smothered feelings, difficulty in swallowing, seizures, etc. When approximately 2000 years later it became established that the uterus was almost totally immobile, another explanation for the symptoms in women had to be found. It was then believed that the uterus gave off internal vapors which did the mischief. "The vapours" too were eventually rejected, and when the sympathetic

---

[22] P. Janet, *Les Obsessions et la psychasthénie* (Paris: Alcan, 1903), pp. 759–761 (Table of Contents). This work was foreshadowed by Janet's two-volume *Neuroses et idées fixes* (Paris: Alcan, 1898), the second volume of which had F. Raymond as the first author.

nervous system was discovered it was decided that nerve impulses from the uterus caused the syndrome. This theory remained secure well toward the twentieth century, being supported by such authorities as Romberg in his midcentury *Manual of the Nervous Diseases of Man* and Horatio Storer in his *Reflex Insanity in Women* (1871). In the meantime, however, some authors referred briefly to the mental and emotional states of hysterics, but not in any systematic way.

Willis (1685)

Among Willis's comments on hysteria is one that applies as well today as it did three hundred years ago.

If at any time an unusual sort of Sickness, or of a very Secret Origine occurs in the Body of a Woman, so that its Cause lies hid, and the Therapeutic Indication be wholly uncertain, and in any unusual symptom, we cry out that there is somewhat hysterical in it; and consequently Physical intentions and the use of Remedies are directed for this end, which often is only a starting hole for Ignorance.[23]

Ryan (1831)

The belief that hysteria was a consequence of unsatisfied or repressed sexual impulses has been mentioned by the writers of every civilized era. Ryan, however, discussed the manifestations in a manner much more perceptive than that of his predecessors.

Absolute continence is seldom if ever observed. It is, however, the ornament of virtuous women, and is well exemplified by the train of nervous and hysterical symptoms, which render their lives distressing and uncomfortable. Hysteria, in nine cases out of ten, arises from continence.[24]

Laycock (1840)

Laycock presented a highly critical analysis of the older ideas about hysteria and stated unequivocally that it was a disorder of the nervous system.

a. First Principle.—The Nervous System the Seat of Hysteric Diseases.

The terms of this generalization comprise an important general principle; one, indeed, acknowledged almost by every writer and observer; namely, that

---

[23] [T. Willis] *The London Practice of Physick or the Whole Practical Part of Physick Contained in the Works of Dr. Willis* (London: T. Bassett and W. Crooke, 1685), p. 297.

[24] M. Ryan, *Lectures on Population, Marriage, and Divorce, as Questions of State Medicine* (London: Renshaw and Rush, 1831), p. 53–54.

the whole class of hysterical affections have their seat in the nervous system.

It is true that the pathology of the early Greek writers had no reference to this doctrine. Hippocrates, or a writer in the books attributed to him, states, that there is a reflux of blood from the uterus to the heart and diaphragm, and these become congested and paralyzed; just as when a person by sitting long is affected with torpor and paralysis of one or other of the lower extremities, which are not relieved until the circulation be restored.

It was not until some light was thrown on the functions of the nervous system that these mechanical and altogether fanciful theories were left in merited neglect. Hysteria and Hypochondriasis came then to be considered analogous diseases. Le Pois, Sydenham, Boerhaave, Whytt, Van Swieten, Flemyng, and many others supporting this doctrine; Hoffman, Cullen, Good, Pujol, Pinel, Georget, and Brachet more lately maintained the distinctness of the two diseases, a difference of opinion easily explicable; but all agreed in the one great principle, that it is the nervous system which is mainly implicated in these affections.

But as regards the particular mode in which this system is affected, and the particular portions implicated in hysteria, there has been much difference of opinion. Sydenham, Stahl, Boerhaave, Cheyne, Flemyng, Whytt, Pomme, Georget, Andral, and others, placed the disease in the brain and nerves; Willis, Van Swieten, and Lobstein, in the sympathetic system; Hoffmann, in the uterus and membranes of the spine. As to the particular mode of disease there was again great variety of opinion. Sydenham and some of his successors considered hysterical diseases to be excited by irregular motions of the animal spirits along the nerves; later writers thought they depended upon irregular vibrations of the nerves; Pomme believed that all the nerves had become corneous from the evaporation of the fluid which should keep them lubricated, and brings forward some ridiculous arguments in support of his opinion. Ludwig attributed hysteria to some acrimonious principle seated in the nerves; and Frank, Bradley, Brown, Teale, Darwall, the Griffins, and Marshall, to spinal irritation; and this appears to be the latest and most novel view; being, however, equally vague and unsatisfactory as its predecessors.

There has been an obscure and indefinite doctrine advanced by almost every writer on the subject, which connects the nerves of the uterus in some way or other, not clearly explained, with the whole nervous system. . . . It will be observed, however, after a careful perusal of these various theories, that they afford no satisfactory explanation of many of the peculiar phenomena of hysteria; of the spasm of the glottis; of the remarkable embonpoint of many hysterical patients under the most meagre diet; of the occasional profuse salivation; of the periodicity observed in the paroxysmal forms; of the more frequent occurrence of the disease in spring and autumn; or, indeed, of a hundred other circumstances connected with its multiform varieties. But although these various opinions be all unsatisfactory, the concurrent testimony of all to one general fact renders it certain that the nervous system is its seat.

This, then, must be received as a synthetical principle to guide us in our future inquiries.

b. Second Principle.—Hysteria Is Peculiar to Females.

The next general fact observed in this class of diseases is, that (with certain exceptions afterwards to be noticed) they are peculiar to the female sex. In this opinion writers are even more agreed than in that we have just considered. It is repeatedly asserted in the Hippocratic writings. Aretaeus states, respecting the hysteric paroxysm, "Young women suffer from this affection, the older are free from it." Paulus Aegineta remarks on the same disease, "This affection is frequently observed during the spring and autumn in lascivious girls, and sterile women, especially if they have been made sterile by drugs." It is quite true that cases have occurred occasionally in the male sex, presenting the phenomena of convulsive hysteria; but so rarely, and under such circumstances, that even if their exact similarity to the hysterical paroxysm of the female be admitted, like other exceptions, they but serve to prove the general rule, namely, that it is the nervous system of women which is implicated in these affections.

c. Third Principle.—Women of Susceptible Nervous System More Liable Than Others.

If the physician cast his eye over the numerous detailed cases to be read in systematic works, and in the medical periodicals, he will find that, for the most part, the subjects of them were women endowed with great affectibility of the nervous system. The extract from Aretaeus embodies this principle. . . . Hippocrates also noticed the circumstance. . . . These quotations sufficiently show that in all ages these diseases have attacked the same class of females, namely, those having great mental and bodily affectibility. This, then, will form a third synthetical principle.

d. Fourth Principle.—Hysteric Diseases Appear Only During That Period of Life in Which the Reproductive Organs Perform Their Functions.

The fourth and last, and least general principle is, that women in whom the generative organs are developed or in action, are those most liable to hysterical diseases. "Seniores immunes sunt;" "In juvenculis salacibus;" "Salacitas major, major ad hysteriam proclivitas." Indeed the general fact is so universally acknowledged, and so constantly corroborated by daily observation, that anything in the shape of proof is unnecessary. According to our rule, it is with this, the least general principle, that we must begin our synthetical analysis of related phenomena.[25]

[25] T. Laycock, *Treatise on the Nervous Diseases of Women* (London: Longman, Orme, Brown, Green, and Longmans, 1840), pp. 6–9.

Wigan (1844)

Wigan emphasized that hysteria also occurs in men of sensitivity; he then referred to epidemics of hysteria in women.

The disease called Hysteria, a word which originally signified that it was confined to females, is well-known to be occasionally inflicted on the other sex. We sometimes see this affection in young men of sedentary and studious habits. It is probably a disturbance of the brain from reflex action, and in both sexes mainly under the control of the will. Men are taught to be ashemed of any manifestation of this malady or passion, as *unmanly,* and the efforts they make to overcome it are generally successful; but many a man of acute feelings must remember instances, in his own person, where the effort has been one requiring extraordinary energy and perseverance—success often doubtful and sometimes impossible. Among females of a certain age, just advancing to womanhood, the disorder propagates itself by sympathy with great rapidity, and will spread in a short time throughout a large school, if the head of the establishment be a feeble-minded person, or the medical attendant of too suave and timid a disposition.[26]

Briquet (1859)

It was Briquet's writings that defined the clinical nature of hysteria. He related its frequent occurrence in women to their difficult role in society and to their greater affectivity.

For me, hysteria is a disorder of the brain, in which the visible phenomena consist principally of disturbances of the vital functions that serve to manifest the affective feelings and the emotion. . . .

Hysteria presents as principal symptoms: extreme sensibility of the nervous system; diverse hyperesthesias, among which the most prominent are pains in the epigastric region, the left side of the chest, along the left vertebral gutter; anesthesias involving principally the skin, the muscles, and the sense organs; spasms, among the most common of which are an oppression in the epigastrium, the sensation of a globe rising from the stomach to the throat, and suffocation; and finally seizures that originate in a constricting feeling in the epigastrium and are accompanied ordinarily by loss of consciousness and which terminate in tears or sobs; symptoms that are totally under the influence of mental feelings.

[Briquet then lists several dozen terms that had been used to designate these manifestations.]

[26] A. L. Wigan, *The Duality of the Mind Proved by the Structure, Functions, and Diseases of the Brain, and by the Phenomena of Mental Derangement, and Shown to be Essential to Moral Responsibility* (London: Longman, Brown, Green, and Longmans, 1844), p. 322.

These names are not good; but should one seek to find another? . . . I shall adopt the term *hysteria* because it was the first one used, because it is the most widely used, because everyone knows it, and finally because I hope that in time it will have lost its etymologic value and will have become a proper name like iron, lead, etc.[27]

One can summarize the influence of sex on the predisposition to hysteria as follows:

1. a man can suffer from hysteria;
2. he is disposed to this illness approximately twenty times less often than a woman;
3. in five-sixths of the cases, the sex organs have no possible connection with this illness;
4. hysteria is very common among women;
5. at least half of them are hysteric or very impressionable, and a fifth of them have attacks;
6. the special tendency does not reside in the sex organs in the physiologic state; it does not reside either in the tangible material arrangements of the brain or its dependencies;
7. woman has in society a noble mission of the greatest importance, that of raising children, that of looking after and maintaining the well-being of the mature years and of old age;
8. to achieve these aims she has been given a special habit of sensibility that is different from a man's;
9. it is in this habit of sensibility that one finds the source of hysteria;
10. this habit of sensibility manifests itself and is appreciated through the series of troubles that produce the emotions and that constitute the basis of hysteric attacks;
11. experience shows that this series of troubles exist for a man only exceptionally, which is the reason hysteria is so rare in a man.[28]

It is because women are so profoundly sensitive to impressions, and because, in life, the painful impressions are more common and more upsetting than gently agreeable ones, it is for this reason, say I, that hysteria is an attribute of woman. In order to fulfill the grand and noble mission given her, it is indispensable that she have a great facility to recieve affective feelings, that she is able in some way to feel everything within herself, and unfortunately as a whole, the bad being born out of the good, hysteria permits this great facility to be effective. . . .

The predisposition to hysteria consists of a mental disposition.

---

[27] P. Briquet, *Traité clinique et therapeutique de l'hystérie* (Paris: J.-B. Baillière et Fils, 1859), pp. 3, 5-6.

[28] Ibid., p. 51.

Almost all hysterics are possessed of a very lively sensibility as regards feelings, and they manifest outwardly the painful impressions that cause these feelings by a series of acts that are appropriate to women and not to men.

The degree of intelligence, greater or lesser, has no concordance, in most hysterics, with the degree of the impressionability.

The main basis of the hysteric character is a disposition toward affective sentiments and a great susceptibility found in all toward painful sensations.

In the very small number of children destined to be hysterics, the character is passionate, violent, and exasperated by all obstacles, although it is gentle and weak.

The principal predisposition to hysteria consists of the facility of women to be painfully impressed.[29]

Charcot (1877)

Charcot objected to Briquet's account, saying that prudery made him deny the primary role of the ovary. Charcot's insistence on the genital origin of hysteria greatly influenced one of his pupils, Freud.

I shall likewise show you a method which I have discovered, or rather re-discovered, which, in the case of some patients, enables us to arrest the course of even the most intense hysterical fit,—I refer to the *systematic compression of the ovarian region*. M. Briquet denies that this compression has any real effect. That is an opinion which I cannot share, and this leads me to make a general remark in reference to M. Briquet's book. The work is an excellent one, the result of minute observation and patient industry, but it has perhaps one weak side; all that relates to the ovary and the uterus is treated in a spirit which seems very singular in a physician. It exhibits a kind of prudery, an unaccountable sentimentality. It appears as though, in reference to these questions, the author's mind were always preoccupied by one dominant idea: "In attempting to attribute everything to the ovary and uterus," he says for instance, somewhere, "hysteria is made a disorder of lubricity, a shameful affection, which is calculated to render hysterical patients objects of loathing and pity."

Really, gentlemen, that is not the question. For my own part, I am far from believing that lubricity is always at work in hysteria; I am even convinced of the contrary. Nor am I either a strict partisan of the old doctrine which taught that the source of all hysteria resides in the genital organs; but, with Schutzenberger, I believe it to be absolutely demonstrated that, in a special form of hysteria,—which I shall term, if you please, the *ovarian form*,—the ovary does play an important part.[30]

---

[29] Ibid., pp. 101, 102.

[30] J. M. Charcot, *Lectures on the Diseases of the Nervous System* [1875], G. Sigerson, trans. (London: The New Sydenham Society, 1877), p. 247.

Charcot and Marie (1892)

The etymology of hysteria (ὑστέρα, uterus) must not be passed by in silence; for it has done too much harm to its proper conception. The comprehension of hysteria as synonymous with *furor uterinus* is the only one known in all classes of society; even among physicians, many have not yet been able to discard the idea that the uterus, or at least the genital apparatus of the female, is more or less the cause of this disease. This, however, does not seem a sufficient reason for altering the name of hysteria, and for adopting one of the terms quite as *bizarre* and quite as little expressive, which have been proposed in its stead. We at least have energetically refused to do so, thinking that the best and easiest way will be to forget that hysteria might possibly have anything to do with the uterus.

Definition.–What, then, is hysteria? According to our notion it is less a disease in the ordinary sense of the word, than a peculiarly constituted mode of feeling and reaction. We do not know anything about its nature, nor about any lesions producing it; we know it only through its manifestations, and are therefore only able to characterise it by its symptoms, for the more hysteria is subjective, the more it is necessary to make it objective, in order to recognise it. Some of the symptoms are most conspicuous, whilst others require careful search; the latter however are much more reliable and constant than the former, and to them one of us has given the name "Stigmata of Hysteria."

Clinically, there is a striking distinction. Hysteria presents itself in *convulsive* and *non-convulsive* forms; although the symptoms of the latter class may vary infinitely, we shall try to arrange them for the purpose of easier description in several larger groups, so comprehensive as to allow of their being studied together. With regard to the *convulsive* forms we have one especially in view, which is known as *Hystero-Epilepsy* or *Hysteria major*.

Aetiology.–Under this head are comprised two distinct matters: (*a*) Aetiology of hysteria proper; and (*b*) Aetiology of the different symptoms of hysteria. Hysteria does not commence with the first more or less boisterous symptom which the patient presents. In most cases the disease was pre-existent, but was ignored, and it only wanted an opportunity for breaking forth; this opportunity has been called by some the "cause," but it only means that nobody had up to that time looked for hysteria in the individual in question. As later on, when speaking about paralysis, we shall have to occupy ourselves with the aetiology of the hysterical symptoms, we shall at present only insist upon general aetiology.

While the mechanism which produces hysteria is almost always uniform, the occasional causes are innumerable. . . .

Symptoms.–These are very variable as such, and also in the way they are grouped. One may, however, divide them into three distince clinical groups.

(*a*) There are convulsive attacks.

(b) The symptoms are either localised in one part of the body or limbs, or manifested by external signs (paralysis, contractures, chorea, cough, sneezing, &c.), which phenomena, however, bear more or less clearly an hysterical character.

(c) There may be only slightly marked symptoms, or they may be without a manifest hysterical character; but on minute examination certain non-apparent symptoms are found to exist, which, however, are in hysteria so frequent and constant, that their presence sufficiently characterizes the affection; these are symptoms which one of us has described as hysterical stigmata.

These groups of symptoms may become mixed, and most frequently we may find in the same individual convulsive attacks, paralysis, contractures, and stigmata. But we, from the first, desired to point out that these three groups may be more or less dissociated. However this may be, we shall study separately—for the convenience of description—the convulsive, paralytic, spasmodic symptoms, &c.[31]

Mental disorders.—It is impossible to study in detail the different mental disorders which may occur in the course of hysteria; they will be treated of under the different mental affections particularised. We mention, however, the *attacks of sleep*, in which the patient presents almost all the objective symptoms of actual sleep, and which last for days and even weeks. But to a certain extent there seems to be an appreciable degree of consciousness; thus the patients eat and drink during this long period of sleep, whenever food is brought near to their lips, and some show a liking for some food in preference to others. Another phenomenon of almost the same kind as the attacks of sleep, but of a quite different clinical order, is the *ambulatory automatism*. In this condition we see the patient lose quite suddenly the consciousness of his personality, and nevertheless continue to accomplish all the actions of life, as though nothing extraordinary had happened. He will go to and fro, take a railway-ticket, go into a *restaurant*, and have a breakfast served to him, for which he pays exactly, but all these actions have no sort of connection with his daily occupation. Then this condition disappears suddenly, and the patient returns to the normal condition, astonished to find himself where he is, and not knowing how he got there; he is also ignorant of the actions he has accomplished during this singular eclipse of consciousness. It is probably a sort of somnambulism, but different from that generally observed; in this category must be classed all the cases of "double consciousness' and "second state," reported by authors.

[31] J. M. Charcot and P. Marie, "Hysteria, mainly Hystero-Epilepsy," in D. H. Tuke, *Dictionary of Psychological Medicine* (Philadelphia: P. Blakiston Son and Co., 1892), Vol. 1, pp. 627–628, 629.

Speaking of hysterical mental derangements, we ought also to treat of the *moral* and *legal responsibility* of the patients, but this will be done in detail in other articles of this Dictionary. We must, however, insist on one point: most authors mention as peculiar to hysteria a certain mental condition—excessive psychical re-action, desire to do something remarkable, love of everything brilliant and extraordinary, a tendency to lying, exaggeration and even simulation, absence of will, irritability, and frequently more or less absolute loss of moral sense. All these mental deviations are doubtless frequently observed in hysteria, but one cannot say that they are special symptoms of this disease; they must simply be associated as symptoms of mental degeneration, which, it is true, lies in most cases at the bottom of hysteria. We always must remember that hysterical patients are hysterical because they are mentally degenerated, and that they do not present symptoms of this disease; they must simply be considered as symptoms of mental degeneration, because they are hysterical. Besides, the symptoms of such degeneration are very variable, and far from being alike as regards quality and intensity in all patients.

We have in the course of this article employed the word patient indiscriminately, to indicate that sex does not make any difference in hysteria, and that the symptoms described may occur in the male as well as female. From a mental point of view, however, we must devote a few lines to *hysteria of the male sex*, which apply especially to cases of hystero-traumatism. Nearly all the hysterical men of the working classes met with in the hospitals are in a melancholy condition, and in addition to this they have a tendency to frightful dreams (wolves, lions, fantastical and terrible animals) even without any alcoholic intoxication. This mental condition differs strangely from the brilliant and sparkling condition of mind, which the exclusive study of hysteria in the female has accustomed us generally to consider as a speciality of individuals affected with this *grande* neurosis.[32]

P. Janet (1893)

Janet's remarkable study of hysteria published in 1893 has never been equaled, much less improved on. His observations on alternating personalities (page 79) and other aspects of hysteria had the added benefit of stimulating thought in different areas of psychology, both normal and pathologic.

Anaesthesias

A great number of patients suffering from hysteria, in conditions in which the normal man would experience a more or less strong sensation, behave as if they felt nothing at all; they do not react, and they do not complain if you pinch them, or prick them, or burn them; if you question them, they declare

[32] Ibid., pp. 638-639.

that they heard nothing, and saw nothing, of the object you placed in a bright light before their open eyes. It is this condition of the patient that is designated by the name *anaesthesia.* This anaesthesia does not exist absolutely with all patients, and we must not reject the diagnosis of hysteria for the simple reason that this symptom in no degree exists; there are, as will be seen, other subjective symptoms, less clear, and above all less pathognomonic, which may in certain cases be substituted for this one. But this anaesthesia exists certainly under one of its various forms in the majority of cases, and may be considered entirely characteristic.

Hysterical anaesthesia may be more or less complete, and be sometimes confined to a diminution of normal sensibility, a hypoaesthesia more difficult to determine. It may bear on all the sensations which the human mind is susceptible of experiencing. Absolutely all the senses—the tactile sense, the muscular, the olfactory, taste, hearing, vision, etc.—may be separately attacked or simultaneously. The sensitiveness of the mucous membranes, at least of those that are accessible, is modified, as well as that of the skin. . . . When a sense is complex, it may be attacked partially, one element disappearing while another remains. The hysterical may lose the so-called tactile sensibility, or only the sensation of pain, that of heat, that which is provoked by the electric current, that which the torsion or pulling of the joints provokes, etc. Sight may be attacked in its various elements, visual acuity, the sense of colours, the extent of the visual field. In a word, there is no sensation acknowledged by psychologists that cannot be modified or suppressed by the anaesthesia of these patients.

Whatever be their seat, these anaesthesias may present themselves under varied forms, which may be gathered into three principal divisions: they may be called *systematised, localised,* or *general.*

Systematised anaesthesias are, we think, more frequent than is generally supposed, for they are not always noticed. They do not bear on all the sensations arising from the excitation of a certain sense or of a certain point of the body, but on a group of sensations forming a system, allowing the knowledge of all the other phenomena which impress this same sense or this same point of the cutaneous surface to reach the consciousness. This kind of insensibility, much studied by the old magnetisers, is easy to establish during the hypnotic sleep by appropriate suggestions. The subject, for example, will see all the persons in the room, but will neither see nor hear a certain person pointed out to him; he will be able to see objects, papers presented to him, but will not be able to see certain papers marked by a cross or an uneven number. The analysis of this phenomenon has been the starting-point of the study of hysterical anaesthesias, which are, more than people believe at first, similar to this model.[33]

[33] P. Janet, *The Mental State of Hystericals* [1893], C. R. Corson, trans. (New York: G. P. Putnam's Sons; London: Knickerbocker Press, 1901), pp. 4-6.

But it should be borne in mind that this phenomenon is far from being general; that, with a number of patients, sensibility and the visual field change very little when it is suggested, and, on the contrary, undergo great modification under the influence of certain excitations—such as drunkenness, or of certain changes of psychological state—as somnambulism. It is very probable that suggestion or other psychological phenomena intervene in the cases pointed out in the preceding paragraph. Maria's sensibility is easily modified by the application of iron plates, but they must be applied by myself. If we trust her to use those plates herself they lose all their power. We should not maintain, however, that all these facts, especially the action of the electric current, are the only suggestions. These suggestions, in fine, may be made in various ways and will be studied later.

Many other psychological phenomena come in to produce, modify, or destroy anaesthesia. For example, strong emotions, preoccupations, reveries, increase it. The association of ideas may in some cases modify it. We say to Maria that she has a caterpillar on her left hand, and she cries out and pretends that she feels the tickling of it; at this moment the whole of her left arm has become quite sensitive. But there is a psychological phenomenon which plays a far more important part than any other, and its study throws a great deal of light upon the problem; we mean attention. To verify this fact, we must remember, as we shall demonstrate later, that with hystericals, attention is altogether the most difficult thing to fix, and that but a few can succeed in directing it.[34]

Do hystericals take any particular interest or pleasure in having their arms pierced through with needles? Do these young girls ... simulate unilateral amaurosis? How is it that, in all civilised countries, hystericals should have agreed to simulate the same thing ever since the middle ages to the present day? If the hystericals *did* simulate, would they allow themselves to be caught in snares as obvious as those that are laid for them? Did they come here to boast of their anaesthesias? All authors have established that these patients are ignorant of them. It is we who reveal them to them, and they might say to us: "If you are not satisfied with our insensibility, do not speak of it; it is not we who have made it known, and we do not particularly relish the reputation of being insensible creatures."

We must not be content with these crude explanations, and since anaesthesia presents itself to us as a psychological fact, we must seek, among the few notions psychology furnishes us, that which best summarises facts of this kind. ... We have maintained for several years hysterical anaesthesia is a certain species of *absent-mindedness*.[35]

Amnesias

To describe hysterical *amnesias*, it will be necessary, we think, to set forth as a prime consideration a characteristic which may be somewhat surprising.

[34] Ibid., p. 22.
[35] Ibid., p. 32.

Amnesias occur *very frequently* and are met with, under various forms, almost as often as anaesthesias. . . . Memory, also, is weak and often null with hystericals. We have seen a patient with whom amnesia had reached a point where she could no longer calculate time. What had occurred the day before did not seem to her any nearer than what had taken place several years before. This diminution of memory is quite a common thing . . .

This continuous forgetfulness must be well understood, for we could not otherwise comprehend the conduct of the patients. As Professor Charcot said, it is from that forgetfulness that arise, not always, but very often, the so-called lies of the hystericals. In the same way may also be explained their whims, their changes of temper, their ingratitude, their inconsistencies, in a word, for the connection of the past with the present, which gives gravity and unity to conduct, depends largely on memory. Finally, these remarks are important from a clinical standpoint; in fact, although it may perhaps appear strange, the cases of forgetfulness of the hystericals—numerous, variable, bearing on movements and on acts as well as on ideas—may simulate the most serious states of dementia, and the diagnosis may here be of primary importance.

These amnesias, in the first place, appear to form three great classes, analogous to those which have been adopted for anaesthesias. They are: *amnesias systematised, localised,* and *general.* But it will be necessary here to add a fourth category, that of the *continuous amnesias,* for a group of lesions of the memory, altogether special, which is separated from all the preceding ones. The first three forms are, as their names indicate, losses of remembrances, and, although this may appear rather naïve, we shall observe that a remembrance cannot be lost unless it has once existed; amnesias bear, then, on real remembrances, which the patient has possessed and which he has been able to manifest for a certain time. It will be seen that this very important characteristic is not found in the last class, which is, consequently, quite distinct from the others.

The first, *systematised amnesias,* are perhaps the most frequent. The patients lose, not all their remembrances acquired during a certain period, but a certain category of remembrances, a certain group of ideas of the same kind, constituting a system. Thus, they will forget what relates to their family or all the ideas relating to such or such a person. A woman, after confinement, will forget not only the birth of her child, but even the facts connected with it; she might likewise forget the name of her husband and even forget her marriage, while she will remember other facts quite foreign to the birth of her child.[36]

The psychological characteristics of the hystericals' amnesia are so like those of their anaesthesia, that in their description we can follow the same order and present the same remarks in an abridged form.

[36] Ibid., pp. 76, 78–79.

1. In the systematised amnesias we see exactly, as in the anaesthesias of the same kind, the *influence of the subject's thought*. We see the remembrance which the subject pretends to have forgotten play its part and determine his choice of things forgotten, like the sensation apparently not felt of the *marked points* (points de repère), which helps the subject in recognising the bit of paper he must not see. In the experiments of suggested systematised amnesia this is evident; but let us consider one that is natural. Celestine pretends having completely forgotten us, having absolutely no recollection of us. Be it so; we question her about what she did this week, and she recovers about all except one incident. She does not remember at all having been examined in the parlour by Professor Charcot. Now, it was we who introduced her to Professor Charcot. How, if she has no remembrance of us, does she so cleverly choose to forget the incident wherein we were concerned? The thought of the subject intervenes in the same way to fix the limits of the localised amnesias. A young woman, married a year ago, has nervous attacks during her confinement. She becomes amnesic and forgets both her confinement and the previous period. Where does this retrograde amnesia stop? At the marriage. The young woman forgets the period that comprises her delivery, her pregnancy, her husband, her marriage. By this delicate association of ideas we recognise an hysterical.

2. In the same way as anaesthesia does not suppress reflexes which depend, however, on sensation, so does amnesia not *interfere with the intellectual function*, which is, nevertheless, the immediate consequence of memory. This is all the more clear when we consider a serious amnesia,—a general amnesia, for instance. Authors, like Dr. Weir Mitchell, always say: "Despite the loss of memory, the intelligence remained intact; as soon as she again learned to speak she expressed herself both sensibly and reasonably." Let us suppose such an amnesia, brought about by the progress of dementia, such forgetfulness of all notions, even of writing and speaking, and we have before us a completely stupid individual. Is it not surprising that an hysterical with so formidable an amnesia should remain intelligent?

3. If we omit quite particular cases, such as continuous amnesia, we can say that the hysterical is as *indifferent* to her amnesia as to her anaesthesia. That the hysterical should have forgotten two or three months of her life does not seem to disturb her much, unless there be very special circumstances that cause her to notice her forgetfulness and induce voluntary questionings. This is so true that hystericals do not complain of it, and that generally they even ignore it, we think. . . .

4. Lastly, we shall find again in amnesia the two primary characteristics of hysterical anaesthesia—namely, mobility and contradiction. Let us first look into *mobility*. Usually a serious amnesia is due to the destruction of traces, of unknown modifications which the sensations leave in the brain, and which allow them to reproduce themselves under the form of images. Let us suppose

a definitive and material destruction of the cerebral cells which have stored up these modifications, and the remembrances of these sensations will be materially destroyed in an irreparable way. Is it so with hysterical amnesias? Certainly not; we may be sure that in every hysterical amnesia the preservation of remembrances is still maintained. This is proved by the mobility of these anaesthesias, which acquire thus a considerable psychological importance.[37]

Abulias

This word *abulia* (ἀ βουλή) designates, in a general way, the alterations, the diminutions of the will; it applies to laziness, to hesitation, to powerlessness in acts, as well as slowness, indecision, to the absence of attention to ideas. This characteristic is well known by the alienists, who observed it in many of their patients; among drunkards, for example, either through opium or alcohol; among delirious neurasthenics, and among patients suffering from melancholia. Certain patients, belonging to a group as yet imperfectly defined, seemed to be especially liable to that alteration of the mind which has been called "the folly of doubt." While recognising that this characteristic is really common to all these patients, we do not think it peculiar to them. Abulia, in all its forms, is one of the most common lesions in the weakening of the mind; it is for this reason that it is also established in hysteria.

We even think that this symptom plays a chief part in hysteria: first, because it is very general and intervenes more or less in many important phenomena, as, for instance, in suggestibility; then because its degree of gravity, more or less great, modifies greatly the prognosis of the disease. . . .

Hystericals present themselves at first sight under two different aspects: some are restless, agitated, gay, like Margaret: others are calm, dreamy, melancholy, like Bertha—in fact, come nearest the type which has been called male hysteria, but which exists also in women. These two types need scarcely be differentiated. Hystericals of either type are no longer good for anything. They have lost all serious and useful activity. If you question the parents touching the beginning of the malady, the story is always the same: the first indication was that they could no longer do their work. . . . This striking inertness of all these young girls, apparently robust, should not be considered only a trait of their personal character. We could not explain why hysteria attacks always inert people. On the other hand, it is easy to obtain information on this point and learn how these same young girls had been before extremely active. Among those we have just pointed out was a talented teacher; another, an excellent domestic; a third, a very industrious seamstress; and their former activity was appreciated by all who knew about them. It is since they are ill that they can no longer work, and their hysterical condition is the only cause of their inertness.

[37] Ibid., pp. 91-93.

Work, except in some very rare cases of purely automatic work, is the greatest manifestation of voluntary activity, and if it disappears, the will with the hystericals must be at a very low ebb.[38]

When the power of attention is simply diminished instead of being suppressed, a number of very complex disturbances may be observed:

1. Attention is very *slow* and very difficult to fix; every moment the subject escapes you and begins either to dream or to babble at random. You have to excite her and encourage her again and for a long time that she may try to pay attention. It lasts much longer when she is alone. When Margaret is about to write a letter she has to take several days to make ready for it. "Indeed, I must set about it; must catch up with time."

2. When the attention is somewhat fixed and the subject really tries to understand what is put before her in the way of reading or ciphering, then all sorts of *sufferings* begin. Anxiety from all sides, very severe headaches often, headaches which sometimes persist and interrupt the patient's movements. The patient, who fears these pains, avoids spontaneously the exercise of her attention, or exercises it only in indispensable cases.

3. These subjective phenomena, which occur during the exercise of attention, are accompanied by objectively appreciable symptoms, new *anaesthesias*, and *disturbances of movement*, which show plainly the difficulty of the effort. In order to give her attention to a thing, the hysterical is obliged to use all of her small amount of mental force, and for the moment sacrifice all the rest. She ceases perceiving the sensations she had conserved. . . . The visual field contracts and can no longer receive any image except the one the subject is looking at. Not only are the sensations, but the movements themselves, neglected by the subject. While the attention is fixed, it would seem as if the motor images had recovered all their independence. Then you see a great number of grimaces, tics, jerks of arms and limbs, of which the subject is not aware. You can take the direction of these movements, their lead, so to say, and make them execute a variety of motions of which the patient has no consciousness. For instance, that young man, a hospital inmate, who was suffering from echolalia while he was playing cards, his comrades caused to say all sorts of things without his knowing it. It is the principle of a variety of subconscious acts, which we shall study farther on.

4. This very painful attention does not last long; it oscillates, ceases, returns for a moment, and ends after a variable time, always sufficiently short, by disappearing completely. It brings often in its wake a certain number of *accidents*. Some subjects just turn their eyes away from their work and say that they cannot continue, complaining of a severe headache. With others it is a more serious matter: such great exhaustion takes place that they can no longer do anything, nor feel anything, for quite a while. Justine fixes her eyes

[38] Ibid., pp. 117–119.

on a book and tries to read; she reads two minutes, then complains, rubs her eyes, which smart, she says, and water; she tries again, but sees no longer anything; she is entirely in the dark. This blindness, however, lasts only a few minutes, and the patient begins to read again. After a little while the same manoeuvre is repeated. It is a part of the phenomenon called *asthenopia*, but we think that here it is simply central and depends on the fatigue of attention. Justine, like many of these patients, reads often without any attention, thinking of something else, and understanding absolutely nothing of what she is reading. This kind of reading does not tire the eyes, nor do they become blinded.

The same exhaustion may become manifest not in the senses, but in the intelligence itself.[39]

Not only after numerous attacks, but gradually after the beginning of the malady is the intelligence of the patients lessened. Of course, this lessening is altogether relative and can be appreciated only by persons who knew the patients well before.

This diminution affects principally a special element of intelligence—the power of advancement in the acquisition of new ideas. It is only gradually and at a later period that hystericals truly retrograde; but, from the beginning of the disease, they cease to develop. Instruction is entirely arrested, whatever be the age of the subject. Louise, up to that time, had been an excellent pupil in her school, but at the age of eleven she ceased to understand anything, to learn anything; for three years now she has passed through the different stages of her malady, but has not recovered the faculty of learning. If she be not cured, her progress in learning will be definitively stopped at the age of eleven. And so with all other hystericals, only at different ages; and this arrest of the mind at a certain period largely determines the special aspect of different patients, the production in them of that generally infantile mind which we observe in all their conduct.

This incapacity for new instruction is bound up with phenomena which have been studied a long time, for example, with the difficulty or the impossibility of attention. It is useless to return to their way of listening or reading, to their difficulty in understanding a new idea, to their perpetual and really specific absent-mindedness. It really all depends on their continuous amnesias, which exist to a certain degree with them all; it depends on the hesitation with which they perceive and apprehend new events, on their doubts, their astonishments; in a word, on all the enfeeblements of the intellectual synthesis.

In hysteria, by a sort of perpetual contrast, all the phenomena of intellectual automatism are, on the contrary, exaggerated. Every time that, by chance, they succeed in understanding a new idea, or remembering an old one, that idea takes on an immense development. . . .

[39] Ibid., pp. 131 ff.

But there is a manifestation of intellectual automatism practically more important than all the others, namely, the tendency to ceaseless reverie. Hystericals are not content to dream constantly at night; they dream all day long. Whether they walk, or work, or sew, their minds are never wholly occupied with what they are doing. They carry on in their heads an interminable story which unrolls before them or is inwardly conceived. . . .

These reveries sometimes have no development; they are variable, incoherent images, which pass before us like the colours of a kaleidoscope, though they have often a certain vague unity about them. It is always the same monotonous story which the patient resumes at the point where she has been interrupted, or unceasingly begins over again. Be that story cheerful or painful, it does not matter; it becomes pleasant to these weary minds, because it is an easy reverie: "How unhappy I am! . . The idea is frightful, but it lulls me, and I am ready to defend it against any one who should want to take it from me; let me think of my little tomb; it gives me so much pleasure. . . ." When reveries get to be systematised in this way, they become more dangerous and are soon transformed into fixed ideas. The predisposition to fixed ideas, of which we see here the germ, is one of the great features of the hysterical mind.

We should also describe here the parallel modifications which activity presents, if we had not insisted, at such great length, on the hystericals' abulia. The lack of will gives hystericals a general aspect which alone enters into our present study. They become indifferent to everything and allow themselves to be led as children. A husband declared that his wife was becoming too docile and that this was not normal. They stop working spontaneously, but sometimes, when constantly directed, they will do something or other. . . . This obedience among hystericals gives but few results, for they do nothing seriously; they have no longer any perseverance and abandon an undertaking before any new and trifling difficulty. They no longer know how to adapt the present to the future, and, in their lack of forethought, they, so to speak, confine human existence to the present moment.

Not to return to known facts, we shall point out here only one of the great consequences of abulia, namely *ennui*. "Ennui is a plague which we try to avoid in society and which more than one unfortunate meets everywhere, even in the midst of the gay world. It is complete emptiness, the extinction of all activity and of all vigour; a depression, a laziness, a lassitude, a benumbing, a disgust, and, what is worse, a mortal blow given to the intelligence and to all agreeable sensations." Ennui finds us because we have no longer either the power or the will to feel; "because our head is empty enough to seek everywhere amusements; because our mind is too dull to seek them anywhere." Is not this a perfect description of hystericals? We shall not be surprised to find among them the true ennui; that which no amusement can dissipate, and which is a malady of the mind composed of desire and impotency.

Along with abulia, there is always the apparently opposite phenomenon, the exaggeration of automatic activity, the indefinite duration of a work once begun. . . .

Without seeking paradoxes, we think we may say that hystericals have in reality fewer emotions than is generally thought and that their principal character is here, as it is always, a diminution of psychological phenomena. These patients are in general very indifferent, at least to all that is not directly connected with a small number of fixed ideas. . . .

. . . Hystericals, above all, lose quickly social sentiments, altruistic emotions, perhaps because they are the most complex of all. . . . All, in fact, very soon fall into a state of unsociability, of misanthropy, which they try in vain to disguise. They wish, they say, to think all alone; and, in fact, their tendency toward revery has something to do with this partiality for isolation. But, really, they do not like society; they lose gradually their friendships and their affections. During their illness, they are generally incapable of acquiring serious sentiments of gratitude and sympathy. With the exception of the somnambulic passion, which is an altogether special phenomenon, they forget people in a short while; in fact, they have never loved them.

This general disposition, more or less developed, explains a well-known characteristic, namely, the selfishness of hystericals. . . . This selfishness manifests itself in various ways; it is that which is added to their want of moral support, a want they all feel, which is the basis of their vanity, their wish to be noticed, listened to, and led by others.

It is indeed curious to see their feeble personality, their very incomplete *I*, play so great a part and absorb all the strength of their intelligence. Yet it is easily explained. To love others, that is, understand others, is, in reality, an affluent mental activity. We must, in order to reach it, add to the synthesis of our own psychological phenomena those of others and construct in our thought a larger synthesis than that of our own personality. These poor creatures cannot understand themselves. They have not strength enough completely to build up their own personality; therefore it is quite natural that they cannot assimilate that of others. Selfishness, in hystericals, is a result of mental weakness, of the diminution of all sympathetic emotions.

We are already accustomed to the contrasts which the mental state of hystericals presents, so we shall not be very much surprised to learn that these apathetic, unemotional patients are, at the same time and from another point of view, extremely excitable and susceptible of very exaggerated emotions. With some of these patients, susceptibility is truly enormous; any kind of accident, a word, a look, provokes an altogether disproportionate scene.

These emotions, whose existence must be recognised, have, we think, very clear characteristics which distinguish them from normal emotions.

1. They are greatly exaggerated in their manifestations. The facility with which they can be modified by amusement, the slight trace they generally leave in the mind, shows that there is very often but little real feeling connected with these loud cries and this great despair.

2. When the emotion is real, it is not in sufficient *rapport* with the circumstances that provoked it. It is disproportionate—without shading, without justice. Instead of changing incessantly, according to the thousand incidents of life, it has a mechanical regularity and remains always the same. . . . Sometimes this lack of adaptation to circumstances on the side of emotion is still clearer, and the patients have contradictory feelings, the reverse of those they should experience in reality. . . . It would seem that there is a mechanism that regulates all this development of emotions and that this mechanism is put out of order, as in the phenomena of allochiria or heterokinesia.

3. Different emotions are not numerous with the same patient. It would seem that each patient has her own emotion and always the same. . . .

. . . There are, in a word, automatic emotions like automatic acts, and the former, as is always the case, are maintained with hystericals, and exaggerated. It is right to add that this exaggeration of the former emotion depends on the general character of hystericals, to the retraction of their field of consciousness, which obliges them ever to adhere to isolated thoughts, without antagonistic ideas, without counteraction. . . . We shall see, in studying suggestion, this power which an automatic phenomenon acquires, thanks to the present weakness of the personal perception.

After having observed this general character of emotions existing in these patients, we must see under what particular forms they oftenest present themselves, what are the most frequent kinds of emotions. Nearly all simple emotions—joy, gaiety, surprise, fear, etc.—can develop, especially in those who are not too ill to understand any longer new situations; and each of these emotions will wholly invade the mind with the same exaggeration and regularity. But we must recognise that the sad, depressing emotions are by far the most frequent. There has often been pointed out a quite correct distinction between the hysteria of man and that of woman. The hysterical woman is represented as full of agitation—restless, gay, laughing loud, doing a thousand strange things; and the man, on the contrary, as more sad, more melancholy, and inert. Things present themselves more commonly in this way, and it is certain that the hysteria of a man, "this upsetting," as M. Briquet says, "of the constituted laws of society, is more painful, more cruel than that of a woman. A man suffers more from this inertia, from this destruction of all vitality, and his moral weakening is more astonishing."

But, behind this apparent difference, there is, at bottom, a resemblance, and hysteria is always essentially the same. Melancholy and sadness are the dominant feelings with women as well as with men. All the patients of whom we have spoken are sad, despairing; continual weariness, disgust of life, fear, terrors, extreme despair, are what they continually express. Bursts of wild cheerfulness are merely accidents in the midst of a very monotonous sadness. They confirm a thought often expressed by philosophers, and recently taken up again by M. Féré: "The sensation of pleasure is derived from a sensation of power, and the sensation of displeasure from a feeling of impotency." We shall go even farther, and, despite hysterical vanity, which sometimes exists, but of which too much has been made, we will say that they are often very humble, incapable of daring anything, discouraged by trifles, and diffident. Those among them who are not conscious of their condition are the rarest; most have discovered before us that they have lost all will and sentiment, and they are disgusted with their miserable existence. . . .

Another group of emotions springs from their selfishness. Very much preoccupied with their feeble selves, they claim all kinds of care and attentions; they ask of others the moral force they have not within themselves, and, finding themselves always helpless, they think themselves always neglected. They are troubled when they represent to themselves the strength, the happiness of others, and are extremely jealous, very irritable, and prone to anger. Jealousy, that great passion of small minds, is the continual torment of the hystericals; it is an almost necessary complement of the somnambulic passion which we have already treated. There is sometimes with them real suffering at the thought of other people's pleasures. We only mention all these moral perturbations, which are very curious and probably quite regular, like all phenomena of hysteria. Their study will later form the starting-point of ethics; at present, psychology is not yet capable of analysing them.[40]

When coquetry exists, it is rather connected with that vanity, that selfishness, which we have pointed out as characteristic, than with the erotic, properly so called.

In a word, with the exception of a few special cases, easily explained, the hystericals are, in general, not any more erotic than normal persons. Their physical and moral anaesthesia, this concentration of the mind upon itself, does not incline them toward amorous passions. They are more frequently frigid than sensual; they are rather inclined to forget their former affections than increase them. We must not grossly deceive ourselves—take for love this infantile need they have of being led and consoled, and consider the temperament of some of them as a characteristic of their malady.[41]

This problem of hysterical simulation is, we think, largely a question of words. What is to be understood by falsehood, by simulation? Do we take the word, as we should, in its precise sense, as indicating a well-planned and voluntary deception? We say that it exists with these patients, as with other

[40] Ibid., pp. 199–214.
[41] Ibid., p. 216.

persons—that is, as an individual indication of character or as the result of a bad education. We also believe that, in exceptional cases, it may exist as a suggested and very accidental fixed idea; but we do not think that we could regard it as a specific characteristic of the malady. If, on the contrary, we take this word "simulation," as but too often happens, in a sense extremely vague, as a certain modification of the truth, as an indeterminate psychological alteration, we say that, in this case, simulation may be a summary of all hysteria and of even all possible mental maladies. It is clear that all these maladies consist in thinking and feeling what a normal man should neither think nor feel. The name becomes true, if you wish it, because it is meaningless, because it confounds all the phenomena, and is no longer good for anything else than to deceive us. Falsehood, like sin, is a word of the language of the moralist, and should have no place in the language of medicine.[42]

Inattention, feebleness of thought, revery, abulia, fixed idea, absence of new emotions, and excess of common emotions are things we meet with very often. Patients attacked by the folly of doubt, the obsessed, the impulsive, present to us the same picture. It is true, they are nearly related to the hystericals. Better still, if we read the beautiful descriptions of M. Lombroso of criminals, we shall be surprised to find again the same observations. It would seem that M. Lombroso refers very often to abulic hystericals. The imbeciles whom M. Sollier described recently, when they are not too inferior, have the same weaknesses and the same defects. Finally, there is a last comparison to be dealt with. This defect of synthesis, this instability, this naïve selfishness, accompanied by jealousy and anger, are found exactly in a state which is in no wise sickly, namely, in childhood. Who, examining an hysterical, has not said a hundred times, "Why, she is but a big child"? The hysterical, like a great category of patients, has no longer any greater power of thought than that of the child. But that which is normal in the child, because it does not act alone, having but few thoughts to understand, becomes a malady at twenty, when the too feeble mind can no longer co-ordinate remembrances and feelings, the accumulations of years. The character of the hystericals is no other than the character of feeble minds, that of children.

If we try to extract from the preceding descriptions traits of character which are not found so clearly in all weak minds generally, and which belong solely to hysteria, we shall observe especially two particular traits: the character is *mobile* and *contradictory*. The patient does not remain long in one and the same moral condition. She passes every moment from affection to indifference, from gladness to sadness, from hope to despair. She seems to be in an unstable equilibrium and to fall every moment from one side to the

---

[42] Ibid., p. 219.

other. On the other hand, there is not a single trait of character that is not every instant contradicted by some action apparently wholly different. Hystericals appear unintelligent and very lively, apathetic and emotional, hesitating and stubborn. These two characteristics should no longer surprise us, since they have been described in all the chapters of this book. They have always, we think, the same meaning. They show the want of mental unity, the diminution of personal synthesis, and the conservation of the automatic phenomena which reappear with exaggerated development.

This mental state is, then, manifest in the character and the emotions, as well as in the sensations and remembrances; but it appeared to us much clearer in the precise phenomena which have been separately studied. It is through the study of mental stigmata that the malday of hysteria must be diagnosed and understood. Each of them shows us very well that the subject has sustained a loss in his personality and that he is no longer master of his own thought.[43]

Suggestion and Subconscious Acts

When we examine the demeanour and thought of certain patients, particularly hystericals, we soon discover that their thoughts are not like those of other people. While with others ordinary ideas, sensations called forth by the sight of surrounding objects or accidental conversations, retain some sort of normal calm—their balance, so to say, along with other psychological phenomena—with hystericals it is otherwise. One particular notion will all at once assume an undue importance,—an importance altogether out of proportion to their other ideas,—and play a chief part in their lives. This fact has been often observed and pointed out by students. They endeavoured to describe and explain the case in various ways, accounting for it as happening at certain periods of the malady; at one time they explained it by the action of the *morale* on the *physique*, of mind on body; now, again, they describe the *power* of the *imagination; at the present day*, they employ the word more in use, "suggestion"—borrowed from the hypnotists. The knowledge of these suggestions, artificially called forth, seems to us the necessary introduction to the study of fixed ideas, naturally developed.[44]

Fixed Ideas

The study of suggestion has shown us that the thoughts of hystericals are not equilibrated; that under diverse influences one of them may develop to an extreme extent and live, so to say, isolated, its own life, to the great detriment of the mental organism. This tendency is not only manifested in artificial experiments; it continually gives place to natural phenomena, which are quite analogous to suggestions. Fixed ideas are for us phenomena of this

[43] Ibid., pp. 221–222.
[44] Ibid., p. 225.

kind; that is to say, psychological phenomena which are developed in the mind in an automatic manner, outside the will and the personal perception of the patient, but which, instead of being, like suggestions, experimentally called forth, are formed naturally under the influence of accidental causes. This difference in the artificial or natural provocation of automatic phenomena has, from a clinical and especially therapeutic point of view, quite grave consequences to justify this distinction. Ideas of this kind have been described at length in the case of patients considered as lunatics. They went under the name of obsessions, impulsions, phobias; they characterise the delirium which develops with some neurasthenics or, as they are often called in France, certain degenerates. We shall repeat here what we have already said in speaking of abulias. Unquestionably, this characteristic belongs to these patients; we in nowise deny it; we shall only say that it also belongs to hystericals; that with them it is very frequent, and that it is the cause of the great majority of their accidents. After having reviewed the different forms which the fixed idea takes with hystericals perhaps we may be able to prove certain characteristics peculiar to these patients and differentiate these phenomena from other forms of obsession met with among divers lunatics.

Description of fixed ideas among hystericals A lunatic tormented with fixed ideas, whether he accords them full credence or struggles against the encroaching delirium, has always an exact knowledge of the thoughts which torment him. He expresses them by words, or, if he does not explain them clearly, it is because he seeks to conceal them; if he meant to be sincere he could always express them. It is quite different with the hystericals: it is rare with them to account clearly for a fixed idea which besets them. Generally, they maintain that their mind is perfectly tranquil, without any preoccupation. It is not always possible to accuse them of dissimulation and their sincerity may be tested. It is sometimes found that these patients are very confiding and very sincere, and that they even confess most hidden things. Is it to be supposed that they could conceal a fixed idea much more insignificant? A large number of authors have not thought so; they have remarked that hysterical accidents do not seem connected with the patient's thoughts. These accidents continued to exist even when the patient was quite absent in mind and appeared to think of something else. It has even been demonstrated that these accidents persisted during the night, during a profound sleep, or during attacks; in conditions, in a word, when the subject did not seem capable of thinking of his fixed idea. These quite correct observations have led to the denial of fixed ideas in hysteria.

We think that it is necessary to admit the existence of a particular form of fixed ideas peculiar to hystericals, which we would designate as *subconcious fixed ideas*. The word "consciousness," when applied to fixed ideas and deliriums, has sometimes taken, in the language of alienists, a particular meaning. It means that the subject is aware of his delirium,—recognises it being false. An unconscious delirium is, on the contrary, a delirium to which the patient abandons himself without judging it, and which he accepts as true. We are sorry that we cannot accept this meaning, in reality incorrect, of the word "consciousness," for we have been obliged to use these terms in another sense. A fixed idea, like any kind of psychological phenomena whatever, is conscious, not when it is judged, but simply when it is known by the subject, and it is in this sense that the fixed ideas of those under so-called obsession may be said to be conscious. We believe that it is extremely important, in order to understand hystericals, to know that with them fixed ideas may lose this character and present themselves under the aspect of subconscious phenomena.

How can the existence of an idea, the definition of which is not known to the patient and cannot be expressed, be clearly demonstrated? We must have recourse to all the processes of observation which the experiments on subconscious acts have brought to our knowledge. Subconscious phenomena are manifested, as we have seen, in various ways: it will be the same for subconscious fixed ideas. 1st. These ideas may develop completely during attacks of hysteria and express themselves then by acts and words. 2nd. In dreams more or less agitated which take place during sleep and natural somnambulisms and which often happen unexpectedly; it is at such moments that fixed ideas are wholly confessed. 3rd. One of the best processes consists in causing the patient to enter artificially into a state similar to the preceding ones—namely, an imposed somnambulism. At one time, abandoned to himself in this artificial condition, he has dreams which he expresses aloud; he gives himself up to acts as in a natural somnambulism, and reveals his thoughts; at another time he talks to us, answers our questions. It is astonishing to see how subjects during their somnambulism find again with precision and clearness recollections, ideas, of which they had no consciousness during their waking state. They explain then most accurately the idea that besets them and give a detailed account of all the sensations, of all the images which have determined and still determine the accidents. 4th. It is well known that subconscious thoughts may be manifested even during the waking hours of the patients and without their knowing it. Certain acts which they perform automatically when they are vacant in mind enable us to guess these ideas. But when it is possible to employ it, the process, which consists in utilising automatic writing, is more exact than all the others. It is useless to go back to the description of this writing discovered by the spiritualists; if it has to-day no longer the religious character the disciples of Allan Kardec assigned to it, it may in many circumstances subserve a medical purpose. Let us also point out a process, less known, which, in very particular cases, may also serve to bring to light subconscious ideas: the process of "crystal gazing," described especially by English authors. Many patients, hystericals almost always, we think, cannot look fixedly upon a moderately shiny surface without having indubitable hallucinations. They see their own dreams filing off in the mirror, and sometimes they thus happen to perceive and express ideas they could not account for previously. Such are the processes, still very imperfect, which permit us to penetrate a little deeper into the minds of patients.[45]

Dysaesthesias and hyperaesthesias Among the many conditions in hysteria the simplest are disorders of sensation. We do not mean by this those diminutions of sensation which have already been studied under the name of anaesthesia, but more accidental disorders, and for the patient more inconvenient. They are mostly alterations or exaggerations of the normal sensibility: dysaesthesias and hyperaesthesias. Many hysterics seem to have imperfect perceptions of the impressions which strike their senses. This is sometimes simply the consequence of anaesthesia; they say, for example, that their food has no taste, that it tastes like sand, and they call for vinegar and very spicy condiments. But the transformation is often more complete and the patient reveals a perception different from that which a normal man would experience under the same conditions. One pretends that everything smells of ether, another complains that her soup tastes of poison, although she would have some difficulty in explaining the taste. One patient delights in red, and the dullest red; she sees "bright rays that penetrate and warm her very heart." A remark of this kind has started the theory which attributes to all hysterics a passion for red. It is far from being a general thing. . . . Certain contacts give to hysterics quite abnormal sensations, and it is partly because of this notion that formerly special studies were made on the influence of magnets and metals.[46]

Among the disorders of sensation those that form the most important accidents are the hyperaesthesias, or rather hyperalgesias. Certain parts of the body seem endowed with so delicate a sensibility that they are constantly painful and become the starting point of sharp pains and other accidents as soon as they are subjected to the least contact. These phenomena seem to us as yet imperfectly known. M. Briquet wished to place them in the first rank with the stigmata. It appears to us that most hyperaesthesias, at least those which we have been able to study and understand, are closely connected with fixed ideas, and it is for this reason that we have described them as accidents of hysteria. . . .

Hyperaesthesias deserve to be called true when a veritable exaggeration in the delicacy, in the acuity of one sense is established. Many authors have described marvellous things attributed to hysterical, sensory acuities, giving the illusion of transparency. We believe that these hyperaesthesias are much rarer than is supposed, and that a certain perspicacity of the subject, reflexions more or less conscious, joined to very ordinary senses, make these pretended marvels generally very comprehensible. We do not, however, doubt certain exaltations of the senses which have been observed either during waking hours

[45] Ibid., pp. 278–282.
[46] Ibid., pp. 291–292.

or more frequently during somnambulism. . . . Hystericals are able to withdraw their attention very easily; in the same way as they can neglect and completely forget certain sensations, they can concentrate all their power of thought upon certain others. Our senses may be put into action by very slight impressions—impressions which we ordinarily neglect to perceive. It has been maintained, and not without reason, that subconscious sensations are much finer than our conscious perceptions. It is these ordinarily subconscious phenomena which penetrate into the personal perception, when our attention is strongly excited. It is probably phenomena of this kind which, by association of ideas, awaken the reveries and divinations of lucid somnambulists. . . . The psychological study of the true hyperaesthesia, when it shall be based on very clear cases, will lead to the discovery of interesting characteristics of unconscious sensation, and will give precision to our knowledge of the power of attention.

Certain hyperalgesias may also be considered true, namely, by the pains hystericals often feel in the head. The hyperaesthesias which most interest the physician when he studies the accidents of hysteria are the false hyperaesthesias, or those which result from fixed ideas. Over various points of the body there is developed, apparently, an extreme sensitiveness. The slightest touch produces great pain, provokes cries, spasms, and even attacks.[47]

This hyperaesthesia is not constant, and several patients, H. and M., for instance, when they are in a state of somnambulism, lose this abnormal sensitiveness. In one word, this variable and contradictory hyperaesthesia is, in reality, not accompanied with any serious modification of the sensitiveness. The tactile sense and even the sense of pain remained normal in this part of the body; this is what we wished to express in calling this phenomenon a false hyperaesthesia.

Wherein, then, does the phenomenon consist? It seems to be evidently connected with psychological phenomena. . . .

This supposition will be verified if we consider, besides, the monotonous regularity of these hyperaesthesias which for years persist in remaining exactly the same. The contact of such or such a spot brings with it always such or such pain, such or such gesture, such or such attitude of the subject. Organic maladies do not thus remain unchangeable; on the contrary, the duration and the regularity of psychological automatism are sufficiently known. . . .

It is not impossible to go further and to determine which is the intervening psychological phenomenon. It is sufficient to examine the initial accident and to compare the phenomena which now occur, when we touch the affected zone, with those of the beginning. There is nearly always a very unmistakable accident that determines real suffering at the beginning of these hyperaesthesias, which seem to prolong indefinitely a momentary pain. . . .

[47] Ibid., pp. 302–305.

Not only may we establish here the fixed idea at the beginning of the malady, but we may be able to show sometimes that it still exists in the mind of the subject, although she may not always be able to account for it. We shall cite only two cases, for they require a detailed presentation to be understood. . . .

We have gradually penetrated the psychological nature of these hysterical hyperaesthesias; they are not exaggerations of tactile sensations, nor even of the sensation of pain provoked by contact; they are false hyperaesthesias, solely due to ideas awakened through association in respect to this contact. As soon as the subject *knows* that the skin of the affected place has been touched, whether he learns it by sight or knows it by a normal tactile sensation, he experiences not a pain, properly so-called and localised, but a general emotion, an anguish, a frightful terror.[48]

Attacks of fixed ideas—ecstasies We have come to a third category of attacks, in which emotional phenomena and convulsive movements are reduced to a minimum. The patients remain, so to say, immovable; sometimes they are completely inert, and seem to have as little thought as motion. However, the study we made some years ago of a patient, Marcelle, interesting in many respects, permits us to recognise that the mind of the subject was far from being wholly inactive during these attacks, but that it was, on the contrary, obsessed by a number of psychological phenomena of an intellectual rather than an emotional order. We have since been able to study examples of these attacks of ideas, which are, we think, very important in hysteria for their frequency and pathological consequences. . . .

It is not rare to meet motionless hystericals, eyes fixed, generally open or half closed, sometimes quite closed. It is rare to obtain any answer from them. Sometimes they appear to waken of a sudden when you shake them; sometimes, again, they cannot be awakened, and come out of this state spontaneously after a certain lapse of time. With some, this kind of sleep is combined with convulsive attacks, which either precede them, or follow them, or take place, as with Bertha, in the interval of the emotional attacks, and in some sort independently. With others, again, these states of immobility are the only attacks to be established, and constitute the principal hysterical condition. . . .

What have we learned by these processes? That attacks of this sort are a kind of "crises of ideas," so to speak. The patients are not without consciousness; they are not without thought; on the contrary, they are absorbed by an obsessing thought which fills their small field of consciousness. Their apparent insensibility is an anaesthesia through distraction due to the ideas which encumber their feeble thought.

[48] Ibid., pp. 307–308, 311, 313.

These ideas, which appear thus during the attack, are most varied, but they have, in common, a few characteristics which we must first point out. They present themselves almost always under the form of images, extremely vivid and complex, which are not contradicted by anything and which give to the patient the complete illusion of reality.[49]

Automatism in the attack and in fixed ideas Hysterical attacks, when considered from their psychological side, seem to depend on certain emotions, images, or ideas which are reproduced in the mind of the patients. They appear, therefore, to differ but little from other hysterical accidents, and to be connected, as most of them are, with fixed ideas more or less complex. It is, then, possible to resume simultaneously the study of these diverse accidents by examining the general characteristics which fixed ideas assume in hysteria. This study, moreover, can be considerably shortened if we remember the characteristics and conditions previously studied in regard to suggestion. It is not difficult, in fact, to establish the very great analogy which exists between suggestions and fixed ideas.

It is not necessary to dwell on the *duration* of such fixed ideas. This characteristic was manifest in all our observations: hyperaesthesias, paralyses, contractures of psychical origin may last for years.... The *frequency* of the repetitions is also evident. Tics, spasms, attacks repeat every day, and even several times a day, the same old incident. Neither shall we study in detail the *ease* with which these fixed ideas develop, when they are once well organised in the mind. The least thing, the most insignificant sign, suffices to release the spring and provoke the apparition of a long succession of images. These images are so precise and so complete that they become constantly transformed into *hallucinations* and *movements*. These are characteristics which have already been described in regard to suggestions, and which are presented here without modification.

We think it more important to dwell on an essential characteristic of these fixed ideas, namely, their *regularity*. A few patients, the simplest, have but one fixed idea, ever the same, and it reappears always, under all circumstances.....

When several fixed ideas, as it very often happens, have developed in the mind of the patient, the regularity of the psychological phenomena will evidently be more difficult to perceive, but it does not the less exist. One may establish, we dare not say laws of fixed ideas, but a certain order in which the phenomena generally present themselves. It is rare that several fixed ideas coexist in the mind of the same patient without mutual influence. It is an exception to the rule when certain hystericals have two or more fixed ideas independently developing, each in its own way, as if it were alone....

[49] Ibid., pp. 383–385, 387.

These fixed ideas conceal each other, and the last appears generally to exist alone. When, in consequence of various circumstances and in particular after a psychological treatment, the last, the actual fixed idea disappears, one will be quite surprised to see another one come up, and this is precisely the preceding fixed idea. This removed, there appears a third, of an earlier date. It would seem that in this case the fixed ideas are arranged in layers, and that they come to light in succession, one after the other. We formerly dwelt so long on this question of the stratified fixed ideas that we will not say more on this subject here.

Lastly, it should not be forgotten that a mind that has been obsessed by a fixed idea remains for some time, even after the disappearance of the fixed idea, in a state of very particular weakness, very open to suggestions and quite in a condition to receive a number of new fixed ideas.[50]

Not only does the fixed idea require no attention or intellectual effort to develop, but it cannot develop unless *the attention and will are very greatly reduced.* All physical or moral fatigue which diminishes the power of psychological synthesis, favours those accidents due to fixed ideas. . . .

As long as the preoccupations, the obsessions, remain entirely conscious, they do not as yet constitute an hysterical accident, so called. . . . The fixed idea, at first conscious, has formed an hysterical attack and remains now in a greater or less degree subconscious. It is true that in certain rare cases the fixed idea, which has been for some time subconscious, may regain consciousness and induce deliriums, which we shall study later. But these are rare accidents, which hardly belong to hysteria proper.

Finally, this subconscious character of the fixed ideas with hystericals plays a great part in the therapeutics of these affections. We formerly showed that it was necessary to look up, so to say, these subconscious phenomena in order to attack them, and that one could not treat the hysterical accident before having reached those deep layers of thought within which the fixed idea was concealed. We are happy to see to-day MM. Breuer and Freud express the same idea. "It is necessary," they say, "to make this provocative event self-conscious; bring it forth to the full light. The accidents disappear when the subject realises those fixed ideas." We do not believe that the cure is so easy as that, and that it suffices to bring the fixed idea to an expression to carry it off. The treatment is unfortunately of a much more delicate nature, but, in any case, it is certain that this discovery of the subconscious phenomena is an indispensable preliminary.

In a word, the fixed ideas of the hystericals present to the highest degree the characteristics of psychological automatism: regularity, repetition of the past, and subconsciousness. They are the same characteristics which have already been established in suggestions. Fixed ideas are phenomena of the same kind, which develop in the same manner in minds of weakened

[50] Ibid., pp. 401–402, 404–405.

synthesis. Both indicate a division of the phenomena of consciousness which we shall see completely manifested in somnambulisms.[51]

Such fixed ideas, existing outside the personal perception, play in hysteria a prime rôle. They can determine the most varied of the disturbances of movement; they give rise to hyperaesthesias; they bring about hallucinations, for the separation of those two states of consciousness is far from being absolute, and a phenomenon that has been provoked in one by a whole series of associations of ideas may appear suddenly in the other; they can disturb and cloud the mind, induce the strangest forgetfulness, and even a sort of delirium. The power of such ideas depends on their isolation; they grow; "they install themselves in the mind in the manner of parasites," and cannot be stopped in their development by the efforts of the subject because they are not known, because they exist aside, in a second thought, separated from the first. . . .

These remarks had formerly induced us to consider these dissociations of the psychological phenomena as an essential characteristic of hysteria: "This fact," we said, "must play in this disease a rôle as great as that of association in normal psychology." A little later, we were explaining divers accidents in hysteria, and in particular contractures, "by a veritable activity of the second group of images, separated from the normal consciousness." "The essential character of this disease of disintegration was the formation, in the mind, of two groups of phenomena, one constituting the ordinary personality, the other being, besides, susceptible of subdivision, forming an abnormal personality different from the first and altogether unknown to it."[52]

[51] Ibid., pp. 409, 411–412.
[52] Ibid., pp. 493–494.

Index